B⊗Y ENTRANT

BOY ENTRANT

by

Brian Carlin

The recollections of a Royal Air Force "Brat"

ISBN: 1-4116-9433-0
ISBN: 978-1-4116-9433-0

Published by Brian Carlin

Cover design by Michelle Carlin, art by Allan Knox.

This book is based on the real-life experiences of the author. The names of certain individuals portrayed in the narrative have been disguised to protect their privacy.

Dedicated to my daughters Michelle and Sarah and to my grandchildren Jacob, Brenden, Lucas and Sophia and those who may come after.

CONTENTS

APPENDIXES

ILLUSTRATIONS

Illustration Credits

The photograph on page 33 first appeared in the *Northern Whig and Belfast Post* and has been provided by the British Newspaper Museum. It is included in this book by the kind permission of the copyright holder, Northern Whig Ltd, and the British Newspaper Library.

The photographs on pages 75; 168; 208; 311; 326; 390 and 391 kindly provided by the Officer Commanding, No. 4 School of Technical Training, RAF St. Athan.

The photographs on pages 243 and 283 first published in the St. Athan Magazine, Vol. 1, No. 4 (December, 1957) and are reproduced by kind permission of the Officer Commanding, Royal Air Force St. Athan.

The illustrations on pages 240 and 300 were specially created for this book by Mickie Collins, whose cartoons regularly appear in the Royal Air Force Boy Entrants Association newsletter, *The Chequered Band*.

The photograph on page 353 was kindly provided by Michael Williams.

The group photograph on page 402 was kindly provided by Tom Dee and restored by Roger Gatti.

The photograph on page 272 is from the author's personal collection.

Acknowledgements

This book would not have been possible without help from a number of sources, including a few of my fellow ex-Boy Entrants - Richard Butterworth, Charlie Cunningham and Eugene Gilkes who filled in my memory gaps, David Williams for lending his copy of the December 1957 edition of the St. Athan Magazine, Michael Williams for specific information and photos relating to the Boy Entrant Trumpet Bands, Tom Dee for the group photograph on page 402, and Norrie Hathaway for lending his Electrical Mechanic (Air) training notes.

Others also lent substantial help - Wing Commander David Orme, Officer Commanding of No. 4 School of Technical Training, RAF St. Athan, and his staff Anne Dawson and Colin Bramley for extending warm hospitality to Charlie Cunningham and me during our return visit to the St. Athan in 2003, and for providing most of the photographs of Boy Entrant activities that appear in the book. Jane Bissett, RAF St. Athan Media Communications Officer, for providing excerpts from the 1958 edition of the St. Athan Magazine and a copy of the "early years" RAF St. Athan Station layout, Richard Powell, for identifying the type of trumpet I played so terribly in the Boy Entrant Band, and my nephew Brian Wisener, for tracking down the copyright ownership of the photograph on page 33.

I also wish to acknowledge the help and encouragement of Cheryl Leedom, Charlie Cunningham and my friend Judy Bowen, all of whom read over all or some of the first draft and provided constructive comments. I am deeply indebted to both Cheryl Leedom and Julie Claydon for proof-reading the second draft, and to my friend Dorothy Eilbeck and my daughter Michelle Carlin for their diligence, dedication and eye for detail in editing the final draft. My thanks also to Michelle for creating the front and back cover designs, to Allan Knox for creating the Boy Entrant figure and Judy Bowen for her suggestions that helped give "him" the appearance of a teenage boy.

Finally, I would like to thank my wife Pam for being so patient with me as I burned the midnight oil nearly every night to record this formative period of my life.

INTRODUCTION

In pre-war and immediate post-war Britain it was considered normal for working class teenage boys to join the workforce after completing their basic secondary school education at the age of 14½ (later raised to 15½ circa 1950). At best, they became trade apprentices and at worst, manual labourers.

In 1934, the Royal Air Force instituted a training scheme that recruited suitable teenage boys between the ages of 15½ and 16½ to be trained in a limited number of trades. The teenagers were required to take the same oath of allegiance to the Crown as the regular servicemen, and were considered to have enlisted for a specified term of service following their training. But because they had entered the RAF before becoming adults in the eyes of the law, they were assigned the rank of Boy Entrant. As such, they were accorded special status within the service. Boy Entrants were subject to normal service discipline, with a few additional regulations thrown in, and could not voluntarily rescind their enlistment after having taken the oath of allegiance to the Sovereign.

Encouraged by the initial success of the Boy Entrant scheme, the RAF expanded it in 1938 to include training for several additional trades, only to suspend all training in 1939 at the outbreak of hostilities with Germany. Many of those Boy Entrants who had completed their training went on to serve during the war. Some became aircrew, some became ground crew, and several of them made the ultimate sacrifice for King and Country.

The Boy Entrant training scheme was resumed in May 1947 when the first post-war intake of young lads was designated the 1st Entry. It was at this significant milestone in Boy Entrant history that boys were first assigned service numbers beginning with the "19" prefix. Thereafter, this distinction was reserved exclusively for Boy Entrants.

Recruitment of boys intensified in the 1950s when manpower shortages anticipated by the approaching termination of National Service needed to be offset. By this time, training in virtually every trade was offered to prospective Boy Entrant recruits. RAF stations Cosford and Hereford became Boy Entrant training schools in 1950 with RAF St. Athan being added in 1955 when the training of several trades was moved there from Cosford.

Boy Entrants wore the standard "other ranks" RAF uniform, but with certain distinguishing marks. The most obvious was a two-colour chequered hatband worn around the service dress (SD) hat in lieu of the black hatband worn by adult servicemen. A brass "wheel badge" (actually a four-bladed propeller within a circle) was worn on the left upper sleeve and usually backed by a coloured disc. Other basic sleeve markings consisted of up to three miniature inverted chevrons worn as "proficiency badges" on the cuff of the left jacket sleeve. These were often supplemented by other badges signifying such distinctions as marksmanship, participation in the Duke of Edinburgh Award Scheme and band membership.

Discipline and organization were administered by a permanent staff of officers and non-commissioned officers (NCOs), who were ably assisted by the appointment of Boy NCOs who wore miniature NCO chevrons surmounted by a wheel badge on the upper sleeves of both arms.

The training period for Boy Entrants lasted for 18 months. The first three months were spent in the Initial Training Squadron (ITS) learning basic military drill, undergoing intensive physical training and being taught the fundamentals of ground combat training that included the safe handling and actual use of live firearms.

General education was not neglected during this initial period. Half of the boys' time was spent in the classroom continuing their education in such subjects as citizenship, current affairs, mathematics, English, geography, mechanics and science—particularly as it related both to the Theory of Flight and fundamental principles associated with their trades. In addition, one period of "Padre's Hour" was set aside each week for Religious Instruction.

At the conclusion of Initial Training, the boys commenced trade training at well equipped workshops-cum-classrooms. Basic workshop practice in the use of common hand tools and practical trade-related work on actual equipment shared equal time with theoretical instruction, whilst individual performance was closely monitored by weekly classroom testing and periodic end-of-term practical and written examinations. Training concluded with exhaustive written and oral tests independently administered by the RAF Trade Standards and Testing Section. Those who were successful—and much to the credit of the quality of instruction they were in the majority— passed out of Boy Entrant service into the regular Royal Air Force as qualified tradesmen, standing firmly on the first rung of a promising career. The few who failed to qualify on their first attempt were usually given a second chance, through relegation into the next upcoming entry. However, if these individuals failed to pass the exams a second time, their training was terminated.

The Boy Entrant training scheme gave many a young lad the basic trade skills and personal discipline necessary to pursue a successful career and rewarding life. But alas, all good things come to an end. The scheme was terminated in July of 1965 when the final entry, the 51st, passed out of training and into Royal Air Force history.

This book is the personal recollections of one who underwent the rigours of Boy Entrant training. Whilst being subjective in nature, the story is representative of the experience of thousands of other youngsters who chose to allow their future lives, characters and careers to be moulded by the training they would receive as Boy Entrants.

Former Boy Entrants, many of whom reside overseas, keep in touch with each other through the Royal Air Force Boy Entrant Association (RAFBEA), which maintains an interesting and informative website at http://www.rafbea.org that was the main source of the information included in this introduction.

Brian Carlin
Former Boy Entrant, 29th Entry
Royal Air Force Station St. Athan

CHAPTER 1

Achieving Escape Velocity

When I look back, life has been good to me—all things considered. And I think I've handled it with some degree of success, even if I say so myself. But it could have turned out so much differently and probably less successfully, if I had failed to make a certain fateful decision at a critical time in my early life.

Many of us make decisions that set the course of our futures—for good or ill—whilst we're still only youngsters. For some it might be a decision to do nothing: the easiest of all to make, just allowing ourselves to be tossed around like corks on the sea of life, washing up on any shore, or maybe never seeing shore at all. For others, it might be a decision to take a path in a new direction that, if followed unwaveringly, will yield benefits in our adult years. I'm happy to say that I made the latter kind of decision at the tender age of 15. It was a very good decision, as things turned out, although I didn't realize that at the time. I'd like to tell you about it.

It was summer of 1956 and I was desperate to escape from what I realized was a dead-end existence. This was Northern Ireland before the Troubles, but not before the trouble that caused the Troubles. I'd just left St. Malachy's Public Elementary School. The school leaving age at that time was 14½, but my father made me stay on for another six months to give him more time to get me apprenticed into a good trade. I really loved working with wood and was good at it, so he tried to get me placed as an apprentice carpenter. But a Catholic lad had little chance of landing something like that in the Ulster of those days, unless his family had exceptionally good contacts. Sadly, mine didn't. So I finally left school at 15 and worked full-time as a message boy for a local grocer by the name of Paddy Corning. My job was to go on errands, mostly delivering large grocery orders to Paddy's customers. A battered bicycle operated by boy pedal power was the means by which I delivered the groceries to our valued customers. The bike came equipped with a large tubular metal pannier mounted in front of the handlebars and supported over the front wheel, which held a wicker basket containing the groceries. Typically, an errand meant pedalling for several miles to deliver a grocery order to the customer's home. The freedom was wonderful after having had to sit in a single classroom all day, especially for six months longer than I needed to. I knew, however, that I couldn't stay in this job forever, not even for very long and so I kept looking for an opportunity that might bring something better. Although, for the life of me, I didn't know what that might be.

That wasn't the only thing troubling me. To put it in the language of today's family psychologists, my family was chronically dysfunctional. I was the eldest of four children, two sisters and two brothers, whose mother had passed away eight years previously. For the first two years after her death my father paid a succession of women to look after us, so that he could go out to work. Some were good and some weren't so good, but not one of them could replace our mother, whom we missed desperately. My father then married again. His new wife was in her forties and had never been married before. Her desperation to find a husband was matched only by my father's desperation to get someone to look after his kids for free, cook him a meal when he came home and share his bed. Maybe it worked out for him, but it sure as hell didn't work out for us. She was a mean-spirited bitch, who did everything she could to make life miserable for my sisters and me. But our brother, the youngest in the family, was a little luckier. Because he was still a toddler, he seemed to kindle her maternal instincts and she adopted him as her own. But as for the rest of us, we were just someone else's brats and she treated us as such. To make matters worse, I didn't really hit it off too well with my father. He believed that I favoured my mother's side of the family and, since he didn't get along with them, any of my personal characteristics that reminded him of them made me a target of his scorn. Young as I was, I realized I just had to get out of that miserably unhappy situation as soon as possible; all I needed was a good opportunity. Then one day, just out of the blue, came the break I'd been looking for.

Leafing through a boys' magazine—probably *The Wizard* or *The Hotspur*—that early summer day in 1956, I noticed a picture of a boy around my own age of 15 looking back at me from an advertisement. He was wearing a round military-style peaked hat with a badge prominently displayed at the front bearing the familiar initials *RAF*, which anyone would have recognized as the insignia of the Royal Air Force. There was an unusual chequered pattern around the outer hatband that I'd never seen before and I'd seen plenty of air force servicemen around and about, since the RAF station at Ballykelly was near my home town. The young man's uniform looked familiar and yet it was different somehow.

"Become a Boy Entrant in the RAF and learn a trade," said the advert, in very large type. My eyes lingered over the words as I wondered what exactly "Boy Entrant" meant, but the words "learn a trade" certainly caught my attention. Could this be the answer to a prayer?

The small print in the advert informed me that if I was a boy between the age of 15½ and 16½, was medically fit and could pass a basic education test, I might qualify for training as a Boy Entrant in the RAF. Well, I was medically fit, reasonably intelligent and certainly had more than a passing acquaintance with the three R's, so it seemed that there was a very good chance of qualifying. Here was a chance to learn a trade and get away from home, all rolled up in one package.

The advert concluded by inviting me to fill out my name, address and age in the spaces provided and then send off for more details. In very short order, I found a pen and filled out the requested information then found an envelope and addressed it, as instructed in the advert, to the Royal Air Force Recruiting Office, Clifton Street, Belfast. A little later, I bought a stamp and posted the application, without telling anyone.

Filling out the application and sending it off was just a simple act, but it had a far-reaching effect on the rest of my life. That's what I was hoping for, in a way, but at such a young age it was all just a vague dream of a far distant future. I wanted to be a success at *something* and rise above the poverty and misery that had been my lot since my mother had passed away. Yet I was groping towards this goal without any real plan, just taking it one step at a time. Little did I realize what a major step I had just taken by posting off that application to the RAF.

If this was a life changing moment, it didn't arrive with any great fanfare of trumpets or off-screen dramatic music. No heavenly ray of golden light shone down on me, no sudden realization of the far-reaching consequences of this deed endowed my countenance with a look of knowing wisdom. Instead, that day life just continued in the very same way it had the day before and the day before that. I pedalled Paddy Corning's message bike, delivering groceries to the customers. And on the way I helped myself to one, well maybe it was two, of Mrs. Mulligan's *Gypsy Crème* biscuits.

This was back in the days when biscuits came in biscuit tins; sheet metal boxes that measured about one cubic foot. The grocer would weigh out the ordered quantity and put them in a paper bag, which he would then hold by the top two corners and twirl it around a couple of times to close it. One day, sitting on the very top of Mrs. Mulligan's grocery order, was just such a paper bag containing half a pound of *Gypsy Crèmes*—my favourite. They were thick, craggy-looking and chocolate flavoured, with a thick layer of chocolate cream filling sandwiched between two biscuits. From time to time I had sampled a few customers' biscuits, but usually they were from bags containing a full pound and not *Gypsy Crèmes* which weighed heavy so that there weren't too many in a pound. Mrs. Mulligan was a schoolteacher at St. Malachy's Girls School and quite an unpleasant teacher, at that. She didn't like boys of my age, thinking that we were always up to no good. But on this occasion, at least, I couldn't fault her for holding that opinion. My guess is that she suspected something because maybe she'd been a victim of my sampling tendencies in the past. In any case, when she answered the door to take the delivery of her groceries, she bade me to wait and then immediately grabbed the bag of biscuits and disappeared into her house. A few moments later she returned with a challenging look in her eye, holding the bag of biscuits before her, up at face level.

"I ordered half a pound of biscuits and I've just weighed these, but there isn't a half pound here," she pronounced in an almost victorious manner, like some prosecuting barrister presenting the case-winning evidence. "Why is that?" Mrs. Mulligan then demanded, her thin lips stretched into a decidedly un-humorous smile.

"Dunno," I mumbled with a half-hearted shrug. But by now I knew the cat was well and truly out of the bag, as well as the *Gypsy Crèmes*.

She waited a few uncomfortable moments for the explanation she must have known wasn't going to be forthcoming.

"Okay, I'm going to phone Paddy Corning and ask *him* why I'm getting short weight in biscuits!" She announced, closing the door in my face at the same time.

Mrs. Mulligan did exactly as she said she would. Paddy was waiting for me when I got back and immediately took me to the storeroom at the rear of the shop, where I got a stern lecture on the importance of the trust customers placed in their grocer's honesty. The desire to escape to pastures new couldn't have been any stronger than it was during that short session getting the sharp edge of Paddy Corning's tongue.

Thankfully, it wasn't too long after sending off my application to the recruiting office that a large brown envelope bearing the boldly printed legend "On Her Majesty's Service" plopped through the letterbox of my home in Windsor Avenue. Hurriedly I opened it and found a booklet describing life as a Boy Entrant, with a list of available trades for which I could apply. There was also a letter requesting that I complete the enclosed one-page form, on which I was expected to provide details of my education, current occupation, parents' names and a history of any illnesses or physical handicaps.

Many of the listed trades seemed very limiting. I ask you, what kind of demand would there be for armourers in normal civilian life? No, I wanted to learn a trade that would stand me in good stead during my life after the RAF. I suppose I was thinking of my father's example. He had joined the Royal Navy as a stoker when he was a young man and in the process was taught skills of brick-laying that were needed for re-lining a ship's boilers with firebricks. On leaving the service at the end of the war, he was able to use these skills to make a living as a bricklayer during the post-war building boom.

With this thought in the back of my mind, the trade of Electrical Mechanic seemed to stand out above all others. One of my former schoolmates was apprenticed as an electrician because fortunately for him his dad practised that trade, so he had a leg up in getting his apprenticeship. Yes, I thought, that sounds like a useful trade, so I made it my number one choice. The instructions for completing the paperwork informed me that I needed to select a first, second and third choice of trades for which to be considered, because all trades might not be available to all applicants. So, I selected Electrical Mechanic as my number one choice, then Instrument Mechanic and Engine Mechanic as my second and third choices. It took a little longer to complete the form this time, but I filled out all of the requested information and asked my father to sign, giving his parental consent.

"I don't want you to go," he said, "but I'm not going to stand in your way."

He had left home to join the Royal Navy when he was 18 and had always commented that a good military training would straighten me out, or words to that effect. My stepmother had no qualms, she said to let me go, that it would make a man of me. So my father signed the form and I returned it in the pre-addressed postage paid On Her Majesty's Service envelope that had been enclosed with all the other stuff I'd received. This edged me a little farther down that fateful road to the future, but still life went on. Oh, I should mention that I told my best pal, John Moore, what I had done. He didn't believe that I would go through with it, but he would soon be proved wrong.

The information I had included on the form must have interested the RAF, because they sent me an even bulkier envelope a short time later. This time, there was much more information on life as a Boy Entrant. Of course it leaned heavily on the glamorous stuff, in the same way that holiday hotel adverts always seem to include those nice pictures framed by bougainvillea, neglecting to mention that the bougainvillea is actually growing in the garden of the much nicer hotel across the street. Included with the glossy books and pamphlets was another form, longer than the first one—four pages this time. It seemed the RAF wanted just a bit more information and some references. I filled out the form in my neatest handwriting and then took the form to my former headmaster, Mr. Murphy, known fearfully as The Boss. I'd been in his class during my last two years at St. Malachy's school and he had given me more than my fair share of a tough time when I was there, so I wasn't sure what to expect.

The Boss squinted at the form through his bifocals for a few minutes, then took out his Parker fountain pen, the one with the solid gold nib and filled with royal blue Quink ink and scribbled something in his sophisticated, grownup, educated, professional-person handwriting. As he handed the form back, he icily told me that he didn't approve too much of an Irish Catholic boy going into British military service and that I should remember my religion and go to Mass on Sundays.

"Don't be like all the others who go to England and fall by the wayside," he said and with that he went back into his classroom. I left too, but as soon as I got around the first corner I opened the form to see what The Boss had written. It took me quite a while to decipher his writing, but when I finally managed to read words he'd scribbled I was pleasantly surprised. He said something to the effect that I was a very intelligent boy and would excel in anything and everything that interested me. He had me to a tee and yet I never dreamed that he held that opinion of me: in fact he had told me once that I'd probably end up being a member of a gang. But when I think about it, maybe he wasn't so far wrong about that after all—some gang!

Paddy Corning wrote up the other reference for me. He told me that he was sorry that I was going to leave my job and go off to the RAF, even offering me a rise if I stayed on with him and promising to eventually promote me to work behind the counter in the shop. Of course, the prospect of staying in Coleraine and working in Paddy's shop for the rest of my life just didn't fit in with the mental picture I had of my future. The siren song of the glossy brochures and the exotic lure of faraway places had me in such a stranglehold that chains and leg-irons couldn't have held me back from going. I politely turned down Paddy's offer, at which he sighed, shook his head and wrote out a glowing reference. This greatly surprised me after the *Gypsy Crèmes* incident and the fact that I continually raided the expensive biscuit tins at tea breaks, instead of being contented with one or two of the more economically priced *Rich Tea* biscuits that seemed to satisfy everyone else.

In August of 1956, just a few weeks after I'd returned the completed form, including the references, another brown envelope from Her Majesty plopped through our letterbox. Inside was a letter inviting me to present myself on a certain date for intelligence and education testing at the RAF Recruiting Office in Belfast. A voucher for free rail travel was included with the letter. I could hardly wait to tell John Moore, but for the first time since we'd talked about it, I detected a hint of sadness that he couldn't quite disguise as he tried to be enthusiastic for me. In the following days, word soon got around and before long I heard that two other boys from Coleraine had also applied and that they would be travelling with me to Belfast.

The day finally came and my friend John came to the house to say goodbye. Then he decided to accompany my father and me on our short walk to the railway station, where I was to catch the morning train. I exchanged my travel voucher for a return ticket at the ticket window and then showed it to the ticket collector at the platform barrier. He punched a neat little hole in it and then all three of us made our way onto the station platform. The other two Coleraine boys, Melvin Jackson and "Bull" McDonald, were already there. Melvin was with his mother, but Bull was by himself as he usually was. There's safety in numbers, so we joined them because, as I recall, we were the only people there.

As we waited on the platform for the Belfast train to arrive, the stationmaster and porters engaged us in friendly banter and soon learned all about the reason for our journey to the big city. Then, as we boarded the train for the two-hour trip to Belfast, everyone including the station staff waved and wished us good luck. It had been arranged that Melvin's aunt was going to meet us at the other end and get us safely to the recruiting office. So, three young boys off on a great adventure would still have adult protection from the big bad world, although it was a more innocent time and we were in no great danger. The wheels clickety-clicked and smoke from the steam locomotive's smoke stack streamed past the carriage window as we sped towards Belfast, stopping with a screech of brakes and a blast of steam at Ballymoney, then Ballymena and finally past Bleach Green as we swept around the eastern end of Belfast Lough and into Belfast's York Road railway station.

Melvin's aunt was there waiting, as promised. She welcomed us then led us to her home a short distance away for some very welcome sandwiches with steaming mugs of tea and freshly baked Irish soda scones topped with butter and strawberry jam. It was mid-morning by now and the time had come to present ourselves to the RAF. So, when we had finished our scones and tea, the kind lady escorted us to the recruiting office in nearby Clifton Street and then wished us well before saying goodbye.

A friendly sergeant welcomed us, introducing himself as Sergeant Malloy whilst he checked our names off his list. If you've seen one recruiting office, you've seen them all. They're full of colourful posters and brochures depicting the glamour of life in uniform, but it was the RAF ensign, hanging from an almost horizontal flagpole over the building's entrance, that really made an impression on me. The ensign was sky blue, with a small Union Jack in the upper corner nearest the flagstaff and a large red white and blue RAF roundel just a little off-centre. This was the first time that I'd laid eyes on the RAF flag, little realizing that, starting from right there and then, I would be seeing it with great frequency for the next 15 years of my life.

We had all received a letter advising that we should be prepared to be away from home for a few days. The arrangement was that we would undergo some testing in Belfast and those who passed this successfully would then travel from there to RAF Cosford in England. I'd never been to England before. In fact, up to that point, Belfast was the furthest distance I'd ever been from home in my entire life and that was only a piddling 60 miles from

Coleraine. So the prospect of going to England had me really fired up. This seemed to be the adventure to beat all adventures.

In all, there must have been close to a hundred boys in our group that day. We came from all corners of Northern Ireland and there were also some boys from Southern Ireland. I remember some of them by name: Niall Adderley, Cecil Burden, Charlie Cunningham, and Billy Cassidy. Most of us were ordinary middle of the road well-scrubbed working class kids, but this was the era of the "Teddy Boys" and one boy showed up in full Teddy Boy attire—long drape jacket with its velvet collar, drainpipe trousers and a shoestring for a tie. His hair was dark, thick and full, heavily Brylcreemed and slicked back into the "DA"—Duck's Arse—hairstyle popular with the "Teds". He looked tough—a real hard-man, as they say in Belfast—so most of us kept our distance. Teddy Boys were reputed to carry flick-knives and cut-throat razors and weren't afraid to use them at the slightest provocation. No point in taking chances with somebody like that.

They paid us—they actually paid us! I couldn't believe it, but we were all instructed to line up and then as our names were called out individually we would step forward, sign on a sheet of paper against our names and an officer then handed us some cash. It wasn't much by today's standards, 21 shillings I think, but it was a small fortune to me. The fact that I was able to buy biscuits and pop from the Sandes Home next door was the height of luxury to me. I told myself that this couldn't be such a bad life, where they give you money just for showing up.

The Intelligence Test was easy. I loved that kind of test and had lots of previous practice, having passed my 11-plus exam a few years before. The next two tests were a little harder, but not really difficult: just basic addition, subtraction, multiplication and division, a few fractions, a little algebra and a few written problems thrown in. The written questions were the kind of arithmetical problems that involve farmers who always want to divide their land up in weird ways so that they can spoil some of their sons and be cruel to the others. The English test was mainly comprehension, although I believe we had to write a short essay on "Why I want to run away from home and join the RAF." No, just kidding, that wasn't what it was about, although it might have been a good topic, suitable for psychoanalysis. Charlie Cunningham, who was one of the other boys there that day, shared memories of this event with me many years later. He mentioned that a person in RAF uniform stood at the front of the room facing us as we sat at some tables. This person held a list of words in his hand and, as he called out the words, we were expected to write them down on our exam answer papers to test our spelling ability. "Hippopotamus" is the only word that Charlie has managed to hold in his memory down through the corridors of time and personally I don't recall the spelling test at all.

Between tests, we went to the Sandes Home next door for lunch—fried egg, beans, sausage and chips, just what a growing lad wanted. The food server was a tall, balding man who was physically handicapped because one of his legs was shorter than the other. A special boot with a very thick sole, which he wore on the foot of his shortest leg, compensated for the difference in length between the two. Although it no doubt helped with his mobility, it looked ugly and caused him to walk with a pronounced heavy limp. In the typically cruel fashion of youngsters, we called him *Clubfoot* amongst ourselves—after a villainous character that haunted many of us through the weekly cliff-hanger episodes of a *Dick Tracy* serial which had made the rounds of Northern Ireland cinemas just a few years earlier.

Later that night, we were accommodated in an upstairs dormitory in the Sandes Home. It was primarily a Christian mission to military people; a place where financially stretched soldiers, sailors or airmen could get a meal and a bed for the night at a reasonable price, if they were willing to behave like good Christians whilst they were there. I learned later that a Miss Elise Sandes wanted to do her bit to save the common soldier's soul, so she founded the Sandes Soldiers' Homes to offer them food, lodging and salvation. I wonder what thoughts might have passed through the genteel lady's mind if she could have seen one of her dormitories packed with around 100 or so loudly boisterous young teenage boys.

Not one of us could settle that night, because we were so excited about being away from home and out in the big wide world. It must have sounded like a riot from downstairs, because it wasn't long before Clubfoot paid a visit to us and read the riot act about all the noise we were making. After his departure from the dorm, silence ensued for maybe all of ten minutes and then the noise level was back to full volume again. Clubfoot made several visits that night, getting angrier each time, but eventually we all ran out of steam and peace finally settled on the dormitory.

Most of us were having a great time, but one boy wasn't. He could be heard sobbing into his pillow. Next morning many of us were surprised to learn that the crying kid was none other than the tough Teddy Boy. He looked very crestfallen and embarrassed as he got dressed in the dormitory, not the preening hard-man of the day before and was gone soon after that. Things like that make you wonder about what goes on behind the façade some people put up. He had only been away from home for one night, in his own city at that and a real tough guy by all outward appearances. So did he miss his mum, or what?

We got the results of our tests after breakfast and I was happy to learn that I'd passed. The bad news was that the other two boys from Coleraine didn't do so well and were sent home later that day. In fact, quite a few fell by the wayside and by the time all the results were called out, we were down to about half the original number of candidates.

After that, they kept us hanging around all day because the boat to England didn't sail until evening. We amused ourselves, talked, played cards, read and filled up on junk food purchased from the Sandes Home with our travel allowance. What the heck, we were rich after all and could afford it!

In the late afternoon, we were rounded up and assembled outside the recruiting office. When everyone had been accounted for, we were paid some more travel allowance to Cosford and given a meal in the Sandes Home. Then, Sergeant Malloy escorted us to Belfast docks, which was just a short walking distance from Clifton Street and ushered us aboard the *M.V. Ulster Monarch* for the overnight passage that evening, across the Irish Sea to Liverpool. This was a ship of some 3800 tons, built at nearby Harland and Wolf's shipyard in 1929. She had been pressed into service during World War II and then decommissioned by the Royal Navy to resume her peacetime role of ferrying passengers between Belfast and Liverpool. Despite being overhauled after her wartime service, she couldn't disguise her venerable age.

Second-class passengers, like us, were located at the stern of the ship, where the accommodation consisted of one large lounge containing parallel rows of bench-like seating. In an apparent effort to make things a little less Spartan, the individual seats were outfitted with faux leather seat cushions and backrests. There was similar seating around some of the walls of the lounge, but a shuttered bar counter took up most of the forward wall. The ship did have some sleeping accommodation, but as I found out later, these "berths" usually needed to be reserved weeks in advance. It didn't really matter, because RAF funds apparently didn't run to that kind of luxury anyway. The lounge was about three-quarters full, so we all managed to find seats on which we dumped our stuff to reserve them before going out on deck to watch the action. I went up there with Billy Cassidy, a Belfast lad that I'd become friendly with. We watched as other passengers boarded the ship until it was time to pull the gangplank away. Soon, a gang of dockworkers cast off the ship's lines and then we were moving down the River Lagan, past the Harland and Wolf shipyard and into Belfast Lough. Gradually, the nearby shores receded on both sides until we were far away from land and the darkness of night slowly settled over the seascape. I could see the faraway lights of Holywood and Bangor twinkling as the ship slowly eased out of the Lagan estuary, carrying me with it on the next exciting leg of this great adventure.

About an hour later the ship emerged from the shelter of Belfast Lough and the wind picked up, now that we were out in the open Irish Sea. The *Ulster Monarch* changed course as we came around the southern headland, now making her way southeast towards Liverpool. At the same time, she met a heavy swell that caused her to pitch and roll in a very noticeable manner. As I later came to learn, this tub was notorious for her poor ability to ride smoothly through rough water and it was even said that she was liable to wallow on wet grass. There was nothing much else to see and the wind had become much chillier, now that we were out in the open sea, so Billy and I then weaved our way back to the lounge. We hung on to anything within reach, in a desperate effort to keep from being thrown around by the up and down and side to side motion of the ship. We were hungry and wanted to find out if we could buy a sandwich from the bar.

Where there had been a closed steel shutter before, there was now a beleaguered looking man wearing a white shirt and black tie. His shirt sleeves were loosely rolled up to just below the elbows and he was doing his best to deal with the undisciplined mob of male passengers that crowded together around the bar. Each man was noisily competing with his neighbour to be noticed by the barman and have his order accepted. Many of the men were buying beer and whiskey, but some were buying mugs of tea and sandwiches. I finally managed to get myself a mug of tea and a sausage sandwich, then went and sat down on the seat I'd reserved earlier. It seemed comfortable at first, but after a while the unyielding hardness of the wooden bench seemed to come right through the thinness of the seat cushion. Many of the seasoned passengers had commandeered more than one seat, then taken the cushions off and laid them on the floor to make a bed. They were the lucky ones! The seats didn't recline in any way. Those of us sitting in them had to sit bolt upright. And if that wasn't bad enough, the wooden armrests prevented any attempt to lie down without an armrest digging into your ribs.

Later, some of the men who had been drinking whiskey and Guinness started singing. These were mostly tough, weather-beaten looking fellows who never seemed to remove their Andy Capp-style flat caps, but wore them always at a jaunty angle. The drunker they became, the jauntier the angle, often with several strands of straggly grey hair poking out from underneath the peak and sticking to their sweaty foreheads. They were mostly Irish labourers going to hard manual jobs in England and representing what was probably Ireland's greatest export at that time—human muscle power. They must have made this journey dozens of times and even if they had ever once thought of it as an adventure, that aspect of the crossing had been lost on them long ago. Drinking was what they enjoyed; it eased the sorrow of leaving their families for a lengthy exile and at the same time was just an extension of the normal social life they pursued with their fellow Paddys in the pubs of England after they'd finished work for the day.

After a while, some of them began throwing up on the lounge floor. No one attempted to clean it up, so the regurgitated Guinness just oozed backwards and forwards, backwards and forwards, as the boat pitched and rolled. It was gut-churning to see and I tried not to look, but the aroma became overpowering, so Billy and I went back out on deck to get away from the awful sight and smell. We found a sheltered spot out of the wind and at about the halfway stage watched as the Isle of Man slipped by on the starboard side. At one point, we saw another ship passing us in the opposite direction. It was all aglow like a small island of light in the surrounding pitch blackness of the sea. Our ship must have appeared just the same to anyone watching from the other vessel, which most probably was the *Ulster Monarch's* sister-ship making the reverse trip from Liverpool to Belfast. Ever since then, whenever I hear the expression "ships that pass in the night", the memory of seeing that ship in the cold darkness of the Irish Sea immediately comes to mind.

We were still on deck when the sky started getting light. It was late summer, so dawn came early. Away on the horizon I could make out the silhouettes of two ornate towers framed in the light of the early morning sun. Each appeared to be topped by some kind of decorative fixture that I couldn't quite identify. Someone told me that these were the twin towers of the Liver Building, a famous Liverpool landmark and what I saw on each tower was a statue of the mythical Liver Bird that symbolized the City of Liverpool. Oddly, the word "Liver" seemed to be pronounced differently ("lie"—as in to tell a lie and "ver"—the first syllable of Veronica) from the way it was enunciated when used in the city's name. If I thought that seeing the Liver Birds meant that we were there, then I was dead wrong. It took something like another two hours from the time that I first spotted them until we actually entered the Mersey estuary and by that time I'd had more than enough of being at sea, even if it was for the very first time.

My first impression of Liverpool was far from pleasant. It was a grimy industrial city and its river, the Mersey, was a stinking polluted waterway. This was all so different to the bucolic land that I'd just left, where everything seemed fresh, green and clean. The smell from the river added to the queasiness that I was already experiencing as a result of having endured the motion of the ship and the sickening aroma created by the drunken navvies of the previous night.

Docking at Liverpool wasn't an easy business. The ship entered a lock, which was then slowly flooded to raise the water level by several feet. The operation lasted for what seemed an eternity until, finally, the upper lock gates swung open and we moved forward a short distance to tie up at Princes Dock. On the shore I caught a glimpse of my first real live British Bobby with his peculiarly English policeman's helmet. The policemen of the Royal Ulster Constabulary that I was used to seeing in Northern Ireland wore flat peaked hats and walked around with holstered revolvers at their waists. This policeman, like all British Bobbies of those days, was completely unarmed. He stood by the gangplank as we disembarked and I somehow expected him to say "Evening all!" like Dixon of Dock Green used to do on TV.

Sergeant Malloy gathered us together and then we walked the half a mile distance to Lime Street Station, as a group, to catch our train for Cosford. This was a huge railway station, making my little Coleraine station seem like something out of Toytown and even making Belfast's York Road look pathetically small. And the sulphur laden smoke belching out of all those coal-fired steam engines filled the air with an acrid odour that was much, much worse than the smell of the Mersey. I remember a popular folk song from around that time that went by the title Maggie May. Not the one that Rod Stewart made popular years later, but an older more traditional one with a chorus that went...

Oh, Maggie, Maggie May, they have taken her away,
And she'll never walk down Lime Street anymore.
You may search from here to China you'll not find a girl that's finer,
That is finer than my darlin' Maggie May.

Every time I heard that song and especially the line about Lime Street, that terrible smell would come right back into my nostrils and my stomach would retch just like it did that morning in Liverpool.

Sergeant Malloy found the train that we needed to board and shepherded us on to the platform. The train was made up of a dozen or so red and creamy yellow coloured British Railways carriages of the era. This colour scheme was popularly known as "blood and custard," and for me, it stood out in stark contrast to the uniform emerald green colour of railway carriages back home in Ireland.

The RAF had reserved a few compartments for us, so we clambered aboard and were pleasantly surprised to discover that these English trains were really very comfortable. More so than those that I was used to back home and the quality of the seating was definitely a huge improvement over that of the *Ulster Monarch*. At last, we were able to spread out and had hopes of catching up on some sleep. But there was a great sense of excitement too and that made sleep impossible for a while. After all, this was another country and there was a lot to see and absorb.

After half an hour or so of waiting, the train finally pulled out of Lime Street station with a shriek of its steam whistle and a violent jerk, then we were on our way. At first we passed through the grimy industrial heart of Liverpool, but then soon found ourselves rolling smoothly through the sleepy early morning English countryside. There were fewer hedgerows and larger fields than in my native Ireland and the countryside seemed flatter too, all of which confirmed what I'd learned from Mr. Murphy during geography lessons at St. Malachy's.

Our route took us to Crewe, a major railway intersection in those days, where we then needed to change to another train that would take us further south to West Bromwich. There was an hour or so to wait at Crewe for the next train, so we grabbed the opportunity to find something to eat. Getting food aboard the ship that morning had been next to impossible, so I was famished in spite of the queasiness brought on by the combination of ship's motion and the unforgettable Liverpudlian aromas. But all we could find in the British Railways canteen were cellophane wrapped egg sandwiches that seemed to have been prepared hours before. Since there was nothing else available, I bought a couple of the sandwiches and a cup of weak lukewarm British Railways tea to wash them down.

About thirty minutes after finishing my sandwiches, the train to West Bromwich arrived at the platform. We climbed aboard and settled down for the hour or two that it took until we pulled into West Brom. After that it was a local train, which wasn't quite as comfortable as the other two main-line trains we'd travelled on earlier, that took us all the way into Royal Air Force Station Cosford, where we arrived some time around midday.

Sergeant Malloy shepherded us from the railway station to the Guardroom at the entrance to Cosford RAF station. There was some paperwork to complete and then, before long, we were issued with bedding, a white pint-sized "china" mug and a knife, fork and spoon. We were then led in procession, carrying our pile of blankets and dining implements, to a group of wooden barrack rooms, each of which contained probably twelve to fourteen RAF barrack-room style beds, but were otherwise sparsely furnished.

The beds, as I was to discover later, were identical throughout the service. The standard RAF barrack room bed consisted of a sturdy metal frame, painted light grey and supporting a horsehair mattress. The actual support for the mattress was a steel lattice stretched horizontally across the frame and held taut by a series of small springs set approximately six inches apart. One end of each spring was hooked into a hole in the frame, while the other end was fastened to a special eye on the lattice. Although the purpose of the springs was to keep the lattice stretched tightly, over time the springs on most beds weakened, resulting in the mattress sagging in the middle so that anyone sleeping on it couldn't avoid rolling into a dip created by the sag. The depth of the dip depended on how old the springs were. In a transit type of billet, such as the ones in which we were being accommodated, the beds all tended to be old so the sag feature was very pronounced.

Bedding consisted of five thin blankets—what the folks back home called army blankets; a feather pillow in traditional striped cloth; a pair of white cotton sheets and a pillowcase. It was all strictly Spartan in nature, but I could have slept on a plank that night so it didn't really matter. I don't think there was any one of us that had a clue about how to make a bed, but we all managed to get our blankets and sheets creatively arranged into something that we could at least sleep in. Later, we would be taught the fine art of bed making, but that was still a little way down the road.

We were hungry. Not one of us had eaten a proper meal since leaving Belfast the previous day. Getting meals outside of the appointed mealtimes was apparently as easy as getting an Act of Parliament passed, but the good sergeant had been given a meal chitty at the Guardroom. He now wheedled the reluctant cookhouse staff into frying up some eggs, beans and potatoes for the ravenous youngsters in his charge. But long before the food was served up, one of the cookhouse staff brought out a big stainless steel urn filled with scalding hot tea, to which they had already added milk. Taking turns, we filled up our china mugs, added sugar and gulped it down. It didn't taste much like the tea that I was used to at home but, as they say, it was wet and warm and I was grateful for it. Not only that, it helped stave off the hunger pangs until the meal was ready. Altogether, the food was plentiful and filling, which was more than I could say about the "home cooked" near-starvation diet that I suffered at the hands of my stepmother, Annie. Yep, I thought, this is alright!

Our visit to Cosford lasted something like four days in all. During that time, in addition to being poked and prodded by doctors, we were interviewed individually by officers whose job it was to gauge our suitability for training and to steer us into the trades they felt we might best be suited for. The Squadron Leader who interviewed me looked at my file and then smilingly informed me that I met the requirements to train as an aircraft electrical mechanic. He told me that this was a difficult trade to get into; that there weren't many openings and that I should feel privileged to have been selected. But, he warned, the training would be difficult and so I needed to work hard if I wanted to pass out as a fully-fledged Aircraft Electric Mechanic at the end of the Boy Entrant training. I was so thrilled that I'd been given the trade of my choice that I really only half heard what he said about working hard and all that stuff. It was the sort of speech that grownups always seemed to make, but my thoughts were soaring up amongst the clouds where I saw visions of the people who would be proud of me and the riches and rewards that learning a trade would bring with it. Here at last was my chance to break free from the chains that had shackled me up until now—my oppressive family life and the unfair Northern Ireland politics of religion that prevented me from getting into a decent trade. Would I be bold enough to reach out and grasp this opportunity? The need to decide loomed just around the corner.

In between interviews and medical examinations, the remainder of our stay at Cosford consisted of being shown something of the Boy Entrant way of life. A "Leading Boy" took us on a tour of the Catering Training School, proudly showing us huge vats in which the food was cooked, mixing machines and a weird implement that was supposed to be used for shredding beef. I'd never before heard of beef being shredded, let alone there being a special piece of equipment for accomplishing the task. As the highlight of the tour, he led us into a room that contained a fine display of little hors d'oeuvres and petit fours. We were allowed to gaze at them for a few moments before the Leading Boy proudly informed us that Boy Entrant trainee caterers had created them that very day. Someone asked what was going to happen to them, maybe hoping that we might be allowed to sample some. But our tour guide loftily replied that they would be served in the Boy Entrants' mess. That took some believing! Such delicacies just didn't seem to go with the class of food we'd become accustomed to partaking in the Boy Entrants' mess.

Another tour guide took us to a room full of desks with the kind of Morse code keys that used to be seen in the old Western films. We were told that this is where the Wireless Telegraphers were trained to send and receive code. The same tour also introduced us to another high-tech item known as the teleprinter. Nowadays, this venerable machine would be classified as a museum piece, having been replaced first by the fax machine and then by the modern miracle of e-mail. But, at the time, it was impressive.

Mostly, however, these were ho-hum tours. I wasn't interested in being a wireless telegrapher and I sure as hell didn't want to be a caterer. No, what really got my juices flowing was a tour of the Boy Entrant training workshops. These were in hangars and they had real live aircraft in there. A Hawker Hunter sat proudly in one of the hangar workshops. It was the first one I'd ever seen at close range and it had to be one of the most beautiful things that I'd ever laid eyes on. Even though its flying days were finished, it was every inch a thoroughbred, looking sleek and shiny sitting there in its dark green and light grey camouflage livery with the swept-back wings and streamlined Perspex canopy gleaming and glinting in the hangar lights. We saw some other planes in the hangar; a Vampire I believe and some prop-jobs, but seeing the Hunter was my epiphany. It made me realize that caring for and being around beautiful aircraft such as this was what I wanted to do.

Up to this point, everything had been something of a boyish adventure—a game, really. Events had just progressed from the time that I'd answered the newspaper advert, like a snowball rolling downhill that starts off small, but grows larger and speeds up with every inch it travels. Now the situation had become serious and I had an important decision to make. There was still time to back out and some boys did, but I didn't want to do that. So I made the decision that this was to be my future—it was what I wanted to do—promising myself that I would stay on this path wherever it led. I rationalized that even though it would subject me to military discipline and training and I'd seen and heard enough to have no illusions about that, it couldn't be worse than the unhappy life from which I was desperately trying to escape. In fact it seemed to hold out great promise. And now, with the hindsight of years, I regard that decision as the most important one that I ever made, without exception, even though I was a boy of only 15 at the time. The space age that was just dawning had a name for it; I had finally achieved escape velocity. There would be difficulties ahead for sure, but I still shudder to think how my life might have worked out if I'd backed off and not made that very important choice.

During our few days at Cosford, the Boy Entrant's uniform became a familiar sight. It consisted of the basic regular RAF blue serge tunic and trousers, but with a few embellishments, the most striking of which was the hat. There was nothing remarkable about it in itself, just the standard RAF issue, but what made it different was the brightly coloured chequered hatband—two rows of alternating colours—worn by Boy Entrants in place of the black hatbands worn by regular RAF servicemen. I recall that the pattern on the hatband of a Boy Entrant being trained in the catering trade, who escorted a party of us on a tour of the Catering Training School, consisted of red and yellow squares. But that was only one colour scheme; there were others, although his was the only one that sticks in my memory from the visit to Cosford.

Two other interesting features elevated the Boy Entrant uniform above the drabness of its regular service counterpart. One of these was what looked like a brass cartwheel about one and a half inches in diameter worn on the upper sleeve and set against a coloured disc that was slightly larger at about two inches in diameter. The other feature was the set of small upside-down stripes worn by many boys at wrist level on the cuff of their tunics. Some had one stripe, some had two and others had three. I could now picture myself in one of those uniforms and was eager to get on with the process of being able to wear one soon. But all in good time. First, we had to go back to our homes and wait until October to be called for our induction into the Service.

* * *

The journey home was less exciting. Going to England for the first time had been a fantastic experience, but there was nothing new to discover on the way back, just the long, long trip to endure. So, we got the train back to Liverpool, then the boat to Belfast. The first stop, after disembarking next morning, was the Clifton Street recruiting office where we were issued with railway passes that would take us to our home towns. We then said our goodbyes and headed off in the direction that would take us to our respective homes. I made my way to the York Road railway station and caught the next available train that would bring me to journey's end.

About two hours later, when I alighted on the Coleraine station platform, one of the porters who'd bantered with Melvin, Bull and me a few days earlier, when we were setting off for Belfast, seemed surprised to see me.

"Hello son," he said, "did you get left behine? The other'uns came back days ago."

"Naw, I went to Englan'. I passed the test in Belfast, so they sent me tae Englan' fur some more."

"Did ye pass?"

"Aye."

"And ye're goin' in the air force?"

"Aye."

He laughed at this. "The other wee fellas said you'd failed too, an' said ye'd be home on the nixt train."

"Naw, Ah passed."

"Well, that's grand, your Da'll be proud o' yeh. When wull y'haff to go away?"

"Dunno," I said, with a shrug of my shoulders, "soon."

"Well, we'll be seein' ye agin soon, then!"

"Aye."

With that, I set off for the short walk home from the station to give the news to the family.

For the next few weeks I found it difficult to settle back down into the old routine of delivering groceries to Paddy Corning's customers, knowing that it wasn't going to be for much longer and that my life was about to change drastically. I saw a lot of my pal John Moore. We had lived near each other when we were younger, had gone to the same school and had been best friends for several years. It was John who introduced me to Elvis the Pelvis. One day he got talking about this record he'd heard played on a jukebox in a little greasy spoon café near the railway station, so I went there with him and listened. That was the first time I heard Elvis—he was singing *Blue Suede Shoes*. It was so different from the usual run of the mill songs that I was used to hearing on the radio around that time and just seemed so new and fresh. We sang the chorus back and forwards to each other when we were out and about, like a young person's code that the older folks couldn't understand. After that, we made many trips to the Railway Place Café to put our money in the jukebox and feed our craving for *Blue Suede Shoes* over and over again until the proprietor must have been going out of his mind. He was probably pleased later, for a little while anyway, when we latched on to *Hound Dog*.

I introduced Melvin Jackson to John. He was one of the two others who had travelled to the RAF recruiting office in Belfast with me. We had become friends and I was sad that he hadn't made it past the initial exams. But now, all three of us went around together during the short time that I had left. Melvin was very self-conscious about having failed to pass the education test. For years he had dreamed of joining the RAF, but now his hopes had been dashed. His mother took me on one side during one of my visits to his home and in an earnest confidential tone asked me not to tell anyone the reason why Melvin hadn't been accepted.

"If anyone asks," she said, "just tell them that he had failed on account of his poor eyesight."

"Okay," I agreed.

One or two people did ask me during the next few weeks, in a way that made me believe they already knew the real reason, but I stuck to the party line about Melvin's bad eyesight.

Coleraine was your typical mid-fifties small town, where all the shops on the main street closed up at six o'clock in the evening and from midday on Wednesdays, which was "half day." There were two cinemas in town, *The Picture Palace* on Railway Road, which was better known around town as "Christie's" after the owner's family name and *The Palladium* in Society Street. Both showed a film for two days—two evening performances and a Saturday matinee—and then changed the programme. They were closed on Sundays, like just about everything else in town. And that was about it for entertainment. Young people in their late teens or early twenties could go to dances at *The Boathouse,* or to *The Arcadia Ballroom* in Portrush, the nearby seaside resort. Older guys always had plenty of pubs to patronize, but there weren't many activities available for us 15-yearolds. We thought of ourselves as oh-so-grownup because we'd left school, were working and had a little money in our pockets, all of which we felt entitled us to a night-life. And for our age group, the "in place" to hang around on Friday and Saturday nights was Morelli's Ice Cream Parlour and Fish & Chip shop, although we never actually purchased very much from that fine establishment.

We'd stand around outside and watch girls no older than we were promenade up and down the street. They were never alone, always at least in pairs and like us they were there to see and be seen. We would behave in really sophisticated ways, like whistle after them, or try out some very witty pick-up lines as they passed by, such as, "Can I see you home? Where've ye been all me life?" Yeah, we really talked like that! Embarrassing, isn't it? The girls would giggle but usually kept walking. If they stopped it was just to trade some banter. At St. Malachy's Catholic School that John Moore and I had attended, the boys and girls were segregated and although I lived with two sisters at home there was still much I had to learn about the opposite sex. Our encounters were awkward to say the least, but it was great fun. Yes, we felt so grown up because we'd left school, but the joke is that not one of us had reached our sixteenth birthday. Hell, we hadn't even started shaving yet.

The Summer of 1956 in Coleraine,—which mainly consisted of rain between the showers—gave way to autumn, when small boys hurled sticks at the high branches of the local Horse Chestnut trees in the hope of dislodging a few prickly seed-bearing cases. This activity was occurring throughout the British Isles. The dislodged chestnuts were used in an ancient children's game that English youngsters called *Conkers* and Irish kids, at least in my neck of the woods, called *Cheesers*.

Around this time another familiar-looking package plopped through the letterbox. It contained a letter officially informing me that I'd been accepted to train as an aircraft electrical mechanic at the No. 4 School of Technical Training, Royal Air Force St. Athan, Glamorgan, South Wales and that I

was to report to the Belfast Recruiting Office on Saturday, 13th
October, 1956. The envelope included a railway warrant that
would take care of my train fare and some consent papers for my
father to sign. I think he gave me the speech again about him not
wanting me to go, but that he wouldn't stop me. I was hoping he
wouldn't, but why would he? Let's face it, there would be one
less mouth to feed and the prospect of a little more money
coming in from the earnings that I was expected to send home.
So he signed the papers and we sent them back to the RAF.

Meanwhile, I continued working for Paddy Corning, but
there was an omnipresent sense that time was running out and
any plans for the future involving friends or home town were
becoming increasingly short term as each day passed. I still
delivered groceries to the likes of Mrs. Mulligan, but now she
always received her full weight of the *Gypsy Crèmes*.

And so it was that I pedalled on into October and into a
new chapter of my life.

CHAPTER 2

The Oath of Allegiance

My final week in Coleraine was tinged with a mixture of excitement and sadness. In addition to giving Paddy Corning a week's notice of my intention to leave his employment, there were goodbyes to be said to family and friends. And one of the most important people that I needed to say goodbye to was my Aunt Maggie, so I made a point of visiting her at home one evening on my way home from work.

In reality, Maggie was my great-aunt because she was my mother's aunt, but I had been brought up to know her as Aunt Maggie. She never married and therefore had no children of her own, but for family reasons Maggie had raised her sister's daughter—my mother—from when she was a young child, all the way into adulthood. The relationship she and I shared was therefore akin to that of grandmother and grandson. Although she was kind and generous to my sisters and me, she had never really hit it off very well with my father. Each tolerated the other, albeit uneasily, whilst my mother was alive, but they had a big falling-out after her death and wanted nothing to do with each other after that. Because of this, my father forbade me to have any contact with Maggie, but I disobeyed him and secretly went to see her at least once a week. She always made me welcome and wanted to be involved in my life, but she wasn't going to be able to come and see me off on the train because she was getting on in years, so I went to see her instead. Aunt Maggie knew why I'd come, and was visibly upset that I would be leaving our home town.

"If your mother was still alive, she'd never have let you go," she said.

For the umpteenth time, I explained that it was the best thing for me because I would be learning a trade.

"You'll write, won't you?" She asked. Then she gave me a little package of writing paper and envelopes so that I wouldn't have any excuse not to. And she gave me some money. "Here, take this," she said as she pressed it into my hand, "it'll buy you something to eat on the boat." She was so kind to me, it broke my heart to have to say goodbye.

When it was time to leave, tears filled her eyes and she repeated what she had said earlier about how things would have been much different if my mother had been alive. Then she gave me a hug and kissed me wetly on the cheek, which I tolerated although I hated being subjected to sloppy stuff like that, like most young boys of my age. When I left, she watched me from her front doorway as I walked down the long straight street. And then just before disappearing around the corner at its end, I turned and waved her a final goodbye.

My father had told me that the Parish Priest wanted to see me, so I made the long trek up to the Parochial House, all the while wondering what I was going to say and what Father Close would have to say to me. He was a brusque kind of a person, so I felt just a wee bit intimidated, although I needn't have worried. The housekeeper answered the door when I rang the bell and I told her that I'd come to see Father Close. She asked me to wait there on the porch and then disappeared into the gloomy interior of the large house. Shortly after that, the middle-aged, balding, grey-haired priest came to the doorway. He didn't invite me inside, but instead asked me detailed questions about where I'd be going as we stood there on the Parochial House porch. He told me that I was going out into the world where there would be a lot of temptation and that I needed to be a good Catholic and keep up my faith. Then he said "Wait, I've got something for you." With that he produced a small metal capsule-like article, about an inch in length, from the pocket of his cassock. It rattled when I took it from him.

"Open it," he urged.

I unscrewed the cap and a miniature statuette of the Blessed Virgin slid out on to my hand.

"This has been blessed at Lourdes. Keep her with you always, she'll protect you."

I did keep the little statuette with me always, and still have it to this day; in fact she should have her own frequent flier account with the amount of travelling I've done around the world. And Father Close was right; she does seem to have protected me wherever I've gone.

As we stood there on the porch, Father Close made the sign of the cross over my head and said a prayer.

"God be with you," he said, shaking my hand. And with that, we parted.

The last two days were difficult, knowing that my life was never going to be the same again. It was tough saying goodbye to my friends John and Melvin, and we all solemnly said that we would get back together when I came home on leave at Christmas, but it was never really the same after that.

* * *

On the day of my departure, both my father and John Moore escorted me to the railway station again, but on this occasion it was for the last time. My Aunt Alice was also there to see me off. She was my father's sister, and had intervened when things had become difficult for me in the family home while I was still attending school. She had rescued me by arranging that I would spend the weekend days at her house. This arrangement had worked out very well for more than a year. I went over there on Saturday mornings, did some chores and ran some errands for her. Then she made lunch for me—a good lunch too—and as a reward for doing her chores, usually sent me off to the Saturday afternoon cinema matinee. I didn't stay there overnight, but went home after having dinner with her and my Uncle Frank. Then on Sundays after Mass, I would go to her house again and take the dog for a walk. That done, I was free to spend the rest of the day as I pleased and would usually go somewhere with John Moore, but I was in her charge for the day, so any misbehaviour on my part would have wrecked the arrangement. And for that reason, I behaved; otherwise the privilege of spending my weekends with Alice would have come to an end. The alternative wasn't too appealing; it would have meant confinement at home under the distrusting eyes of my stepmother, Annie, who was always of the opinion that I would only get up to no good if I was out of her immediate supervision. Even after I left school and had started working for Paddy Corning, I still spent Sundays with Alice, right up to the end. And now, she had come to the station to say goodbye.

The train came and my father shook hands with me; he
told me to be careful and wished me luck. I knew he felt
awkward, but no more awkward than me. Aunt Alice gave me a
hug and told me to remember to go to Mass on Sundays. John
shook hands with me too, but he also had an awkward air about
him. The Irish male culture that the three of us shared didn't
provide us with the tools necessary to deal with a sentimental
moment like this. So we shuffled our feet, fidgeted and engaged
in small talk, wishing that it was all over and we could get back
to our respective comfort zones. Then the train Guard blew his
whistle, which meant it was time for passengers to get aboard
the train. I climbed the two steps into the train, went into a
compartment and put my suitcase up on the luggage rack, then
pulled up on the big leather strap that lowered the window and
leaned out. We made some more small talk until the Guard blew
his whistle again, at the same time waving a green flag and with
a few powerful chuffs from the steam locomotive, the train
started to move out of the station. We all waved as the distance
between us increased and we became small in each other's eyes.
Then, when my little send-off party had completely disappeared
from view, I closed the window and settled down in a corner of
the compartment. There came an unexpected twinge of
homesickness that moved me to drink in the vision of the
emerald green fields and autumn tinted trees and hedgerows of
Ireland as they raced swiftly past the train window, as though
they were passing symbolically out of my life.

The nostalgia lifted, however, when I got to the recruiting
office in Clifton Street. Sergeant Malloy was there again and so
were the friendly faces of the other boys. I joined the group and
talked and joked with the others, as we all waited for something
to happen.

They gave us a meal at the Sandes Home again and we
then lined up for our travel allowance—I always liked that part!

Sergeant Malloy said, "Gather round lads." And, when
we all got around him in a circle, he briefed us. "We're going to
take the Stranraer boat this time. It's a shorter sea journey," he
explained, "but there'll be a longer time on the train when we get
to the other side." He then went on to tell us that we would travel

to Cosford first, drop off those boys who would be training there and then the remainder would continue on to St. Athan in South Wales, a total journey of around 500 miles. He also proudly informed us that our group was the largest ever to have left Northern Ireland to join the Boy Entrants' service and that a press photographer was there to take our picture. The photographer was from the *Northern Whig & Belfast Post*, one of the morning papers I used to deliver to people's homes as a newsagent's delivery boy in my earlier years. He went to an open upstairs window of the recruiting office and leaned out, aiming his camera at us as he called out directions. At his urging, we squeezed tightly into a group, then tighter, and tighter still. Finally, he took the picture and it appeared the following Monday, on page 3 of the October 15, 1956 edition of the *Whig*. I know this because Melvin Jackson's mother saved it, and showed it to me a few months later.

The Scottish town of Stranraer is due east across the Irish Sea from the port town of Larne and coincidentally, the distance between the two ports is the narrowest stretch of sea separating Ireland from its neighbour, Great Britain. In 1956, the average crossing time between Larne and Stranraer was only about two hours, which was nothing when compared to the eight or nine hours of overnight sailing across the wider stretch of sea and longer diagonal route from Belfast to Liverpool. So Stranraer did seem to be the better choice, especially since we had a lot of territory to cover the next day. Sergeant Malloy might also have known that there was a threat of fog in England the next day that would surely delay our arrival into Liverpool, while the more northerly Stranraer route had the reputation for being less troubled by that particular weather phenomenon.

The crossing was calm, and in truth really did take only two hours. The only downside was that Sergeant Malloy managed to get himself drunk. I don't know why that happened, but it was a Saturday night, which, for all I know, might have been his pub night. Ordinarily, he was a very pleasant, patient man, but his darker side came to the surface courtesy of a few pints of Guinness and by the time we docked at Stranraer, the sergeant was several sheets to the wind. He swore profusely at us for no apparent reason as he fumbled around trying to get us organized on the dockside, frequently calling us little fuckers and angrily throwing our luggage around. Fortunately, the train was waiting for us right next to the dock, so it was just a matter of stepping a few feet from ship to train and finding our reserved compartments, in spite of the sergeant's inebriated state. It was easy, now that we knew the drill and so we settled down with plenty of reading material and waited to start on the long rail journey ahead. It was still the middle of the night and chilly in the compartment without the heat that would come only when we got under way, but there seemed to be some delay. That's when we heard about the fog further south, across the border in England. A "pea-souper" the railway people called it. Progress was going to be slow as we headed south.

I wasn't very familiar with fog. We rarely had it at Coleraine's latitude. All we'd get was an occasional sea mist that cleared in a few hours. Nothing like the thick fogs—the pea-soupers—that we had often heard blanketed England for days on end. Now I was going to experience thick fog firsthand. Everything was clear for the first few hours, as the train rattled through the pre-dawn hours towards Carlisle. It was certainly no express, and seemed to stop at every station along the way, but we were making progress. We were scheduled to catch a mainline train at Carlisle that would take us on to Crewe, our next destination, but the mainline train was late in arriving. I can still hear the sound of the barely understandable station announcer's echoing voice announcing something like, "The train to Crewe will be late arriving at platform three," over the public address system. We waited in the cold early morning air for what seemed like hours, drinking endless cups of British Railways tea and smoking Woodbines. Yeah, I smoked in those days, like most people, and had been at it since I was about 13. "Wild Woodbines" was my weed of choice because it was the cheapest and besides, that's what my father and Annie smoked like the good role models they were. The Woodbines cost one shilling and tuppence for a packet of ten, or eightpence for a little open-ended packet of five.

OFF ON AN
R.A.F. CAREER

Sergeant J. M   (right), with the 47 boys who left Clifton Street R.A.F. recruiting centre, Belfast, on Saturday for England, where they will commence training.

Photograph that appeared in the Northern Whig and Belfast Post *after our departure on the Larne – Stranraer ferry for RAF Cosford. The author is on the extreme left.*

Eventually, the train pulled into the station and halted in a cloud of hissing steam and with a long, eardrum-piercing screech of brakes. Doors came open and then slammed closed with the loud noise that only those old solidly wooden railway carriage doors could make, as some passengers alighted and others climbed aboard. Sergeant Malloy was looking more sober by now, but a little white around the gills as he led our little party along the platform until we found the compartments that had been reserved for us. As before, this was signified by white "Reserved" notices pasted on the insides of the windows. We climbed aboard the train and waited. Eventually, the guard's whistle-blast preceded a sudden jolt, as the locomotive took up the slack in the large chain links that connected the carriages of the train to one another, and then we were off on the next leg of the journey.

Everything seemed to be going well for a while, but then the train's speed dropped off to a snail's pace. It was impossible to see anything in the darkness outside, but occasionally harshly yellow sodium lights would come into view as they floated eerily past the compartment window in a disembodied kind of way, each ringed with a halo of swirling fog. Other than the lights, there wasn't anything else discernible. Then, as daylight gradually seeped into the world, it became obvious that we were travelling through a thick grey blanket of fog. Visibility was maybe 20 feet and I could only make out the railway embankment, with everything else beyond swallowed up in the impenetrable greyness. The trees and undergrowth that I was able to see were dripping wet, and the fog swirled around as our train made its painfully slow way south. Frequently, the brakes would screech on and we'd come to a jarring stop, then sit there for what seemed ages, probably waiting for a signal to change. And it was like that all the way to Cosford, where we arrived several hours later than scheduled.

The stopover at Cosford was short, but long enough for us to get a meal. Then, it was time to say goodbye to those of our friends who would be staying there. In a way, I was feeling envious because it was over for them while we had to battle on through the fog to Wales. But at the same time, I felt that Cosford was ancient explored territory with nothing new to offer and I was eager to tackle the new and unexplored—namely, St. Athan. With only another 200 miles or so to go, we set off under the trusty eye of a slightly fragile-feeling Sergeant Malloy who, by this time, had mostly recovered from his bout with the demon drink.

For a few hours the name-boards on stations that we passed through had seemingly English names, like Kidderminster and Hereford, but then I started seeing strange names like Abergavenny and Pontypridd and Llan-this and Llan-that. Meanwhile, day had turned back into night again before we arrived at our last-but-one destination, the town of Barry. At least its name sounded English and was easy to get my tongue around, unlike those Aber and Ponty places that we'd passed through earlier. Our dwindled-down party of about twenty souls climbed down from the train and onto the platform. We groaned with relief as we exercised our stiff limbs while waiting for the local train that would take us to Gileston, the nearest railway station to our final destination, RAF St. Athan East Camp.

This train, when it came, was rickety and cold. There was no corridor, just separate compartments and it was just too bad if you needed to heed the call of nature. Fortunately, the journey was mercifully short—no more than thirty minutes and then we were there. Well, not quite! We still had to get from the railway station to the camp itself and it was much too far to walk carrying luggage, especially at that late hour. Sergeant Malloy, stone cold sober by now, went to the Station Master's office and used the telephone to call the Camp Guardroom, asking them to send transport to pick us up. Waiting for that took up another chunk of time, but we were too tired to care.

It was half an hour later that a 3-ton lorry pulled up at the station entrance. Like most military lorries, its cargo space was covered by a tarpaulin supported on a metal frame to form an enclosed shelter, with the tail-end open. After the driver got out and dropped the tailboard, we heaved our luggage on board before grabbing a hefty rope that hung down from the metal framework and hauled our tired bodies up after it. There was slatted bench-type seating along both sides of the cargo space, so we sat ourselves down and hung on to the nearest metal stanchion as the lorry lurched and bumped off into the night. Sergeant Malloy, exercising the privilege of rank, sat up with the driver in the warmth of the cab.

This final short journey wasn't very comfortable; it was cold and draughty as the wind blew through the flapping canvas that supposedly sheltered us from the elements and the fumes sucked into the back of the lorry from its exhaust pipe made the air nearly un-breathable. To make matters worse, the combination of hard wooden bench seats and what seemed like a lack of springs in the lorry's suspension system inflicted such punishing treatment to my rear end that I joined some of the others who had already stood up and were now hanging on to the overhead part of the frame, swaying with the motion of the lorry like strap-hangers on a crowded bus. I tried to see something of where we were passing through, but it was too dark to see anything except a small part of the road surface and nearby grass verges that were dimly illuminated in the glow cast by the lorry's rear lights. Thankfully, Gileston railway station was only one mile from the camp, so it wasn't too long before we pulled in through the brightly lit St. Athan main gate and stopped at the Guardroom. The driver hopped out of his cab, then came around to the back and lowered the tailboard so that we could all jump down. As we were getting down, Sergeant Malloy came around to meet us, accompanied by a tall Service Policeman who towered above him. The huge police corporal wore a red and black armband bearing the letters "SP", with a white hat, a white belt and white gaiters complementing his immaculately pressed uniform.

Although the initials "SP" properly stand for "Service Police," they also conveniently give rise to the derogatory terms "Snoop" or "Snowdrop," either of which we commonly used in referring to this particular sub-species of the Royal Air Force population. And the Snoop now standing alongside Sergeant Malloy, who happened to be the first one I'd ever set eyes on, appeared sinister in the extreme. The gleaming black peak of his hat dropped in a sheer vertical direction down over his eyes, almost like a blindfold, to press tightly against the bridge of his nose, requiring him to keep his head tilted back at an angle to be able to see anything to his front. This, together with his height advantage, gave the appearance that the Snoop was looking down his nose at anyone on whom he had reason to fix his gaze. It was a deliberate psychological tactic, successfully employed by many of the Snoops to be more intimidating in the furtherance of their work. It was certainly very disconcerting, when confronted by one of these much-feared individuals, to stare up into the darkness underneath the peak of his hat, searching for the eyes that we knew were hidden somewhere in there and looking down at us along that lofty nose, only to be frustrated in our ability to make human-to-human eye contact.

"Inside the Guardroom you lot, and sign for your bedding," he barked.

We made our way to a counter just inside the Guardroom doorway. An area of woven-fibre matting protected the floor at this particular spot, but on the other side of the counter it appeared as though we were gazing on the Holy of Holies. The tan coloured linoleum floor was so highly polished that I could clearly see reflections in its glassy surface. The same kind of matting that we now stood on was laid along the boundaries of the floor, allowing access to the inner areas of the Guardroom, where cell doors were plainly visible. Clearly, no one was allowed to walk on the highly polished area of linoleum. There seemed to be an unspoken message in its pristine brilliance, that to defile it in such a pedestrian manner as walking on it would be at the peril of a person's miserable life.

Each of us waited our turn at the counter to sign on a form for bedding and eating implements, before being ushered back outside and around to the bedding store at the rear of the Guardroom. In the process, we discovered to our horror that the lorry had disappeared, taking our worldly possessions with it. Sergeant Malloy calmed us down by explaining that our luggage had been taken on to our quarters, and that we'd be able to pick it up when we walked there. Then, still wondering if we were ever again going to be reunited with our meagre belongings, we each collected our heap of bedding and staggered off in a straggling line into the darkness and away from the island of light that surrounded the Guardroom. I followed some distance behind the person in front of me, who was just about at the limit of my vision on the sparsely lighted camp roads. Likewise, someone followed me at a similar distance. I only hoped that someone up front was following the lorry, but as it happened we only had to go about a hundred yards to our new home, where we were reunited with our luggage.

The lorry sat outside a black, creosoted single storey wooden hut, commonly referred to as a billet in RAF parlance, similar to those we'd stayed in at Cosford during our visit earlier in the year. It was the first hut in a double row of identical interconnected billets and was identified by a 3-foot high "G4" painted in neat white characters against a square green background, on the left side of the billet entrance. There were three other huts in the same row, labelled successively as G3, G2 and G1. Although the front entrances to all billets were independent of each other, the rear entrances opened onto a connecting corridor between the other three huts. The second row of huts, G5 to G8, was a mirror-image of the row that contained our billet and had the same interconnecting corridor

arrangement as our row. Both corridors opened onto a series of
latrines, washrooms, bathrooms and other utility rooms
sandwiched between both rows of billets. Huts G4 and G3
shared one set of latrines and washrooms with G5 and G6, while
G2, G1, G7 and G8 shared the other set. We soon learned this
complex of billets was known as "G-lines".

A concrete path provided access to the front doorway of
the billet and beyond that, a small entrance hall led to an inner
doorway that opened into the billet proper. Two small rooms
opened off the entrance hallway; one of these was a one-man
bedroom known as a bunk; the other was a storeroom. On passing
through the inner door, I discovered that the billet was furnished
in much the same way as the one I'd stayed in at Cosford.

As well as the familiar row of beds on both sides of the
billet, there were two Formica-topped tables arranged
lengthways down the centre of the room, each with a set of four
wooden chairs tipped forward on their front legs at a 45 degree
angle, with their backrests supported against the long edge of the
table. In the centre of the billet, between the two tables, there
was a carefully set up arrangement of two brooms, a waste-bin
and a strange-looking implement the likes of which I'd never
seen before. The unknown object possessed a cylindrical shaft
similar to that of a broom, except that it was thicker by half as
much again and probably about 5 feet in length. The business
end consisted of what appeared to be a solid rectangular block of
cast iron about one foot long, six inches wide, three inches high,
and painted black in colour. The handle was attached to this
metal block (or the head, as it came to be known) within a
centrally located recess in such a way that it allowed the handle
to swivel back and forth to describe an arc the long direction of
the head. An array of very short densely packed bristles, no more
than half an inch in length, covered the underside of the head
and these were caked with the residue of ancient floor polish,
which provided a vague clue to the implement's purpose.

On entering the billet, I had noticed another person
dressed in civilian clothes standing just inside the doorway of
the bunk. He followed us into the billet and then introduced
himself as Corporal Hillcrest, adding that he was the NCO in

charge of the billet. Hillcrest inquired as to where we'd travelled from and seemed interested and friendly, even helpful, as we each selected a bed and then dumped our blankets on it. Someone offered him a cigarette, but he said he didn't smoke. That didn't stop the rest of us taking time out for a smoke break and a chat. We had a million questions, because there was so much we wanted to know about this brand new world. Hillcrest was baby-faced and didn't appear to be very old, but he was a little older than any of us and it later transpired that he was 19. Having lived all my life in Ireland up to this point, I wasn't able to pick out regional English accents—they all just sounded "English" to my ears—but we learned that Hillcrest came from the North-eastern corner of England. That was "Geordie" country, with its own distinctive accent and dialect. He confided that we were the first group of new recruits of the current intake to arrive at St. Athan and that the others would be arriving over the next few days.

I can't recall what we did for food that evening. I believe that we were all so tired, having travelled for more than 24 hours without a break, that we just went to bed right away and quickly slipped into blissful unconsciousness.

Next morning, Corporal Hillcrest directed us to the cookhouse—the Boy Entrants' Mess. There were two routes available to get to the Mess; one was a short direct route that passed through the middle of another set of billet lines and the other was a longer, less direct route that paralleled the main runway, but at a reasonably safe distance from it. Hillcrest strongly advised against taking the short route. He said it would take us through "The Wings", and that the Wings people wouldn't take too kindly to us using their territory as a shortcut. His advice left us a little puzzled, but we did as he said and headed off to the Mess by way of the long route, carrying our white china mugs and eating irons.

Breakfast was served from a long stainless steel counter that we learned was referred to as a servery. The food items were contained in separate metal trays, some deep and some shallow, that were set into recesses in the servery so that their rims were flush with its surface. Steam was piped into the space beneath

the servery surface to keep the food in the trays hot and small wisps
of this could be seen escaping from around the rims of the trays.
Kitchen staff, dressed in white cotton jackets above thin blue and
white chequered trousers, served food to the individuals ahead of
me as they shuffled in a line along the front of the servery. Picking
up a plain white plate from the stack at the end of the servery, I took
my place in the queue and joined in the slow but steady
progression. When I got to the first server, he scooped up a pre-
cooked fried egg with a spatula, from one of the trays in front of
him, and slid it unceremoniously onto my plate. The tray contained
about twenty identical eggs, all cooked only on one side with a
covering of clear slimy uncooked "white" lying atop the yellow
yolks. And the white part of the eggs that had actually been cooked
was shiny and plastic looking. I would have much preferred to have
had the eggs cooked on both sides, with bubbly parts in the white
that made the edges appear all lacy, maybe a little browning around
the extremities and even a few little black specks from the fat in the
frying pan embedded into them. But the temperature at which these
eggs had been cooked was far too low to endow them with such
desirable gastronomic qualities and they just lay there staring up at
me with their single yellow eyes, like toy fried eggs made from real
plastic. Sadly, this was the style of fried eggs I would be obliged to
get accustomed to for many years to come—these weren't gourmet
fried eggs, they were RAF fried eggs!

Other members of the kitchen staff served me with fatty
bacon, sausage, tinned stewed tomatoes, baked beans and fried
bread as I shuffled my way along the front of the servery. There
were also some scrambled eggs in a deep metal container, but
they looked vaguely grey, watery, and altogether unappetizing. I
helped myself to cornflakes from a large container and ladled
some milk over them out of a large vat. Then I picked up a few
slices of white bread and a dollop of a yellow greasy substance
that everyone referred to as axle grease. The substance was
allegedly butter whipped with margarine, although whatever
percentage of butter the mixture contained, it was completely
overpowered by the unappetizing taste of margarine. Having
now reached the other end of the servery, I headed off to find the
others sitting at one of several long Formica topped tables, six

people on each side. The food certainly wasn't gourmet fare, but we hadn't had much to eat for many hours, so we scoffed it down. Some even went back for more. When everyone had finished their meal, we left the Mess and washed our mug and irons in a large tank of scalding hot water that bubbled and belched loudly because of the steam that was being continuously piped into it to maintain its temperature. Then we made our way back to the billet.

A little while later, some of us went out to explore the camp. Initially this took us along the road that we had staggered down the previous night under a pile of bedding, but in the opposite direction. In daylight and unburdened, the walk seemed very short and before long we came to the major camp thoroughfare. The main gate was a short distance off to our right and the southern end of the Station Headquarters building, also known as SHQ, was immediately to our front. On its western frontage, SHQ faced a huge square-shaped expanse of tarmac of about 500 feet in length on each of its sides. A thin layer of fine grey gravel covered the black tarred surface. At the northern side of this square, opposite to the side on which we were walking stood a large flagpole from which the Royal Air Force ensign wafted gently in the breeze. Actually, the ensign didn't fly directly from the vertical flagpole, but rather from a shorter pole about quarter of the way from the top of the main pole that jutted out over the Square at an angle of about twenty degrees to the horizontal. This arrangement allowed the flag to be fully extended, even on the calmest of days. A smaller flag, with a swallowtail-like notch in its free end, fluttered from the very top of the flagpole. Its dominant colour was the same light blue as the RAF ensign, but it bore a red horizontal bar the length of its centre and two darker blue bars, one along its top edge and the other at the bottom. It turned out that this was the Station Commander's pennant; its shape and design signified that he was an Air Commodore.

There weren't any nearby buildings on our side of the Square, but we could see an interesting collection of brick structures diagonally across from the corner at which we were now standing. Being practical people, who were not given to walking further than was really necessary, we set off in a beeline across the gravel surface of the Square towards the buildings that now held our attention. All was going well until we were about halfway across, when a loud bellowing voice from somewhere to the rear caught our attention. Reacting instinctively and in unison, we immediately looked backwards towards the source of the voice to see a red-faced Sergeant standing facing us on the road from which we had departed only moments before. He looked as though he was about to have a fit as he yelled for us to come to him—on the double! We kind of understood from the way he emphasized the word, and from his body language, that "double" meant "get there very fast," so we ran.

"Just where do you bloody lot think you're going?" He angrily demanded to know, when we reached the spot where he waited for us.

One of our group mumbled something about looking for the swimming pool, but the sergeant wasn't interested in explanations.

"Hasn't anybody told you bloody people that you don't go walking across the Square as if you're out on some bloody Sunday school picnic?" He yelled in our faces.

"No, Sergeant," we all answered meekly.

"Well, I'm telling you now. The Square is like sacred ground and you only go on it when you're marched on there by an NCO," he continued, calming down slightly, but still highly agitated. "When did you lot get here?"

"Last night Sergeant," we replied.

"Well okay, you've been warned. Just keep off it in future. You'll be on there sooner than you think anyway, laddies, and believe me you'll then wish you weren't. But for now, just stick to the roads. And don't walk on the grass either, okay?"

"Yes Sergeant," we all answered.

"Okay, that's all. Get on your way then."

We turned around and walked away from him, but I couldn't resist a quick glance over my shoulder only to see him still standing there watching us, while shaking his head and appearing to mutter something to himself.

We continued along the road that ran parallel to the Square and finally arrived at the buildings we had been heading for, prior to being so rudely interrupted. Most of the structure consisted of a large gymnasium that included an Olympic size heated indoor swimming pool. I gazed at it mesmerized, never having seen anything so grand in all my life. I couldn't swim a stroke, but had always wanted to learn, so I knew that this pool was going to be a magnet for me. The others seemed to feel the same way too. The remainder of the gymnasium complex was enormous. It housed all kinds of athletic apparatus, a boxing ring, an indoor running track, vaulting horses, parallel bars, and punch bags—just about every piece of athletic apparatus a person could think of. This wouldn't have been so surprising if we had been aware that St. Athan was also home to the RAF Physical Training Instructor (PTI) School.

Further exploration of the complex resulted in our discovery of the Astra cinema. All RAF cinemas were—and I believe still are—named *"Astra,"* taken from the Latin service motto *"Per ardua ad astra"*—*"Through endeavour to the stars"*. Whoever came up with the idea of borrowing "Astra" from the RAF motto obviously intended to associate the name with the stars appearing on Astra cinema screens rather than those stars that appear in the heavens.

The YMCA canteen stood directly opposite the Astra and the prospect of sticky buns, sandwiches and tea or pop proved too strong an attraction for our hearty teenage appetites to resist. So we went inside to find out what it had to offer and then sat and talked, whilst stuffing ourselves with the goodies and liquid refreshment we'd purchased.

Around lunchtime it seemed a good time to make our way back to the billets, so we departed from the YM, taking the little concrete pathway down to the road and then turned left, heading towards what looked like a boiler house. On our left we passed the tall brick-built water tower that served as the major station landmark and approached an intersection where the main camp road crossed the road on which we were currently walking. We needed to turn left here, which would then take us back past the Square that we now knew wasn't there for the purpose of taking casual strolls! As we neared the intersection a faint musical sound came to my ears, growing louder by the second.

And then, from the direction of some hangars that I had noticed earlier, there came a parade of Boy Entrants marching in columns of three and led by what appeared to be a drum and bugle band, the latter being the source of the music. But it couldn't be a bugle band, because the instruments appeared to be longer than bugles and in fact looked like brass trumpets minus the valves. As the band approached our position, the trumpeters and drummers ceased playing, save for only a single rhythmic beat from the bass drum to keep the marchers in step.

The band leader was taller than the most of the other boys and carried a drum major's mace that he spun and twirled around in a dazzling display of dexterity, occasionally tossing it into the air as he swaggered along at the head of the column, then skilfully catching it on the way down. I noticed, however, that there were several dents on the ornate silver head of the mace that bore silent witness to the fact that not every toss in the air ended in a successful catch. A row of drummers marched immediately behind him, some with side drums and others with deeper tenor drums. Behind them a hefty fellow carried the big bass drum strapped to his chest. He was the one beating out the time with one drumstick for the marchers. Most members of the band, those that surrounded the bass drummer, carried the trumpet-like instruments tucked under their right arms, with the flared trumpet end pointing rearwards. Then, as the band drew nearer to where we stood, the leader grasped the narrow end of the mace in his right hand and then fully stretched his arm above his head to hold the mace in vertical position, so that its head was the high in the air and visible to all members of the band. At this signal the side drummers started to beat out a tattoo in synchronism…drrr-drrr-dit, drrr-drrr-dit, drrr-drrr-drrr-drrr-drrr-drrr-dit. Simultaneously, one of the trumpeters at the rear yelled out what sounded like an incomprehensible order. At the first drrr-dit, the trumpeters thrust out their trumpets at a full arms length in front of them with the mouthpiece pointing vertically up and the flared end pointing down towards the ground. Then, at the end of the third and longest drum roll, they brought the trumpets to their lips, in perfect unison and started playing. The sudden blast of noise startled me since I was so close, but it wasn't unpleasant. I didn't recognize the tune and in truth, not everyone seemed to be playing perfect notes, but what they may have lacked in musical skill they certainly made up for in enthusiasm.

The band turned right and then proceeded down the road that we had been following up to this point, marching past the boiler house and towards a complex of billets that I could see in the distance. By this time, the column of marchers was passing in front of us. They were all carrying bundles of khaki coloured clothing of some kind under their left arms, but exactly what these bundles were, I couldn't tell. As our small group stood there gaping, one of the marchers yelled in our direction, "Hey you sprogs, go back home while you still have a chance!"

Immediately, a boy entrant with a stripe on his upper arm, who was marching alongside the column, loudly ordered the commenter to be quiet or he'd be put on a charge, whatever that was. We continued to watch as the last of the parade passed in front of us before it too turned right to follow the band down the road that took them away from us. Meanwhile, the sound of the drums and trumpets became ever fainter as they marched off into the distance, until finally it finally ceased altogether.

What we'd just witnessed was the 2 Wing Drum and Trumpet Band leading Numbers 3 and 4 Boy Entrant Squadrons from Workshops for the midday meal break. And later, I learned that the instruments were indeed valveless trumpets. One other thing I had noticed was that most of the marchers wore berets, not the big hats that we had seen at Cosford.

As we continued our walk in the relative quiet that now surrounded us, I reflected on the comment that the marcher had flung at us. I'd never heard the word "sprog" in my life before that day, although its meaning was fairly clear from the context and I soon learned that it was RAF slang for a new recruit, sometimes also known as a rookie. But with regard to the comment, as far as I was concerned the marcher was wasting his breath because I hadn't the slightest intention of taking his warning to heart. For me, the journey here had been a long one, in more ways than one, so I certainly wasn't going to give it up now.

When I arrived back at the billet, many of my travelling companions were still lounging around reading, playing cards, or just chatting. Corporal Hillcrest came through the rear door on his way to his bunk. This time, he was in uniform, wearing a sharply creased battledress blouse and trousers and heavy boots that were studded with hobnails on the soles and steel tips at the heels. An immaculate blue/grey webbing belt with its gleaming brasses was clipped snugly around his waist. The loose material of the beret he wore on his head was pulled sharply down over his right ear. Some of the lads called out "Hi, Corp" in a familiar manner. He acknowledged the greeting in a friendly way, and stopped to chat with them and answer their questions. During this exchange, we learned that we were in the Initial Training Squadron, or would be when we took the oath of allegiance. Usually, the squadron was known just by its initials, ITS. Hillcrest was one of several drill instructors attached to ITS.

Long before coming to St. Athan, I'd heard scary stories about drill instructors, but this chap didn't seem the slightest bit fear-inducing. In fact he would come into the billet and chat with us most evenings. Usually, during these visits, he would pick up a broom and use it to sweep the main area of the floor, whilst chatting and patiently answering our unending questions about life in the RAF. On occasions, he would even ask us, in friendly manner, to sweep the areas around our own beds.

Hillcrest also demonstrated the use of the strange-looking implement I had noticed nestled with the brooms on the day of our arrival. It turned out to be a floor polisher and was known as a Bumper. RAF issue wax floor-polish, which was bright orange in colour, was usually dolloped onto the linoleum floor and then spread around and worked in by pushing the bumper backwards and forwards over it. "Swinging" the bumper was very hot work and took a lot of energy, especially as the polish spread out and the liquid component evaporated, leaving behind a stubborn coating of wax paste. Buffing off the wax to obtain a polished surface entailed placing a felt pad underneath the bumper head and then repeating the process, although it did get a little easier as shine started to appear. The result, after a lot of hard work, was a brilliantly gleaming billet floor.

The billets started to fill up as more new recruits arrived that day and the next. In the meantime, I continued to explore my new surroundings with several others of the Irish contingent. We discovered the Navy Army and Air Force Institute, better known as the NAAFI (pronounced "naffy"), which operates recreational and canteen facilities on most military installations, where servicemen can relax, buy snacks, watch TV, or play games such as darts, snooker, billiards, and table tennis. There was also a separate NAAFI shop where I was able to buy some more Woodbines, having smoked all the ones I'd brought with me.

During this time, we met most of the drill instructors, the DIs, who would be in charge of our training. In addition to Corporal Hillcrest, there were also Corporals Blandford and Kaveney who were both married and therefore lived with their wives and families in the Station Married Quarters. The squadron disciplinary sergeant went by the name of Clarke and he manned the squadron office. Sergeant Clarke seemed reluctant to take part in any of the activities connected with the obnoxious horde of teenage boys who had suddenly burst into his calmly ordered life. Most of the time, he walked around with his nose in the air, exuding a detached demeanour that seemed to say I'm-above-all-of-this-distasteful-stuff, like some Jeeves-like butler.

Within two days of our arrival at St. Athan, we were all gathered into a large room and instructed to be seated at some tables and chairs arranged in parallel rows. Sergeant Clarke then handed out mimeographed form letters to each of us and told us that we were to address them to our parents and sign them. The letter briefly advised "Mum and Dad" that the supposed writer had arrived safely at St. Athan and was being well cared for. It also went on to say that his civilian clothing would be mailed home in the coming days. We were allowed to add a personal sentence if we wished, so I scribbled a few words about how long the journey had taken, about the fog, and what the local weather was doing. After signing my letter, I folded and placed it inside the 'On Her Majesty's Service' envelope that I had also been given, then licked the gummed flap and sealed it before passing it along to the end of my row of tables, from where it was collected by Sergeant Clarke.

After breakfast the next morning, which was Wednesday, we were shepherded into the same room again and, after being seated, a plump sweaty-looking little Pilot Officer took the floor. His opening statement is forever burned in my memory, "My name is Pilot Officer Morgan-Williams," he said, "and I'm here to tell you about the R. A. F." He enunciated each letter separately—"Arr Ay Eff."

Morgan-Williams' puffy white face was crowned by a thick oily mat of slicked-down jet-black hair and the pale upper part of his face stood out in contrast to the heavy dark shadow that covered its lower half. In fact, he looked more than a little foreign to me, an impression that was reinforced by what sounded like a strong foreign accent when he spoke. I later discovered he was Welsh, and that his "foreign" accent was overwhelmingly shared by a rather large Welsh population that was spread out for many miles from the gates of Royal Air Force St. Athan. Morgan-Williams, a teacher in civilian life, was in fact doing his 2-year National Service stint by serving in the RAF Education Scheme teaching RAF history, the subject on which he now proceeded to lecture us. We learned that the service had first come into being as the Royal Flying Corps during the First World War, as a branch of the army, but then evolved into a separate service in 1918, changing its name to the Royal Air Force at the same time. Because it was the first "air force" ever to be created as a separate entity, it has always had the distinction of being known simply as "The Royal Air Force" in contrast to all other air forces that have their national identity incorporated within the title.

The portly little Pilot Officer finished delivering the history lesson and left. Now it was Sergeant Clarke's time to brief us on more down to earth matters.

"Pay attention, now," he called out in his strained manner, as though the very act of addressing us was painful for him. "Tomorrow you will be inducted into the Royal Air Force and you will be asked to take the oath of allegiance." He paused to let this sink in. "Now, if there is anyone amongst you having second thoughts about going through with this, this is your last chance to back out." He looked around briefly to see if anyone had reacted to this solemn announcement and then continued, "If you should decide *not* to continue with induction, the Royal Air Force will provide you with a travel warrant back to your home town and you will be free to return there." He paused again and looked around, "Okay, anyone who doesn't wish to be inducted tomorrow, put his hand up."

A small number of boys decided to take advantage of this final offer and were politely but quickly ushered out of the room. The sergeant then addressed those of us in the majority who had remained.

"Following induction, you will be known as the 29th Entry. Your training will consist of three months of initial training here in ITS, followed by fifteen months of technical training after you have passed-out of ITS and go to the Wings. On completion of your technical training, you will pass out of Boys' service into the regular RAF, with the rank of Leading Aircraftsman." He paused for breath and then added, "The training you will receive here at the Number 4 School of Technical Training is the finest in the world—second to none!"

Such a claim could easily be taken as a gross exaggeration, but having personally been the beneficiary of the training he spoke of for the greater part of my life, in retrospect I have no doubt that he was completely truthful in this regard. Of course, he was referring specifically to the technical training we would receive, but in a wider sense his words also included another form of training that came as part of the package. This other training, which also turned out to be second to none, involved the acceptance of discipline and learning to live in an ordered world, whilst developing initiative and the ability to be self-assertive. These were traits that would prove invaluable for successful and productive lives in a future that few of us could have imagined at that particular moment.

That evening, after eating in the mess, I entered a NAAFI canteen that I had noticed nearby. The ITS NAAFI was a long way from the mess and I needed to buy some cigarettes, so why not use this more convenient NAAFI, I thought? One of the other boys came with me and as we walked up to the counter, the ambient noise level in the place dropped several notches. It was like in one of those Westerns, where the sheriff walks into the saloon to confront the baddies and everyone in there knows that a big showdown is about to happen. Immediately, we knew that we had made a mistake by coming into this NAAFI, but there was no turning back now. The lady behind the counter didn't appear to realize anything was wrong and served us, but very soon a tough looking kid with stripes all over his arm came up to us as we stood at the counter.

"What are you sprogs doing in here?" He sneeringly demanded.

"Just getting some cigarettes," I replied.

"You've got your own NAAFI over there at ITS," he growled, "this is the 2 Wing NAAFI and we don't let sprogs like you in here." He stopped, waiting for some kind of response.

Meanwhile, the NAAFI lady completed the transaction and handed me the cigarettes and some change. As this happened, several others gathered around in a circle, hemming us in.

"Didn't you understand what I just said?" The toughie resumed, while his friends sneered at us and egged him on.

"Yes," I answered, and then said by way of explanation, "We didn't know we weren't supposed to come in here."

There was more sneering by the others, as they made fun of us while taking turns at pushing us around in the circle. To say I was scared is an understatement. At that moment, I just wished that the earth would have opened up and swallowed me.

"Well you know now," the tough guy finally retorted, "so just take your stuff and get out…and don't come back again or you won't get off so easy next time."

The gang surrounding us supported this threat with "yeahs" and calls of "get out of here."

We didn't need any second bidding, but just muttered, "Yes", and then beat a hasty retreat to the sound of loud jeers and catcalls, all the while expecting that someone would pounce on us from behind before we could make it to safety. That was my first encounter with the Wings people while I was an ITS sprog. It wasn't entirely my last, but that came later.

* * *

The next morning, Thursday, the 18th of October, we were split into several large groups, each under the supervision of a DI. My group was shepherded into the same large room where we'd been the previous day. When we had been seated, hand-book-sized Bibles were passed around to everyone for the administration of the oath, although Roman Catholics were invited to come forward and all place their hands on a large Catholic bible. Several of us went to the front of the room to take advantage of this offer. Induction then commenced when we were each given a card printed with the following:

RAF Form 60
OATH TO BE TAKEN BY RECRUIT ON ATTESTATION
I, ..., swear by Almighty God that I will be faithful and bear true allegiance to Her Majesty Queen Elizabeth the Second, Her Heirs and Successors, and that I will, as in duty bound, honestly and faithfully defend Her Majesty, Her Heirs and Successors, in Person, Crown and Dignity against all enemies, and will observe and obey all orders of Her Majesty, Her Heirs and Successors, and of the Air Officers and Officers set over me. So help me God.

An officer then told us to stand up, take the Bible in our right hands, or in our case place our hands on the Catholic Bible, and read the oath out aloud all together from the card, stating our own names when we reached the dotted line.

When we had completed this brief swearing-in ceremony, the officer congratulated us on being brand new recruits into the Boy Entrant service of the Royal Air Force. Then, when we were seated once more, an orderly distributed a package of paperwork to each of us. First amongst these was a blue "Arrivals" card about eight inches long and six inches wide. We were instructed to print our names neatly in block capitals on a line at the top of the card, last name first, first name last. Another line was reserved for our service number, but we were warned to leave this blank for the time being. Underneath, there were several columns of names such as Bedding Store, Pay Accounts, Sick Quarters, Bicycle Store, and many more, each with a blank underline alongside that was obviously intended for someone's signature. We were then led into another series of rooms in which numerous separate tables and chairs had been set up. Uniformed airmen were stationed at each of these tables, which we were obliged to visit in a certain order. At the first table I visited, the orderly stamped a long number on a blank piece of paper, which he handed to me; he then took my blue card and stamped the same number on it. He told me that this was my service number and advised me to keep the white scrap of paper somewhere safe until I had memorised it. I did exactly what he told me to do, hardly realizing that in the course of time the number on the paper would become as familiar to me as my own name. I was then instructed to sign on a sheet of paper attesting to the fact that I'd been issued with my service number, after which the orderly signed my blue card on the blank line against "Records" and handed it back to me.

As the morning wore on, we trooped from table to table, each one representing a particular Section of the station Administration, where our personal details were noted and fed into the bureaucracy. The person manning each table signed my blue card on the line appropriate to his particular interest in me; Pay Accounts, Rations Clerk, and so on. Eventually, everyone in my group visited every table and our cards were filled with signatures proving that we had been duly recorded and processed into the Royal Air Force. By then, it was time for lunch.

After Corporal Kaveney had shepherded us out on to the roadway, he gave the order, "Fall in, in threes!"

Having spent some time as a Sea Cadet, I knew what this meant as did several others, but not everyone understood. Eventually, the corporal managed to get us lined up in three columns, facing toward the building that we'd just left.

"Flight, attennnn-shun!" He commanded.

We all seemed familiar with this command, so everyone knew to bring both of his feet together and stand erect with arms vertically down by his side. Corporal Kaveney seemed to be reasonably satisfied as he surveyed the motley crew in front of him.

"Okay, good," he announced with a moderate amount of praise in his voice. "Now pay attention while I demonstrate the actions on being given the commands "Stand at ease" and "Stand easy." He then proceeded with a brief demonstration of the movements in time with the commands that he gave himself. Then it was our turn.

"Flight, stand at eeeeease!" He commanded.

We copied the first movement he had shown us, which seemed to satisfy him.

"Flight, stand easy."

We relaxed as he now he explained, in barking military fashion, that when he gave the order "Right dress", we were each to turn our heads smartly to the right, and raise our right arms horizontally to touch the shoulder of our neighbour with end of our closed fist. Those at the right end of columns were to continue looking ahead, and the two boys at the end of columns 2 and 3 were to raise their arms to the front and touch their fist to the shoulder of the individual in front of them.

"Okay," he said, "let's try it. Flight, ri-ight dress!"

Much shuffling of feet ensued, as Kaveney urged us on with shouts of "C'mon, c'mon, look lively. We haven't got all day."

After a few minutes, the ragged appearance of our ranks was replaced by three reasonably straight lines of equally spaced boys in an assortment of civilian dress. Apparently, our training had begun.

The corporal stood us easy again, and now demonstrated that when he gave the Right Turn order, we were to swivel our feet and bodies to the right so that we would face in the direction of the road. At this point the right foot would also be pointing in the correct direction, but the left foot would be at an awkward angle, so we were to then bring the left foot smartly alongside the right foot. The interval between first and second movement was to be timed by numbers that he instructed us to call out aloud, turn—two—three, and then bring the left foot smartly alongside the right foot. Following this demonstration, he brought us back to attention so that we could try it.

"Flight, ri-ight turn!"

We all made it. Now we were to march as a column.

"When I give the order 'By the left, quick march'," Corporal Kaveney now instructed in clipped tones, "you will step off with your left foot, and swing your right arm up shoulder high." He paused momentarily to take a deep breath before giving the order, "Flight, by the le-eft, qui-ick, march!"

This didn't work out quite as smoothly as the right turn. Some boys, who seemed to have difficulty in differentiating between left and right, stepped off with their right foot instead of their left and, in the process, trod on the heels of the boys in front. The latter reacted by either hopping in pain, or turning around and angrily confronting the person responsible for inflicting the injury. The combined result of both reactions caused others in the column to collide and stumble, bringing total disarray to the marching formation. The DI ordered us to halt.

"That was a shambles," he shouted. "An utter bloody shambles! Let's try it again shall we?"

So, we had another try, and yet another, until we eventually started moving off down the road in what can only be described as semi-military fashion with our guardian DI calling out the step, "Yeft, yoyt, yeft, yoyt, yeft, yoyt, yeft—yeft, yeft, yeft, yoyt, yeft. Get those bloody arms up shoulder high you lot in front!"

He called a halt when we got to the Mess, but it was more of a controlled crash. I caught a momentary glimpse of the corporal's pained face as he closed his eyes and shook his head, silently mouthing, "Mother of God, give me strength." Then we were dismissed, with the admonition to be back on the road in thirty minutes.

The RAF served the main meal of the day at midday in those days—we called it dinner. Usually, it consisted of three choices of meat, with potatoes prepared in various ways and vegetables—always the canned variety. There was soup if we wanted it and a few choices of dessert to follow. Sounds mouth-watering, but it certainly wasn't *cordon bleu* dining by any stretch of the imagination, just very plain fare. I never knew of anyone who over-ate; we just took in enough to dispel the feeling of hunger. But the desserts were enjoyable, usually some kind of sponge-cake or pastry concoction with a jam filling and a ladleful of warm custard poured over it.

Thirty minutes later we were out on the road again, falling-in in threes. A repeat of the Right Dress manoeuvre, then a left turn that most of us accomplished this time—although some still needed to figure out their right from their left—and we were off again, headed for Sick Quarters and the Dental Section.

The Dental Section was first. It operated like a production line. We were each called in turn to sit in a dentist's chair while a Dental Officer inspected our teeth. He called out the state of each tooth to a dental orderly, who recorded the information on a standard dental chart. On completion of the examination, the Dental Officer commented on each person's dental hygiene. I'm ashamed to have to admit that in my case he pronounced my hygiene as "poor". I had never been encouraged to go a dentist at home because it cost too much.

After the dental examination, we marched to Station Sick Quarters where we were subjected to the old push, prod, turn-your-head-and-cough routine, but with an added bonus—we were to be inoculated against Typhoid A & B and Tetanus—TABT in the medic's lingo. And so, after being examined, we queued up to run the needle gauntlet. Some boys fainted as the needle was buried none too gently into their arm by a burly male nurse. Others didn't even get that far, their knees folded up at the mere sight of the hypodermic, or maybe it was the strong medical aroma that permeated the room. Personally, I made it through the ordeal and although my fear of needles was equal to most others there that day, I was at least able to remain conscious during the process.

The dental and medical examinations took up all of the afternoon, most of the time being spent on filling out questionnaires about whether or not we had ever been afflicted by any of an amazing variety of exotic diseases, and then having to wait around until everyone in the group had been through the various inspections and inoculations. By now my left arm, the one that had been subjected to the needle, was feeling sore and becoming stiff. It was not only very painful to the touch, but hurt badly as I swung it shoulder high during the march back to our billets. I wasn't the only one affected in this way. As I found out later, the pain and stiffness was an unpleasant side effect of the TABT inoculation, which was also usually accompanied by flu-like symptoms.

By the time I got back to the billet, I wanted to do nothing more than lie down on my bed while trying not to jar my arm against anything that would aggravate the pain. As I lay there, some of the others in the billet, who had not yet been subjected to the inoculation process, were sitting around on a bed on the opposite side of the room talking and smoking. During the course of their conversation, the door at the end of the billet opened and Corporal Hillcrest came through en route to his bunk. One of the group, who had apparently developed a friendly relationship with the corporal, called out "Hi Corp, how ya doin' today?"

The corporal stopped by the bed where the group was gathered, smiling his usual friendly smile.

"I'm fine," he replied. Then, in what seemed to be an afterthought, he innocently asked, "By the way, did any of you boys take the oath of allegiance today?"

"Yes Corp, we all did," replied the boy.

On hearing this response, the smile abruptly vanished from Corporal Hillcrest's face and was replaced by a hate-filled sneering look. Before our very eyes, Dr Jekyll suddenly became Mr. Hyde.

"Well, you're in the Royal Air Force now," he screamed, "On your feet laddie. Put that cigarette out and stand to attention when you're addressing an NCO! From now on, when an NCO enters a room the first person to see him will come to attention and yell out 'NCO present!' Is that understood?" All of this issued from the corporal's mouth in a continuous stream of words delivered in a screaming voice not more than six inches from the poor unfortunate boy's wide-eyed frightened face.

The boy was utterly dazed, as we all were. "Yes corp— ORAL," suddenly remembering to add the second syllable.

Hillcrest turned to look around at all of us. "This place is a shit-heap," he pronounced with a look of disgust. "Take hold of those brooms and the bumper and get it cleaned up, NOW!" With that he turned on his heel and stomped off towards his bunk.

We all looked at each other in the aftermath, for what seemed an eternity, then someone picked up a broom and started sweeping around his bed area. No one said anything because we were all still too stunned by witnessing the unexpected transformation of our friend into the monster he had just become. The monster lived on thereafter, and we would never again see the friendly side of Corporal Hillcrest.

CHAPTER 3

Out of the Frying Pan...

At 8 o'clock the next morning—or oh-eight-hundred hours (0800 hours) in the military language with which we were now expected to become familiar—all new recruits in ITS were ordered to parade on the road near our billets in the same groups into which we had been sub-divided on the previous day. Everyone still wore civilian clothing, combined with a variety of hair styles ranging from crew-cuts to Teddy Boy "DAs". In retrospect, I can only imagine that our overall appearance must have given the DIS nothing short of acid indigestion. Although it was less than 24 hours since having been sworn into the service, we had nevertheless learned how to come to attention and dress off in ranks that were reasonably straight, so most of us were able to respond to these commands when the order was now given. The DIS in charge of our groups took a few minutes of strutting backwards and forwards to look us over and then with little more than grudging satisfaction, ordered us to stand at ease. Having done that, they all spent the next several minutes in a huddle with Sergeant Clarke before returning to their respective groups, each one carrying a sheet of paper in his hand.

Corporal Blandford addressed my group, "Okay, pay attention!" He paused for a moment to make sure we were all listening before proceeding. "We're now going to assign you to the billets that you will occupy for the remainder of your time in ITS," he said, then continued: "When you hear your name called, listen for your billet number and then, when you're dismissed, go on the double to the billet that you're now in, collect your belongings and take them to your new billet." He paused and looked around, "Are there any questions?"

No one spoke, so Corporal Blandford then started to read off the names and billet assignments. When he got to my name, it was "Carlin—G6." I made a mental note that I would now be housed in hut G6.

When all the names had finally been called out, he asked if everyone knew which billet they were assigned to. No one spoke, which apparently satisfied him that we all knew where we were supposed to move our belongings to, so he brought us to attention again and then dismissed us. We had been taught how to respond to the "Dismiss" command the previous day, at the conclusion of our march to the Mess; it was executed by swivelling the feet and body one-eighth of a turn to the right, then bringing the left foot to the right foot while still in the position of attention. Like any drill movement, it was performed by everyone in unison, but at its conclusion we broke ranks as individuals and usually just walked away. However, in this particular case the follow-up order had been to go at the double to collect our belongings, which meant that we were expected to run.

As soon as we were dismissed, there was a stampede of feet on concrete that very quickly transformed into a loud pounding noise on wooden corridor floors as we all ran to the billets we now occupied to collect our gear. Because G4 was the nearest billet, I got there almost right away and quickly threw what belongings I'd brought with me into my battered old suitcase, then folded my blankets, pillow and sheets, and carried the whole load to G6, which fortunately wasn't very far away. Just through the rear door, a jog to the right, cut through the communal washroom—the Ablutions—into the corridor that served the billets on the other side of the complex, a second jog, to the left this time, and I was there. My immediate plan was to stake a claim to the best possible bed-space in G6 by wasting no time in getting there. But the plan turned out to be all in vain when I discovered that the beds had already been assigned by name. What was more, there was no preferential treatment involved because they had all apparently been assigned alphabetically. My bed-space was near the midway point in the billet, on the right as viewed from the front entrance.

To the best of my recollection, the following are the names of the people who were assigned to hut G6. Starting from the left side on entering from the front door: Niall Adderley; "Bertie" Bassett; John Beech; "Dicky" Bird; Geordie Brand; Howard "Ginge" Brown; Cecil Burden; Richard Butterworth. Opposite Butterworth, on the other side of the billet: "Barney" Barnes; "Jock" Campbell; "Jock" Callaghan; myself; "Charlie"

Chaplain; Derek Chinnery; "Cokey" Cole; and George Coaten.

When everyone had found his assigned bed-space and all belongings had been transferred, Corporal Blandford proceeded to give us the first of many lessons on military life. The subject of this particular lesson was on how to maintain a smart, military-like billet, by showing us how to make our blankets and pillows up into bed-packs and demonstrating the manner in which our personal bed-space areas were to be left each day, so that they would be ready for inspection at any time during "duty hours".

The first step in making a bed-pack was to strip all sheets and blankets from the bed, except for one blanket that was used to cover the bare mattress. This blanket needed to be stretched as tight as a drum so that there were no wrinkles, and the loose ends tucked beneath the mattress on both sides and at the foot end of the bed. When tucking the blanket in at the foot, we were to use "hospital corners," which are little diagonal folds that are made by folding and tucking the blanket in a certain way. Next, three of the blankets and both sheets each had to be folded in half three times and then stacked on top of each other, starting with a blanket on the bottom and then alternating with sheets and blankets on top of each other. The remaining blanket was then folded once lengthwise and wrapped around the stack of sheets and blankets. This pack of sheets and blankets was then placed at the head of the bed, with its folds facing towards the foot. To complete the arrangement, the pillow was plumped up and placed on top. The final result of all this was a bed-pack. That, at least, was the theory, but it took some practise to get the bed pack to appear anything like it was supposed to. Managing to fold the blankets so that they were all the same size seemed to be the greatest challenge. Next, and only slightly less challenging, was acquiring the ability to wrap the final blanket tightly enough around the pack so as to endow the completed construction with an appearance that closely resembled the perfectly square contours of the model bed pack featured in a poster pinned up on the billet bulletin board for our guidance. Achieving these important skills didn't happen overnight, so it wasn't unusual to make the unpleasant discovery, on returning to the billet at lunchtime, that your bed pack had been pulled apart and strewn all over your bed during the daily barrack room inspection.

In addition to making our bedding up into a bed-pack, we were required to display our mug and irons on the top of our small bedside locker. The china mug had to be positioned upside down in the exact centre of the locker top, with the knife, fork and spoon arranged around it in a pattern that mimicked a table setting. Needless to say, all of these implements were to be spotlessly clean. Dirty mug or "irons" would be thrown on the bed, but if the white porcelain of the mug exhibited even the faintest of hairline cracks, the inspecting NCO would immediately break the vessel and toss it into the billet waste bin, leaving the unfortunate owner with little choice but to buy a replacement from the NAAFI.

But the unpleasant experiences of toppled bed-packs and smashed mugs were to come later. On this particular day of learning about bed packs and the locker-top layout, we finished around lunchtime and were then formed up in threes on the road outside the billets—that is in three ranks or columns—and marched to the mess for our midday meal. Directly after lunch, we were marched to the camp barbershop to be confronted by three middle-aged Welsh barbers from nearby Barry who quickly busied themselves in converting our assorted civilian hairstyles into the standard military "short back and sides". They weren't much given to barber shop chatter with the customers, although they prattled incessantly to each other in their almost unintelligible Welsh accent as they efficiently, and none too gently, sheared us of our cherished locks.

Having been collectively relieved of such a great weight from our shoulders but now suffering the irritating torture caused by those tiny hair clippings that stubbornly insisted on clinging to the insides of the neckbands of our shirts, we were marched off to our next destination. This was to be the clothing store where we would be issued with our kit. When we arrived another group was still in the process of being kitted out, so we were permitted to "stand-easy". Those in possession of a smoking pass, duly signed by a parent, were allowed to smoke. I didn't have a pass, but I lit up a cigarette anyway. No one challenged me, so I continued, smoking half of the cigarette before carefully putting it out to save the remainder for later. Then it was our turn to be kitted.

"Flight, attennn-shun," yelled Corporal Blandford.

We were then marched in single file into the clothing store, which was in reality a huge warehouse. A long wide counter separated us from the racks and racks of clothing and equipment. On the other side of this counter a team of weary and bored looking storemen waited to fulfil our every need. On our side of the counter, Sergeant Clarke from our squadron office supervised the proceedings.

The plan was simple; we moved forward along the counter in single file until every storeman had a "customer" facing him from our side of the counter. The storeman then made a note of each person's name, rank and service number—we were all the same rank; Boy Entrant, or B/E in RAF shorthand— and then proceeded to issue us with items of kit, calling out the name in military-style reverse order as he did so. "Drawers, cellular, six"—that was six pairs of loose-legged underwear that came down to mid-thigh made from a cellular cotton fabric. We would later learn that the RAF slang name for these garments was "shreddies" because of their tendency to become threadbare and shred at the crotch where they rubbed against the harsh worsted material of our trousers.

The items were dumped onto the growing heap of clothing before us, and whilst a complete listing of every item of kit we received would be prohibitive, not to mention boring, it can be recorded that our mounting pile included three collarless shirts, the kind our fathers and grandfathers were more likely to wear, and six separate collars to go with them, plus two black ties. We were also issued with six pairs of knitted woollen socks, two pairs of leather lace-up boots, a V-necked sweater, one pair of canvas gym shoes known as plimsolls, two cap badges, one pair of blue-grey knitted gloves, three pairs of dark blue gym shorts and three white gym shirts, a service dress hat, a beret, and the oddest thing of all—a housewife. This was a little cloth wallet-like object containing sewing and darning needles, white and black thread, blue darning wool for our socks, a thimble, and several buttons. It was a sobering thought that if there was any darning or sewing to be done, we were going to have to do it ourselves. And this wasn't the only non-clothing item to be issued, we also got a set of four brushes, two boot-polish brushes—one to apply the boot polish with and one to shine it off—a clothes brush, and a button brush to be used for cleaning our brass buttons and cap badges. There was also a little brass gadget called a button-stick to be slipped under any button being cleaned, to hold it in place and also to protect the fabric underneath from being soiled by metal polish. There was more brass-work on the square-shaped shoulder bag known as a small-pack, and on the webbing belt, both of which were included in the kit issue.

The webbing belt was standard British military issue; only its colour separated the services. The RAF version of the belt was blue-grey. It was made from a heavy woven material known as webbing, and had a fastener at the front comprising of two sturdy brass pieces that fitted together in a tongue and slot clasp arrangement. Two brass slides that were used to adjust the length of the belt, fitted snugly up to the clasp, and two buckles at the rear completed the brass-work. Probably the most attractive example of someone wearing this kind of webbing belt was Ursula Andress, when she first appears in the James Bond film "Doctor No." However, hers was white, and it certainly looked a lot better on her than it did on me.

A dapper little middle-aged civilian tailor moved along our side of the counter, taking measurements of our chests, waists and inside leg, as we continued to receive items from the clothing clerk. Each time he did this he would call out a size to the storeman, who would then issue the individual with two uniforms and a greatcoat in that size. One of the uniforms was to be used as our "Best Blue" and the other as our "Working Blue." When it was my turn to be measured, he called out, "36 regular." The storeman disappeared amongst the racks of clothing and then returned a short time later with a bundle of blue serge, which he dumped on the counter in front of me. I was then directed to go into a small curtained-off cubicle to try on both uniforms and the greatcoat for size. The uniforms were both a good fit, which the tailor confirmed with a few tugs and a check of the waistband, but the legs of the trousers needed to be shortened. Also, the greatcoat was loose around the waist and needed a slight alteration. The tailor gathered in the surplus material and marked it with tailor's chalk. Then I took it off and filled out three labels with my rank, name and serial number, one of which I tied on to the greatcoat and the other two on to each pair of trousers before leaving them in a pile with other clothing that needed alterations, having been told that I could pick them up from the tailor's shop in a few days.

The uniforms were made from a hairy worsted material, which was standard RAF issue at the time. Both were identical. The jacket-like tunic was buttoned down the centre by a row of four brass buttons and came complete with a detachable belt, made from the same serge material, which was held fastened round the waist of the tunic by means of a brass buckle. The tunic included four pockets in all. Two of these were large side pockets positioned over each hip, while the other two were smaller breast pockets. All of the pocket openings were covered by a flap, which in the case of the side pockets just fell loosely over the pocket. But the breast pockets were different; they were held fastened by a small brass button that was otherwise identical in design to the larger tunic buttons. Each button was embossed with a representation of Her Majesty the Queen's crown above an eagle in full flight. The regal bird was portrayed to be flying towards the viewer, but with its head turned towards the viewer's right. The same eagle image, embroidered in pale blue silk, was also worn as a small badge, known as a "shoulder flash", which was worn at the very top of the tunic sleeve on each arm. It was a curious feature of these embroidered eagles that their heads were turned to face rearwards.

There is a service legend that answers the question of why the eagle's head pointed rearwards. During the Battle of Britain many of the brave Spitfire and Hurricane pilots were NCOs—sergeants and flight sergeants—who wore this very same shoulder flash. The legend has it that the eagle's head originally faced forward until one NCO pilot removed his, during those hectic September days, and switched them around to be on opposite shoulders, (there's a "right shoulder" flash and a "left shoulder" flash). This, he said, was "because he needed to have a pair of eyes in his arse" when he was up there dog-fighting with Jerry. The idea quickly caught on, and eventually all NCO fighter pilots followed suit and wore them like this. As a tribute to their bravery, the RAF adopted the reversed eagles as the official shoulder flash for all "other ranks" airmen—including Boy Entrants. The RAF is a young service and doesn't have too many traditions of its own, so we liked this particular one because it gave us the feeling that we'd inherited a tangible connection to the Battle of Britain heroes from the generation immediately preceding our own. The tunics and greatcoat were issued with these shoulder flashes already attached, which was at least one sewing task that we wouldn't have to fumble our way through. But that wasn't the case with the brass wheel badges that I'd first noticed at Cosford. We were issued with three of those; one for each tunic and one for the greatcoat.

When everyone had been issued his full complement of kit, Sergeant Clarke told us to pay attention. Grabbing someone's white canvas kit bag, he dumped the contents on the floor, and then proceeded to hold up each item as he called out its name. We were instructed to do likewise. When both he and Corporal Blandford were satisfied that each and every one of us had been issued with that particular item, he put it in the kit bag, and instructed us to do likewise.

"Button stick! Hold up your button stick! Has everyone got a button stick?" He looked around in all directions as Corporal Blandford walked around and assisted those who were unable to tell their button stick from their elbow. The corporal then nodded his head towards Sergeant Clarke, who took this as a signal that everyone possessed this item of kit.

"Okay," the sergeant announced, "put it in your kitbag."

This was really a good thing, because we might have otherwise been unaware that something was missing. But, it was a two-edged sword because it also removed the option of being able to claim later that we hadn't been issued with a particular item if it somehow went astray. Being short of an item of kit would get us into serious trouble, so now if anything went missing later on, it could only happen through carelessness on our part.

When we'd finished making sure that all kit was present and correct, we were instructed to wear our big hats, the SDs, even though it had neither hat badge nor hatband. This was so that it wouldn't be crushed out of shape in the kit bag during our march back to the billet.

Before being dismissed on our return to G lines, Corporal Blandford instructed us on the order of dress for the next few days. "Pay attention!" He commanded. "Until you receive the items of clothing back from the tailor, you will wear your denims instead of working blue. That means you will wear your RAF issue shirt, collar and tie, beret and working boots."

"Those of you with tickets for collection of clothing from the tailor on Monday, Tuesday, etc., will be taken there to collect those items on the specific day. Thereafter, you will wear full working blue during working days and best blue on Sundays for Church Parade." He paused briefly before asking, "Is that clear?"

We all replied in a staccato response, "Yes corporal!"

The terminology of "working blue" and "best blue" was new to us, but we understood it to mean that one uniform would be worn throughout the week and one would be kept in good condition, like the "Sunday suit" that was worn only for church and special occasions that most of us were familiar with in civilian life. It didn't matter that, at this point, both uniforms were brand new and equally in good condition. It was simply a matter of choosing between the two.

Denims referred to an olive-green coloured one-piece work overall made from sturdy denim material. We had all been issued with one set of these on a personal loan basis from the squadron.

By this time, we were aware that we would be confined to camp during our first three weeks in ITS, so it wasn't surprising that our weekend assignment was to get our uniform into a wearable condition, and also prepare for a kit inspection on Wednesday morning. This meant cleaning our brass accessories, which were covered in some kind of tough preservative coating, pressing any item of uniform that wasn't with the tailor, ironing the wrinkles out of shirts then folding them in a special way, and polishing our boots. That may sound simple enough, but it wasn't—we had to "bull" everything. In military slang, "bulling" means senseless cleaning for its own sake, like the mirror-like shine on the Guardroom floor, or the mirror-like shine that we were expected to put on our black leather boots. Now there was a challenge!

The entire boot uppers consisted of knobbly black leather that refused to take on any semblance of a shine, yet the toecaps and the heels needed to be so mirror-like that a person, especially a corporal person, could actually see his own reflection in them.

According to Corporal Kaveney—we needed to employ the old spit-and-polish routine, literally, to achieve the desired effect. "First, take a spoon," he told us, "and use a match or a cigarette lighter to heat up the business end. Then put plenty of black boot polish on the toecap and the heel of the boot. Press down with the underside of the spoon and rub the polish into the leather in little circles." He turned to leave, "Won't take more than a couple of days, lads." And then he was gone, his evil little smirk still lingering like the after image on a retina that has been exposed to a too-bright light.

After many hours of rubbing, the pressure of the hot spoon on the leather smoothed out the little knobbly bumps, meanwhile the polish was absorbed into the leather. Then, when the toecaps and heel area were completely smooth, I put some spit on the area that I'd been rubbing and used a yellow duster wrapped around one or two fingers to rub the spit mixed with polish in little circles with my fingertips. Finally, the duster served as a polishing cloth to buff the leather until the toecaps and heels took on the smooth gleaming appearance of patent leather.

Although we'd been issued with all necessary items of kit, we still needed to provide our own cleaning supplies. For instance, boot-polish, Brasso, and the blanco paste needed to clean our webbing. We had to buy these supplies from the NAAFI shop, as well as the front and back studs needed for attaching a collar to its shirt. In the meantime, our NCOs came around and gave each of us a chequered hatband to be worn around our SD and a painted metal disc to be worn behind the RAF hat badges on our berets. The check pattern on the ITS hatband was a double row of half-inch squares that alternated emerald green and black.

The same pattern was repeated on the aluminium disc, but on a larger scale so that the disc was simply divided into quarters with alternating quadrants of green and black. The hatbands and discs weren't actually issued as kit, but were on a personal loan basis, like our denims, for the duration of the time we'd spend in ITS.

I continued getting my uniform ready to wear. This included sewing a wheel badge on the left arm of both tunics and the greatcoat. When examined up close, it became obvious that the wheel badge wasn't really a "cartwheel". Although the outer circle was a wheel of some sort, the "spokes" were in fact the representation of a four-bladed propeller within the wheel. The wheel badges were to be sewn directly onto the sleeve of our uniform minus the coloured discs that I'd seen both at Cosford and here at St. Athan; those would come later when we graduated to the Wings. Sewing buttons back onto my clothing was something I'd been taught to do early in life, so using the materials in the housewife wasn't any problem for me. I opened it up and took out a small sewing needle, then broke off a length of black thread. As I threaded the needle, it brought back memories of my maternal grandmother, Hannah McElhone, who used to ask me to do this little job for her because she said I had "good eyes". With the needle threaded, I positioned the first wheel badge about four inches below the eagle shoulder flash with the propeller oriented so that it looked like an "x", as we had been instructed, and then sewed several loops of thread over two opposing propeller blades, close to the rim of the wheel. There was a full-length mirror at the end of the billet, so I tried the tunic on and checked to see if the wheel looked okay. It seemed to be at the correct location on my arm, and the propeller blades looked like an "x". My eyes ceased to focus on the wheel badge and instead strayed to take in my whole reflection in the mirror. Somehow, it seemed that I wasn't looking at myself, but at some other person who just vaguely resembled me. However, this other person was partially dressed in the uniform of the Royal Air Force. For a few fleeting moments, the vision seemed to signal a new life, a new person—and then the moment passed. I cleared my head of this daydream and got back to the task of sewing the wheel badges onto my other garments. After that, I slid the little button stick underneath each wheel badge and cleaned it with Brasso.

All day Saturday we bulled our kit, trying to get the best possible shine on our buttons and badges, and performing near miracles in getting a mirror shine on our boots. Sometimes helping each other, sometimes offering or receiving advice. The spoon trick worked well for smoothing out the knobbles in the leather, but all the rubbing was hard work and my arms and fingers ached long before I'd finished. Finally, I took my turn at using the table at the end of the billet as an ironing board to press my tunics with a hot iron, putting a damp cloth over the area being ironed to prevent scorching. It was simple to cover the table with a blanket, and it served just as well as the provided tables in the ironing room miles away at the other end of the long corridor that interconnected the billets. And at some point, we all fitted the chequered hatbands around our SDs and put the coloured metal discs in place behind the cap badges on our berets.

Everything needed to be tried on for fit and size, but it was a major struggle with the detachable collars because they were so stiff and uncomfortable. The front collar stud invariably stuck into the wearer's throat at an angle, and after knotting the tie with the collar up, it was difficult to fold the collar over without getting it all crinkled up. Mercifully, the RAF phased out detachable collars several years later, and issued more modern shirts with collars that were permanently attached. But those of us who had to wear those uncomfortable detachable collars will forever remember the small circular semi-permanent red indentation on our throats, just below the Adam's apple. It was always such an exquisite relief just to take that damned uncomfortable collar off.

On Sunday, I took a break to go to Mass with Niall Adderley, who was also Catholic. We went in our civilian clothes because we both had items of our uniforms in the tailor's shop. The RC (Roman Catholic) church was on the other side of the camp, in 1 Wing territory, but this posed no problem. The denizens of the Wings had enough to keep them busy on any Sunday morning; most of them were nominal members of the Church of England, and were therefore required to be on Church

Parade. Other Protestants were also required to participate, but not Catholics since it was assumed, I think, that we would voluntarily attend church anyway without the coercion of the RAF hierarchy.

Niall and I walked the mile or so from our billet to the church. He was from Dublin, the Drimnagh area to be precise, and was a very easy person to get along with. I was fascinated by his soft Dublin accent, which sounded so much more melodious to my ears than my own Ulster accent. Niall was endowed with a lot of wisdom for such a young person, coupled with a warmth and genuineness. Frequently, he was a steadying influence on my own brash impulsiveness and I certainly looked up to him. We stayed good friends throughout ITS, but got separated later when we went to the Wings and were housed in different billets.

At the RC church, we were welcomed by several 1 Wing and 2 Wing Boy Entrants and given hymnbooks to use during the service. Apparently, this was neutral territory. Afterwards, we were offered refreshments in the common-room adjoining the small chapel where the Mass had been offered. The Priest, or Chaplain as he was referred to in the RAF, mingled with us and had a friendly word for all the newcomers. I was surprised by the fact that he wore a light coloured jacket, unlike the sombre black clothing worn by every priest that I'd ever seen in Ireland. He was also English, which didn't seem right, but he came across as a compassionate human being. When Niall and I finally decided to leave he escorted us to the door, and said that he was looking forward to seeing us again later in the week, at Padre's Hour. We didn't quite know what that meant, but nodded and said yes as though we did.

We had lunch after Mass, although it always seemed to be called dinner since it was the main meal of the day. Afterwards, Ginge Brown came up with the idea of going to the huge indoor pool that we'd discovered just a few days before, and asked if anyone else was interested. I immediately jumped at the chance. Although I couldn't swim, I certainly wanted to learn. Bertie Bassett and "Cokey" Cole both said they were coming too because they also wanted to learn how to swim.

None of us possessed swimming trunks, but we did have the PE shorts that had just been issued to us, so we rolled them up in a white towel (Boy Entrant, for the use of) and headed for a dip.

The pool was accessed through the large gym complex that we had seen a few days previously. Actually, there were two gyms. There was an outer gym with a concrete floor that was used for activities such as callisthenics, which would very soon become part of our training. The second inner gym had an immaculate hardwood floor that included an indoor running track. This was also where most of the gym equipment could be found. A blanket of warm humid air hit us as soon as we opened the door in a corner of the outer gym that led to the pool. The strong aroma of chlorine clung to my nostrils as we made our way alongside the pool to the changing room, taking in the immensity of the huge body of water as we walked through. It seemed enormously long and wide and the large room echoed hollowly to the splashes and voices of the people who were already having fun in the water. The doorway through which we had just entered was at the shallow end and facing us at the far end was a high diving board and a lower springboard. A number of swimmers were busily showing off their skills on the springboard so we stopped and gaped at them for a little while. Other people watched from an upper spectator gallery, applauding each time one of the divers made a clean entry into the water.

When I'd changed into my PE shorts, I followed the others to the shallow end, and eased my way into the water. It wasn't cold, just a pleasantly comfortable temperature. We recognized a few other denizens of the shallow end as ITS boys, so we joined up with them and for the next couple of hours we all splashed and jumped around in the water, getting used to moving around in it, gradually gaining the confidence we needed before we'd ever be able to swim. Bassett was having a great time flipping somersaults in the shallow water. He would stand up and then plunge his head into the pool. The next thing I'd see was his feet come up and then disappear before his head popped back out again. It looked like fun, so I tried it but only managed to get water up my nose and quickly resurfaced coughing and choking.

"No, no," he said. "Do it like this," and he pinched his

nose between thumb and forefinger before ducking below the surface once again.

I followed his example and this time managed to turn a complete loop under the water. It surprised me that I could hear the noise made by others splashing while I was submerged, although it sounded muffled and far away. The experience was exhilarating, and I spent the remainder of the time in the pool, flipping somersault after somersault until it was time to go back to our billets and get ready for the evening trip to the mess hall. But I knew that there would be many return visits to the pool—and very soon.

Back at the billet I resumed preparation for the kit inspection on Wednesday morning. Indeed, these preparations consumed the next two days of our lives, interspersed by brief excursions when we were marched, denim-clad, to the tailor shop to collect our items of uniform and to the mess for meals.

Tuesday night arrived, and the kit inspection loomed large in everyone's consciousness. On Wednesday morning, all items of kit needed to be laid out on our beds in a very precise arrangement, so it was just as important to get everything folded in readiness as it was to iron, clean and polish. A poster prominently displayed in every billet, illustrated the exact layout we needed to abide by.

The bed pack was a basic part of the layout, but on top of it we needed to place our greatcoat, folded in three with the buttons facing outwards. Then, our Best Blue, trousers on the bottom and tunic on top folded in two with the buckle at the fold. The small pack came next with its bottom brass buckles facing towards the foot of the bed, and finally the SD hat, complete with gleaming hat badge and ITS hatband, topped off the stack.

The remainder of our kit had to be displayed in rows across the blanket-covered mattress. The first row consisted of three equal-size stacks of garments, all folded in the prescribed manner. Midway down the bed, a snow-white towel was to be stretched lengthwise across it and tucked under the mattress on either side. On top of the towel we were supposed to set out an array of small articles such as socks and gloves, folded in some cases or tucked into tight little balls in others. The array needed to be balanced so that whatever went on the left side was mirror-imaged on the right. Just about everything we had been issued with and that we weren't going to be wearing at that particular moment was to be displayed on the surface of the bed, including our brushes and the button stick. We also needed to include personal items such as soap and toothbrushes, and the cleaning materials we had purchased.

On the floor at the foot of the bed we had to place one pair of our highly polished bulled boots that had their laces pulled tight and the ends tucked away out of sight. These were flanked on either side by our plimsolls, with laces similarly tightened.

If getting our stuff ready for kit inspection wasn't enough, we also had to polish the billet floor until it too gleamed. This meant slopping dollops of orange floor polish on the linoleum, then spreading it out and rubbing it in with the bumper. After that, we put a "pad" made from an old blanket under the bumper to buff the floor into a shine. Everyone swept and bumpered his own bed-space and we all took turns at bumpering the central billet floor until it gleamed. In the morning we would only have to give it a quick once-over again with the bumper, and it would be ready for inspection.

As 2130 hours, lights-out time, approached we were all more than ready to collapse into bed, but there was one last ritual to be completed—bed check. This was a nightly routine that took place during all phases of Boy Entrant training. At 2100 hours or thereabouts, the Duty ITS Corporal made his rounds of all billets. As he entered our billet, someone yelled out the mandatory alert, "NCO present!" We all sprang to attention.

"Stand by your beds," the corporal ordered.

Each of us made our way to the end of our bed, and stood there to attention, facing the centre of the room. The corporal then walked the length of the room to make sure that each bed had a Boy Entrant standing alongside it. When he had satisfied himself that everyone was present and correct, he dismissed us with "Carry-on," as he went on his way to pay a visit to the next billet on his rounds.

I put my kit in neat piles under my bed in readiness for the morning, and then went to the washroom to clean up before turning in for the night. At 2130 hours, the lights were switched off and then, as we lay in the darkness, the sound of a trumpet playing "Last Post" played softly over the Tannoy, the billet public address system. This was from Radio St. Athan—not a true radio station, but a closed system that was wired to speakers in every billet throughout the camp. The solo trumpeter's notes played out clear as a bell, interspersed by a soft orchestral rendition of the "Evening Hymn". This was no Boy Entrant trumpeter, but a professional recording, made by someone who could really play the instrument. The music stopped and there was silence, all talking had to cease by 2200 hours, but we were all too tired to talk anyway. I fell fast asleep recalling the strains of that beautiful music that somehow seemed so comforting in this seemingly hostile new world that I had gone and committed myself to.

A different trumpet sound woke me up at 0700 hours. It was Reveille! At almost the same time the door of the billet was flung open and the Duty Corporal was in the room yelling, "C'mon, c'mon, let's have you. Out of bed. Feet on the floor!" Incredible as it seemed, one or two individuals continued sleeping regardless of the racket going on around them, so the corporal shook them roughly by the shoulder to wake them. The heavy sleepers each grunted and one muttered something completely unintelligible before coming fully awake.

There was a Service myth about being unceremoniously awakened in this manner. Supposedly, a sleeping person was immune from being held accountable for the first few semi-conscious utterances made when awakened in this way. I don't really know if this was true, but if so, it theoretically granted us the right to indulge in downright insubordination to our superiors during that brief moment. In reality, I never knew of anyone who actually put it to the test.

Wednesday morning. It was the big day! We scrambled out of bed, got washed, and struggled with the unfamiliarity of putting on our new uniforms. The collars again—they were so difficult to work with, but the lace up boots took time for a group of people who had been used to wearing shoes. Most of us skipped breakfast; there was so much to do before the kit inspection at 1000 hours. The process of just laying everything out took about an hour, but then the billet needed to be cleaned up as well. We swept and bumpered our bed-spaces, then swept the central floor and gave it a final bumpering. Corporal Blandford, who was the NCO in charge of our particular billet, had shown us how to move around on the floor like skaters, using pads made from old blankets to protect the shine on the lino. So we glided backwards and forwards on the pads as we tried to get everything ready for the big event. We even had several pairs of pads available at both entrances to the room so that anyone entering could pick a pair up, and then drop them off at whichever door they left from. The Flight office was located in one of the small rooms at the front of our billet that usually served as a Corporal's bunk, so through traffic was heavier for us than for most other billets. Blandford and most other NCOs who traversed the billet to the Flight office used the pads to protect the floor, but as we were to discover, there would be one notable exception.

By 0945 hours we were all standing by our beds finally and officially dressed in our full uniforms for the very first time. Most of us fidgeted, frequently checking our buttons to make sure we hadn't inadvertently smudged them, or making minute adjustments to items of our kit where it lay on the bed. Corporal Blandford hovered around outside the hut watching for the inspecting officer, but also occasionally checking our individual displays or uniforms to make sure everything appeared acceptable. Getting a bunch of raw recruits to this stage was a big reflection on him, so he certainly wanted the inspection to go well.

During one of the periods that Corporal Blandford was outside, the rear door suddenly opened. We all sprang to attention, but it wasn't the inspecting officer, it was our erstwhile friend Corporal Hillcrest. Instead of using the floor pads, he just ignored them and deliberately stomped the entire way down the centre of the billet floor, from door to door, all the while displaying a nasty little smirk on his face as the hobnails and steel heel-tips on his boots carved scratches in the linoleum. Corporal Blandford returned a short time later, after Hillcrest

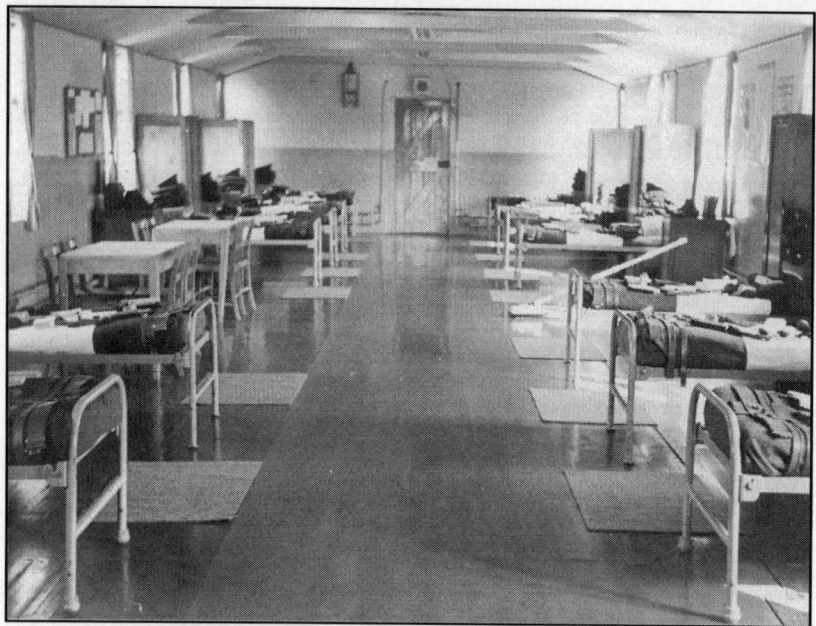

A Boy Entrant billet with items of personal kit laid out on beds ready for Kit Inspection. Note the "bumper" at middle-right of the picture. The door leads to the interconnecting corridor between billets.

had disappeared into the office, and when he saw the damaged floor surface he must have strongly suspected who the culprit had been.

"Did Corporal Hillcrest come through here?" he asked of no one in particular, while arching one eyebrow.

"Yes corporal," several of us replied.

Both eyebrows came down together as Blandford's face took on a grim look. He said nothing more, but he didn't have to; his expression said it all. It didn't take any great measure of intuition to learn from this little incident that Corporal Blandford, together with Corporal Kaveney as we later learned, considered Hillcrest to be a snide little snake-in-the-grass who was thoroughly disliked by his peers. In fact, Blandford helped us to plot a small act of revenge on Corporal Hillcrest for this and the other tribulations he would subsequently inflict on us, but that was several weeks later. For now, we had no choice but to tolerate Hillcrest's spiteful act.

The inspecting officer, Flight Lieutenant Hubbard, who was actually our Flight Commander, entered the billet with his entourage.

"Billet, attennnn-shun!" barked Corporal Blandford, as he sprang to attention himself and threw a stiff salute in the officer's direction.

Flight Lieutenant Hubbard, returned the salute by raising his brown leather-gloved hand to the peak of his hat in a relaxed officer-like way, "Thank you corporal, stand the billet at ease."

Blandford immediately turned to us and gave the order, "Stand *at* ease! No talking!"

Starting at Niall Adderley's bed, Hubbard led the way down one side of the billet and back up the other, followed in single file by Sergeant Clarke and Corporal Blandford. Hubbard stopped in front of each person and as he did so, the Boy Entrant under scrutiny came to attention, as we had all been instructed to, and gave his name and the last three digits of his service number. The officer examined him closely and then his kit layout, picking up some items to look at them more closely. Occasionally, he made a comment to Sergeant Clarke, who then scribbled something into a small pocket-size notebook that he carried in one hand. Most of the time this was due to a problem with a Boy Entrant's kit—maybe some buttons that weren't quite as clean as they needed to be. When this happened, the Sergeant lingered behind to make a note of the offender's name and number before catching up again with the inspecting party. It took some time to get to me since I was halfway down the opposite side of the billet, but when it was my turn I came to attention like the others.

"Sir! Carlin, 153," I managed to say in a loud voice, in spite of the nervousness that had me quaking in my boots.

Flight Lieutenant Hubbard stood immediately facing me and looked at my buttons, at my hat badge and then down at my boots. He stepped back a little way and took in a full-length view to check my general appearance. Were the creases sharp enough? Any wrinkles in the uniform? He stepped forward and reached up to adjust my hat. It was an anxious moment. Then he looked at the kit laid out on my bed for a few minutes.

"Very good Carlin. Carry on," he finally said, and moved on to "Charlie" Chaplain, whose bed-space adjoined mine.

I felt great relief that the ordeal was over and I had come through inspection without any hitches.

Altogether, the kit inspection in our billet took about thirty minutes. When Flight Lieutenant Hubbard finished inspecting the final boy, he turned to face Corporal Blandford and said, "Carry on, corporal."

"Thank you sir," said Corporal Blandford, whilst saluting.

Flight Lieutenant Hubbard returned the salute and then left by the front entrance, followed closely by Sergeant Clarke.

We all immediately felt very relieved, including Corporal Blandford, who also seemed pleased.

"Okay lads, stand easy," he said. "That wasn't bad, but there's a lot of room for improvement." He then continued, "Some of you got picked up by the Squadron Commander," then, looking at a piece of paper in his hand, he read out the names of the boys who had been picked up by Flight Lieutenant Hubbard. "Sergeant Clarke wants to see you in the Flight office at thirteen hundred hours. Be outside the office door by twelve fifty-five hours."

It was getting on for 1100 hours by now. A little too early for lunch, so we quietly put our kit away in our lockers, took our berets off and unbuttoned our tunics carefully so as not to get fingerprints all over the buttons, then sat on our beds and relaxed for a while. At around 1130 hours, someone said, "Anybody coming to the cookhouse?"

A few people answered verbally, but most of us responded by just picking up our mugs and irons and heading for the door. It was a ten-minute walk to get there by the safe but roundabout route that avoided the dreaded Wings, and the queue started to build up for quite a while before the mess door was unlocked at midday, so it was good to get there early. We were all hungry, so the thinking was that if we left now we'd get a place near the head of the queue. A few others were already making their way to the mess along the road that ran parallel to the runway, everyone walking in little groups of three or four.

Our earliness paid off, because we found only four or five people waiting on the step leading up to the closed mess door. Even though it was obviously locked, I still walked up to the door and tried to open it, unaware that in the next few moments I would learn that not all English people speak in what we like to call the Queen's English. Standing with his back to the door, as though guarding his place of first in line, was one of my fellow Boy Entrants by the name of Swaley.

"Wha's tha think tha's doin? Can't tha see bluddy doh-ah's shoot," protested Swaley in a broad Yorkshire dialect, "ah were 'ere fest."

He might as well have been speaking Outer Mongolian for as much sense as it made to me. Although my ears heard sounds, my brain that had been tuned to a regional Northern Irish dialect since birth just couldn't process them into intelligible words.

"Eh?" I responded, screwing my face into a questioning grimace.

A small ginger-haired lad standing nearby piped up, "He says 'what do you think you're doing, can't you see the bloody door's shut, and he was here first.' He's from Yorkshire and that's how they talk."

I looked at Swaley and said, "Am surry, ah wusn't try-in' tae go in frunt a yeh."

But this time it was Swaley's turn to look blank, as though I had spoken to him in something akin to Swahili. Richard Butterworth, the ginger haired kid, jumped in again to interpret for Swaley.

"He says he's sorry, he wasn't trying to push in front of you." Then he added helpfully, "He's from Ireland," as though it explained everything, which it probably did.

That's how I became friends with Butterworth. He was from Liverpool, which people jokingly called the capital of Ireland because of its large Irish population, so he was used to Irish accents and had little trouble understanding my broad brogue. And since Liverpool was in the neighbouring county to Yorkshire, he also understood Swaley's thick dialect. This was a good guy to know, I thought, he could be of some help. As for

Swaley, he and I spared each other any further attempts at conversation that day, but as time went on we all found an ear for regional accents and dialects, so understanding each other became a lot easier.

Finally, the mess door was unlocked from inside, and we made our way in line to the servery. The Wing boys were also making their way in there through another door, and queued up on the opposite side of the servery to ours. This was just as well because, as we had already started to discover, there was a definite pecking order amongst the entries, in which members of the newest entry came last—we were low men on the totem pole or at the bottom of the food chain, whatever you want to call it. Although we were protected by having a section of the mess specially set aside for us, the pecking order amongst the Wing boys didn't escape our notice. Those with the most inverted stripes on their cuffs seemed to be able to push in front of those with fewer stripes. Some of the Wing boys had no stripes at all and it appeared that the one, two and three-stripers could all push in front of them. It appeared that by being down at the bottom of the food chain, it was going to take us a long time to swim to the top.

We were all back in the billet a little before 1300 hours, where we noticed that the boys who had been summoned to the Flight office were joined by several more from the other billets. Then, at a little after 1300 hours, they were ushered into the office, and given a bollocking—a stern lecture—for not meeting the standards of preparedness required for a kit inspection. A common problem was buttons that weren't clean enough, which was something that dogged most of us at one time or another during our time at St. Athan. This was also one of Sergeant Clarke's pet peeves. "You need to get the shit out from between the crowns," he proclaimed. "Get an old toothbrush and really get in there."

He was referring to the intricate little nooks and crannies on the embossed crown on our buttons, and the little gap between the crown and the eagle. It was difficult to clean these by just using a regular button brush or a cleaning cloth, and it could easily become a trap for metal polish residue, which had a tendency to turn green in reacting with the brass. Using a toothbrush was the best way to clean the tiny areas involved and all it took was a little more time and patience, but sometimes both of those commodities were in short supply.

Corporal Kaveney made an appearance soon after everyone had returned to the billet. The contrast between our drill instructors' personalities was interesting. At one extreme we had Hillcrest the Snide and at the other there was Blandford who treated us like human beings for the most part, although he still maintained good discipline. Kaveney, tall, quiet, lean and straight as a ramrod, was somewhere in between the other two. He was what you might call a little tightly wrapped, but at the same time he was fair. Although he never picked on anyone, he didn't joke with us either. The expression on his face never altered and it seemed that not even the hint of a smile ever crossed his face. For Corporal Kaveney, it was all just business. His entry into the billet initiated the alert, "NCO present!" We all jumped to attention, in what now seemed to be second nature to us. Corporal Kaveney carried a large roll of brown paper and a large ball of twine, both of which he dumped on the table. The paper appeared to be of the type used in shops of that era to wrap purchases, but it differed in that on one side it had a shiny green waterproof coating.

"Pay attention," he announced in his calm, bland voice. "You will send your civilian clothing back home to your parents. From now on you must always be in uniform and must be properly dressed at all times, on or off duty, except when you are here in the billet after duty hours. Is that clear?" He looked around to emphasise the point that it should be clear, then continued, "That means tunic buttoned all the way up, belt buckled, hat properly placed on the head, unless you are indoors, in which case you may remove it." He looked down at the paper and twine on the table in front of him and gestured, "Use this paper to parcel up your clothes. Tie it well and then label the parcel with your parents' name and home address." As he said this, he pulled a pad of gummed labels from his pocket, "Here are some address labels." He then pointed to a corner of the billet, near the table. "When you've finished, pile your parcels in that corner. Okay? And don't take all afternoon. I'll be back in an hour and expect you to be finished." With that, he turned on his heel and departed by the front entrance.

The act of parcelling up my civvies hit home as a moment of truth because of the symbolism it embodied. This, more than anything else I had been through in the past few days, brought a strong dose of reality to the situation. Those clothes had hung in my locker as a link with my old life. Up to now, a thought had persisted at the back of my mind that I could very easily take the uniform off and put my old clothes back on to end this adventure if things didn't seem to be working out. Now, by sending the clothes home, that link with my former life was gone and it was a case of sink or swim from now on.

I parcelled the clothing up in the brown paper as neatly as a 15-year-old boy possibly could and wrapped enough string to moor the Queen Mary around the package. Then I filled out the address label and licked the gummed side, getting the foul taste of the glue in my mouth, and smoothed the label on the outside of the parcel before adding it to the growing pile. And that was the last I ever saw of those clothes.

That night I wrote my first real letters home—the form letter that we'd been forced to send a few days earlier didn't count as far as I was concerned. Ironically, I was feeling homesick, brought on partly by the separation from my civvy clothes. It's true that I was glad to be away from there, but home meant more than just being in my father's house. It meant familiar surroundings, sisters, a brother, friends and uncles and aunts to whom I could turn when things got difficult. There was something else—in spite of the misery that I suffered at the hands of my stepmother Annie, I had learned lots of ways to get around her and snatch some small comforts in life. But here in ITS there were no friendly relatives to turn to, nor long-time friends. And the DIs had seen it all before, so there was no getting around *them*. They would often say things like, "You might have broken your mother's heart, laddie, but you're not going to break mine!" It really felt as though I'd traded one tough life for another—out of the frying pan into the fire! And although there seemed to be a far off light at the end of this dark tunnel holding out a promise that at least the journey's end would be worthwhile, the feeling of loneliness at being stranded in an uncaring, hostile world made me miss the comfortable familiarity of my old life.

Before my departure from home, Annie had made sure I understood that I was expected to send some of my weekly earnings home, meagre as these would be. She had told me in no uncertain terms that I wouldn't be welcome to come back there on leave if I didn't do this. A person needs somewhere to come back to, so there seemed to be little choice but comply. Therefore, one of the things I'd done during my induction a few days earlier was to assign a weekly allotment of ten shillings to Annie. The government would send her a coupon book that she would present every week at the Post Office to receive the allotment, much the same way as elderly people drew their pensions. My letter told her about this, which in a way I suppose was to secure my reservation when the time came to go on leave. The short letter, written in postcard fashion, told her of some of the happenings of the past few days and included my new address in the hope that I would receive a letter in return. As every serviceman will tell you, getting any kind of mail is a big morale booster when you're far away from home. I also mentioned that my civvies should arrive in the very near future, so that she'd know to expect the parcel. Then I wrote to my great aunt Maggie. This second letter contained a lot more of myself, as I told her of all that had happened since the last time she'd seen me. Finally, I wrote a third brief letter to Aunt Alice, then sealed all three letters before walking over and posting them at the NAAFI. There seemed to be comfort in this, even if it was just one way contact with home. I felt much better on the way back to the billet.

CHAPTER 4

Recoil on the Range

The next morning Corporal Kaveney stomped noisily into the billet, shortly after we had returned from breakfast. "Fall in outside, on the double" he ordered.

We sprinted outside and headed for the road, joined by the other boys who were also streaming out of their billets. On reaching the road, everyone formed up in the usual three ranks. Corporals Blandford and Hillcrest were already there and when we'd right-dressed and been stood easy, the corporals divided us all into three smaller groups. I found myself in Corporal Hillcrest's group: he brought us to attention and then put us through the right-dress manoeuvre before standing us at ease.

"I hope you've all been busy cleaning your buttons," he announced with a malicious little smirk, as he strutted around in front of us, "because I'm going to be inspecting them very closely." He stopped strutting and faced us, "But first I'm going to give the order for you to open ranks," he continued. "On the command 'open order march' the front rank will take one step forward and the rear rank will take one step back. The middle rank will *not* move and don't forget—the word of command is 'march'. Do not move until it is given. Is that understood?"

"Yes corporal," we answered together.

He demonstrated, marching forward with his left foot as he voiced the command 'march'. He then completed the movement by bringing his right foot smartly alongside the left. That, he explained, was for the front rank only and then he showed us how the rear rank needed to take one step backwards. It looked easy enough, but as we learned time and time again with new drill movements, it was rarely as simple as it looked.

"Flight...! Waiiiit for it, waiiiit for it,"—some people had started to move before the actual command was given. Hillcrest paused until stability and equilibrium returned once more to the ranks and then completed the command, "opennnn orderrrr *march*."

The front rank took one step forward, the rear rank took one step back, some of the middle rank took one step forward, some stayed where they were and some took a step back.

"You bloody *shower*," screamed Hillcrest. "You're an *absolute* bloody shower! As you *werrrrre*!"

With his North Country accent, he always pronounced "bloody" as "blue-dy". I recognized the word, distorted though it was, but I didn't know what a shower was in the particular context in which he used it, although to judge from the manner in which he screamed the word, it didn't sound as though it was very complimentary.

We shuffled back into our original three ranks, only to undergo another 'right-dress' and then, after one or two more attempts, we eventually responded to the 'open order' command without major disorder. Having managed to get us into open order, Hillcrest then walked along the front and rear of each rank, inspecting our buttons, boots, uniforms and personal appearance in general. In particular, he was having a field day with our berets. Many of us were still grappling with exactly how this piece of headgear should be worn. The correct way was to adjust the head band so that it was horizontal all around the head at a level that was two finger-widths above the bridge of the nose, with the hat-badge located directly above the left eye. The loose material was then supposed to be pulled over the right ear. But styles varied amongst Boy Entrants. A few wore their berets in the regulation style, whilst an even smaller number wore theirs with the headband pulled all the way down until it rested on their ears, leaving no material to pull over to the side and endowing the wearer with a moronic appearance. Most of us, however, wore our berets in the sophisticated style affected by the Wing boys. This was really a modified regulation style— after pulling the material over the right ear in the approved manner, the wearer grasped the backing plate that supported the badge and pulled it to an upright position, at the same time putting a tuck in the material behind the backing plate. Hillcrest didn't like this style, however and wore his own beret in a strictly regulation way.

"I don't want to see any little bloody duck ponds in those berets," he informed us as he made us adjust the headgear to suit his style.

But we always adjusted our headgear to reinstate the "duck pond" as soon afterwards as we could get away with it. This was a continual source of irritation to Hillcrest and it became an ongoing battle between him and us. Few of us ever relented and always wore our berets in the Wing style, which we believed to be a hallmark of the true Boy Entrant. Many of us, in fact, wore it in this manner throughout our entire RAF service careers and very often it served as a recognition signal between ex-Boy Entrants, even after we had left Boys' service far behind us.

Although we may have made a stand for individuality with regard to our berets, there was little we could do with our brass buttons except try to keep them clean. The problem with the buttons was that they tarnished at the slightest touch of a finger, or a light sprinkle of rain, or just by being exposed to the damp or foggy air of a winter morning. Hillcrest and the other DIS were constantly on our backs for dirty buttons, or "shit between the crowns," as they frequently called it. If we failed to pass inspection because of our buttons, we would be ordered to perform extra chores—known as fatigues—that evening. These were menial jobs, like washing dirty pans in the cookhouse. Afterwards, we would be required to report to the corporal's bunk with all of our buttons, hat badges and boots clean and shiny, ready for the next morning's daily button inspection. If they weren't up to par, we were sent away to do them over again.

When Hillcrest finished inspecting our buttons he gave the command to "close order march," which meant that the front and rear ranks reversed the steps they had taken earlier to restore the Flight to its regular formation. When that was completed and we had performed a right-dress for the umpteenth time, he gave the order to right turn and then "By the left quick march!"

We moved off in a column of threes, approximately thirty boys with no idea of where we were headed, but it soon became very apparent that our destination was the Square. Hillcrest called out the time as we marched, left, right, left, right, with everyone in unison—all except for one poor unfortunate misfit. Potter must have been somewhere else when right feet had been given out, because he seemed to be cursed with two left ones. The poor lad couldn't keep in step to save his life. Whilst most of the Flight moved forward in a reasonable semblance of order, a minor tempest raged in the immediate area surrounding the unfortunate Potter. He was stepping on the heels of the people marching in front and tripping up those behind. People were stumbling all around him, getting kicked and kicking back in retaliation. Hillcrest suddenly became aware of the problem, like noticing rough water on the surface of an otherwise calm lake. He called a halt just as we got on the gravel-covered approach to the Square and marched back to where Potter was located in the column, obviously relishing the crunching noise that his steel-shod boots made on the fine gravel. Many pairs of eyes were glaring at Potter, so Hillcrest knew exactly who the culprit was right away.

"What's your name laddie?" he demanded, in his tough-guy voice.

"Potter, corporal," came the timid reply.

"Well Potter," Hillcrest shouted, "don't you know your bloody left from your right?"

"Yes corporal."

"Well, it doesn't look like you do. Pay attention to the step that I'm calling out, I'm not doing it for my health y'know!"

"Yes corporal," responded Potter.

We recommenced our interrupted march to the Square and actually made some progress before Potter lost his synchronicity again. This time, he caused even more mayhem than he had on the previous occasion. Corporal Hillcrest, who had been keeping a careful eye on the situation, called us to a halt once more and then ordered Potter to the rear of the column in the hope that he might be less of a problem there. We then continued on to the Square without further incident.

This was the first day of the infamous square-bashing that we'd all heard about, which was to become a part of our everyday life for the next three months. Drill, as it was officially known, started with the basics of marching in step and coming to a halt when given the order. The two other Initial Training Squadron groups of boys were also on the Square, but the separation between all three groups was sufficient to avoid confusion by any one group mistakenly responding to orders given by the DI of another group. Potter continued to be a problem, but as an individual I was secretly glad that someone else was getting all of the unwelcome attention that might otherwise be focused on me, and I suspect that I wasn't alone in nursing that selfish little thought. Potter was eventually taken out of the flight and given some special drill tuition, which must have worked because he didn't seem to have too many problems with drill after that.

* * *

Although drill occupied a large amount of our time in the Initial Training Squadron, it was only one part of our training. In fact, the mission of the Initial Training Squadron was to provide us with four pillars on which to build our future service careers: to mould us into disciplined members of the Royal Air Force; to train us in the skills of personal combat and defence so that we would be prepared in the event of a hostile ground attack or nuclear war; to build up our physical strength, fitness and stamina; and to endow us with an appropriate level of education that would prepare us for the trade training that would come later. And although our drill instructors were all experts in their own field, they could only teach us how to march and perform drill movements on the parade ground. It took a team of experts in all four fields to accomplish the wide spectrum of training that the RAF expected us to absorb in the three months of our initial training.

Drill, or square-bashing as it was unlovingly referred to, started off with the fundamentals like how to make right, left and about turns from the standing position. Everything was done by numbers, which we were instructed to chant out loudly whilst performing the movements. For example, when the order for a right turn was given, I had to swivel my body around to the right whilst keeping both of my feet on the same spot. The intermediate position of the movement left me with both feet pointing in the same direction as my body but my left foot slightly behind me, as though I had been frozen in the act of taking a step forward. For the final part of the movement, I needed to bring my left foot forward alongside the right. And whilst performing all three parts of the movement, call out "turn," as I swivelled, "two," when the swivel was complete and "three," as I brought my left foot forward. The left-turn movement was exactly the same except that the swivel was to the left and it was the right foot hanging back waiting to be brought alongside the left. An about turn was similar to the right turn, also with the same chant, but in this case the swivel was made through 180-degrees, which left me facing in the exact opposite direction.

We learned how to salute. On hearing the command, "Officer on parade, to the front salute!" We were instructed to bring our right arm up in a sweeping motion until it was parallel to the ground, then hold the upper arm in that position whilst the forearm, with palm fully extended, rotated at the elbow until the fingertips gently touched the right temple, just behind the eye— all of this in one fluid movement.

Then we progressed from stationary movements to marching drill. Performing about-turns on the march, like the guards at Buckingham Palace, or the more difficult manoeuvre of making an abrupt right or left turn on the march—so that instead of moving forward in a column, we would suddenly be moving in line abreast at ninety degrees to the original direction. When marching, we were always exhorted to swing our arms shoulder high. The DIs told us that this was only required during our time in the Initial Training Squadron and that when we went to the Wings we would only need to swing them as high as our waists.

The commands for the drill movements were always given in such a way that the marcher could anticipate when the actual word of command would be given and be mentally prepared to execute the movement. When the order to march was given, the first step was always with the left foot. Then once on the move, commands for simple drill movements were always given just as the right foot made contact with the ground. For example, when the command to a halt was issued it would be just as the right foot touched the ground. We knew to continue the stride with our left foot and then to stop when it hit the gravel and bring our right foot to a halt alongside of it, instead of continuing on through with the step.

An about turn on the march was also given on the right foot. The command for this was "Flight, about turn," with the word "turn" coming simultaneously with the right foot's contact with the parade ground. Again, the left foot would continue in the same direction, but this time, when the right foot followed, it would be planted in such a way that it formed the crossbar of a 'T' with the left foot. At the same time, the arms would be clamped stiffly to the sides. When the left foot came up, with an exaggerated lifting of the knee, it would then be turned by 180 degrees to point in the opposite direction. The upper body would meanwhile be following the left foot around to face in the new direction and finally the right foot would also be raised up and brought around, also with an exaggerated knee lift, before continuing to stride through and march off in the new direction, with arms swinging again.

Just when it seemed that we had got the hang of marching, the DIs introduced us to rifle drill, which seemed a little more interesting to me than ordinary drill. The Lee Enfield .303 rifle has now passed into the realms of history, but the drill movements that we were taught using this rifle are still as real to me today as they were when I learned them on the Square at Saints all those years ago.

First we were marched to the Armoury, where we were each issued with a rifle and then it was on to the Square and after several days of practice, it became second nature.

In the Stand at Ease position, the rifle butt would rest on the ground, snugly alongside my right foot and the muzzle would be thrust out in front of me as far as my right arm could reach. When the DI shouted, "Flight, attention," I would pull my arm rapidly back towards me to bring the weapon alongside and perpendicular to my right side. In doing so, I would slide my right hand down from the muzzle to grip the body of the rifle somewhere just above the breech. At the command, "Flight, slope arms," I would flick the rifle vertically upwards with my right hand, briefly letting go and then catching it at the stock—the narrow point of the butt just behind the trigger guard. At exactly the same moment, I would bring my left hand across my chest to grasp the rifle at the midway point of the barrel to steady it. This latter movement caused the taut rifle sling to slap against the wooden cladding of the rifle, creating a noise that was loudly multiplied by all of the other hands slapping their rifles in synchronism. The drill instructor paced the first movement by chanting, "Up, one, two." Then, for the second movement, he would chant, "Across, two, three," at which I would raise the rifle vertically upwards, the fingers of my right hand closing around the stock, using this grip to bring the rifle up and, still holding it vertically, bring it across my chest to lay it on my left shoulder. At the same time, I would transfer my left hand to cradle the end of the butt and take the full weight of the rifle. The DI would then chant, "Down, two, three," and I would bring my right arm smartly back down to my side in the final movement, whilst adjusting my left arm so that the forearm was parallel to the ground to complete the Slope Arms movement.

The rifle at Slope Arms was in the most versatile position of all. From there we could march, or perform other movements, such as Present Arms—the ceremonial salute for someone of high rank. We also learned how to make a normal, non-ceremonial salute whilst holding a rifle at the Slope Arms position. This was done by bringing the right open hand across to slap the flat face of the rifle butt, where it would remain until the salute was returned by the officer to whom it was directed.

After becoming sufficiently proficient at rifle drill, we advanced to bayonet drill, which is basically rifle drill with the additional complication that we fixed bayonets onto the rifle muzzle, whilst in the Stand at Ease position, when given the order, "Prepare to fix bayonets!" This movement was executed by withdrawing the sheathed bayonet from its scabbard, which was suspended from the webbing belt and dangling on the left hip. When everyone had withdrawn his bayonet and was holding it out in front of him at arms' length, with the blade pointing upwards, the command was given, "Fix bayonets". I would then fit the opening in the bayonet hilt over the end of the muzzle and click it into place, but my hand would remain in the Fix Bayonets position until commanded to resume the normal Stand at Ease.

The type of bayonet normally used for drill was a short, round spike known as a pig-sticker, but for ceremonial occasions we used a wicked-looking bayonet, shaped like a bowie knife. Since they were lethal weapons, the bayonets were always returned to the Armoury, together with the rifles, when the drill period ended each day. After all, nobody in their right mind would have trusted a bunch of teenage Boy Entrants with possession of either of these weapons any longer than was absolutely necessary and only then under the strictest supervision. Rifle drill with fixed bayonets might sound dangerous, but I never knew of anyone being inadvertently stabbed or otherwise injured during these drills.

We were, however, to become even more intimately acquainted with rifles during Ground Combat Training, or GCT as it was more often called. For this we needed our groundsheets and denims. The denims were difficult to get into because of our thick serge uniforms and once inside the feeling was one of bulkiness. Snap fasteners served as buttons up the front and closed the garment off at wrists and ankles.

Members of the RAF Regiment, the Royal Air Force's own internal army, directed this particular part of our training. Our drill instructor simply marched us to the RAF Regiment section and left us to their tender mercies. I noticed right away that they were different. They looked different, dressed differently and behaved differently from all other members of the RAF. They'd even earned themselves the special nickname of "Rock Apes", which was a less-than-reverential comparison to the Barbary Apes that inhabit the Rock of Gibraltar. Some even said that the Gibraltar apes were the more intelligent of the two, but that was mere hearsay. Rock Apes wore *RAF Regiment* shoulder flashes above their eagle flash, so that they wouldn't be mistaken for normal run-of-the-mill airmen. They also wore gaiters and webbing belts as everyday items of their uniform.

The major function of the Regiment was to provide the nucleus of basic protection for RAF airfields and installations against ground and air attack. For this reason, their skills lay in armed and unarmed combat. But they were small in number—a nucleus—so all normally non-combatant members of the RAF were expected to take up arms and do their bit to defend the turf under the Regiment's supervision, if we ever came under direct attack. In addition, because of the nuclear threat that hung over all of us in the nineteen-fifties, the RAF Regiment had been given the role of overseeing and developing personnel defensive measures should a nuclear attack become reality. In retrospect, it was unkind to belittle them by calling them Rock Apes and questioning their intellect, because they knew their job and taught us well. Besides, most of our GCT was a lot more fun than square-bashing—except for the nuclear-preparedness part, which tended to be very dull and boring for a bunch of teenagers.

The first thing we acquired from GCT was an intimate familiarity with the two main combat weapons we would be expected to use if push ever came to shove. One was the Lee Enfield .303 bolt-action rifle and the other was a light machine gun, or LMG, much better known as the Bren gun. The Lee Enfield rifle was actually in service during the First World War and both weapons were used in the Second World War. These same reliable weapons had also been used successfully in the Korean War, which had ended in 1953, just three years prior to our induction.

Most of us had never even seen a firearm up close before, let alone handle one, but during the next twelve weeks GCT transformed us from being almost certain cannon fodder into lean mean fighting machines. Well, maybe that's a slight exaggeration, but at least we could load, aim and fire a .303 rifle and a Bren gun, strip them down to their basic parts, then reassemble them into fully workable weapons again in a matter of minutes. Yes, rumour had it that the Russians trembled at the mere mention of our names.

Training in the safe handling of weapons came first, as it rightfully should.

"Never point a weapon at anyone unless you intend to kill them!" was the first thing the instructors hammered into our heads. That was a tough message for most of us to swallow—to point a gun at someone with the intent of actually killing him.

One brave boy asked, "Couldn't we just wing them or something Sarge, the way Roy Rogers does?"

"No lad, a weapon is made for killing. It's very difficult to aim to wound someone, you'll most likely end up missing him altogether and then he'll get you. No, you must always aim for the largest target on the enemy's body, his chest, and shoot to kill! And if you don't intend to kill a person, then don't point a weapon at him."

"Okay, Sergeant."

Eventually, we would be firing live ammunition on the rifle range, so range discipline was the next important lesson to be learned. We were told that when a red flag is flying from a high point on the range, it means that the range is in use. Another red flag down in the range meant that no one could proceed beyond the line of fire until it was lowered. We were also told to always point weapons towards the bank of sand against which targets are displayed and follow the range master's instructions at all times.

Weapons were stored in the Armoury, so we had to pass through there in single file, in one door and out another, to be handed a rifle by the Armourers as we passed through. The air inside the Armoury smelled heavily of gun oil as I walked through and took the rifle that was handed to me, being surprised to find that its 9 pounds of weight felt much heavier than I expected. Once outside, we were shown how to strip the rifles down into their component parts and clean them, using the cleaning tools and materials stored in a nifty little compartment that opened in the heel of the rifle butt. We were then shown how to fill a charging clip with ten dummy rounds and use it to load the rifle's magazine. Next we learned the method of unloading the weapon and then how to operate the bolt five times to make sure all rounds had been cleared from it before pulling the trigger to fire the action.

With the Bren gun, it was a matter of how to change barrels when the one that was in use became overheated, or how to crawl up alongside the weapon and use a spare round of ammunition as a tool to adjust the gas flow regulator, if the automatic firing action stopped. Loading the magazine with ammunition was easier than the rifle. We just pushed 28 rounds into the spring-loaded magazine until it was full and then clipped it to the gun.

We were taught how to aim. With the rifle, it was, "Put the tip of the foresight on the target and line it up with the middle of your back-sight, then squeeze the trigger gently. Squeeze, lads! Squeeze the trigger with the second joint of your forefinger, don't pull it or you'll jerk the weapon and come off the target. Feel the first pressure, then the second pressure and keep squeezing until the weapon fires. That's it." The training ground echoed with sporadic clicks as we fired the actions of our individual weapons.

The Bren gun was a little different. It was fired either in short bursts of three rounds or long bursts of five. Longer bursts would cause the barrel to overheat. The rate of fire was 120 rounds a minute. So that we'd know how long to keep the trigger pulled for short bursts, we were instructed to say to ourselves "Fire, release," pulling the trigger as we did so, then letting it go when the short phrase was complete. A number of short bursts could be fired off by muttering "Fire, release"—pause—"Fire, release"—pause, and so on. For long bursts, the phrase we were told to say was,"One, two, three release," before letting go of the trigger again. Of course, that didn't sound very long or exciting to many of us. It would have been much more thrilling if we had been able to stand up with the machine gun at hip level and fire off long bursts, like actors in a war film.

Mostly we used the Lee Enfield .303, shooting it from the prone position. That meant we had to learn how to get down on the ground quickly while still holding the rifle. This was accomplished by first planting our left hand down on the ground, putting all of our weight on it and then kicking both legs out and behind to splay them on the ground, all the while gripping the weapon at its midpoint in our right hand to keep it clear of the ground. Once on the ground we then needed to go quickly into the aim position and be ready to shoot at the imagined enemy. Luckily, we each had already spread our groundsheet out to lie on, so we weren't exactly grovelling in the mud. After mastering this manoeuvre to end up in the position of aiming the rifle, we then had to crawl on our bellies with the rifle held in both hands. The Rock Apes would yell out, "Keep your arses down or you'll get them shot off!" My arse went down, but it was hard to crawl like that, elbow over elbow, while trying not to dig deep furrows in the soil with the pointy end of the gun. But to let that happen was to invite a bollicking for getting soil and grass into the muzzle of the gun.

Achieving this level of proficiency took more than one session of GCT and after we had spent several sessions crawling around on the ground with rifles, we were more than ready to go on the range for live fire practice. Now, I thought to myself, the fun stuff would really begin.

Going on the range for the first time was an exciting experience. First, we went to the Armoury where six rifles were issued to the Flight. Six lucky lads were each given the privilege of carrying a rifle all the way to the range. They marched along at the head of the column swinging only their left arm shoulder high. Their right arms were fully extended downwards with the middle finger supporting the weight of the rifle by its trigger guard. The rifle itself was held in a vertical position, butt downwards with the tip of the barrel just about level with the bearer's ear.

At the range, I couldn't believe I was actually going to fire a real live weapon. Most boys of my age wouldn't normally get the opportunity to do this and I wouldn't have traded the experience for all the money in the world. I was just afraid that it might be snatched away at the last moment for some spoilsport reason, so it was a great relief when my turn finally came around and I was motioned to move towards the ammunition boxes to load a charging clip with ten live rounds.

We didn't use the .303 that first day—the rifle lying waiting for me was a .22 calibre. It looked like a .303, right down to the wooden cladding that enclosed the barrel, but it was smaller. But I didn't mind because it was still a real gun and fired real bullets. Six of us stood in the firing line facing the targets, after we'd spread our groundsheets out on the earth bank that served as the firing position. The weapons lay at our feet; ammunition clips were clutched in our right hands. Then, the sergeant Rock Ape gave the order to get down. Immediately, I put my left hand on the groundsheet, took my weight on it and kicked my feet and legs out behind me as I'd been taught. My denim-clad torso made contact with the hard-packed earth underneath the groundsheet.

"Clear weapons!" The sergeant ordered.

I worked the bolt ten times and then left it open.

When the sergeant was satisfied that none of our rifle breeches held any leftover ammunition, he called out, "In your own time, load weapons!"

I took the little metal charging clip of ammunition and slotted it into a special recess at the rear end of the breech and then pressed down on the top round with my thumb to push all of the rounds into the magazine. Having done that, I slammed the bolt home to cock the rifle, applied the safety catch and then waited.

We lay there forever, or so it seemed, until the order came, "Target at your front, range 500, ten rounds—in your own time. Fire!"

I set the sight for 500 feet. The distance was only 25 yards, but 500 feet was the smallest possible distance to set the sights. I pushed the safety catch off and started squeezing the trigger. The first pressure was an easy pull, but the inside of the second joint of my trigger finger felt the stronger resistance of the second pressure. My target was a human-shaped cardboard cut-out depicting a fierce-looking soldier running towards me with a bayonet fixed to his rifle. Several oblong target areas were nested on his chest and my job was to aim for the innermost rectangle and try to hit it. I continued squeezing the trigger until suddenly the action released and the weapon fired with a loud bang that left a ringing sound to my right ear. A puff of smoke blew briefly across my face and my nose instinctively puckered at the sharp smell of burnt cordite. Everyone had warned me to expect a kick from the rifle, but I felt hardly anything. I let go of the trigger and reached forward with my right hand to push the bolt up and then pulled it back towards me, causing the still smoking shell to eject from the breech. Then I closed it and took aim once more. The target was too far away to see where the first round landed, so I just hoped for the best, aimed and fired again. This time the noise and the smoke weren't any surprise and my ear was still ringing from the first time, so it didn't matter any more. I continued firing until the last round had gone, cleared the rifle ten times, fired the action and then laid the weapon down with the breech open to await further orders.

When it was certain that everyone had fired off all their rounds and cleared their weapons, the red flag at the target area was lowered. We were then told to go and inspect our targets. Mine had four holes in an area off to the left of the inner oblong and one hole several inches away from the others.

"Good grouping, Carlin, but try and keep the same aiming point so that you get all five together," said the sergeant, who had suddenly materialized beside me.

Apparently getting a good grouping was more important than hitting the centre of the target area. I nodded affirmatively and then went outside of the range enclosure to wait around with those who had fired and those still waiting their turn. Time for a woody-Woodbine!

Eventually, everyone fired off their ten rounds and came outside to wait for our DIs, who had turned up to march us back but then had gone inside the range. The DIs knew that ammunition signed-out for target practice could not be returned to the armoury, once the seal on the ammo box had been broken and therefore it all needed to be fired off at the range. Since there was still quite a lot of ammunition left over, they wanted to take advantage of the opportunity and were now having a great time showing off with their fancy shooting, or so they would have us believe. I clearly remember Corporal Blandford standing and firing one of the .22's from the hip. This wasn't really a good example for us, but just another example of the old adage: don't do as I do, do as I say!

That was both the first and last time we fired .22 calibre rifles. At our next GCT session, a few days later, we were taken to the range again. This time it was the real thing—.303 calibre. We followed the same procedure—getting down, loading, aiming and squeezing the trigger. This time, however, when the trigger released the firing pin there was such an almighty bang that it hurt my right ear, but I barely noticed that because it felt as though I'd just been kicked in the shoulder by a mean, angry mule. That was bad enough, but I had to fire off nine more shots and be rewarded with nine more similar mule-kicks. The second shot hurt an already aching shoulder and each successive shot only increased the agony. By the time I was squeezing off the third shot all thoughts of grouping them had disappeared; I only wanted to get it over with so that the torture would end. Later, when I went to look at the target my poor aim was very obvious, because the bullet holes were all over the place. In fact, I'm not sure that more than five rounds landed on the target. Rifle practice lost a lot of its allure that day and just became something else unpleasant that we had to do. Most of us felt the same way and all nursed bruised shoulders and painful ringing ears for days afterwards. And this wasn't helped by repeated visits to the range at regular intervals for the next few weeks, until we were deemed proficient with the Lee Enfield .303 calibre rifle.

Next, we moved on to the Bren gun, which was a lot more fun to fire. The internal action absorbed all of the energy from the exploding cordite charge in the round that gave the .303 its kick and used it to automatically reload the next round and re-cock the action. I suppose that's why it was called a machine gun. It could fire single shots or bursts and we were required to try both. The safety catch had three positions, A for automatic fire, S for safe and R for "rounds" or single shots. For this reason, it was referred to as the ASR lever. The sights were offset to the left side, instead of being directly over the centre-line of the weapon as they are on a rifle. This was because a carrying handle was mounted atop the barrel, creating a visual obstruction between the foresight and back-sight, if they had been mounted directly above the barrel. When aiming over a long distance the offset wasn't a problem, because the sights were slightly angled to compensate for the difference, but this didn't work for the short length over which we were shooting at the range, so our targets had an additional faint "ghost" image target to the left of the aiming point. The idea was that although we would aim for the bull's eye, the shots would actually land on the ghost target, hopefully in the offset bull's eye.

The drill for getting down on the ground was the same as before, except that this time I was holding the slightly curved

Bren gun magazine that I clipped onto the top of the breech, after first checking that the ASR lever was in the S for safe position. The gun had a set of bipod legs at the front end, so it was just a matter of picking up the butt and nestling it into my shoulder, right hand on the pistol grip and the other hand across my chest gripping the top of the stock to steady the weapon.

"Target at your front, in short and long bursts fire, in your own time, fire!"

I eased the ASR lever to A for automatic and manually cocked the gun to fire the first round, then let loose with my first short burst. Firing the Bren was like driving a Rolls Royce on a smooth highway after having suffered the equivalent of a ride across rugged terrain in a Landrover when comparing it with the Lee Enfield .303 rifle. There was no nasty recoil. The only indication that deadly rounds of ammunition were spewing from the weapon was the sight of sand kicking up in tiny spurts, as bullets slammed into the sandbank behind the target. This was accompanied by the "blat-blat-blat" sound of the gun, as its recoil action drove the automatic firing mechanism. Fire, release, fire, release—that got two short bursts off, then—one, two, three, release for a long burst of five rounds. I did this several times whilst resisting the temptation to hold the trigger for longer, fully aware that the eagle eyes and ears of the range master would know immediately if any burst endured longer than it was supposed to. His vigilance wasn't in vain. Despite the strong emphasis on safety that had been drilled into us, someone further along from my position started firing his Bren before lifting the butt off the ground and up to his shoulder. The front of the weapon was angled upwards because of the bipod legs and suddenly bullets started pinging off the top of the high wall behind the targets. Several chunks of masonry flew off the top of the wall before the sergeant was able to cover the distance from where he stood to where the shooter lay and give him a solid kick on the soles of his feet. The surprised boy looked around and was immediately yanked unceremoniously to his feet and expelled from the firing area. Another sergeant went to the gun, applied the ASR to safe and removed the magazine. With order restored, I continued short and long bursts and then a few single shots with the ASR lever in the R position until the magazine ran out of ammunition. Then I put the lever to S for safe, manually cocked the action a few times, fired the action and then lowered the butt to the ground as I raised my hand to indicate that I'd finished. A few others were still firing, but eventually the blatting sound was replaced by comparative quiet. We were ordered to get to our feet and when the red flag at the target area was lowered, we trooped out in single file to retrieve our targets so that we could discuss the grouping of the holes with the sergeant. Yes, firing the Bren was an altogether more pleasant experience than firing the rifle.

Our training with the RAF Regiment, however, wasn't all shooting and crawling around in the dirt. In fact the next part of it was named Ground Defence Training, or GDT, and mainly involved teaching us what we needed to do in the aftermath of a nuclear attack. To us, this wasn't as interesting as shooting and handling weapons and required that we sit in a classroom, instead of being out on the range. They showed us films taken during nuclear tests so that we could see the awesome power of The Bomb for ourselves. As I watched buildings and vehicles blowing away on the screen, I wondered if anyone would survive such an attack. But the training was geared more towards going into an area that had had already been attacked.

We learned that a nuclear explosion resulted in a blinding flash that travelled outwards from the site of the explosion at the speed of light, blinding anyone whose eyes were unprotected. A wave of radiation followed close behind and after that, the physically destructive blast wave. If we survived all of those, we would then be faced with radioactive fallout as dust and debris that had been irradiated by the explosion returned to earth. To guard against all of this, we were taught how to use an instrument called a survey meter, which was something like a Geiger counter that measured the radiation level in units known as Roentgens, except that it didn't make a clicking noise like those featured in films in the Astra. We were also shown how to use small personal radiation measurement devices called dosimeters that were designed to indicate the amount of accumulated radiation a person had been exposed to whilst wearing it. The dosimeter was shaped something like a fountain pen and could be clipped to the wearer's clothing. We were shown how to peer through it to see if a specially charged quartz fibre indicated that we were still safe, or if it had moved into the get-to-hell-out-of-there zone.

Part of our Ground Defence Training involved learning about how to use a gas mask. To provide us with practical experience, we were taken to a smoke filled tunnel-like structure and instructed to don a gas mask and walk through the tunnel. As my friend Butterworth and I waited our turn, we noticed that the first people through the tunnel emerged coughing and spluttering, even though they had been wearing the gas masks. We watched this for a while, noting that an air of chaos and confusion seemed to accompany the whole exercise. Exchanging knowing looks, but without saying a word, we each donned our gas masks and edged slowly away from the tunnel entrance and gradually covered the short distance to its exit where small groups of boys were coming out enveloped in clouds of smoke. Surreptitiously, we joined one of these groups and stumbled along with them to an area of clear air, then removed our gas masks with the others, coughing and spluttering just as they were. Nobody seemed to notice in the confusion, so we got away with not having to suffer the smoke. It's interesting to reflect that both of us were willing to smoke a Woodbine, but took the risk of being punished to avoid going through the smoke filled tunnel.

* * *

The third pillar of our training in the Initial Training Squadron was Physical Training, which we usually just called PT.

There seemed to be a graduated plan for developing our physical flexibility and strength, and for the first few weeks we would be taken to PT on alternate days. The first sessions usually consisted of group callisthenics under the supervision of a physical training instructor. As with the RAF Regiment, PTIs were another separate breed with their own unique working uniform that consisted of a V-necked white wool sweater, long navy blue trousers and athletic shoes.

The PTIs demanded discipline, but less harshly than the DIs. Mostly, PT was a welcome relief from drill and education since it was less rigorous than drill and we didn't have to stand still for long periods. As time passed and we became stronger and fitter, we moved on to more physically demanding challenges like vaulting and somersaulting over a vaulting horse. It was safe because the instructor always positioned himself on the other side, grabbing us as we came over and it was just a matter of making contact with the rough coconut fibre mat on the landing side of the horse. We experienced quite a bit more gym equipment than the vaulting horse: walking on our hands along a set of parallel bars, doing chin-ups on a bar in the corner of the gym and tossing medicine balls around to each other.

Eventually, the frequency of our PT sessions became a daily activity and during much of the time we were subjected to Circuit Training. The "circuit" consisted of a number of stations, each dedicated to a specific exercise. In small groups of two or three boys, we had to spend five minutes at each station in rotation, performing the required activity. For example, at one station we were obliged to step up and down on a bench repeatedly for five minutes, until the PTI blew his whistle as a signal for us to rotate to the next station. The next station just might have been the one equipped with a number of sand-filled metal ammunition boxes. The required activity here was to bend over at the waist, grab a box by its two handles and then continually raise and lower it to the chest until the whistle blew to signal the next rotation.

Physical Training wasn't confined just to our sojourn in the Initial Training Squadron; it was a solid part of the curriculum throughout our entire 18-months' long Boy Entrant training. Even at the very end, when it came close to the time for our final passing-out parade from Boy Entrants, we were taken on daily five-mile route marches—on the double! Although a general improvement in our physical fitness wasn't noticeable in the short term because it was so gradual, we were all in excellent physical condition at the completion of our Boy Entrant training.

Sports were also an important part of the physical training regime at St. Athan. Wednesday afternoon of each week was dedicated specifically as Sports Afternoon, during which we were expected to participate in an organized sporting activity. St. Athan catered to almost every sport one could think of. In addition to the usual football, rugby, cross-country, cricket, basketball, boxing and field hockey, there were more exotic activities such as fencing, small bore rifle shooting and of course, the unofficial but ever-popular Egyptian PT—the latter being best performed in a horizontal unmoving position on one's bed with the eyes closed. Unfortunately, as well as being unofficial it was also strongly discouraged and heaven help any Boy Entrant caught in the billets engaged in this somnolent activity by the ever-watchful DIs. If one wanted to practise Egyptian PT, rather than one of the more physically demanding Sports Afternoon pursuits, it was advisable to find a hidden nook far from prying eyes where such inactivity could be enjoyed undisturbed. Some Boy Entrants became experts at finding such hidey holes and on any given sports afternoon a small dedicated number of them participated in this less than physically demanding "activity" whilst most of the Boy Entrant population engaged itself in the healthier fully-approved physical sports. Personally, I took the opportunity to pursue my current passion—learning to swim—and so enjoyed this and many other sports afternoons thrashing about in the pool.

* * *

Not all of our time in the Initial Training Squadron was devoted to the physical. Further education was the fourth pillar of our overall training.

The Education Centre consisted of a conglomeration of classrooms and offices built in the same single storey wooden style of construction as our billets. Corporal Hillcrest marched us there on the first day that we were scheduled to start classes. As soon as he dismissed us, we gathered around a bulletin board to find our first classroom.

It was an odd sensation. When I'd left school back in Coleraine, I thought I had left it forever, but here I was back in the familiar surroundings of a classroom again. There were desks and blackboards, and the smell of chalk dust mingled with the aroma of freshly sharpened cedar-wood pencils. RAF history was the first item on our agenda and waiting to welcome us was our old friend Pilot Officer Morgan-Williams, who had briefly lectured us on this very same topic during our induction.

"Be seated lads," he said to no one in particular as we flooded into the room. I chose a desk by the wall in a row midway between the front and the back of the class. The chubby little officer, whose dark jowls always seemed to imply that he'd forgotten to put a blade in his razor that morning, waited patiently until everyone was seated and then started roll call. When each person's name was called out he answered by shouting "Sir!" Morgan-Williams then handed out some notebooks and pencils and for the next hour we learned about the organization of our service by listening and copying the notes he chalked up on the blackboard. First, he described how the service was divided and subdivided into increasingly smaller units and then he explained the rank structure.

We learned that, starting from the top, the RAF is divided into several Commands. Famous amongst these, from their wartime exploits, were Fighter Command and Bomber Command. But in addition to those, there were Transport, Coastal, Flying Training and Technical Training Commands. We, of course, were current members of the latter.

The Commands were then subdivided into Groups: No. 1 Group, Fighter Command, for example. Groups were made up of Units—a Unit being usually a Station, although not necessarily so. And Units were broken down into Wings. At St. Athan, we had No. 1 Wing and No. 2 Wing. Wings, in turn, were made up of Squadrons and Squadrons were made up of Flights. Although a Flight is the smallest official subdivision in the RAF, a very small group of people organized into marching order was generally referred to as a Squad.

At the conclusion of our lesson on RAF history and a short break, during which I took the opportunity of having a few puffs on a Woodbine, we moved to another classroom and a different education officer. This one was also a Pilot Officer, who wore a hairy battle dress with the almost invisible thin stripe that signified his rank on the epaulettes. The hairy uniform marked him as a National Service conscript—probably a teacher in civilian life, like Pilot Officer Morgan-Williams. The measly pittance of a salary earned by the poor souls suffering through this compulsory duty, didn't quite afford them the luxury of purchasing one of the nice smooth uniforms favoured by career officers.

Shortly after we had taken our seats at our desks, another education officer entered the classroom and then both officers proceeded to pass out exam papers. This, they informed us, was an exam to test the level of our individual knowledge. The results would be used to break us into a number of smaller groups with different levels of competency, whose specific needs would be easier to meet.

Following this exam, most of us were assigned into the groups as promised, but two or three boys did so well that they were head and shoulders above everyone else. Significantly, they were all from Scotland, which at that time was reputed to have the highest educational standards in the United Kingdom. These boys were immediately offered transfers to the Apprentice training school at Halton, where lads of our own age went through a 3-year training course, emerging as skilled tradesmen with the rank of Junior Technician. By contrast, our 18-month training course would send us out into the regular service as semi-skilled tradesmen, who would then need to take an additional Fitter's course to reach skilled technician status.

For the remainder of our time in the Initial Training Squadron, we spent at least two half-days in the Education Centre each week studying Mathematics, Physics, English, Geography and RAF History combined with Current Affairs.

Not surprisingly, Current Affairs dealt mainly with situations in the world that directly impacted the Royal Air Force, with most of the focus being on events of the recent past rather than those that were strictly "current" affairs. The Suez crisis had just ended, so we learned a lot about Colonel Nasser and the British and French invasion of the Canal Zone. We were told that Nasser had scuttled ships in the middle of the canal to block it. Also, that the Americans disapproved of the entire invasion and had been successful in putting pressure on Britain and France to withdraw.

The topics were interesting, but my favourite classroom subject was Physics. There was so much interesting stuff to learn. The two important subjects for my group were the theory of flight and electromagnetism. The Physics education officer frequently used clever demonstration models to show us how things worked, like lift on an aeroplane wing, or how iron filings could be used to show the normally invisible lines of force between the North and South poles of a magnet.

At the beginning, my knowledge of both subjects was just about zero. I didn't have a clue how an aircraft managed to remain up in the sky and as far as electricity was concerned, all I knew was that if I turned the light switch on, lo and behold the bulb would light, or if I poked around in an electric socket it would give me an unpleasant shock.

As time passed, I learned that an aircraft wing is lifted because the airflow across it develops low pressure on the top surface and high pressure on the bottom surface. As the high pressure tries to get to the low-pressure area it pushes the wing upwards. Theory was reinforced by a demonstration using a cross-section model of an aerofoil—the end-on shape of an aircraft wing—as a fan blew smoke across it. This made the normally invisible flow of air visible, revealing that the smoke molecules were squeezing together as they passed under the bottom surface, creating high pressure and moving apart in the low pressure flow over the top of the aerofoil.

The effect was further reinforced by another aerofoil model, but this time there were rows of little transparent plastic tubes inserted into the upper and lower surfaces of the wing from within the model. The tubes all led to a small rack, where they were arrayed vertically alongside each other. Each tube contained the same small volume of red ink, so that all ink levels were horizontally equal. When the fan started blowing air across the aerofoil, the level in each tube went either up or down, depending on which surface the other end of the tube was located. Levels in the tubes attached to the lower surface tended to drop, while those attached to the upper level tended to rise. This gave us a visual demonstration of the pressure differences at multiple spots on the wing's surface.

Electromagnetism was probably the most important subject for those of us who were going to train as aircraft electricians. In addition to his demonstration of the magnetic lines of force emanating from a magnet, our teacher used a little instrument known as a galvanometer to show us how an electric current was induced into a length of wire when it was passed through the magnetic field. Of course, this is the basic principle on which the production of electricity depends, but I hadn't known that previously. We learned important physical laws of electricity, like Faraday's Law, Lenz's Law and Ohm's Law. Overall, the education was excellent and by the end of our time in the Initial Training Squadron I was very well prepared to tackle the more practical aspects of my chosen trade.

CHAPTER 5

Home Sweet Home?

B y the time we had finished our first session at the Education Centre, Corporal Hillcrest was waiting outside to march us back to the billets. I was looking forward to getting back there so that I could dump my newly acquired notebooks and go to tea. We "fell-in" in threes on the road adjacent to the Education Centre and set off marching when Hillcrest gave the order. I don't know whether it was weariness, or just the fact that we still hadn't got into the habit of swinging our arms up to shoulder level, but halfway back to the billets Hillcrest called a halt.

"You're marching like a bloody shower of shit again," he bawled. "Well, I've had my tea laddies, so I'm in no hurry to get back. We can just bloody-well wait here for a while until you bloody-well decide to get your bloody arms up shoulder high." He paused briefly for breath, very red in the face by this time. He then continued in a quiet, but sneering voice, "Don't think you'll break my heart, laddies. You might have broken your mothers' hearts, but you won't bloody-well break mine!"

Corporal Hillcrest kept us standing at attention for a good ten minutes before finally calling out the command to march. We were famished and I know that I swung my arms shoulder high with so much force that it felt they were going to fly off. Mercifully, we soon arrived back at the billets and were dismissed so that we could get to the mess for much needed sustenance.

Hillcrest seemed to enjoy making our lives miserable, which he did as often as possible and in many ways. For the most minor of infractions, he would frequently detail people to perform evening fatigues, or make them run around the Square on the double, with a rifle held in both hands at arm's length above their heads. But what could we do? We were the lowest on the pecking order with no one to complain to. It was just a case of tolerating the punishments and indignities with the knowledge that they couldn't last forever.

Over and above what Corporal Hillcrest might have dished out in his mean-spirited manner, we got our fair share of normal fatigues during the weekly Tuesday bull-nights. Everyone in the billet was expected to pitch in to help in the task of applying floor polish with the bumper, then bumpering it off with the blanket pads. On top of that, Senior Boy Willie Burns doled out additional cleaning tasks, because each billet had a responsibility to provide representatives to perform cleaning duties in the communal areas. The worst of these assignments was to clean the toilets and washbasins in the ablutions area. Of course, we didn't call them the "Ablutions", but instead called them the Bogs—the RAF slang name by which they were universally known. There were also the ironing room, bathrooms, windows and the exterior of the billet area.

Wednesday mornings always involved some kind of inspection. Usually, it was a "stand-by-your-beds" type of inspection by the Flight Commander, during which our billet would be inspected for microscopic specks of dust and our persons for the slightest hint of tarnish on our buttons or cap badges, lack of creases in our uniforms, or a less than perfect shine on our boots. That was on a good day. Periodically, on not-so-good days, we would experience the thrill of a full-blown kit inspection.

Willie Burns was a no-nonsense Scottish lad who was the oldest and probably the most mature boy in my billet. From Corporal Blandford's point of view, he must have been the perfect choice to appoint as the billet's Senior Boy. The DIS couldn't be everywhere and besides, with the exception of Corporal Hillcrest, they all lived in married quarters, which was a considerable distance away. Therefore, one person in each billet had been appointed to the position of Senior Boy. It wasn't exactly a promotion, but they were given a dark red-coloured lanyard to wear around their left shoulder and a limited amount of power over the other inhabitants of their respective billets. A Senior Boy's job was to make the corporal's life easier by shepherding the inhabitants of his billet out on parade in good time, supervise bull nights—"domestic evenings" in official parlance—and keep an eye on the daily schedules to make sure everyone was prepared for the day's itinerary.

* * *

On the day that Corporal Hillcrest had deliberately halted us for the first time to make us late for our meal, essentially putting us at the very end of the long queue, I returned to the billet after tea and cleaned my buttons, badges and boots ready for the next day. I wanted to get this over with so that I could go back to the swimming pool with the others and continue pursuing my goal of learning to swim.

Once in the pool, I splashed and somersaulted in the water for a while, continuing to develop confidence in my body's natural buoyancy. Then Basset showed me a new technique that looked as though it could be helpful. He stood at a spot in the shallow end, maybe ten feet from the edge of the pool and crouched down with arms outstretched like Superman getting ready to leap from a tall building. For a moment he crouched there, concentrating, then he launched himself towards the handrail around the edge of the pool. His feet came off the bottom and for a few seconds he was gliding through water, arms outstretched in front of him and without any visible means of support, before he grabbed onto the handrail. Putting his feet back down on the bottom of the pool, he turned to face us with a look of self-satisfied triumph on his broadly grinning face.

"Come on, try it," he shouted.

And that's what I tried to do for the remainder of the evening in the pool, although it certainly wasn't an instant success. At first, each time I tried to launch myself forward it took more courage than I could summon up to let my feet leave the security of the pool's tiled floor, so that I made countless false starts. But by moving inch by inch nearer to the handrail after each failed attempt, I finally got to a position where it only took a forward fall with outstretched arms to be able to catch hold of it. Bassett had made gliding from about ten feet out look so easy, but I found it to be the most difficult thing in the universe that evening. So I lowered my expectations and just stayed close to the edge, falling forward and only allowing my feet and legs to come off the bottom when I had securely grasped the handrail. But it was a start! I was able to feel the resistance of the water as it buoyed me up when I fell forwards and so I warily started to trust it. Impatient as I was, learning to swim

wasn't going to happen overnight, but just being in the pool was
enjoyable by itself and every little improvement towards my
eventual goal felt like a major triumph.

Next morning it was drill on the Square as usual, but first
the button inspection. The weather had turned colder and we
were in winter dress, which meant wearing our greatcoats, which
also meant having another set of buttons to clean each evening.
At 0755 hours, we all started tumbling out of the billets, falling
into three ranks on the road. Corporal Blandford seemed to have
drawn the short straw this morning and was calling us to look
lively and get fell in—with less of the talking. Then, by 08:00,
we were all on parade.

We went through all the usual preliminaries leading up to
inspection: attention; right dress; open order march, and then
Blandford started at one end of the front rank and worked his
way from one person to the next, scanning buttons, hat badges
and boot leather with a practised eye in his search for the
slightest blemish. All was going well, with everyone seeming to
be up to par and there being nothing much more serious than an
occasional tug at someone's uniform here, or a beret straightened
there—that is, until the corporal arrived in front of Potter—he of
the two left feet. Blandford's calm, business-like manner
suddenly disappeared when he beheld Potter and was replaced
by a look of horror, as if he couldn't believe his eyes. Somehow,
Potter looked all bundled up under his greatcoat; his buttons
were buttoned in the wrong buttonholes and his face wore the
look of a helpless lamb being offered up to the slaughterhouse.
Just for a moment, although it seemed like an eternity, Corporal
Blandford was speechlessly transfixed to the spot, his mouth
open, unable to do anything but stare at the DIS nightmare before
him. Potter just stood there, pale, innocent and wide-eyed,
waiting for the inevitable.

Finally, Blandford found his voice. "Potter," he roared.
"What the *bloody hell* has happened to you?"

"Dunno, corporal," Potter replied weakly.

"Well, you look like a bloody pregnant fairy," Blandford
bawled, right into Potter's face and spacing out the last three
words for additional emphasis.

Cruel as it seems in retrospect, we all burst out laughing. It was a reflex action that had more to do with Blandford's remark breaking the nervous tension, than actually laughing at Potter. For one thing, the laughter came as a spontaneous reaction to the sense of relief each of us felt that because the spotlight was so narrowly focused on Potter, it enabled us to escape close scrutiny. But it was also because there was something comical about a "pregnant fairy". In my youthful innocence, I had a clear mental image of Tinkerbell wearing maternity clothes. Many years later, armed with the knowledge that "fairy" was a slang term for a homosexual, it suddenly dawned on me what Blandford had really meant that day.

Poor old Potter turned bright red with embarrassment. He was such an inoffensive little chap and I felt very sorry for him, despite laughing at his expense, because he seemed so vulnerable, yet was having a tougher time than most of us. Corporal Blandford ordered him to unbutton his greatcoat and then pulled and tugged on the uniform underneath until the lumps and bumps disappeared. He then made Potter button the greatcoat up again—but properly this time—and the situation was defused.

* * *

Thursday arrived, the first of many such Thursdays—all of them a special day of the week to look forward to. It was Pay Day! Or, as some wags crudely, but aptly, referred to it—The Day the Golden Eagle Shits.

Following the morning drill period, we were marched to the Drill Shed: the concrete-floored building adjoining the gym and swimming pool. It seemed as though everyone else on camp had got there before us and all of them were in large, separate formations spread over the vast Drill Shed floor area. We were marched to a vacant area where we found ourselves facing a row of three or four tables pushed together end to end. Three officers faced us from their seated positions behind the tables. On the table in front of two of the officers, metal boxes lay open to reveal bank notes and silver coins, whilst the third officer surveyed a large ledger that also lay open before him. We were brought to a halt in front of the tables and then Corporal Blandford explained that, on being dismissed, we were to form ourselves alphabetically into rows with those having the same first surname initial as ourselves. The first row was to comprise the "A's" with the other rows following in alphabetical order towards the rear. Corporal Blandford also instructed us to have our identification card, the RAF form 1250, in our left hand ready to show it to the officers as verification of our identity, although on this, our first Pay Parade, we still had not received our 1250s. The photographs had been taken (no smiling—look straight into the camera) shortly after we'd been issued with our uniforms, but it took time for the RAF to process the identification cards. For the moment, each of us had been given a temporary ID chit, a piece of paper signed by the Squadron Commander bearing our name and service number, as proof of identity.

Blandford continued with instructions on what we needed to do. "When your name is called out," he said, "come to attention and shout out the last three digits of your service number at the top of your voice. Then march smartly up to the table," he said, ignoring the fact that there was more than one table, "and come to a halt facing the officers. Remain standing to attention and salute the officers, then show them your twelve-fifty."

He then went on to explain that on receiving our cash, we were to make a left turn, march smartly away and exit the Drill Shed. Once outside we could individually make our way back to the mess for dinner. After receiving these instructions and being asked the usual "Any questions?" we were dismissed to reform ourselves into alphabetically-ordered rows. Then, when we had reassembled, the senior officer nodded to a sergeant standing near the tables who then faced us, took a deep breath and called out, "Pay parade, attention." He then turned smartly towards the officer, saluted and informed him, "Initial Training Squadron present and correct, sir!"

The officer returned the salute from his sitting position and at the same time responded with, "Carry on Sergeant."

The sergeant swivelled around on his heels to face the pay parade once again and then ordered us to stand at ease. A short pause followed to allow the combined echo of our feet to die away and then the officer at the ledger began announcing our surnames in alphabetical order. Each person sprang to attention at the mention of his name, yelled out his "last three" and then headed for the table. Some came smartly to a halt, others slid to a stop, while some just simply stopped walking. The officer did not return the salutes, which wasn't surprising, considering all the salutes he would have had to return during the hour or so that it took to get through with the pay parade.

First the A's, then the B's. Ginge Brown's name was called and then Richard Butterworth's. I knew that mine couldn't be far off. The voice calling out the names wasn't too loud and that, coupled with the terrible acoustics of the Drill Shed and the general hubbub, made it difficult to hear. Campbell, Callaghan, I strained to hear and then there it was—Carlin.

"Sir, 153," I yelled, as I came to attention, marched forward to the tables and came to what I hoped was a smartly executed halt and snapped up my salute. The officer on my right glanced up and I thrust my ID chit towards him to read. He looked at it and checked my name off on a long list, then announced "Boy Entrant Carlin, seven and six."

The officer in front of me counted out three half crowns and pushed them across the table towards me. I took the money with my left hand, took one step backwards, saluted again before executing a smart left turn and then headed for the Drill Shed exit. Once outside I dared to look at the coins in my hand. Seven shillings and sixpence! I was rich—rich, yippee!

Seven and six was approximately equal to 33 pence in present day decimal money, but of course it had greater purchasing power in 1956. This was my spending allowance. We were actually paid a total weekly wage of £2, but the remainder was withheld and then paid to us in a lump sum when we went on leave. I had, however, arranged for a weekly allotment of 10/- (ten shillings) to be sent to my stepmother Annie (at her insistence), which left £1-2s-6d (one pound, two shillings and sixpence) per week to be withheld for my going-on-leave pay.

Anyone who grew up with the pre-decimal currency will probably never forget it. Just like inches, yards and miles, or ounces, pounds and tons, the relationships between the separate units had to be learned at an early age, because they weren't based on any rational system. The Pound (£) was the basic unit, as it is today. But under the old system it consisted of 20 shillings. The shilling was made up of 12 pennies or pence, which were huge, copper coins measuring approximately 1-1/4 inches in diameter. If that wasn't bad enough, the coinage also included a large heavy silver coin, slightly larger than the penny, known as the half-crown, which was worth two shillings and sixpence—there being eight of these to a Pound. Then there was the florin, which was another heavy silver coin, but slightly smaller in diameter than the half-crown, and worth two shillings. Besides those two, we had a small silver sixpenny piece and an octagonal brass coloured threepenny, or thruppeny, 'bit'. There was no other coin of greater value than the half-crown and so the next highest denomination of currency was the ten-shilling note, worth half of a Pound and equal to the present-day 50 pence coin. The smallest denomination was the halfpenny, or hae'penny as it was pronounced. Prior to my time there had been a smaller coin known as a farthing, which was equal to a fourth of a penny, but this was no longer legal tender by the time I was able to count my pennies.

Because the initial of my surname was near the beginning of the alphabet, I got paid before most of the others and was able get to the mess before the queue became long. Then after dinner, I made a beeline for the NAAFI shop. My cigarette hoard lay somewhere between dangerously low and non-existent, so I needed to replenish it with some Woodbines. Knowing that the money wouldn't burn any holes in my pocket, I bought five packets of ten cigarettes all at once, each costing one and tu'ppence, which came to total of five shillings and tenpence. I also bought a bottle of Corona orangeade, a locally made soft drink, for about 9d (ninepence). The price of the Corona included a small cash deposit, which would be refunded when I returned the bottle. Having made these important purchases, I headed for the billet to enjoy a cigarette and some orangeade, but with very little left of my original seven and sixpence.

The intensive weekly training programme contained one or two oases: Sports Afternoon and Padre's Hour.

Most of the religious denominations, namely Church of England and PM & UB (Presbyterians, Methodists, Unitarians and Baptists were collectively grouped together as the PM & UB denomination) actually took religious instruction during Padre's Hour, but not the Catholics, who were referred to as RCs in the RAF. Father Carberry was rarely in attendance when we arrived at the RC church for Padre's Hour. Instead, we made ourselves comfortable in the common room, where we were free to spend the time as we pleased. There was a gramophone and a selection of ancient 78 rpm records to play on it. The records were all favourites from the previous generation, mostly Glenn Miller recordings. They were okay to listen to, but an Elvis or a Tommy Steele record would have been much more welcome. A ping-pong table occupied one end of the common room and bats were provided so that we could indulge in some table tennis—if we could find a ball that wasn't cracked. And there were books and magazines to read, mostly about church issues or foreign missionary work. Yes, Padre's Hour at the RC church was like a little refuge in an otherwise hostile world. Perhaps that was Father Carberry's intention; maybe not, but it was okay in my book.

Usually, after Padre's Hour, Niall Adderley and I would make our way back to the billet a little early, pick up our mugs and irons and then head for dinner at the cookhouse before the C of E hordes arrived from their Padre's Hour. The duty billet would already be there dressed in their white aprons and white sleeve protectors, waiting to serve that day's dinner to their fellow Boy Entrants. Getting to the mess early meant having the pick of all available choices, especially the desserts. Sometimes Eve's Pudding was on the menu and that was my favourite— sponge cake with stewed apple underneath and hot custard poured on top. I was more than ready for something good like that after crawling around with a rifle and keeping my arse down so that it didn't get shot off, then playing ping-pong with a cracked ball at Padre's Hour.

I usually headed back to the billet after finishing the meal, stopping to wash my mug and irons in the steaming, bubbling tank of scalding hot water that waited just outside the mess entrance. During mealtimes the water was heated to a high temperature by steam injection, causing the tank to bubble and make strange rumbling and gurgling noises. A person needed to be careful in order to avoid being scalded by the hot water whilst washing his mug and irons and it was very easy to receive a painful burn from the overheated metal of a knife, fork or spoon. Sometimes a mean-spirited Wing boy might sneak up behind an ITS sprog—unsuspectingly washing his utensils—and then quickly reach around to rap him on the knuckles with the heavy handle of a knife, making the unfortunate victim drop his mug or irons into the bubbling cauldron. On other occasions, the assistance of a Wing villain was completely unnecessary when some of us managed to let go of a mug or eating utensil purely by accident. Whatever the cause, it would take considerable patience and ingenuity for a victim to rescue his lost property from the bottom of the two-foot depth of roiling water. And retrieval certainly wasn't aided by the ever-murky water that made visual sightings of lost items virtually impossible. It all had to be done by feel.

On returning to the billet, we usually had time for a few minutes of relaxation, to smoke a cigarette and to read our mail, if we were lucky enough to get any. Mail was an essential lifeline. We desperately needed the contact it brought with the outside world, when the small closed universe we occupied seemed to consist of nothing more than being ordered around by our superiors, continually cleaning buttons and boots, performing drill movements on the Square and always, always being surrounded by people dressed identically to ourselves. Hearing my name being called out and then being handed a letter in a sealed envelope, when the Senior Boy distributed the mail that he had picked up from the squadron office, always gave me a jolt of adrenaline. Usually, it was a letter from Annie, my stepmother. I have to give credit where credit's due because, despite our difficult relationship, she wrote to me regularly, keeping me up to date with all the family news from home. In fact, we both maintained this correspondence for many years.

* * *

After spending our first three weeks confined to the camp, most of us were impatiently chomping at the bit by time the third weekend arrived. Now we would be allowed to go out to one of the local towns and be able to rub shoulders with ordinary people for a little while. The magic key that gave us access to this outside world was a personal Permanent Pass, commonly referred to as a PP, which would be distributed by the DIs that very Saturday morning. The Permanent Pass was a pocket sized blue-coloured cardboard permit that gave us written permission to be absent from our quarters from "after duty hours" daily until 2000 hours, as long as we remained within a five-mile radius of "station bounds". The permit allowed us to stay out until 10 PM on Saturdays and Sundays and venture a little farther afield by virtue of a handwritten endorsement on the back of the pass that stated: "Permitted to proceed up to a 10-mile radius (including Barry) on Saturday and Sunday only."

Orders had been circulated regarding where we could and could not go, how we should be dressed and how we should conduct ourselves. Certain areas of Barry were out of bounds, like Thompson Street, near Barry Docks, which was reputed to be the local red light district. Nor were we permitted to go as far afield as Cardiff, which was outside of the ten-mile radius. Dress was to be best blue and in winter we were either required to wear our greatcoat, or carry it neatly folded over the left arm with buttons fastened and sleeves tucked into the half belt at the back of the coat. We were to conduct ourselves in a manner that did not bring disrepute to the service and to wear our uniforms properly at all times. Smoking cigarettes in public was also forbidden, except when in certain situations such as in a restaurant or similar establishment—and so was walking "arm in arm" with females. The DIs warned us that SPs, the Snoops, regularly patrolled Barry in their Land Rovers and were more than willing to give anyone a free one-way ride back to the camp if they found him breaking any of the rules.

At last, the long-awaited Saturday came around. We had to parade in the morning for a "best blue" inspection so that the DIs could make sure that our uniforms were up to the standards necessary for appearing in public, so we weren't permitted to

leave camp until noon at the earliest. As soon as the inspection
was over and we'd received our PPs, it didn't take Butterworth
and me long to get ready. 'Ginge' Brown decided to come with
us and since we were all already wearing our best blues for the
inspection, it was just a matter of folding our greatcoats so that
we could carry them with us. The day wasn't cold, even though
it was the beginning of November. We made sure we had our PPs
and our newly issued 1250s, the RAF identification card that bore
a small head and shoulders photograph of the bearer. The Snoops
at the Guardroom would need to see both of these before they
would allow us to sample the sweet taste of freedom that lay on
the other side of the perimeter fence.

As we approached the main camp road we noticed that
there was already a steady stream of Wing boys making their
way towards the gate. The ITS boys ahead of us were joining this
flow, making it appear as though we were the waters of a
tributary joining and widening a blue-grey river that was heading
towards the sea. The Snoops were busy inspecting the uniforms
and general appearance of those ahead of us, so we waited our
turn. Most boys made it through the inspection, but not without
suffering a few belittling remarks from the fearless SPs. When it
was my turn, I approached the open Guardroom window, tensed
and hoping that my buttons were clean enough to pass the
Snoop's cynical eye.

"Permanent pass," he ordered, holding out his right hand
in anticipation and then, "Twelve-fifty," he demanded without
looking up, but still continuing to study the PP.

Both documents were examined minutely, even though
there wasn't enough written information on either one to justify
the amount of time that it took.

"Okay, Carlin," he barked, as he handed both documents
back to me. "Sign out in the book," motioning to the large
ledger-type notebook on the window sill between us.

I picked up the pencil that was held captive by a length
of string securing it to the sill and printed my last three, name,
squadron, billet number and the time that I was signing out.

Richard and Ginge were next. Both of them made it
through inspection too and then they signed out. We walked

towards the main gate, trying not to hurry but instinctively wanted to make a run for it, half expecting to be called back at each step. Then we were through the gate, but not quite out of the woods, because we were still visible from the Guardroom. We headed for a bus stop that was diagonally across Cowbridge Road from the main gate, finally passing out of the direct view of the Snoops as we did so. When we made it to the bus-stop, each looked at the others and breathed an exaggerated sigh of relief. All we needed to do now was just wait a few minutes until the next bus came along. Soon, a dark-red coloured single-decker bus, displaying the name Western Welsh Omnibus Company in large gold-coloured lettering along its flank, appeared from around a bend in the road and pulled up at the stop. It seemed somehow alien to me. The buses operated by the Ulster Transport Authority back home were green in colour. They had been an ever-present part of my environment as I'd grown up and evoked the comfort of the familiar, whereas the unfamiliar appearance of this bus made me feel just a little ill at ease. Once again the sensation of being a long way from home stole over me, but I shrugged it off. After all, being in a strange place amongst unfamiliar things was all part of the experience, all part of the fascination.

We all three climbed aboard the bus with the other waiting passengers and made our way down the aisle until we found some vacant seats. When everyone was aboard, the conductor reached up and tugged twice on a thin black cable that was suspended from the ceiling for the entire length of the bus. A bell rang twice somewhere up front, followed by a grinding noise as the driver engaged the first gear. Then the bus lurched off, even as some passengers were still trying to find a place to sit down. A series of lurches took us up through the gears as the bus increased speed, slowing down only when it wound its way through several small villages and past a sign identifying a small civil aviation airfield on our left as Rhoose Airport. About half an hour and several stops later, the bus pulled to a halt on Broad Street, Barry's crowded main thoroughfare where we got off and stood on the pavement with no idea of what to do next. We didn't stand there undecided for too long because our grumbling teenage stomachs soon prompted us to think that some food might be a good idea. We were in need of appetizing food far removed from the variety dished up in the Boy Entrants' mess.

There was a coffee bar on Broad Street, not far from where the bus had dropped us off. Coffee bars were all the rage in the mid-fifties. They were the kind of places that attracted young people, where sixpence would purchase a cup of frothy, milky coffee that could be slowly sipped for two hours at a time. In this case, the coffee bar was, in reality, an ordinary little café that had adopted the grandiose title because it appealed to the clientele the management wished to attract: people like us. Peering through the plate glass window, we could see that there were other Boy Entrants inside, so we entered. The café sold only snacks, but it was different—no one was ordering us around, or pushing in front of us. And even though there were Wing boys in there, they just ignored us. We bought some food, took it to a table, then sat down and ate it. Having temporarily taken the edge off our hunger, the question now was, What were we going to do next? Someone mentioned an amusement park at Barry Island, which seemed like a good idea. So before heading out into the cool November air, we asked for some directions, which were given together with the sage advice that it was quite a long walk.

Harbour Road, two miles long and dead-straight, was the only access to Barry Island. It seemed much longer than two miles, giving some validity to the old saying about it being a long road that has no turning. But we were young and strong and certainly used to walking, so it didn't seem too much of a challenge. Not surprisingly, road traffic to Barry Island was very light on this early-November day, although an RAF Police Land Rover, easily identified by the red and black plates it bore on both front and rear, passed us at one point. The two Snoops inside, one driving and the other in the passenger seat, turned their heads to keep their gaze locked on us as they cruised past.

Out of the corner of his mouth, Ginge Brown muttered, "Keep walking and pretend you don't see them."

We behaved as he suggested, but I still fully expected them to turn around and come back to pick on us for something.

But no, they just kept on going and it was with a feeling of relief that we turned to watch the Land Rover disappear in the direction of Barry. We resumed our trek towards the fabled Barry Island and a short time later saw some figures in the distance that appeared to be Boy Entrants coming towards us. Recognition of brothers-in-arms, comrades, a sense of kinship: all these feelings burst into my head as they drew closer. They were Wing boys—from 2 Wing according to the red and blue check on their hatbands; it was the wing to which we would go after passing out from the Initial Training Squadron. There were three of them and they were all were smiling. Foolishly, we mistook this for friendliness and smiled back, preparing for some friendly conversation as they approached. But they weren't intent on stopping to chat and instead just cannoned right through us as though we weren't there. One boy out in front of the others smirked continuously as he looked dead ahead to avoid our questioning eyes and charged shoulder first into our midst, scattering us to left and right. His two grinning companions followed closely behind him, but neither one made any attempt at physical contact. We had become accustomed to this sort of behaviour on the camp, but we felt that here in Barry we should be on neutral territory, so the attack was a very unpleasant and unexpected incident. I didn't know the leader of the three then, but I remembered his face and recognised him when I went into the Wings a few months later as a boy named Lackland. He was 28th Entry, just one entry ahead of us and not long out of Initial Training himself. No doubt he liked being able to bully someone that he perceived as weaker, now that he had climbed a short distance up the pecking order. We had unwittingly played into his hands, because all Wing people seemed godlike to sprogs like us. We didn't even realize that there was a definite pecking order in the Wings and Lackland was at the bottom of that particular heap.

Poetic justice was eventually meted out to Lackland, because he flunked his final trade test and was relegated to join us in the 29th entry for one more try. Indeed, I felt a great deal of satisfaction on seeing that the smirk had been wiped completely from his face on the day he slunk into our classroom, whilst his

erstwhile 28th friends passed out of Boy Entrants and left him
high and dry to develop his skills at the delicate art of fence-
mending. Suffice to say, he didn't do too well in that regard, but
did manage to pass out with the 29th entry. But I'm getting
ahead of myself a little, because that happened several months
later. On the particular day that he charged his way through our
small group, I didn't know him from Adam.

Eventually, we arrived at Barry Island after our long
walk. It was windy and we could see whitecaps dotting the
waters of the Bristol Channel. The amusement park was there,
no mistaking that, but it was closed! This was November after all
and Barry Island was the haunt of summer holidaymakers. We
hung around for a little while, looking at the boarded up rides
and stalls, then retraced our footsteps back along Harbour Road
to Broad Street in Barry. Then, having returned to civilisation
once more, we made our way towards the centre of the town,
threading through the crowds of Saturday afternoon shoppers. At
one point Richard dug me in the ribs and hissed, "Look!" He
was pointing to a street sign high up on the corner of a building
that signified we were at the intersection of the infamous
Thompson Street that led off at right angles from the main
thoroughfare on which we were walking. We stopped and
allowed our gaze to travel along the "out of bounds" street, even
if we couldn't go there physically. We were hoping to notice
some clue to its forbidden illicit nature, but were disappointed in
not seeing even one lady of easy virtue, or anything else that
might indicate the steamy sordid goings-on that we just *knew*
must be happening behind the lace curtains and closed silent
doors, even as we stood there. After a few moments, we gave up
on seeing anything exciting and moved on, finally going into
Woolworths for a wander around and to smile at the girls behind
the counters. I bought some sweets and enjoyed the simple
pleasure of just mingling with ordinary people who would have
seemed a lot like Irish people, if only they didn't speak in that
strange-sounding Welsh accent.

It was around teatime and we were hungry again. But it
wasn't difficult to find a good place to eat this time—we just
followed our noses to a fish and chip shop. This was a real

treat—something we didn't get in the Boy Entrants' mess. There are few pleasures in this world that surpass eating fish and chips drenched with salt and vinegar and wrapped the traditional way, in several layers of old newspaper. The combination of hot chips and battered cod reacting with the vinegar and newsprint creates a sensuous aroma that's unmistakable and just irresistible. The tasty flakes of cod were of just the right moistness and the chips were crisp on the outside, but soft and delicious on the inside. We had to conclude that no matter what else could be said about the Welsh people, there was no mistaking that some of them had learned the secret of how to make great fish and chips. We finished the best meal we'd had in weeks and licked our fingers clean, then wiped them on the newsprint before tossing it in a nearby rubbish bin. Our appetites were satisfied for the moment, so what next?

We remembered having seen a cinema during our travels up and down Broad Street and therefore decided to see a film in surroundings that were a little plusher than the Astra back on camp. Some instantly forgettable film was playing, but I think we enjoyed it anyway. I always became absorbed in any half decent film and the next hour or so transported me away from reality and into the world up there on the screen.

The early darkness of winter had fallen and the temperature was plunging towards freezing by the time we emerged from the cinema. Since it was about time that we needed to get back to camp, we made our way to the bus stop near the railway station. From the bus stop, it was just a stone's throw to the platform where I had alighted from the mainline train just a few weeks earlier after the long journey from Cosford. In terms of weeks, it hadn't been all *that* long ago that I had walked stiffly up and down the platform, but after all that had transpired since then, it seemed like a dimly remembered event in the distant past.

The bus back to camp rumbled and jolted through the darkness towards Cadoxton and then past Rhoose Airport on its way back to St. Athan. The interior lighting made it impossible to see anything in the outside darkness except street lights and their immediate surroundings in the built-up areas, but only pitch blackness when the city lights gave way to the dark countryside between Barry and the camp. Eventually, the lighting of the main gate came into view, signalling that we had returned to the rigid discipline of Boy Entrant life. Immediately on alighting from the bus, we were uncomfortably aware of being under the Snoops' intense scrutiny as we approached the Guardroom on foot, but surprisingly we were allowed to pass without interference, other than be reminded to sign the book against the entry we had made when signing out, to show that we had returned. The three of us then made our way back to the billet in a glow of happiness related to the little bit of freedom we'd been able to enjoy after three long weeks of confinement.

Next day, in order to further indulge the privilege of our new-found freedom, Butterworth and I went to the small town of Llantwit Major, which lay in the opposite direction to that of Barry. Calling it a town was something of an exaggeration: it seemed more like a large village. It was the kind of place where High Street gets rolled up at 5 o'clock each Saturday afternoon and doesn't get unrolled again until 9 o'clock on Monday morning. It was completely dead. We wandered up and down the High Street for a little while, but could find nothing or no one of interest. We weren't interested in the pubs, of which there seemed plenty, and besides, we were too young. Apart from the local watering holes, the only other establishment showing any signs of life was Llantwit's sole cinema. There and then, we decided that Barry was the going to be the destination of choice for most of our future ventures into the wide world. Giving up on Llantwit Major, we caught an early bus back to camp.

* * *

Drill, Education, Physical Training and Ground Defence Training came at us in a never-ending cycle as our weeks in the Initial Training Squadron marched relentlessly onwards. In the process, what had been a motley collection of civilian youths was slowly but surely being transformed into a smartly uniformed squadron of young men who exhibited an increasingly noticeable military bearing. During this time, I continued to make my frequent trips to the swimming pool and within a few weeks was able to swim with confidence. There was never a risk that I would be selected for the Olympic team, but I could easily swim a few lengths of the pool doing the crawl or the breaststroke. In the meantime, life in ITS had become very routine with Wednesday sports afternoons, pay parades on Thursday, Padre's Hour, swimming and going to the Astra and Barry at the weekends. But it would soon all come to an end with our passing out of initial training, which would then be immediately followed by our first home leave, which happily coincided with Christmas.

By now, we had completed nine weeks of the twelve-week Initial Training Squadron programme and a mounting sense of excitement had gradually started to permeate our ranks, raising our spirits. Even Corporal Hillcrest's favourite mean trick of deliberately halting us on our way back to the billets seemed tolerable, even though hunger gnawed at our innards. His mocking taunt, "Ah've had mah dinner laddies. Ah can wai-it here al day," had become all too familiar, but we had become immune. We would soon be passing out of ITS and away from the likes of him. We didn't care any more! Even now, it seemed as though we were spending the greater part of our remaining three weeks practising for the passing-out parade. And although Education, GDT and PT still continued to be a part of our lives, it seemed as though we spent most of the time either on the Square—or in a blister hangar if it was raining—rehearsing for the passing-out parade, so intent were the drill instructors on getting us ready us ready for the big day.

Then the day finally arrived. On 20th December, 1956, the 29th Entry of Boy Entrants, Royal Air Force St. Athan, celebrated the completion of their initial training, formalized by a ceremonial passing-out parade complete with rifles and fixed bayonets.

The usual procedure was to hold such ceremonial parades on the Square, but a thick blanket of fog on that particular date made this impractical, so our ceremony was held in the Drill Shed instead. We were marched there in two squadrons, wearing our winter uniform of greatcoats and gloves, both of which provided some protection against the penetrating cold of the freezing fog that enveloped us on the march from the squadron billets to the Drill Shed. Empty bayonet scabbards dangled from our webbing belts. They were empty because the actual bayonets glittered at the ends of the rifles we carried at the slope arms position as we proudly marched onto the parade ground area that had been marked off in the Drill Shed. All of us felt buoyed up by the sense of achievement of having made it through the trials and tribulations of the Initial Training Squadron and the knowledge that we would soon trade our green and black hatbands for the coveted Wing hatbands. In my case, this would be in the red and navy blue check of 2 Wing.

All of our drill training now came into play as we went through the various manoeuvres of a parade that included presenting arms as the RAF Ensign was being hoisted and marching into open order so that our ranks could be inspected by the Station Commander. Then it was time for the final march past the saluting base, in line abreast. The Station Commander took the salute and we then left the parade ground, symbolically marching out of the Initial Training Squadron.

Some two weeks previously, Corporal Blandford had gathered us together in a classroom and distributed Leave Application forms. He told us that we would be granted 21 days leave from "after duty hours" on Thursday the 20th of December, the day of our Initial Training Squadron pass-out parade, which meant that we would be due back on camp by 2359 hours—midnight—on the 10th of January. Submitting the Leave Application would ensure that travel vouchers would be prepared in time and that we would receive the held-back portion of our pay at the pay parade immediately prior to going on leave. Blandford supervised as we filled out personal details on the form—name, rank and serial number—and the amount of leave requested. Two weeks still to go before we passed out of ITS and then went on leave! I was impatient for it all to happen right now, instead of just applying for it. We finished by signing our applications and then handed them to Corporal Blandford for the Flight Commander's signature of approval. They would then be sent to Personnel Records at SHQ for processing.

Now, with the parade behind us, the time had finally arrived—this was my first leave home since joining the Boys. We were destined to move to the Wings on graduating from Initial Training, but that was going to be organized when we returned. We were, however, instructed to take all our kit with us when we went on leave and that nothing was to be left behind. I had already started packing my kitbag with items that probably wouldn't be needed during the two weeks leading up to the pass-out parade. Now, on the eve of our departure on leave, I packed the remaining items in gleeful anticipation of going home the very next day. My white canvas kitbag was cylindrical in shape, about two feet in diameter and stood at around three feet tall. It held a deceptively large amount of kit—a lot more than I possessed, as soon became obvious.

The next morning, we were called on parade immediately after breakfast. There was no button inspection this time. Instead, Corporal Blandford passed up and down the ranks distributing leave passes and travel warrants that we each needed to exchange at the railway station for the return rail ticket home—my warrant also included the fare for the sea passage between Liverpool and Belfast. Then, we were taken to the rooms where we had sworn the oath of allegiance several weeks previously. Once there, we were treated to a special pay parade, during which we received the back-pay that had been saved for this very occasion. On top of that, we received a ration allowance for the days that we wouldn't be eating in the camp mess. The back-pay and ration allowance together came to about twenty pounds—more money than I'd ever had of my own, all at once, up to that moment. I felt like a millionaire.

Before I even opened my eyes the following morning, I felt a great eagerness to set off with the other Irish lads on the journey back to Ireland. Each of us was faced with the certain prospect of a long day and night before we reached our final destinations. Just the train journey to Liverpool by itself was going to take us several hours, with one or two changes on the way. Then there was the long sleepless overnight sea crossing to Belfast to look forward to. But it didn't matter because we were going home. They could have made us walk on hot coals all the way and we would still have cheerfully made the journey. The train for our first leg of the journey was due to leave Gileston railway station at around lunchtime.

After a hurried breakfast, I packed the remainder of my worldly possessions into my kitbag and marvelled at how the canvas sack could still be half-empty. In the past, I had seen soldiers and sailors and airmen lug around large well-filled kitbags when they travelled and wanted mine to look the same way, but apparently they must have owned more kit than I did. Not to be outdone, I took the pillow out of my locker and stuffed it into the empty space and that did the trick. Now the kitbag looked the way I imagined it should be.

The squadron admin. office had organized a service bus to take us to the station. When it arrived outside the billets at around 10 o'clock, I waited my turn to stow the well-stuffed kitbag into the cargo space, then joined the queue to climb aboard and sat down next to Billy Cassidy. I hadn't seen much of him in ITS because we were in different flights. We were still friends, however and enjoyed talking and joking around with the other Northern Irish lads with whom we travelled as a group.

Finding seats aboard the train from Gileston was relatively easy, but when we arrived at Barry station it suddenly became apparent that we had joined up with the holiday rush. Never having had to travel around the festive season before, I was unprepared for the hordes of other travellers also making their way home for Christmas. The train to Crewe was packed with not a seat to be had, which meant that we had to be content with travelling all the way in the corridor, using our kitbags as seats when the guard wasn't around. At Crewe, it wasn't any better. In fact, it was worse and the train on our next leg of the journey, to Liverpool's Lime Street station, was even more crowded than the one from Barry to Crewe. But if we thought it couldn't get worse, we were dead wrong. It could and it did.

The watery winter sun had long since set by the time we arrived on foot at Princes Dock. A long queue of assorted travellers had formed, patiently suffering the steady rain that was falling unceasingly from the heavens, as they stood at the closed dock gate waiting to board the ship. Someone mentioned that we needed sailing tickets, although that's the first that any of us had heard of it. I didn't even know what a sailing ticket was. We'd been told that a return railway ticket was all that was needed for the passage between Liverpool and Belfast. So, we joined onto the end of the queue and thankfully lowered our kitbags to the ground, easing the ache in our arms that came from holding the bags up on our shoulders during the long walk from Lime Street station. The queue didn't move forward a single inch for what seemed an eternity. Meanwhile, the relentless rain fell in a fine drizzle, hissing softly as it made contact with the wet road and the numerous puddles in my immediate surroundings. The tiny splashes made by the raindrops on the wet pavement momentarily reflected the harsh orange glare of the street lights, taking on the hypnotic appearance of a firefly swarm that dances continuously above the surface of a pond. Occasionally, the soft hiss of the rain was overpowered by much louder swishing noises, as cars and buses splashed by on the wet road, the imprint of their tyre tread pattern being quickly obliterated by the thin film of surface water that jealously reclaimed the territory from which it had been so rudely displaced.

A shipping company official eventually came along the queue, informing servicemen in uniform to make their way to the front. We immediately detached ourselves from the main queue and waited in a small separate line as our tickets were inspected before being allowed to go on board the ship. It was also explained to us that a sailing ticket was usually needed during busy times such as this. Talking amongst ourselves, we resolved to pass this nugget of information on to the travel warrant clerk back at Station Headquarters. Although being called forward turned out to be a stroke of good luck, we still had to deal with a severely crowded ship. Every seat in the passenger lounge had been filled by the time we got on board and the ship's crew had gone to the unusual step of opening the cargo hold to accommodate the extra passengers. Having no other option, we clambered down into the hold and tried to make ourselves as comfortable as possible under an overhang. At least we were more or less out of the rain, but it was cold and miserable as we huddled down into our greatcoats and used our kitbags for makeshift pillows. I can remember looking across at Cassidy as he tried to get some sleep and seeing that he had the high collar of his coat pulled up around his neck and the peak of his hat pulled down over his eyes, so that barely anything of his face was visible. Some civilian wag nearby commented that Billy looked like a member of the Gestapo. And, just to add to our misery, the boat was late in sailing.

Finally we got under way and the first hour was relatively calm as the ship sailed within the shelter of the Mersey estuary. But as the estuary widened, the swell grew noticeably heavier until we were taking the full brunt of a gale force wind and the tempestuous waves it stirred up on the Irish Sea that dark December night. The ship continuously groaned and creaked as it pitched and wallowed in the roiling sea. Occasionally it would ride high on the crest of a wave before plunging steeply into its trough, accompanied by a screaming sound from ship's propellers as they briefly emerged from the water and spun with little resistance in the air, before plunging back once again into their element and to their normal speed. At other times a large wave would collide head-on with the bow and break over it, creating a loud boom that resounded through the metal bulwarks of the vessel. The noise and motion made sleep utterly impossible, although I desperately tried. In the end I spent much of the night wandering around on the decks, watching and hearing the ship battle its way through the turbulent sea as its lights illuminated the spray flying from the crests of the waves. At all times I was hanging on to something solid so as not to be thrown off balance and fall. Many more people were suffering from sea-sickness than there had been on my first trip and although I wasn't physically sick myself, there was an uncomfortable queasiness in the pit of my stomach.

It was a relief to everyone aboard when we finally entered the shelter of Belfast Lough in the early hours of the morning and even more so an hour later, when the ship docked at Donegal Quay just as a watery dawn lit up the morning sky and I was able to step onto solid, unmoving dry land once again. It had been a rough crossing for sure, but after experiencing many Irish Sea crossings during the next few years, I eventually came to know that a rough ride such as this was fairly common in the winter season.

After wishing the other lads a merry Christmas, I set off walking along Corporation Street in the damp early-morning Irish air, towards York Road railway station, carrying my kitbag over my right shoulder, then over my left shoulder and then back to the right shoulder again. By now, the glamour of carrying the kitbag had worn a bit thin. I cursed it for its awkward shape and for the fact that I'd filled it with more than just my kit. I could still feel the motion of the ship as I walked along, even though I was now firmly on dry land. The sensation stayed with me for the remainder of the day and was probably due to a lack of sleep as much as anything else. But in spite of the awkwardness of the kitbag and the queasy feeling that still grabbed at my stomach, I was happy and excited to be back in my homeland again.

My sense of excitement increased with the miles on the train journey from Belfast to Coleraine. My heartbeat sped up at seeing familiar names on the platform nameplates as the steam locomotive hissed into one station after another along the single gauge line: names like Ballymena and Ballymoney. Then finally, just over an hour after leaving Belfast, we pulled into Coleraine station. I had already left my seat several minutes before and was at the door, with the window pulled down to feel the hometown air on my face, whilst the train was still moving. Then it lumbered to a stop with a loud hiss of steam and squeal of its brakes. I reached outside for the large brass carriage door handle, turning it a full quarter turn until it clicked open, setting me free to walk on my home turf.

My old friend the station porter was there and he greeted me with a question. "Home for a wee bit of leave, son?"

I grinned and replied, "Yeah," forgetfully using the English way of saying yes, instead of the local "aye".

"When d'ye haff tae g'back?" It was question that was to become only too familiar in the following days. Everyone seemed to ask it, unintentionally of course, but just hearing it always reminded me that leave wouldn't last forever. Right now, going back seemed a long way off and there would be time enough to think about it later. All I wanted to do at that moment was to enjoy the next two weeks. There was money in my pocket and a whole lot of plans in my head.

There were big grins all around when I walked in through the door of the pre-fab—the pre-fabricated house—that was home. I felt proud and embarrassed all at the same time, very conscious of my uniform which still looked relatively smart in spite of the rough journey it had just suffered.

Annie spoke first, "Huh! Wid ye luk at the Brylcreem boy," she mocked, ending the sentence with a cackle that, in her mind, was intended to "cut me down to size". It didn't work. I was proud of my progress and allowing her mockery to get to me was a thing of the past as far as I was concerned.

My father studied my uniform, eying the eagle flashes on my shoulder. "I thought you had to *earn* your wings," he said.

"These aren't wings. It's only pilots who have wings and they wear them here." I pointed to the left side of my chest, just above the breast pocket. "Everybody has these," I continued, gesturing with my head towards the eagle flash on my right shoulder.

"Aw," he nodded, accepting the explanation without further comment.

I dropped my kitbag on the floor, happy that I could put it down at long last and then took off my hat and greatcoat. There wasn't any locker here to hang my clothes up in, so I went out into the hallway and found a hook to hang them on with all the other coats. Then I came back, unbuttoned my tunic and sat down. Annie asked me if I wanted something to eat. The queasiness was still there, but I felt hungry too, so I nodded yes. Soon the appetizing aroma of eggs and bacon filled the kitchen and before long I was eating the most enjoyable meal I'd had in a long time. One thing I had to admit—her eggs and bacon were a lot more appetizing than those dished up in the Boy Entrants' mess. Being fed like that also gave me the sense that I had "arrived"—eggs and bacon hadn't come my way too many times from Annie's frying pan in the years before I had left home to join the RAF.

So it was with great relish that I polished the whole meal off and washed it down with a mug of her weak milky tea.

When I had finished and we were sitting around talking, Annie picked her moment and brought up the subject of money by remarking that I would be expensive to feed while I was home on leave. I reached in my pocket and gave her five Pounds, but she only looked at it disdainfully. "Surely they paid you more than that?" she protested.

I mumbled something about giving her some more and handed her another fiver, which seemed to satisfy her. The subject then changed to something else and for the next hour or so I answered questions about life as a Boy Entrant in the RAF. My father countered with some of his stories of life when he was in the Royal Navy during the war and we compared notes on the differences and similarities of the two services. I had always enjoyed his stories of the Navy and now felt that I had some of my own to bring to the table. Yes, it was good to feel that I was getting some respect, now that I was "making something of myself".

Later on, my sisters Veronica and Pauline and brother Thomas arrived home from their last day at school before breaking up for Christmas. They were delighted to see me and plied me with questions about my experiences "across the water". Being the big brother who was now such a man of the world, I'm afraid I laid it on a bit thick.

After the tea-time meal, I casually mentioned that I was going to see Maggie, our maternal great-aunt. This was greeted with an awkward silence that implied disapproval, but nothing was said, so I put on my tunic, greatcoat, hat and gloves and set off on the mile or so walk through the lamp-lighted streets to Maggie's house. In Coleraine most people either walked or rode bicycles, because the town wasn't large enough to have its own municipal bus service and most working people didn't own cars in those days. The walk only took about twenty minutes and when I reached Maggie's house in Bellhouse Lane I tapped on the lighted window as I'd always done in the past. Then I went to the front door of her two up—two down terraced house and heard her open the inner door.

"Who is it?" She called out.

"Brian," I answered.

The door opened and her small frame stood there, a warm smile lighting up her face as her eyes began to fill up with tears. "Och, it's you son," she said, "I'm glad you could come and see me." I stepped into the small hallway and she hugged me, which made me squirm uncomfortably like any 15-yearold boy. She laughed at this and then said, "Let me have a look at you." I stood there as she weighed me up and down. "You look very smart in your uniform," she said, "I just wish your mother could see you." The thought made us both feel sad: she missed my mother probably as much as I did, having raised her from a child to an adult young woman. Then Maggie added, "But if she'd been here, you wouldn't have had to go away and join up." By which she meant enlist in the RAF. She then made some tea for us both and I sat and told her as much as I could about life at St. Athan.

"Are the higher-ups hard on you?" She asked, meaning my superiors. I immediately thought of Hillcrest.

"Naw," I replied, shrugging off the question. How could I explain to Maggie—my grandmother in all but name—that I needed to tough it out without complaining? The officers and NCOs expected us to take the hard knocks of training like men. My fellow boy entrants were even more demanding, just as much as I expected the same of each and every one of them. There was no place in boy entrant training for cry-babies, and anyone who might have initially exhibited some weakness had either toughened up quickly or had already fallen by the wayside. The truthful answer would have been "Yes, it's no picnic." But I couldn't say that.

Maggie dropped the subject, perhaps because she understood better than I did that it was a rite of passage that would help me to make the transition from childhood to adulthood, building my self-confidence and self-respect in the process.

"They seem to have got you to stand up straight and not slouch," she remarked.

"It's the marching," I replied and then offered, by way of further explanation, "We have to swing our arms up as high as our shoulders and it makes us straighten up."

"Aye, you look a lot better straightened up and very smart in your uniform," she remarked. This observation made me feel pleased and proud.

I told her about the sea crossing and how rough it had been. Maggie had never been out of Ireland in her life, but had heard many similar stories from those who had crossed the Irish Sea. She was very interested to hear about Wales and the Welsh people and laughed when I mimicked their accent and the words they used. We talked for about two hours like this and then it was time for me to leave and make my way back home.

On returning back there, I discovered that I would be sharing a bed with my younger brother. It was just like old times in our little overcrowded house. Ever since I'd arrived home I'd been struck by how small and claustrophobic everything seemed after the large open space of the barrack room I'd become used to. Just finding space for my kit was a challenge. And everything seemed to be damp. The only source of heat in the house was a fireplace in the living room that also heated the water. Having become used to the central heating system that we had in the billets and just about everywhere else on camp, I had forgotten about the damp feel of the bedclothes that made them seem cold and damp until our body heat warmed them up. Going to bed in the dead of winter at our house was like taking the plunge into a cold icy pool. It was a case of just gritting your teeth and getting in there, braced for that first shock of coldness until the body got used to it. Getting dressed in the morning was a similar experience because the clothing accumulated moisture from the dank air during the night, but with clothing the shock passed sooner. Despite the initial damp chilliness of the bedding, I slept well, making up for lack of sleep during the previous night on the boat.

The very next morning after my first night at home was the Sunday before Christmas. There wasn't any other choice but to dress in my uniform, because I didn't have anything else to wear. I don't know what happened to the clothes I'd sent home in the brown paper parcel, but they weren't available. Nevertheless, I was proud of the uniform and wanted to show it off. At around half past ten I set out with Veronica and Pauline to walk the mile or so to St. Malachy's church for the 11 o'clock Mass. I could sense that they felt proud of their big brother as we walked together and were enjoying the escort.

Most things seemed small when I had come home on leave, but this was one instance where it was the reverse. St. Malachy's is a huge church, almost cathedral-like in size, so when I entered into the high, vaulted and cavernous interior it seemed to be a dramatic contrast to the little wooden building that housed the RC church I'd been attending at St. Athan for the last three months. It also seemed more formal, lacking the intimacy of the much smaller church that I'd become used to. Gradually, I began to notice that many people who would have normally greeted me with at least a "Hello," before I left home to join the RAF, now pointedly ignored me. And then I understood why; they didn't see me so much as they saw the uniform. The realization came that attending a Catholic Church service in Northern Ireland whilst wearing a British military uniform wasn't exactly the smartest thing in the world to do. But there wasn't much I could do about it. The religious teaching I'd received when growing up told me that it was a mortal sin to miss attending Mass on Sunday and in any case, there was my father to deal with if I didn't go. Besides, this uniform was all that I had to wear. It would be Christmas day on Tuesday, which was another day when a Catholic was supposed to attend Mass under the pain of mortal sin, so it looked as though I would have to go through the same embarrassing situation all over again. It was too late now, but I promised myself that I would get some civilian clothes before next Sunday came around, so that I wouldn't find myself in this uncomfortable situation once more.

After the service, I parted company with my sisters and took a different route from theirs, one that took me to my Aunt Alice's house—just like I'd always done for the past one or two years before becoming a Boy Entrant. Alice, my father's spinster sister, always went to early Mass, so she was at home when I arrived. She beamed when she saw me and told me that I looked very smart. Did I want something to eat, she wanted to know, as if she hadn't already correctly guessed my answer. There was a large pot of delicious Irish broth bubbling on the cooker, which I knew because its mouth-watering aroma had hit me as soon as I walked through the door. She made me sit at the table and then set a large soup plate full to the brim with the thick broth, full of vegetables and a few small chunks of mutton, into which four or five medium-sized potatoes had been plopped. As I spooned the nourishing broth into my mouth, Alice asked about all that had happened since she'd seen me off on the train back in October. Was I going to Mass on Sundays, she asked sternly in her brusque manner? Were "they" treating me all right? Was I getting enough to eat? Had I made any friends? I answered her questions and expanded further on the subject by relating a few additional experiences concerning my new life, as all the while she listened to me with an indulgent smile playing on her face. The good news was that she didn't ask me to take the dog for a walk. Apparently, that was a thing of the past. So, after spending an hour or so with my Aunt Alice, I said goodbye and made my way home.

Sometime in the early afternoon, my pal John Moore came to see if I wanted to go out. He had called at the house a few times during my absence, so he knew when I would be coming home on leave. I saw him coming up the street and opened the door to let him in, but he just stood there in the doorway grinning at me.

"So they let ye out, did they?"

"Yeah," I grinned, forgetting once again to use the local word "aye".

"Ye're talkin' like an oul' Englishman," he mocked.

Annie joined in, "Och, he's too posh for us now. Put a tramp on horseback and he'll ride tae the divil." It was one of her favourite expressions.

The banter continued for a while, which was typical of any time that John visited our house. He took a perverse delight in always feeding Annie enough ammunition to get her going on about all my faults and then kept stirring the pot. Good friend that he was, it was one trait that pissed me off about him, so it seemed to be time for a tactical withdrawal.

"D'ye want tae go out?" I asked.

"Aye. Where'll we go?" He replied.

"Dunno. What about goin' over for Melvin?" I suggested, referring to our mutual pal, Melvin Jackson, who had tried but failed to become a Boy Entrant during that first trip to Belfast that now seemed so long ago.

"Okay," he agreed.

I went into the bedroom to put on the rest of my uniform. I had given the family a demonstration on using a button stick the previous evening and the buttons were still clean, despite my outing to Mass that morning. Even my father had been interested. It was something new to him, since his navy uniform didn't include brass buttons or badges.

John looked me up and down now that I was wearing the full regalia. He didn't really say anything, but his face took on a serious look. I could tell that for a moment he saw me in a very different light. Then the moment passed and the usual smile returned to his face.

"Ready?" I asked.

"Aye," he answered, getting up from where he'd been sitting and following me out into the chilly December air.

When we were growing up, John lived just a few houses away in one of the other pre-fab houses and we went to St. Malachy's School together. That's how we had met and became friends. Then, about two years ago, his family had moved two miles away, to a better house in the Kilowen district of town on the other side of the river Bann: the same part of town in which Melvin Jackson lived. On leaving school, John had been taken on as a trainee projectionist at Christie's Picture Palace, a cinema not far from where we both used to live. He still worked there, which brought him back to his old home area every day and that's why he was able to call at my house on a fairly regular basis.

We walked and talked. First, I grumbled at him for stirring things up for me with Annie, but he just laughed as always like it was water off a duck's back. Then we talked about life in the RAF. He wanted to know if the drill instructors were as mean and nasty as he'd heard. I told him that they were, relating some of the dirty tricks that Hillcrest had played on us and probably exaggerating more than a little, to accentuate toughness at being able to survive in such a hostile environment.

When we arrived at Melvin's house, his mother greeted us as old friends, which in a way we were. Mrs. Jackson had served school dinners to us during most of the years that we'd attended St. Malachy's, so she knew both of us well.

"I've got something for you, Brian," she said, almost as soon as we arrived at the house, then she disappeared somewhere into the rear of the house, returning a few moments later with an old newspaper. "Your photo's in here," she beamed, while ruffling through the pages to find the correct one. Finally, she found the photograph on one of the inside pages, folded the pages back on themselves so that the object of her attention was at the front, then deftly doubled the bottom half of paper up behind the top half before presenting it to me in a triumphant gesture. It was the group picture taken by the "Northern Whig" photographer on the day I'd set off with the other lads on our way to St. Athan. I had completely forgotten about it until she showed it to me.

"I saw it after you left for England," she explained, "so I saved it for you."

I had never had my picture in a newspaper before and it made me feel important to see it there now.

"You can keep it," she added with a kind smile.

I thanked her and accepted it.

Whilst all of this was going on, Melvin was cleaning his shoes. He seemed to have some kind of fetish about cleaning them and we always had to wait ages for him to perform this personal chore that took only five minutes for most other people. We ragged him about it and his mother joined in. It was like a repeat performance of what had happened at my house earlier, but now I was on the winning side and that felt a whole lot better. Melvin just smiled, a little like Stan Laurel's smile in the Laurel and Hardy films, but just kept on shining his gleaming black shoes. I silently wondered how long it would have taken him to bull his boots, had he been successful in joining the Boy Entrants. Maybe that would have cured him, but then again, maybe not.

Eventually, we managed to drag Melvin and his highly polished shoes out of the house. I said goodbye to Mrs. Jackson and thanked her again for the newspaper, then we headed back towards the centre of the town. On the way there, Melvin admired my uniform and remarked on the wheel badge.

"It means I'm a helicopter pilot," I explained, as straight-faced as possible, repeating a corny old Boy Entrant line of bullshit.

"Naw," he said. "Is it really? Are they training you to fly a helicopter?"

No longer able to remain deadpan, I grinned as I said yes. He laughed and then punched me playfully on the arm.

"Watch out for the uniform," I shouted in mock horror and we jostled and fooled around during the mile walk back into Coleraine town centre.

I was getting plenty of looks and stares from passers-by and was particularly aware that girls of around my age were taking notice. In Barry there were so many of us wearing the same uniform that hardly anyone took any notice, but here it worked its magic and I felt like the fabled one-eyed man who was king in the country of the blind.

But, as much as I enjoyed the company of my friends, there seemed to be an undercurrent that disturbed me more than just a little. I felt that sometimes I was out of the loop when the other two frequently discussed experiences and people of which I knew nothing. It was understandable; after all I hadn't been hanging around with them for the past three months, but these were my friends. John and I had grown up together and had known everything about each other since the time we first became best friends at around age 10. Now I had the feeling of being on the outside looking in, like a new kid at school listening and smiling and nodding along with everyone else when he really hasn't a clue what the conversation is all about. Sometimes I would ask them questions in an attempt to fill in the background knowledge that I was missing. When this happened, they would stop and patiently explain, but then the flow was lost, the subject changed and I felt even more of an interloper.

But we still had fun. As day turned into evening, we ate fish and chips at Morelli's. We could afford that now, at least John and I could—Melvin didn't have a job yet. Later we hung around the main street and, with the sophistication of our advanced years, were actually able to engage some members of the opposite sex in conversation, although it was more about joking and smart-alecking with some girls. One of them grabbed my hat and ran off with it. She laughed and giggled as I chased after her, then screamed in mock terror when I caught up with her, and then we were in a corner a little way off from the others. There was some playful scuffling and awkward kissing, combined with a lot more giggling and "accidental" contact between body parts. It was typical teenage stuff, but that's as far as it went. Sex education hadn't been on the curriculum at St. Malachy's Catholic school and in fact boys and girls were strictly segregated in two separate schools-within-a-school. So, my level of sophistication when it came to interacting with the opposite sex was close to zero. Looking back on it, I'm reminded of the old joke about the dog that chased cars. He could make lots of noise barking and running after them, but wouldn't have known what to do if he had ever actually caught one. There was a lot of growing up to do and this was just the kindergarten level. Little did I realize that in just a few more days, the pace of my growth from boy to man would be given a slight boost of acceleration.

The next day was Christmas Eve and my sisters asked if I would take them to Midnight Mass. They were still too young to be out that late at night by themselves, but they would be allowed to go if I went with them. It was a good idea because the congregation at this service was usually more relaxed and cosmopolitan, many of them feeling quite mellow after the pubs had shut and not all were Catholics either. It was common knowledge that many Protestants attended the service to experience the "bells and smells" of a High Mass. Therefore, my exposure to the kind of embarrassing wall of silence I had experienced the previous Sunday, for wearing my uniform to church, would be considerably lessened at Midnight Mass. In the end, Annie decided to come too and so the four of us trudged through the lamp-lit streets to St. Malachy's Church.

Midnight Mass had its own special air of excitement: the sung mass with its three celebrants instead of the usual one, the heavy smell of incense in the air and the joyful feeling of

Christmas in everyone's heart. When it was over, we made our way home to a darkened house and crept quietly to bed. Now we didn't have to get up and go to church in the morning, but could stay at home and enjoy Christmas.

Christmas dinner wasn't a grand affair, there wasn't too much money to spend on luxuries, but we had a nice dinner of roast goose and Annie had baked a cake and made some mince pies. She may have had her faults, but she certainly knew how to cook and bake when the notion took her. Christmas presents were simple and inexpensive. I got an inexpensive watch from Annie, my first ever and that was about it. I gave my sisters and brother Thomas some money, which to them was better than getting a present, but expected nothing in return because they didn't have the means of buying presents. Later, I went to see Aunt Maggie to wish her a Merry Christmas and took her a little gift. She received it gratefully as if it were something rare and expensive, which it was not. She gave me a pen and pencil set, which was a welcome gift.

Before long, the warmth of feelings around the family hearth seemed to evaporate like the morning mist, replaced by the old status quo. Once again, I became the frequent target of belittling criticism and the urge that prompted me to leave home in the first place surfaced strongly again—although I was in no rush to resume the disciplined life at St. Athan. The solution was to spend as little time as possible in the family home, so I either spent time out and about with my friends, or visited my many relatives in the Coleraine area. Eventually, on the second day of 1957, and with a great sense of relief, I set off on the return journey back to South Wales.

* * *

The boat to Liverpool was just as crowded on the way back as it had been coming over, but I was able to find Billy Cassidy and the others without any trouble. As before, all available seating in the passenger lounge was occupied, so we made our way down into the hold again and carved out a reasonably comfortable little area where we could possibly get some sleep.

Two regular RAF people in uniform were also taking shelter in the hold, although they weren't actually travelling together. One was an airman in his early twenties and the other was a member of the Women's Royal Air Force, a WRAF. She was also in her twenties, slim, with slightly reddish blonde hair and attractive in a girl-next-door kind of a way. Both seemed to gravitate towards our small group from different directions and we all got talking together. Boy Entrants were something of a rarity to most members of the regular service, so they were curious about us and the meaning of our chequered hatbands and brass wheel badges. We, for our part, were curious about life in the regular service so everyone had lots of questions. But, because she was the only woman in our midst, the WRAF got most of the attention and, young though we were, we all tried to impress her and gain her attention. She responded to our juvenile adulation in an engaging flirty kind way, obviously enjoying it.

The sea was calm during this crossing and after two or maybe three hours the other boys and the regular airman gradually dropped out of our little discussion group as they started getting settled down for the night. I was the last one left talking to Sandra, the WRAF girl (by this time we were on first name terms), but in the process had managed to clear a little area on the floor and had laid my kitbag down as a pillow and then used my heavy greatcoat as a blanket. Sandra seemed to be travelling light and had little protection from the cold night air, other than the thin uniform she wore, so I offered her my greatcoat to keep her warm.

"Thanks," she said, "but why don't we share it?"

"Okay," I agreed, wondering exactly what she had in mind.

I soon found out when she came over to where I lay and then lay down alongside me, pulled half of the coat across her body and snuggled up close to me. Her nearness and warmth had an electrifying effect on me, but also made me feel tense and unsure of how to position my body. We could both see that other passengers in the hold were watching us intently under the bright floodlights that illuminated the hold.

"Try to keep the coat down over me," Sandra said, "I don't want anyone seeing up my skirt." Then she added, "And I haven't anything on under my shirt!"

I had no difficulty understanding the first part of her statement, but the second thing about wearing nothing under her shirt had me puzzled. "What do you mean you've got nothing on under your shirt?" I asked.

She didn't answer, but instead took my hand and placed it on her breast. She had unbuttoned her tunic, so I could feel the soft yielding flesh through the thin fabric of her shirt.

"Shhhh," she whispered in my ear, "I'm not wearing a bra."

My hormones, which by this time were already wide-awake, now thundered into a full-scale stampede. My pulse raced, my throat went dry and my head throbbed as I gently caressed the tender softness, feeling the small hard lump of her nipple pressing into the palm of my trembling hand.

She reached up and gently took the hand away again. "You're too young for that," she laughingly hissed into my ear.

"I'm not," I protested, "I've been out with girls!"

"Can you kiss?" she asked.

"Yes," I said defensively and planted a closed-mouth tight-lipped kiss on her mouth. She quickly broke away and quietly giggled.

"That's not how to do it," she said. "You need to keep your lips open like this," she demonstrated by slightly parting her lips.

"Okay, let me try again," I said, very eager to learn as I moved my now parted lips towards her. She met them with her warm moist mouth and our lips crushed together. My head suddenly seemed to be filled with lightning flashes and ringing noises sounded in my ears. Never in my life, up to that moment, had I experienced anything so sensually wonderful. But the best was yet to come—suddenly and unexpectedly I felt her tongue thrust itself into my mouth, increasing the pleasure of the kiss a thousand-fold. Then it was all over as she quickly pulled back.

"That's enough," she said, "you're really far too young for this. Let's just get some sleep."

That was much easier said than done, as far as I was concerned, because sleep was the furthest thing from my mind right then. I moved my hand around to the front of her shirt again and found the softness that I had suddenly become hopelessly addicted to. But almost immediately, her hand came quickly up to grasp mine and firmly move it away to a neutral area, where she continued to hold on to it tightly. The passionate interlude was over and I could tell she really meant it, so I tried to relax and go to sleep as she suggested. We had been like that for another half hour or so when the regular airman suddenly approached us. He told Sandra that he'd got a much more comfortable place to sleep, which was away from the light and with cushions to lie on. He then suggested that she come and share it with him. To my dismay she agreed and saying only that she was sorry, went off with the airman.

It could be said that Sandra was merely toying with a young boy's emotions for her own amusement—and I dare say there's a lot of truth in that. But, whether she knew it or not, I learned more during that brief encounter than I could ever have learned in months of fumbling through the awkward teenage courtship rituals that had seemed so enjoyable only a few days prior to my encounter with Sandra underneath the greatcoat. That night, my transition from boy to man took a giant leap forward.

I never travelled by the Liverpool route again after that. The apparent absence of Wing boys during the crossings had puzzled me, but long before going on my next leave, I discovered the reason for that. It turned out that they all used the Heysham to Belfast ship, which was owned and operated by British Railways. The ships on the Heysham route were modern, much more comfortable and had better catering services than those that sailed from Liverpool. There was also the added advantage that the railway station at Heysham was right on the dockside, making it a matter of simply getting off the train and walking a short distance to where the gangplank led onto the ship. So, even though Heysham was a little farther north than Liverpool, the slightly longer rail trip was well worthwhile.

* * *

On the first day after returning from leave, we were instructed not to unpack the bulk of our kit, since we were going to be moving from the ITS lines to the Wing lines on the following day. Other than giving us that instruction, the DIS mostly left us alone during our final day in the Initial Training Squadron. In fact, Corporal Hillcrest seemed to have disappeared altogether.

That evening Corporal Blandford came into our billet to wish us good luck for the future. He'd been drinking. Not heavily, but just enough for him to be much less inhibited than usual. His tunic was unbuttoned and he wore his hat on the back of his head as he sidled into our billet in a very relaxed manner. We all gathered around to talk to him because, even though he represented discipline in our lives, he was a very likeable person who had always treated us fairly. For a while, he entertained us with anecdotes from his years of service and commented on some of the funnier things that had happened during our time in ITS. When Potter's name came up, Blandford rolled his eyes and remarked that there was always one like him in every entry. We just lapped it all up. Then the topic of conversation changed to his views on the other drill instructors. When someone mentioned Corporal Hillcrest, Blandford confided that none of the other DIS liked him.

"What are you going to do about him?" He asked, as his voice dropped to a more conspiratorial tone.

We all looked at each other dumbly. Not one of us had thought much about doing anything.

"If it was me," said Blandford, "I wouldn't let that little bastard get away with all the things he did to you."

Somebody asked, "What do you think we should do Corp?"

Corporal Blandford didn't answer, but instead looked around and stared pointedly at the row of four fire extinguishers that stood in the entrance to the billet. Two were painted red indicating that they were soda-acid extinguishers and two were painted a cream colour to signify that, when activated, they discharged a fountain of thick foam for extinguishing oil or grease fires. Then he looked back at us, arched his eyebrows in a theatrical way and said, "Well, that's up to you boys now, isn't it? I couldn't encourage you to do anything unpleasant against a brother NCO, now could I?" With that he smiled, said goodnight and good luck and then left the billet.

We called out, "Bye Corp," as he disappeared into the darkness of the night. Then we stood around for a little while thinking and talking about what he had said, before somebody had the idea of going to check if Hillcrest was in his bunk. One or two people went around on the outside of the billets to see if his light was on, coming back a few minutes later with the news that his bunk was in complete darkness. On hearing that announcement, four boys grabbed an extinguisher each and, with several of us accompanying them, set out once again around the outside of the billets. Sure enough, the bunk window was in darkness.

"The window's locked, what are we going to do now?" someone asked.

"Break the fuckin' window! That's what we're going to do," another voice answered.

With that, there was the tinkling sound of breaking glass. Next came a wooshing sound as the contents of both soda-acid extinguishers were released into the bunk through its broken window pane. Then it was the foam extinguishers.

"Somebody's coming!" a voice called out in a loud whisper.

In a panic, the person holding the last foam extinguisher heaved the whole thing through the hole in the window, while it was still disgorging its foam, and we all pounded away across the grass towards our billet, under cover of darkness. When we got inside there were great sighs of relief and laughter and joy that we'd finally taken a little revenge on someone who had quite deliberately made our lives much more miserable than was really necessary. We moved to the Wings the very next day and never heard a single thing about the incident after that.

CHAPTER 6

Life in the Wings

Psychologically speaking, moving into the Wings was a huge leap forward, even if it was only one small step upwards in the general pecking order. The most immediately important event was that our green and black chequered ITS hatbands were forever consigned to a place in the 29th Entry's history. Instead, those of us who moved into No. 2 Wing would now wear a red and navy blue chequered hatband, whilst our brother entry members, who went into No. 1 Wing, would wear a red and green checked band around their hats.

The Wings were divided into four squadrons: 1 and 2 squadrons were part of No. 1 Wing and consisted of U/T Airframe, Engine and Mechanical Transport Mechanics— U/T signified "Under Training". No. 2 Wing comprised 3 and 4 Squadrons, with U/T Instrument and Armourer Mechanics assigned to 4 Squadron, whilst 3 Squadron, the one to which I now belonged, was made up entirely of U/T Electrical (Air) Mechanics. The parenthetical word "Air" indicated that we were destined to be Aircraft Electricians, in contrast to Ground Electricians who worked on all non-aircraft electrical systems and who were not represented in the Boy Entrant training scheme at that time.

In addition to being entitled to wear the hard-won red and navy blue hatband, I would also now wear a red disc behind the wheel badge on my sleeve to identify me as a member of 3 Squadron. Both of these outward symbols of my new status were like battle honours that we had all earned—by suffering from blistered feet after square-bashing sessions on the parade ground, crawling through mud in GCT and withstanding the cynical tongue lashings and indignities heaped on us by the ITS drill instructors. We had come a long way in just ten weeks, having somehow been transformed from a bunch of gawky raw civilians into disciplined members of a military unit. It was a proudly earned achievement, but there was still a long way to go.

The actual move up to the Wings itself occurred, without ceremony, on Saturday, 12th of January, 1957. We were given new billet assignments that morning and told to move our kit and bedding over there that afternoon. Although there was transport available, since Richard Butterworth and I had both been assigned to hut E7, we decided not to wait for it, but instead worked together to move our belongings and bedding over to the Wings by simply carrying it there on foot. We reasoned that the sooner we got everything over there, the sooner we could relax. It took at least two trips backwards and forwards between our old G lines hut and our new home in E lines, but at least we were now able to use the short route between ITS and the Wings that had once been forbidden, since we were now Wing members ourselves.

Leading Boy Entrant "Gerry" German, the NCO Boy in charge of billet E7, met us at the entrance and indicated four empty bed-spaces that had recently been vacated by 25th Entry members, when they had passed out of Boy Entrant training just before Christmas. Two other 29th Entry boys, Ron and Bill, had been assigned to the same billet, so each of us chose a bed and claimed it by dumping our kit on the bare mattress. All of the other bed-spaces were occupied by a cross-section of the Wings population, members of the 26th, 27th and 28th Entries, who eyed us with either interest or disdain, depending on the personality of the individual concerned.

Shortly after we'd stowed our kit away in the bedside lockers and made up blanket packs on our new beds, Leading Boy German returned with a message that all 29th Entry people were to parade immediately on the road outside E7, my new billet. All four of us struggled into our greatcoats and put on our hats and gloves as we headed out to the roadway where other entry members had already started forming up into three ranks. A group of NCOs consisting of one sergeant and three corporals waited around patiently, but chided the few inevitable stragglers to hurry up and get fell-in. We were then ordered to come to attention, the chatter ceased and a blanket of silence descended on our ranks. Nothing happened for a few moments, but then the sergeant stepped forward from the group of NCOs and addressed us, after first standing us at ease.

In a strong Cockney accent he announced: "My name is Sergeant Savoury and this is Corp'al Longfellow, Corp'al 'ubbard (Hubbard) and Corp'al Calloway behind me." Each corporal nodded once as the sergeant mentioned their individual names, without actually looking at them. "I am the sergeant in charge of free Squadron discipline," he continued, "assisted by Corp'als Longfellow, 'ubbard and Calloway." As he spoke, he tried to enunciate his words in a clipped manner, but was heavily handicapped by the pronunciation he had inherited from his upbringing in the East End of London. The result was an affected kind of posh Cockney, if there is such a thing, which would have been comical if the situation hadn't been one of great seriousness. Sergeant Savoury continued, "And on be'alf 'em and myself, I want to welcome you to the squadron." He paused for a moment or two, either to think about what say next or to let that part of his speech sink in. During the pause, he paced up and down on the slightly elevated grass verge that lay between where we stood and the billets. Seeming to have collected his thoughts, he stopped pacing and came around to face us again. "You may 'ave noticed that you 'ave been billeted wiv members of the uvver entries. We 'ave a good reason for mixing you in wiv the uvvers, but you don't need to know wot that is." He spoke the last sentence in a dismissive kind of way, as if this mysterious reason was a great secret that we were too unworthy to have revealed to us.

Sergeant Savoury continued with his speech, "You will find that fings are much different 'ere than they were in ITS. We won't be babying you 'ere; instead we expect you to act as responsible members of the squadron. Your main duty will be to attend trade training at Workshops and you are expected to study 'ard so that you will gain proficiency and pass out as qualified mechanics, along wiv the uvver members of your entry. You will take end-of-term exams and, if you pass, will be awarded proficiency badges." He was referring to the inverted stripes that were worn on the cuff of Boy Entrants' tunic sleeves.

Having stood still whilst speaking to us, the sergeant now started pacing backwards and forwards in front of us again, all the while looking at the ground as though seeking inspiration.

Then he stopped walking, faced us and drew himself up again before continuing with the address. "We 'ave assigned Boy Entrant NCOs to maintain discipline. Each billet is under the supervision of a Leading Boy Entrant. You will obey 'is and the uvver Boy Entrant NCOs' orders as though they were mine. Is that understood?" Some of us mumbled a response, at which he bellowed, "Is that *understood*?"

"Yes Sergeant," we chorused in response, startled that he had unexpectedly raised his voice.

"Leading Boys, Corp'al Boys and Sergeant Boys have been given the aufority to charge anyone in breach of regulations and that includes Queen's Regulations, Station Standing Orders and Wing Routine Orders. If you are put on a charge you will be marched in front of the Flight Commander, who will assess your guilt or innocence. If the offence is serious, you may then be remanded to appear in front of the Squadron Commander and so forf."

Savoury paused, paced briefly before stopping again and then continued, "Punishment may be anyfing from an award of confinement to camp for a number of days, to spending some time in detention in the Guardroom. But you have only to keep your nose clean, do as you're told and this will not 'appen to you."

Another pause and more pacing, then: "You will parade out 'ere in your respective flights at oh-eight-hundred each workday for inspection, before marching to Workshops to start classes at oh-eight-thirty hours. Is that understood?"

"Yes sergeant!" We didn't mumble this time.

"That's all I 'ave to say. Any questions?" Despite his spoken invitation, the look on his face challenged anyone who might dare to ask a question. "Okay," he barked and then turning to one of the NCOs arrayed behind him he said, "Corp'al Longfellow."

Corporal Longfellow stepped forward and took over the spot now vacated by Sergeant Savoury, who proceeded to leave the area entirely. The corporal looked much less forbidding than the sergeant, as was reflected in his calmer voice. "Okay, pay attention. I have the new hatbands and discs for your berets," he said, indicating some cardboard boxes sitting on the grass. "And, red discs that you need to sew in behind your wheel badges."

Then he added, "Don't come on church parade tomorrow without having the hatbands on your SDs and red discs behind your wheel badges." He eyes scanned along our ranks as he let this sink in, before continuing, "We're also going to issue you with working greatcoats. These will be on loan from the squadron and need to be handed in when you leave St. Athan." He stopped again briefly to catch his breath, then continued, "When I dismiss you, come up here and pick up your hatbands and discs, then go to the squadron stores and sign out a greatcoat." He paused for a moment then asked, "Any questions?" There was no reply so he said, "Okay, Flight dismiss!"

As soon as we were dismissed, I joined the crush of bodies that immediately surrounded Corporal Longfellow and jostled with the others until I got my goodies. Then I headed off to the nearby squadron store to collect a working greatcoat.

On our first visit to the clothing store, during those first few days in ITS, we had been issued with one greatcoat to be worn with our best blue as formal winter uniform and with our working blue in those same winter months. The long heavy coat was especially welcome when we were standing still for lengthy periods of time during morning inspection parades. They hadn't been worn for anything other than drill or when going out of camp in our best blue uniforms, so after just twelve weeks of intermittent use the coats were still in very good condition. The Wings' administration obviously foresaw that our greatcoats would quickly become the worse for wear and therefore unsuitable for best dress if we continued to use them every day. Therefore, they apparently came up with the solution of lending us old hand-me-down greatcoats for everyday use, strictly within the confines of the camp. Many of these coats were ancient and had probably warmed many bodies before they encountered ours, whilst others were of more recent vintage, but all had one thing in common: they lacked the eagle flashes on the shoulders, which was probably to indicate that they were on loan. The old greatcoats came with a huge built-in advantage, however: the buttons had been cleaned so often by our predecessors that all the small nooks and crannies around the embossed eagle and crown had been worn away, leaving a smooth surface.

Keeping them clean was going to be very easy.

After receiving my "new" working greatcoat, I went back to the billet to do a little sewing. The wheel badges had to be removed from both of my uniforms and my best greatcoat, then sewn back in place with the red no. 3 Squadron disc behind each one. The red and blue chequered hatband was easy to fit on my SD hat because it was held in place by a row of sharp little metal hooks on one end that hooked over and into the excess fabric of the band after it had been looped around the hat, in much the same way that Velcro works in today's world. The red and blue quadrant disc that was to be worn behind the badge on my beret was easy to install, because it was just a matter of removing the badge, as we would to clean it, and fitting the disc behind it. Finally, there was a fourth wheel badge and disc to be sewn on to the working greatcoat that I'd just picked up and *voila*, the transformation from ITS sprog to Wing Boy was complete.

Well, we might now be Wing Boys but the 29th Entry was still the lowest form of life on camp, as we were soon to find out.

That night, at 2130 hours, Leading Boy "Gerry" German came into the billet from his bunk and announced, "Stand by your beds for bed check!" With that, an adult NCO entered the billet wearing an "Orderly Corporal" armband. Later on, I recognized him to be one of our technical instructors, but on this first night in the Wings I had yet to meet any of the instructional staff. The Orderly Corporal—the name given to the duty corporal after normal "business hours"—moved quickly through the billet to check that either everyone was by his bed or otherwise legitimately accounted for. Gerry German accompanied him as far as the back door and then returned to his bunk. After that I performed my evening ablutions and got into bed ready for lights out. Then, at exactly 2200 hours, Leading Boy German came back into the billet to make sure that everyone was in bed before turning out the lights. Conversation stopped and all became quiet as the familiar solo trumpet notes of "Lights out", backed by the orchestral "Evening Hymn", played over the Radio St. Athan speaker high up on the wall. I never got tired of hearing this music, nor did anyone else judging by the silence that settled over the darkened billet as it played. On this night it signalled the end of a very busy, stress-filled milestone of a day and gradually induced a sensation of comfort whilst I began nodding off to sleep in my new surroundings. This blissful state must have lasted for all of ten minutes before I was brought back to full wakefulness by the glare of several torches suddenly piercing the darkness. Four or five people holding the torches then got out of bed and noisily left the billet through the rear door, their footsteps fading into the distance as they galloped off along the corridor that interconnected the billets.

"What's going on?" I heard a voice ask in a stage whisper, recognizing it as coming from one of my fellow 29th Entry.

"It's the 26th," answered a second voice, "they're going to be coming round on a raid."

Now I could hear the sounds of several distant voices and footsteps out in the corridor between the billets, sometimes walking and sometimes running. Loud crashing sounds frequently accompanied the sound of the voices and footsteps and, to make matters worse, it sounded as though they were getting ever closer to where we lay.

The second of the two voices that I'd heard before spoke again, "Whatever you do—don't try to resist them. They're tipping people out of bed and they'll make it worse on you if you make a fight of it. Just take it like a man and then wait until they've left and then make your bed again."

As I listened to this advice my stomach knotted up; meanwhile the voices and footsteps drew ever closer until they were right outside our door. I held my breath as the doorknob rattled as it was being turned, then the door was flung open and several torch beams flashed around the room in random directions, piercing the comfortable blanket of darkness as the intruders entered. Almost at once, the air was filled with sounds of bedsteads crashing to the floor as the raiders moved through the billet, leaving a trail of tangled mattresses, bedding and struggling bodies in their wake. Some of the torch beams found me and I instinctively froze where I lay, like a rabbit caught in the headlights of an oncoming car. Then, two unseen pairs of hands grasped the frame on one side of my bed and heaved it upwards so that the entire bedstead was thrown on its side, dumping me unceremoniously out onto the cold linoleum floor.

The entire billet was now in a shambles as we all tried to extricate ourselves from the wreckage of what had, until very recently, been our beds. But the raid wasn't over just yet.

"Where are the sprogs?" A voice hissed.

A torch suddenly turned in my direction, forcing me to shield my eyes from the blinding glare.

"Here's one!" Answered the voice behind the light beam that was pointing at me.

Other torch beams homed in on me until it seemed as though I was an aircraft caught in a cone of searchlights. There was no escape! The lights drew nearer.

"Stand up!" One voice commanded.

I managed to untangle myself from the bedding and stood up, feeling nervous and sheepish, especially since I couldn't see anything in the glare of the torches.

"What entry are you, sprog?" Demanded the disembodied voice behind the torch.

"Twenty-ninth," I answered as confidently as I could, which really wasn't very confident.

"That's a *shitty* entry, isn't it?" The voice taunted.

I didn't answer.

"Say it, sprog! The twenty-ninth is a shitty entry!" He shouted in my ear.

I mumbled, "The twenty-ninth's a shitty entry."

"Louder! We didn't hear you!" The voice shouted in my ear again.

Identification with one's own entry was strong amongst Boy Entrants and being forced to make a statement like this seemed like a betrayal. But I remembered the advice we'd received immediately prior to the raid and hastily decided that it was a minor thing compared to what might lay in store if I didn't go along with them.

"The twenty-ninth's a shitty entry," I said, speaking louder.

"What's the best entry?" The taunting voice now continued.

"The twenty-sixth," I replied, giving what I thought was

the obvious answer.

"No! Say 'the twenty-sixth's the best entry'," he demanded.

"The twenty-sixth's the best entry," I parroted.

Apparently satisfied, the torch beams left my face as the raiders turned their attention away from me and sought out the other 29th members. Two were subjected to the same treatment that I'd just suffered, but Ron was left alone. The fact that he towered above most of the other boys, and was powerfully built into the bargain, probably had something to do with that. And then, just as suddenly as they'd arrived, the 26th raiding party left, on their way to the next conquest.

We couldn't turn the billet lights on because it was after "Lights out", but a few people had torches of their own and these provided enough light for me to upright my bedstead and replace the mattress before remaking my bed and getting back into it. The voices and footsteps of the raiding party were still audible somewhere in the distance, as the band of Senior Entry raiders inflicted mayhem on some other hapless billet, but eventually the noises subsided and peace returned once more. A little later, our own billet's small detachment of 26th entry returned, still chuckling over their adventure. They climbed into their intact beds, which had been spared in the raid because each had been marked by a white towel laid across its end to signify that it belonged to a member of the senior entry. The night's raid was over and we were finally able to settle down and get some sleep. Strangely, our Leading Boy was noticeably absent during all of the excitement. It seemed that he preferred to keep a low profile while all the shenanigans were going on. It turned out that he was 27th entry and was following an unwritten law that said he shouldn't interfere in senior entry affairs. Later, when the 27th entry came to power it was a slightly different story, but more about that later.

Reveille was half an hour later next morning because it was Sunday and we were allowed to sleep in a little longer. Church parade wasn't until 1000 hours, so most of us skipped breakfast to enjoy an even longer lie-in, safe in the knowledge that nobody would be around to bother us for a while.

Church parade that morning was the first time that I wore

my newly-embellished uniform. The corner of my eye kept catching the splash of red on my left arm from the disc behind my wheel badge, as I marched to the RC church. It moved rhythmically in and out of view as I marched along swinging my arms at the more relaxed waist-height level, like the other Wing boys, instead of having to swing them up shoulder high as we had been required to do in ITS. Those around me wore red and blue chequered hatbands and I knew that the SD hat on my head also matched theirs. I felt proud and elated to be in the Wings, even if the 29th was the lowly junior entry. That very same evening, I was rudely reminded of my entry's lowly status.

It was after tea and I was sitting on my bed cleaning my buttons and boots in readiness for inspection next morning when Mac, one of the 26th, came over to my bed-space carrying his greatcoat and tunic draped over one arm. He was taller than average and close to 18 years old. Mac had been one of the inhabitants of the billet who had regarded our initial arrival in E7 with a look of utter disdain. Although trying not to let him see me looking, I had noticed that he always seemed devoid of humour and his face appeared to wear a permanently angry expression. This formidable presence now stood not two feet from me and I wondered why? Maybe he had seen the stealthy glances I had cast his way? Whatever the reason, I felt a great sense of intimidation.

"Here, clean these buttons while you're at it," he said, tossing his garments down on my bed beside me.

I looked up at him, but was unable to say anything due to the sense of dread that had gripped me. This evidently made him think that I needed some further explanation.

"You're going to be my bull boy," he announced with a cynical little smile, as though that explained everything.

But I already understood. Being someone's bull boy was just another rite of passage. It was something that nearly everyone had to do when his entry was the most junior. The only consolation was the potential of a deferred reward: an ex-bull boy could enlist the services of his own bull boy at a later date, when his own entry finally became the senior entry. The strictly unofficial privileges claimed by those in the senior entry didn't just end with having their personal bull boys clean buttons and boots for them. In fact, they felt entitled to opt out of anything and everything of a menial nature. So, on bull nights they would go out to the NAAFI or the Astra, leaving all the cleaning and floor polishing to the other non-senior entry billet occupants. Junior entry bull boys were also expected to sweep and polish the senior entry boys' bed spaces. To refuse, or under-perform to the extent that the recipient of these favours got into trouble for having dirty buttons or an unacceptable bed space during billet inspection, meant even bigger trouble for the bull boy. He would be hauled before a "court martial" hastily convened by the senior entry, tried, sentenced and then punished. All of this was very unofficial, of course and Sergeant Savoury and his corporals didn't seem to know that it went on. Actually, I believe that they vaguely knew that some things like this went on, but were unable to do too much about it because they were up against the universal code of silence observed by teenagers, that discourages them from ratting on their peers.

On Monday morning the events of the weekend were only a memory, as we tumbled out of our billets at 0745 hours and paraded on the road for the daily inspection. Everyone on parade carried a rolled up pair of denims under his left arm. Most had classroom notebooks rolled up inside their denims, but since we of the 29th hadn't been to "Workshops" yet we didn't have anything to carry except our denims. The squadron was divided into two flights, based on billet numbers. Those of us in billet E7 belonged to "A" Flight and I now followed the others to where it was forming up into three ranks, a short distance up the road, near the boiler house that supplied hot water for the camp. For inspection, we faced towards the billets, sandwiched between "B" Flight on our left and the drum and trumpet band on our right. A corporal-boy called us to attention and then proceeded with roll call, after which he moved through the ranks to inspect us, picking up a few people here and there for having tarnished buttons. During the time that we stood there at attention, I watched the boiler house workmen arriving, one by one, for work. The casualness that marked the beginning of their day was enviable compared with the beginning of mine. Each

man that arrived went to the boiler-house office window and
rapped with his knuckles on the glass, then waved to the person
inside before entering the building through its main door. They
didn't have to suffer standing to attention for roll call, there was
no button inspection for them and no marching to work. Besides
that, what could be cosier than working in a nice warm place like
a boiler house?

With inspection finished and the time approaching 8:15,
it was time to set off for Workshops. The sergeant-boy, who had
been overseeing the squadron inspection, now took over by
ordering the whole squadron to make a right turn. On his
command, each person swivelled from the line abreast position,
transforming our formations into columns of three ranks that
faced in the direction of travel, with the trumpet band at the head
of the parade.

"Number 3 Squadron! By the left, quick march," yelled
the sergeant-boy, at the top of his lungs.

As one, all three formations stepped off on the left foot,
keeping time with the slow rhythmic boom of a single-stick
drumbeat from the large bass drum. This lasted for several paces
until we'd travelled a short distance up the road, then all of the
side drummers suddenly started beating out a full tattoo. I heard
a voice in the band briefly yelling out some unintelligible
command and next thing the trumpeters started playing a tune. It
was one that I'd vaguely heard before somewhere, but couldn't
quite place. Music to march to work by! This was a lot better
than having someone like Corporal Hillcrest call out "Yeft, yeft,
yeft-yoyt, yeft"!

The march to "Workshops" lasted no more than ten
minutes and then I was able to discover what the word actually
meant, within context of Boy Entrant training. The outward
appearance of the structure where we came to a halt was that of a
light-brown, brick-built aircraft hangar, but when we entered
through a set of red-painted steel fire-doors set midway along
the length of the building, it became apparent that the building's
function was very different from that of a hangar. Most of the
floor area was partitioned-off into classrooms that were accessed
from a grid pattern of aisles. In addition to the classrooms, there

were also a few open areas in which work-benches were used to support brown coloured panelling surmounted with complicated-looking electrical equipment and wiring.

On entering, we were led along one of the aisles to a classroom, into which we entered through a door-sized opening in the light-green painted partition. An elderly civilian, who wore a light brown coat-style overall and an armband with the word "Instructor" on his right arm, was waiting for us. He indicated that we each find a place to sit at one of the tables arranged in four or five rows in the classroom. After finding a seat and sitting down, I turned my attention to the instructor. He had a kindly face and appeared to be in his late fifties. A full moustache, sandy in colour, covered his upper lip and his thinning hair was of a similar shade. He wore a clean white shirt with a neatly knotted tie and gave off the appearance of orderliness and self-confidence. His name—Mr. Edridge—had been chalked at the top right corner of the blackboard to the left of "Instructor" and above the line that read "Subject: Basic Tools".

This class would last for a few weeks, with the object of teaching us the correct use and maintenance of hand tools, in a practical sense. But first, we needed to learn about the tools themselves and this meant spending the first two weeks in the classroom. Here we learned everything that anyone would ever want to know about screwdrivers, which were referred to in the peculiar backwards military fashion—*screwdrivers, ratchet-handle; screwdrivers, general service (GS); screwdrivers, non-magnetic.* Then there was the family of pliers—*pliers, insulated, sidecutting; pliers, long-nose; pliers, wire stripping.* And then there was one of my favourites. It came under the general heading of "files"—actually, it was one file in particular: the one that was known as a bastard file. This was during a more genteel time, when the word "bastard" was considered taboo in polite society. It was the kind of word that was nearly as bad as the "eff-word"; a get-your-mouth-washed-out-with-soap class of word. Yet here we were, being given official permission to use expressions such as "Hand me that bastard," in the serious pursuance of our high calling as tradesmen and with the noble awareness that we were merely using a technical word that just happened to have an evil "bad-language" twin.

To learn about tools we would also need to use them, however, so at one point during our instruction we were taken to another workshop hangar and each issued with a basic toolkit that came in a tough fabric carryall bag. The issuer was Corporal Simpson, an unsmiling skeletal-looking man who bore the unfortunate nickname "Gummy", for a reason that wasn't particularly obvious. Rumour had it that at one time all of his teeth had been removed because of some gum disease. For some time after that, he didn't wear dentures and unfortunately his appearance during this period saddled him with his unflattering nickname. Gummy wore the same kind of brown overall as worn by Mr. Edridge, with the addition of another armband worn loosely on his left arm bearing a heavily soiled set of corporal's stripes.

After issuing us with our personal toolkits, Corporal Simpson ordered us to fan around him in a wide semicircle and then instructed us to empty the contents of the bags out onto the floor. Then he went through a checklist of the tools that we were each supposed to have in our toolkit. As he called out the name of a tool, using its RAF nomenclature—*hammer, ballpane*—we would hold up the appropriate tool to indicate that we had it. When Gummy had scanned around to confirm that everyone was holding up the correct tool, he told us to put it in the bag before calling out the next item on the list. Checking that we had all of our tools after performing a task was a good and necessary habit, we were told. This was because of the danger that a loose tool can create if carelessly left behind in an aircraft. Loose objects are very likely to move around during flight, possibly jamming the controls, or even causing injury to someone during military style flying, when the pilot might be rolling or looping the aircraft.

This was no exaggeration because I recall an incident from later in my RAF service career when a large, heavy screwdriver struck the pilot of a Meteor on the head while he was performing an inverted manoeuvre. The screwdriver bounced off his helmet and then struck the cockpit canopy. He was lucky that the helmet saved him from injury and it was with great presence of mind that he remained inverted long enough to reach out and retrieve the wayward tool from where it had come to rest in the inverted canopy, before making a hasty return to base. The owner of the screwdriver denied that he had lost it in the cockpit, but an identifying mark on the blade provided evidence to the contrary. A subsequent tool check then revealed that the screwdriver was indeed missing from his toolkit although, in this case, carrying out a tool check after the event was like closing the stable door after the horse had gone. The airman was punished, but worse, he was permanently banned from working on aircraft and was forced to work in a non-aircraft trade for the remainder of his service. Tool checks were rigidly enforced for many weeks after the incident and eventually a new system of keeping better control of tools was established on the squadron.

When Gummy Simpson had completed the tool check, he ordered us to close and padlock our tool bags. He then told us that they would be stored at Workshops under his supervision, but we would have possession of the key to our own personal tool bag so that no one else could open it. Trustingly, we believed him.

During the following two weeks, I learned to identify many of the tools that I would be using in my everyday working life. They consisted mostly of screwdrivers and pliers. We then moved on to some of the other tools we would be expected to use from time to time, for the purpose of cutting and shaping materials. This category included hacksaws and files. We were also introduced to some of the less common tools, such as a scribe used for marking guide lines on metal prior to cutting it, in the same way that one would draw a line on a piece of wood with a pencil before sawing it. There were surface tables and vee-blocks, both of which are precisely machined to provide true, flat surfaces that enable measurements to be made with a high degree of accuracy, and there were tri-squares for checking the trueness of right angles. Next, we moved on to micrometers and Vernier calipers, both of which are used for making precise measurements down to 1/1000 of an inch.

All of this was a prelude to going into the workshop, where we could put our new knowledge into practise. And when that time came, we were taken to an area of the hangar that was equipped with workbenches, for the first of many sessions of workshop practice. The object of this initial session was to start us off simply with some basic work, but first we collected our tool kits from storage, which naturally called for a tool check as an essential part of the training.

Just as before, we all stood around in a semi-circle with a pile of tools at our feet while Corporal "Gummy" Simpson went through the checklist. All went well until he called out for us to hold up *hammers, ballpane, one*. I dived into the pile, but couldn't find the hammer. I then began frantically rummaging around in the pile, but it just wasn't there. So I looked in my toolbag, expecting to find that it had lodged in there when I had emptied the other tools out, but the bag was empty. Then I looked at the other piles of tools near me, thinking that maybe my hammer had strayed into one of those, but that also drew a blank. In the end I had to admit to the corporal that my hammer was missing, even though I couldn't for the life of me understand how it could have disappeared when the only other time that I'd taken it out of my tool bag was during the previous tool check. I mentioned this to the corporal, but he dismissed my reasoning and told me that I must have been careless and hadn't put the tool back in my bag after that last tool check. He took my name and serial number, telling me that a report would be sent to Pay Accounts on some kind of RAF debit form and that the cost of the tool would be deducted from my pay. At this point he had me doubting myself—maybe I had left the tool out of the bag, or maybe someone else had picked it up by mistake? In any event, there was little I could do but go along with the debit charge against my meagre pay.

For our first project at Workshop practice we were provided with a roughly cut piece of aluminium that was slightly larger than six inches square and was half an inch thick. The object of the practice was to file the edges of the piece until its dimensions were exactly six inches by six inches, with each edge perfectly level and each corner a perfect right angle. The task was designed to give us practise in the use of a scribe, a tri-square, the surface table and of course a whole series of files, from coarse file all the way to a very smooth finishing file.

Like everyone else, I clamped the metal piece in a vice and worked on it throughout the morning. Then, when I thought it was very close to the required dimensions I checked all four edges with the tri-square, only to find that none of them were level—when I held it up to the light I could see gaps between the tri-square and the aluminium. It took quite a lot more work with a smooth file to get all the edges square and then, when I was satisfied that each edge seemed level and at right angles to all the others, I was ready for the next step. This entailed sliding the work-piece around, one edge at a time, on a surface table that had been lightly coated with oil and then checking to see if the entire edge of the work-piece was uniformly coated with a film of oil. Not surprisingly, that happy result was not achieved the first time. There were a number of low points that remained dry, indicating that the edge was uneven. This meant more careful filing and many more trips to the surface table to reduce the high spots so that they were at the same level as the low points. Finally, I was able to get the film of oil to completely coat all of the surfaces and the job was done. I carried my work-piece to the instructor, who checked it before giving his approval. Work assignments such as this were marked and the results placed in our training records, counting towards the award of a proficiency stripe at the end of each term.

Workshop practice took up one day of instruction each week and on the other days we sat in the classroom, being instructed in subjects that were designed to give us the knowledge and skills we'd need to become the best aircraft technicians in the world. That's not to say that we were finished with our general education. We still went to classes at the Education Centre once a week for maths, physics and current affairs. Then there was PE, which was always a welcome break from sitting in a classroom. And of course, the weekly Padre's Hour and Sports Afternoon all helped to provide some variety in our week. Thankfully, the drill sessions and Ground Defence Training had been removed from our curriculum and we went to Workshops for trade training instead. Other than that, the activities involved in our training seemed to remain just about the same.

* * *

Life in the new billet settled down into a routine of sorts. When we finished Workshops for the day, we were expected to do homework in the evenings, which involved transferring the scribbled notes that we'd copied down from the blackboard during the day into our "best" notebooks. The theory behind this was that the information that we had received in the classroom during the day would be reinforced by transcribing our rough notes and diagrams into the "best" notebooks, using better handwriting and draughtsmanship. I didn't agree with this theory, because I felt that the act of transcription was somehow automatic and that the knowledge didn't sink in very well this way. In retrospect, it would have been better for me if I'd read over the notes after having neatly written them out into my notebook, but by the time I'd finished writing them out I wasn't in any mood to read them again. That's really a pity, because I think it would have helped me a little later on. Sometimes, when transcribing notes, I had difficulty in reading my own scribble or the hasty free-hand sketches that I'd made during the day. At such times, it was difficult to produce neat copperplate hand-

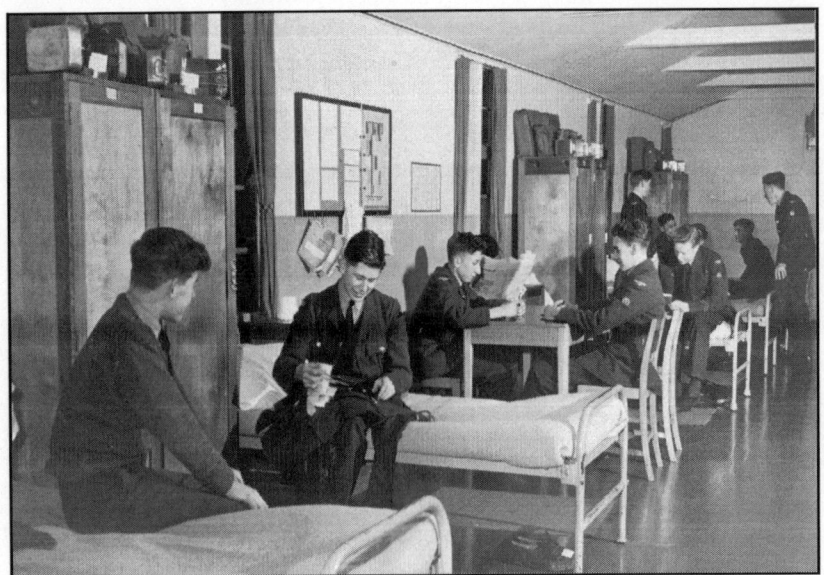

Boy Entrants relax "at home" in their billet. One boy, second from left, is busy cleaning his buttons.

written notes and elaborately-coloured diagrams from my scrappy, rough information. It was a necessary evil however, because our "best" notebooks were subject to weekly inspection by the current instructor and lapses in keeping them up-to-date could easily land an errant boy entrant an interview with Warrant Officer Dimwiddy, who was in charge of instruction in Workshops. Ginge Brown invented an apt expression for that particular experience: he referred to it as "having coffee and biscuits with Mr. Dimwiddy".

Raids by the 26th still continued after "lights out", but as the weeks wore on it seemed that the senior entry had become bored with that particular activity and so the frequency of the after lights-out disruptions lessened progressively.

One of the seemingly exciting benefits that appealed to me when I first moved into my Wings billet was discovering that one of the occupants possessed a record player. We never had that kind of luxury in ITS, so at first I enjoyed listening to the "Rock around the Clock" LP by Bill Haley and the Comets and another LP featuring "The Platters". Unfortunately, that was the full extent of the collection possessed by the owner of the record player. The result was that both LPs were played over and over again, until I was sick to death of hearing both of them and longed for lights-out so that they couldn't be played any more. One dubious advantage of this exposure is that, to this very day, I can easily remember the lyrics on each track, word for word, on the odd occasions that I am unfortunate enough to hear either of them again.

* * *

The bond of friendship between Butterworth and me, that had been born in ITS, was strengthened somewhat by the fact that we had both ended up in the same 2 Wing billet. But to a larger extent, the bond had already found considerable reinforcement due to similarities that we shared in our backgrounds. At an early age, we had both helplessly felt the pain of losing our mothers to untimely death, only to suffer additional salt being poured into our wounds when their places were unworthily taken by less than loving stepmothers. By becoming Boy Entrants, we had each found the very same escape route from our miserable home lives. The circumstances under which we both had suffered were so similar that, after listening to me telling of mine, Richard commented that I could just as easily have been describing how life had been for him. In many ways, it seemed as though we had truly lived in each other's shoes. The only major divergence we could identify was in the jobs we held before joining the RAF. It was difficult for us to decide which of our previous forms of employment could possibly have been the better: mine as a message-boy or his as an undertaker's assistant. I kidded him that his was a dead-end job—a joke he appreciated. We did lots of things together, such as going to Barry at weekends and the Astra cinema during the week. We also got ourselves into the same kind of trouble. Butterworth was a non-smoker when he first joined the Boys, but he took up smoking within a few months of falling into my bad company. It's not something I'm particularly proud of, but it seems that my regular bouts of puffing away at a Woody Woodbine influenced him to also become addicted to the "weed". And that's what got both us into hot water and introduced us to "Jankers", shortly after moving into E-lines.

Smoking in the billets during "duty hours" was forbidden, including the period in the morning when we were tidying the place up before going out on parade for inspection. But the "standing orders" that forbade the practice didn't stop us from lighting up and having a few puffs, as we made our bed-packs and swept out our bed spaces during the short period of time remaining between breakfast and the parade. Unfortunately for us, the squadron Sergeant Boy sometimes patrolled the billets to make sure that everyone was out on parade on time. He was a large, overbearing, 26th entry non-smoking youth who had no understanding of the craving that we tobacco addicts suffered. On one particular morning the Sergeant Boy caught both us with cigarettes in hand and late for parade as well. He read us the riot act and ended by warning us that if it happened again we would be put on a charge.

Being put on a charge was very much like being booked for some misdemeanour by a policeman and was always accompanied by the same sinking feeling in the pit of the stomach. It was something that we had been sheltered from up to now. During our time in the Initial Training Squadron, punishment for minor infringements was dispensed directly by our DIs and usually involved us in performing some type of fatigues, such as cleaning greasy pans in the mess kitchen, or an equally menial task. But being put on a charge was to find oneself in a situation that had similarities to a court appearance in civilian life, from which a more formal type of punishment would be meted out. It usually began when an NCO accosted an individual with the accusation of a perceived transgression. The NCO would inform the accused that he was being placed on a charge and would then proceed to record the details of the transgression on a Charge form, better known by its RAF form number, "Form 252". The "court" equivalence was a nerve-wracking appearance before an officer, usually the person's Flight Commander if the offence wasn't of a too serious nature. And the most common punishment for minor offences was confinement to camp for a specific number of days, unofficially called "jankers". But the punishment wasn't *just* being confined to camp. There were activities that those on jankers were expected perform during the confinement that made the whole experience of jankers something to be avoided if possible.

Although the Sergeant Boy gave us fair warning, we must have been slow learners or didn't take him seriously, because neither of us gave up dragging on a Woody each morning. And just as sure as night follows day, he caught us smoking again a few days later. This time there was no getting off with a warning.

"Okay you two, I'm putting you both on a charge this time," said the Sergeant Boy as he unexpectedly entered the billet and caught us cigarette in hand. With that, he unbuttoned his breast pocket and took out a pad of the little RAF form 252s. "Let me have your twelve-fifty," he demanded of me, referring to my RAF identity card.

I produced the blue identity card from out of my pocket and handed it to him, then watched in silence as he copied down my personal details on to the 252. Next, he repeated the same process with Butterworth.

"Okay, you'll hear when you have to go before the Flight Commander. Now get out on parade before I put you on another charge for being late."

We grabbed our hats and coats and hastily left the billet, struggling to put them on as we ran out to the road where the others had already formed up in the ranks.

All morning long, in class, I wondered when we would be called before the Flight Commander, but we didn't have long to wait because at lunchtime the same day, Leading Boy German ordered Richard and me to report to the Flight office right away. Sergeant Savoury was waiting there to meet us, together with the Sergeant Boy and two other boys who had been picked at random to be our escorts.

"Carlin and Butterworff," Savoury barked, "you 'ave been put on a charge and will be taken before the Flight Commander. Remove your 'ats!"

This was standard procedure for someone appearing on a charge, the reason for which I am completely ignorant, but we did as we were told and left our berets on a hat rack in the Sergeant's office. Everyone else involved was required to wear their hat.

Sergeant Savoury then explained the protocol of going up on a charge. "You will bofe go in to see the Flight Commander togevvah, and will be referred to as 'the accused'. Understood?"

We both answered, "Yes, sergeant."

He continued, "When I give the order: 'Accused and escort quick march', you will march into the Flight Commander's office between the two escorts. Listen for my order to 'mark time' and mark time in front of the desk. Then, I'll give you the order to 'alt, whereupon you will cease marking time. Izzat understood?"

"Yes, sergeant."

On hearing that we understood, the sergeant continued, "I will order you to 'right turn' so that you will be facing the Flight Commander, you will 'en remain at attention at all times and look straight ahead. Do not speak until the Flight Commander asks if you have anyfing to say." He continued, "If you 'ave some mitigating circumstances, although I doubt it in this case, speak clearly and loudly enough for 'im to 'ear. Okay? If you have noffink to say, just say 'no sir' and 'en be quiet. Izzat understood?"

We both meekly answered, "Yes, sergeant."

"Okay, get fell in over 'ere," he said, pointing to a spot adjacent to the corridor wall, just outside the Flight Commander's door.

We lined up along the wall, both of us sandwiched between the two escorts, with the Sergeant Boy taking the lead ahead of us to make a fifth person in our party. Sergeant Savoury went into the Flight Commander's office, presumably to check if he was ready to hear the charge. Then, reappearing in the doorway, he called out "Accused, escort and witness, attention! Qui-ick march, left wheel, left wheel, mark time, 'eft right, 'eft right, 'eft right!"

We marched the short distance to the office door, turned left to pass through the doorway at "left wheel" and then immediately made another left turn at the second "left wheel", to bring us in front of the officer's desk, marking time for a few moments. Flight Lieutenant Grafton, also wearing his hat, gazed at us with a bored, disconnected look as he sat with both elbows propped on the desk, supporting his chin on clasped hands. His demeanour suggested that, for him, this was just another dreary day at the office. More petty Boy Entrant shenanigans to suffer through, when he would really prefer to be flying off up into the wide blue yonder, perhaps hurtling through the sky at the controls of a Javelin or Hunter, or anything with some horsepower behind it, instead of being stuck behind a damned desk and forced to participate in all this bloody schoolboy stuff and nonsense.

We seemed to mark time longer than was really necessary, but finally Sergeant Savoury gave the order, "Accused and escort, 'alt! Right turn! Stand still, you're at attention!" With that he gave a smart salute in Flight Lieutenant Grafton's direction, which was half heartedly returned by the Flight Commander's hand flopping limply to the peak of his hat.

"Sir, Boy Entrants Carlin and Butterworff are charged wiff smoking during duty hours. The charge has been preferred by Sergeant Boy Entrant Jones."

"Thank you Sergeant Savoury," said Flight Lieutenant Grafton. Then, addressing Jones, "Sergeant Boy Jones, present the evidence."

Sergeant Boy Jones produced a small notebook and whilst reading from it, barked out the details of his confrontation with us that morning, "Sir, I entered billet E7 at oh seven fifty hours on ....." and here he gave the date, "and found both of the accused smoking during duty hours. I had previously cautioned them about this behaviour, so I informed them that I was placing them on a charge."

"Thank you, Sergeant Boy," the Flight Commander said and then turning to the sergeant he said expectantly, "Let me see their one-oh-ones."

RAF form 101 was a document that was used to record all charges brought against an individual, together with the punishments handed out for each transgression. Flight Lieutenant Grafton saw that each form 101 was completely blank. His gaze returned to us.

"Do you have anything to say Carlin?" He asked.

"No sir," I replied.

"Butterworth, do you have anything to say?

"No sir," replied Richard.

The Flight Lieutenant studied our blank forms again for a few moments, before directing his attention back to us as we stood stiffly before him.

"You know that you're not allowed to smoke without permission during duty hours, don't you?" He said, in what sounded suspiciously like a fatherly tone of voice.

"Yes sir," we both answered in a timidly muted manner, one after the other, responding to his fatherly tone by playing our part as the errant sons.

"Well, since this is your first offence I'm going to be lenient with you," he said, still speaking in his fatherly voice, "but you must follow orders." Now he raised his voice slightly, "If the Sergeant Boy, or anyone else in authority, tells you not to do something then pay attention to them." He glared at us for a moment from under the peak of his hat, allowing time for his words to sink in. Then, "Is that understood?"

"Yes sir," we answered in unison, the eagerness in our voices betraying our anticipation of being let off the charge.

"Well, I'm going to give you a little taste of the type of punishment that we have here in the Wings. Perhaps it will convince both of you to keep your noses clean in future and not appear in front of me again." Then, in a change of tone, he loudly and officiously pronounced, "I award you both the punishment of one day confined to camp." And then, barely pausing for breath, "March them out sergeant!"

Sergeant Savoury immediately sprang to life, with a look of surprise clearly etched on his face. "Accused, escort and witness, mark time, 'eft right, 'eft right. Ri-iight turn, quick march, ri-iight wheel, ri-iight wheel." And then we were back in the corridor, outside the Flight Commander's office. "Mark time. Accused, escort and witness, 'alt!"

We came to a standstill.

"Accused, escort and witness, into line 'eft turn."

We swivelled around to face the opposite wall of the corridor.

"Boy Entrants Carlin and Butterworff, you 'ave been awarded one day of confinement to camp," the sergeant intoned in his Cockney accent, even though he was making a huge effort to speak "proper-like". "Report to the Guardroom forfwiff and sign out your defaulter's webbing." Then he dropped the pretence of trying to speak correctly as he added in a quieter tone, "Cor blimey! In all my years, I've never 'eard of anyfing like it! Getting only one day's jankers! You got off very loightly moy lads!"

It seems that we made history that day because nobody else had ever heard of such a light sentence and everyone was at a loss to understand why Flight Lieutenant Grafton was so lenient with us. As far as Richard and I were concerned, it didn't matter too much because the only important outcome was that we got off so lightly, much to Sergeant Boy Jones's disgust.

We both headed for the Guardroom right away, where we were issued with a large haversack made of blue coloured webbing material, several other accessories and a tangled mass of webbing straps. The snoop at the Guardroom sneered, "You brats are going to be kept busy sorting this little lot out," as he dumped the equipment on the counter in front of us. Then, when it appeared that he had put everything out, he said, "Sign here," in a more officious voice, whilst indicating a large ledger-like notebook, labelled "Defaulters".

We signed in the notebook, then gathered up our bundles of webbing and hurried back to the billet where we threw them into our bedside lockers, just managing to get out on parade in time for afternoon workshops.

When we returned to the billet after workshops, there wasn't any time for the evening meal because we needed to prepare for the Defaulters' Parade at 1830 hours. This meant changing from our working blue into our best blue and wearing the webbing that we'd picked up earlier from the Guardroom. There was only about an hour available in which to clean and assemble the webbing, clean our buttons and polish our boots. Thankfully, the other older, more experienced boys in the billet rallied round to help us. The foundation for the complete webbing assembly was the webbing belt, which was used to anchor a harness arrangement that supported the large haversack that we would be wearing on our backs. We then needed to attach our satchel-like small-pack to a set of straps that hung from the left side of the webbing belt, so that the small-pack dangled at about hip level. A water bottle was suspended from a similar set of straps to hang at the right hip. Finally, two ammunition pouches needed to be clipped to the front of the harness, one on each side of the chest. There was brass-work all over the webbing, which we started to clean, once our helpers had finished assisting us with the assembly process. But cleaning the brass-work wasn't the only part of the preparation. There seemed to be square yards of webbing that needed to be blancoed, otherwise we wouldn't pass inspection. Somehow, we managed to get it all done before the time came to go on parade in the Drill Shed with our fellow *janker wallahs*. We got a great send-off from the other boys in the billet, which cheered us up as we struggled along the road to the Drill Shed, under the weight of the webbing and items that we were required to carry in its various packs.

A *janker wallah* was, and probably still is, a slang word often used in the RAF for someone unfortunate enough to be on Defaulters' Parade. The word *wallah* is a Hindu word that was probably assimilated into the military vocabulary during the time of the British presence in India. It means a "fellow" who performs some type of menial activity. For example, a man who launders clothing and bed linen is known as a *dhobi wallah*— "*dhobi*" being another Hindu word meaning "laundry". Similarly, a person assigned to make tea is known as a *char wallah.* Jankers, whilst not being performed as a service to others, somehow attracted *wallah* as a companion word. And although the root of *wallah* is known, the origin of the word *jankers* is not.

The Defaulters' Parade was conducted by the Orderly Officer, assisted by the Orderly Sergeant. Different junior officers and senior NCOs were assigned to fulfill these duties on a daily basis. Defaulters' Parade was just a small part of their overall responsibilities. Other duties included handling and managing incidents that occurred on the camp outside of normal operating hours; raising the flag in the morning and lowering it again at sunset; supervising mealtimes in the Boy Entrant messes and of course making sure that *janker wallahs* were appropriately occupied in performing fatigues during their confinement to camp.

When Butterworth and I arrived at the Drill Shed, we formed up with the twenty or so other defaulters in three ranks.

At 1830 hours, the Orderly Sergeant took up his position in front of our three ranks and commanded, "Defaulters," followed by a slight pause before continuing, "Defaulters attention! Right dress."

We shuffled around for a few moments, getting an arm's length spacing between each other. Then, when the shuffling stopped, the Orderly Sergeant called out "Eyes front."

We stood at attention, staring straight ahead for a few moments, before receiving the next order, "Defaulters! For inspection, open order march!"

Smartly, both front and rear ranks took the necessary one pace forward or backwards to open up the ranks. Then the sergeant turned to face the Orderly Officer, who was waiting a short distance away.

The Orderly Sergeant threw up a smart salute as he addressed the officer, "Defaulters ready for inspection, *Sir*!"

The sergeant held his salute until the officer walked forward the few paces necessary to bring him to an arm's length distance from the sergeant, before returning the salute.

"Thank you sergeant," he responded in a normal speaking voice.

With that, the officer walked to the end of the front rank which was nearest to him and began inspecting us, followed closely by the sergeant. His inspection was detailed and meticulous, taking several minutes for each person. Apart from checking our buttons and boots, the officer also ordered several of the defaulters to reveal the contents of their small pack, their large pack, or their water bottle. It was a requirement that each of these contain certain specific items: the large pack was supposed to contain certain articles of clothing such as shirts and underwear, whilst the small pack was required to contain toiletry items and the brushes that we used to clean our buttons and boots and of course the water bottle needed to be filled with clean fresh water. Only the ammunition pouches were to be left empty. Any *janker wallah* unlucky enough to be found wanting of any of these mandatory items would probably be placed on another charge. It was common barrack-room wisdom that it was a very difficult accomplishment to finish the original "award" of jankers and avoid being put on another charge, during the usual course of these defaulters' inspections. More often than not, the original award became a self-perpetuating vicious circle, because the risk of getting even more days of punishment seemed to increase exponentially with the length of time that a person remained on jankers. Much depended on the mood and personality of the daily Orderly Officer and Orderly Sergeant, many of whom took their duties very seriously with regard to defaulters, often to the point of mean-spiritedness.

Happily, Butterworth and I both managed to sail through the inspection that night. After the parade, we performed an hour of fatigues in the mess, scraping congealed gravy from greasy cooking pans, before taking a one-hour break and then going back on parade at 2100 hours. There was no inspection during this short parade, since its main purpose was simply to inconvenience us and make sure that we weren't out somewhere having fun. With that, we came to the end of our single, solitary day of CC. Had we been unlucky enough to have been "awarded" more than one day of punishment, it would have been necessary for us to report to the Guardroom early next morning for the first parade of the day, and to perform some fatigues, before returning to the billets for the workshops parade. Indeed we had been let off lightly on our first charge, but not so the next time, nor the countless times after that.

Back at workshops we progressed through our training, covering topics such as "Instruments", during which we learned how voltmeters and ammeters worked. We then progressed on to "Aircraft Wiring", during which we were taught familiarity with the different types of electrical wire used on the aircraft of that era. Our instructor for that topic, Mr. Edridge, involved us in practical work to help the learning process along, which turned out to be typical of the overall instructional technique as our training advanced.

For this particular topic, we were each assigned to bench-mounted panels on which several types of the small cockpit lights, switches and terminal blocks had been mounted. These components were typical of aircraft of that time: lamps with red bulbs for general cockpit lighting that didn't compromise the pilot's night vision and ultra-violet lights that caused the indicators and numbers on the cockpit instruments to glow when the other cockpit lighting was turned off. The ultra-violet effect had even less of an effect than the red lighting on the crew's ability to see into the outside darkness during night flights. The task before us was to wire up the lamps, using information from a simple wiring diagram. The work gave us practical experience in reading and using the information available in wiring diagrams. It also helped us to develop the skills of cutting the wire to size and stripping back its insulation in the manner we'd been taught, before connecting it securely to the correct terminal screws. I had to borrow a screwdriver from someone else to make the connections. For some inexplicable reason, my screwdriver was found to be missing during the pre-work tool-check ritual.

In fact, quite a few of my tools seemed to be missing and I wasn't the only one: many of the other boys complained that tools were missing from their tool kits also. This discovery was unfortunately accompanied by the bad news that those of us with missing tools were going to be docked some money from our pay, to cover the cost of replacing them. It seemed as though some funny business was going on—our tools were going missing when they were supposed to be in Corporal Simpson's safekeeping. Could there be a connection? We started speaking up about this to anyone in authority who would listen.

I finished wiring my panel and then raised my hand to let Mr. Edridge know, but by this time he had several others already waiting to have their completed work inspected. If Mr. Edridge was satisfied with their wiring, he rewarded them by turning on the 24 volts D.C. power supply to their panels. These early birds were then able to savour the satisfaction of operating the switches they had wired up on their panels and see the results of their handiwork when the cockpit lighting illuminated. The circuits also included dimmer switches that enabled the brightness of the lighting to be adjusted, which gave the lucky few something to play around with, in addition to simply switching the lights on and off. Something about my wiring didn't meet with Mr. Edridge's approval, which meant that I had some rewiring to do before getting his approval and the application of the power supply. Finally, I got it right and was then able to proudly light my lights and tweak them through all the intervening intensities between dim and bright.

Although we had the impression that our complaints about tools mysteriously and systematically going missing were being ignored, we were wrong. One day, at the beginning of a workshop practice session, two other corporal instructors took us through the tool check procedure, whilst Corporal "Gummy" Simpson was very conspicuous by his absence. I could tell from the whispered comments passing between the two corporals each time they discovered that not everyone possessed each category of tool, that there was more than the usual emphasis on what was missing. By this time, most of my tools had disappeared and the tool-bag felt embarrassingly light. When a few of the boys began to sense that something was in the air, they strongly protested that their tool-bags were being systematically looted when the bags weren't in their possession. Very soon, most of us jumped on the bandwagon and echoed the same protestations. The corporals conducting the tool check openly sympathized and, to our relief, informed us that we wouldn't have to pay for the missing tools. A few days later, we heard that Gummy Simpson had been charged with stealing the tools. Apparently, he unlawfully retained duplicate keys to our tool-bag locks and had been using them to open various bags and remove tools, which he then sold at a local market. For him, it was more than just being awarded jankers because he had used his position of trust as an NCO and instructor to commit theft. Corporal Simpson quickly disappeared from St. Athan and we never heard exactly what became of him. But he was most probably demoted to the ranks, possibly spent some time "inside" and most certainly had to pay restitution for the tools that he had stolen and sold. We, on the other hand, had our tool kits fully replenished with the items that had gone missing and never lost any more after that.

* * *

On the 14th of February, St. Valentine's Day, the 30th Entry was inducted into the Royal Air Force Boy Entrant Training Scheme. In doing so, they relieved and replaced the 29th Entry from the unenviable position of being the lowest form of life to crawl on the earth.

CHAPTER 7

Farewell to the 26th

After the first few weeks, life in the Wings settled down into a regular routine. Whilst discipline remained strict, there seemed more of a willingness on the part of the authorities to treat us as thinking individuals. We no longer suffered from the "herd instinct" mentality that seemed to have featured so prominently during our time in the Initial Training Squadron. This was most evident at mealtimes, especially during the midday meal when we observed the 30th entry going through the same painful introduction to Boy Entrant life that we had only recently suffered ourselves.

Instead of being marched to the mess, as we were during our time in ITS and then participating in the ensuing mad stampede to be avoid being last in the queue, we were marched to our billets instead. This gave us the individual freedom to casually stroll a short distance to the mess and have our meal at any time during the allotted midday break. Usually, most of us wanted to find out if we had mail, or perhaps visit the toilet, before going to the mess. The advantage in doing this was that it allowed time for the queue to die down, which meant less time standing in line waiting to be served. By way of contrast, the ITS boys were marched to the mess and dismissed *en masse*, precipitating a giddy race for a place near the head of the queue. And, as in life, the race always went to the swift.

The mess was actually split into two halves. The Initial Training Squadron had one half all to themselves, whilst we in the Wings had the other half. One of the reasons that it was beneficial for me to wait for a while before going to the mess had to do with the seniority culture of the entries. One of the senior entry privileges that the 26th wielded was the right to move to the head of the queue for meals in the mess and ahead of everyone else, except other senior entry members. The pecking order proceeded from there; members of the 27th could move ahead of the 28th, who in turn, could move ahead of the 29th. Since we were the junior entry, we found ourselves perpetually at the end of the line. At first, having been used to the free-for-all in ITS, I began to object when this happened to me, but only until I caught sight of the chevrons on the cuff of the other person's sleeve that marked him as a member of an entry senior to mine. At that point, my objection would wither on the vine and I would reluctantly make room for the senior person to squeeze into line in front of me. It therefore paid for me not to go to the mess immediately on being dismissed at mealtimes, but to wait instead for the queue to become shorter. This meant being served a meal much quicker and with less risk of having someone pushing into the line in front of me.

Entry seniority culture was unfair and the recollection of it would trouble my sense of fair play when I had matured to adulthood, but at that time it was the nature of the world we lived in. It was the unwritten law that an entry member had precedence over those in entries junior to him, but he deferred to those in entries that were senior to his. The proficiency stripes on the cuff of our tunics indicated the level of seniority. Three stripes identified the wearer as a senior entry member, which was the 26th when we first became the junior entry. The next entry in seniority sported two stripes, as worn by the 27th who were the next entry in line of succession and one stripe by the 28th. We of the 29th, just being new to the Wings and not having taken any proficiency tests as yet, were devoid of stripes. So, although we now wielded some puny seniority over the ITS boys, anyone with a stripe on his cuff could and would push into the queue ahead of us, two-stripers would push in ahead of the one-stripers and the senior entry would go straight to the head of the line.

The seniority system also extended to the Astra camp cinema. The senior entry occupied the rear rows of seats and junior entry members knew very well not to sit there. The lesson was driven home with each new ITS intake, when several sprogs would learn the hard way that their place was on the front rows. Although there was no set number of rows reserved for any specific entry, the rule was that if any senior entry members sat in a particular row, it immediately became exclusively reserved for them. Any lesser entry members already occupying seats in that row were obliged to move—or else! Of course, the 27th didn't allow less junior entries to sit in rows that they had taken over and so it flowed on down the pecking order to the front rows where, if the cinema was full, the ITS kids were forced to crane their necks back at an uncomfortable angle to view the flat distorted images on the screen. Luckily for them, it wasn't too crowded most of the time.

But there is an exception to every rule and the exception in this case was Marianne (which is not her real name), who could sit in any row she chose.

There were two performances per evening at the Astra: the early show catered to Boy Entrants, who were subject to "lights out" at an early hour. The later performance was aimed at the adult camp staff and their families, who understandably avoided the early performance. Marianne, however, seemed to prefer attending the early performances. She wasn't an adult, but just a teenager of around 16 years old like ourselves. Needless to say, her female presence in that all-male, teenage, testosterone-charged environment was polarizing to say the least.

Marianne usually sat about a dozen rows back from the screen where a wide aisle traversed the cinema. This allowed her to stretch out her long legs and provide many of us with the kind of view that maintained our interest until the house lights went down and the film began. Most of the time, she wore provocative short skirts and clothing that was intended for women a few years older and on top of that, her makeup was very much overdone for someone of her years. Rumour had it that she was an officer's daughter who lived with her family in Officers' Married Quarters. But the really exciting rumour concerning Marianne was that she had a "reputation". It was whispered around in hushed, confidential tones that she was a "sure thing" and the tales of her exploits with any number of Boy Entrants were legendary. Strangely, it was always someone who knew someone who had heard that someone had been "all the way" with her and how eager she had been to cooperate.

If Marianne chose to attend the first sitting at the Astra for the sole purpose of meeting boys, it didn't seem to work very well for her. In fact, most of the time it seemed that she sat alone for the simple reason that few of us had the courage or the confidence to approach her. But occasionally a brave lad would throw caution to the winds to go and sit next to her. This move was generally accompanied by cheers, jeers, catcalls and explicit offers of advice from those of us who were made of less courageous stuff. Bill from my billet, who was coincidentally in the 29th entry, was one such person. I'm not sure whether it was an act of blatant bravado on his part, or his reaction to the irresistible attraction of the opposite sex, but at least he waited until the house lights went down before making his move and slipping into the seat beside her. Perhaps he hoped to avoid detection by waiting until then, but his sly move failed to go unnoticed and the usual great cheer went up from those in the immediate vicinity who witnessed it. The cheer set off a loud buzz of interest that spread around the dark, cavernous interior like wildfire. Interest then faded for a while, as everyone became more interested at what was happening up on the screen, but the catcalls resumed with a vengeance when the lights came up for an intermission prior to the screening of the main feature. Bill, to his credit, turned around, looked at the chanting faces and just grinned in a way that said, "Don't you envious bastards just all wish you were sitting here instead of me?" Of course he was right—we both envied and hated him in equal quantities.

He and Marianne left together before the film ended, but this didn't go unnoticed either and their departure was accompanied by another huge cheer as he escorted her out by way of a side aisle.

Later that evening, when Bill returned to the billet we crowded around him, wanting to know all the lurid details. He was grinning from ear to ear and milking the moment for all it was worth as he proudly described how far he had been able to get—that is, if we were to believe his whole story.

Physically, the Astra occupied the north end of the drill hall and gymnasium structure. Apart from a neon sign above the main entrance, its rows of utilitarian theatre seating inside and the curtained stage that supported the silver screen, it bore little resemblance to the plush cinemas in the external civilian world. The walls were of plain brick that had been painted a drab yellow and above our heads the skeletal steel trusses that supported the roof lacked the benefit of a false ceiling to modestly cover their nakedness. The acoustics were dismal, but it didn't really matter very much given the juvenile fare, such as "I Was a Teenage Werewolf", that was served up to the eager Boy Entrant audiences.

The price of admission was very reasonable, at around one shilling, which was much cheaper than those same plush civvy cinemas. But that didn't stop some people from trying to sneak in without paying anything at all. One of the several dodges employed to this end depended on someone actually buying a ticket. Once inside he would make his way to the toilet, where he unlatched and opened a window, allowing several of his friends to climb inside. Another more elaborate scheme took advantage of a management blind spot. Cinemagoers were permitted to temporarily leave during the intermission to buy snacks at the YMCA across the street. Re-admittance was based on a cursory inspection of the torn off ticket stub as proof that a ticket had been purchased. Little did the Management suspect that a few wily lads were busily retrieving discarded ticket stubs from the cinema floor and then taking them to the YM at intermission time. There, they either gave the stubs to friends or sold them to eager buyers at a discount price. With all this going on, I just wonder if the St. Athan Astra was ever able to make a profit during the Boy Entrant era.

The Astra was more than a place of entertainment. Occasionally, we were marched there to view educational films that acquainted us with the horrors of venereal disease, or VD as it was more commonly known. All of the films, which had been made by the US military authorities for their own military, graphically featured stomach-churning close-up views of the symptoms of unpleasant sexually transmitted diseases such as syphilis and gonorrhoea. As the images flitted across the screen, an American narrator warned us about the risk of catching these terrible diseases if we didn't "take precautions", whilst most of us were thinking that we weren't lucky enough to even be slightly at risk of catching any of them. Fortunately, the films were in black and white, which at least meant we were spared the horror of having to view the graphic symptoms in full colour.

Later in the billet, when we told the senior entry boys where we had been, one of them smirkingly told us that it was common knowledge in the service that only very senior officers or padres caught VD from a toilet seat—everyone else got it the old fashioned way. Topics like this that centred on sex were endlessly fascinating for a mere 16-year-old.

In fact, my 16th birthday occurred in February, shortly after going into the Wings. I got a small parcel from home and one from Aunt Maggie, both of which contained sweets. When the other boys saw this, they immediately guessed the reason. I was then quickly hustled outside and tossed in a blanket sixteen times—and one for luck—to mark the occasion. I had protested loudly, but several strong arms grabbed me, while someone pulled one of the blankets out of my bed-pack. Outside, the blanket was spread out and the corners grasped by four individuals. I was then dumped unceremoniously into the middle, only to have my feet quickly jerked out from under me as the lads pulled upwards on the corners, tossing me into the air and then catching me in the blanket as I came down. Going up wasn't so bad, but they deliberately allowed my rear-end to make contact with the ground on each downward trip. I laughed along with everyone else, but suffered a painfully bruised bum for several days afterwards.

* * *

Safety precaution lectures in our education curriculum weren't confined only to the remote possibility of extra-curricular activities. There were other dangers that we would come across when working in and around military aircraft. Our technical training therefore required that we become intimately familiar with the lethal systems that we would almost certainly encounter later, when we were dispersed from Boy Entrant service to work on operational aircraft. The most obvious dangers were aircraft weapons systems—guns, bombs and missiles—but there was one other dangerous system with which we were more likely to come into frequent contact that wasn't actually a weapon, although it could be every bit as lethal. Ironically, it was (and still is) an item of so-called safety equipment. This is the ejection seat—the system of last resort that saves the lives of aircrew members by rapidly removing them from a stricken jet aircraft when all else fails. Since we were expected to work in the cockpit around ejection seats within very restricted spaces, it was essential that we knew how the seat operated and how to ensure it was safe.

Western military aircraft equipped with ejections seats display a warning on their exterior in the form of a red inverted triangle with the words "Ejection Seat" printed in white letters within the triangle and the word "Danger" printed around its three sides. The warning is not an overstatement because, although intended to save the life of the person sitting in it, the seat can very easily kill or, at the very minimum, severely injure anyone who behaves carelessly on coming into close contact with it. On being activated, this amazing piece of equipment performs a number of actions that taken together will safely preserve the seat occupant's life. Yet the general public knows very little about it, other than brief stories in the media that might typically state something along the lines of "the pilot ejected safely".

Simply stated, the ejection seat is mounted on a large gun that shoots the seat out of the aircraft when its occupant activates the firing mechanism, usually immediately on having decided that something has gone so badly wrong that the plane has become uncontrollable and is doomed to crash. But that's just the beginning of the story and not the end. As soon as the initial ejection has occurred, the seat takes on its role as a life support system, performing several necessary actions that culminate in the seat's occupant being returned safely back to earth.

From the inception of the ejection seat, RAF aircraft have been equipped exclusively with those provided by the Martin Baker Company—the company that pioneered the original concept and development of the seat.

As an electrical mechanic in training, my ejection seat education consisted only of familiarization because, as the armament instructor patronizingly informed us, "You electrical people will no doubt be disappointed to learn that there isn't a single electrical device on any part of this seat." By that time, the ejection seat had already benefited from considerable development and new aircraft were equipped with models such as the Mark V or Mark VI. Understandably, however, these up-to-date models weren't available for us to "boy entrantize" them, which meant that we had to be trained on a much earlier model known as the Mark II. Using a disarmed seat as an instruction aid, our instructor explained that from the moment of initiation, the entire operation became a self-sustaining process from ejection until the pilot's parachute landed him safely on the ground.

As has already been mentioned, the reason that people such as us needed to be familiar with an ejection seat's potential danger, and be able to behave in a knowledgably safe manner when around one, was because of the likelihood that we would come into close contact with armed ejection seats in the performance of our everyday duties. There was also another reason. Part of our job would probably involve assisting aircrew members to strap into an ejection seat and help them to get out of it at the end of a sortie. We therefore had to be capable of arming the seat just before flight and making it safe when the aircraft returned. This meant being able to tell at a glance whether or not the seat was "safe" by looking for the safety pins.

Understandably, the intensive and frequent training on ejection seats was very important, even though as electricians we had no direct role in their maintenance. The training didn't stop when we left Boy Entrants' service and took our place in the regular RAF. As new marks of seat were introduced, we would always receive training before being permitted to come into contact with them.

* * *

As January and February gave way to March, our routine remained the same: Workshops during the week, a day out in Barry on Saturdays and church parade on Sundays.

It was on one of those Sundays, just as I stood up to leave the church after Mass had ended, that I was surprised to hear a female voice suddenly exclaim my name: "Brian Carlin?"

There was something vaguely familiar about the voice, but I couldn't quite place it until I turned around and recognized a long-time family friend from my home parish making her way up the aisle towards me, against the crush of people intent on leaving the church. Her name was Maureen Doherty and although she was a few years older than me, there was a connection. We had both gone to St. Malachy's school, as had both of our mothers before us. What's more, they had been good friends during their school years and the friendship continued through their adult years. I had also been in the same class as Maureen's younger brother John, from when we had both started school until we left. Maureen had moved away from Coleraine to become a nursing sister, some years prior to this encounter and I had vaguely followed her career because John had always eagerly bragged, to anyone who would listen, each time she achieved some particularly notable career milestone.

On seeing that I recognized her, she spoke my name again: "Brian Carlin!" This time it was with more certainty and an edge of pleased excitement. "I never expected to see you here!"

I responded by letting her know that I was just as surprised to see her and then happily answered her questions, telling her when I had arrived at St. Athan and what I was being trained for. Maureen was in civilian clothes, but an officer in a Squadron Leader's uniform stood closely behind her. She turned and introduced him as her husband. We then talked for several minutes, exchanging information about our families. I learned that although she had served as a nursing sister in Princess Mary's Royal Air Force Nursing Service, she had now retired from military service and lived in Officers' Married Quarters with her Squadron Leader husband.

"You'll have to come over for tea sometime," Maureen said.

"Yes, that would be nice," I replied, but it was about the last thing on earth I wanted to do. Going to the officers' "married patch" would be like walking the gauntlet for a Boy Entrant. I could hardly imagine a less comfortable situation than having tea with a Squadron Leader in his home, although I genuinely appreciated her offer.

After that, we would meet at Mass every Sunday and always have a brief chat. This went on for several months until one day she confided that her husband had received a posting to another station. We wished each other well and said our goodbyes. Sadly, we lost touch after that.

* * *

Bleak winter weather slowly gave way to less bone-chilling days, as the green shoots of spring began to make their welcome appearance on the stark skeletal trees that dotted the camp. Instead of marching head down with teeth clenched against driving sleet and rain that drove in mercilessly from the Bristol Channel, it became a pleasure to hold my head up and savour the cool clear sunlit air of the new season.

By this time, members of the 26th entry were beginning to prepare for their passing out parade. They had been issued with white webbing belts and rifle slings for the all-important ceremony and were spending much of their time between parade rehearsals applying fresh coats of white blanco to the webbing, polishing brasses until it seemed they might wear the yellow metal away and bulling their boots to such a mirror shine that the inspecting officer would have no trouble seeing his face in their reflection. The 26th entry boys in my billet performed these chores as a labour of love. The amount of care needed to achieve the desired standard of perfection was much too important to be entrusted to mere bull boys and, more importantly, all of the blancoing and polishing for the last great hurrah was filled with a great amount of symbolism that needed to be experienced by the lucky graduate himself. For a change the senior entry were performing many of the personal bull tasks that up until now had been dumped on the junior entry. We would have a short respite until the 26th had passed out. The 27th would then, unfortunately, want to exercise their new senior entry privilege, so we would continue to be bull boys for new masters until the 30th entry came up to the Wings from ITS.

In the last few days as Boy Entrants, the graduating entry members were issued with the new badges of rank they would be entitled to wear just as soon as the pass-out parade was over. Most Boy Entrants passed out with the rank of Leading Aircraftsman (LAC), signified by a two-bladed propeller embroidered in light blue silk on a blue cloth backing. This badge was worn on both arms, with the blades of the propeller aligned horizontally. In addition, the senior entry boys had been taken to the clothing store where each had been fitted out with a new battle dress that would be their normal daily working uniform on entering the "men's service".

The most significant feature of this new uniform was its waist-length blue serge jacket, known as a blouse, which fitted snugly at the waist but ballooned out from there to fit loosely around the upper body. Although its name might conjure up the mental picture of a female shirt-like garment, it had little similarity to a woman's blouse. Because it was derived from a uniform that was literally used in battle, the jacket lacked the highly visible brass buttons featured on our Boy Entrant tunics. Instead, a row of ordinary black buttons, concealed within a flap, fastened the battle dress blouse at the front. The only two visible buttons were those that fastened the breast pocket flaps. These latter two bore the eagle and crown motif, but were made of a dull black plastic material. This was in deference to the concept of a battledress uniform, which avoided light-reflecting components, such as shiny brass buttons, that would give away the wearer's position on the battlefield. The thought of finding ourselves in actual battle didn't really ever cross our minds. For us, the most important aspect of wearing a battle dress was the achievement of "airman" status, but a close second was the added bonus of finally being freed from the chore of having to clean brass buttons every day as part of our normal routine.

The proudest moment for each and every boy entrant was taking part in his entry's passing out parade. Everything that had gone before led up to this highly ceremonial occasion. The parade was considered so important that it was presided over by a very high-ranking officer, such as an Air Vice Marshal, who would review the graduating entry. He would then take the salute during the exhilarating climax to the graduation ceremony when the entry marched past the reviewing stand, symbolically passing from boy's service into the "real" air force. Parents of the graduates were invited to witness the ceremony, so that they too could share in this proud event with their sons. The parents were provided with overnight accommodation in a block of billets across the road from the main gate. It wasn't The Ritz by any means—they slept in the same type of beds and surroundings that we accepted as the norm. The experience probably gave them an idea of the conditions in which their sons had become accustomed to living for the past eighteen months. Of course, the males were segregated in separate billets from the females and the only small concession was that they weren't expected to make up their own beds. No prizes are offered here for guessing who actually made up those beds. Yes, it was yours truly in a working party with several other non-senior entry boys. We all volunteered: one of our corporals came along and said, "I need a few volunteers, you, you and you…"

On the day of the parade, 9 April, 1957, we of the non-graduating entries were assembled in squadrons and marched on to the parade ground, keeping in step to the music of the Station Band. Well almost! Initially, we were quite some distance away from the parade ground, where the Station Band was located. Because of the intervening distance between us and the band, the rhythmic booms of the base drum that we heard were mixed with its echoes, as the sound waves bounced off the surrounding buildings. Instead of a strong beat that we could keep time with as we marched, our ears picked up a confusing mixture of double and triple beats, making it impossible to sort out the real beat from the echoes. To prevent us from tripping over one another, the NCOs in charge of the squadrons were forced to call out the step until we got close enough to where the drumbeat was loud enough to drown out its own echoes. The NCOs ceased calling out the step as we marched on to the Square, bringing us to a halt at pre-determined positions. Still carrying our rifles with fixed bayonets at the slope arms position, we were ordered into line abreast and then commanded to order arms before being given the "stand easy" to await the Senior Entry's triumphant entrance onto stage centre.

And finally they came—led by the combined Boy Entrant Trumpet Band—the morning light glinting off the shiny stainless steel of their bayonets and with the gleaming whiteness of their webbing belts and rifle slings signifying their hard-won status: the stars of this long-awaited ceremony. The wearing of white webbing was a special privilege granted to the graduating entry as a mark of honour, in contrast to the normal undistinguished-looking blue-grey webbing worn by the "supporting" entries. As they drew nearer I was able to see that they somehow managed to look proud, smug and happy all at the same time. I'm certain that I wasn't alone in wishing that I was also marching in that proud, happy group, but this wasn't our moment of fame. It would be several months and two more attendances at similar ceremonies before the 29th entry could be the bride instead of a bridesmaid.

The 26th came to a halt in the centre of the Square, in two formations that represented No. 1 Wing and No. 2 Wing. They were then given the command to order arms and stand at ease by their Flight Sergeant Boy Entrant, who would now have the high honour of being the Parade Commander.

When an entry achieved Senior Entry status, one of the small number of Corporal Boys in each of the four squadrons was selected to be the Sergeant Boy for his particular squadron. The selection was made on the basis of trade proficiency, leadership qualities, appearance and an exemplary record of good conduct. Of the four Sergeant Boys, only one would eventually be elevated to the highest rank—that of Flight Sergeant Boy. The promotion came late in the entry's life and was deliberately timed to coincide with the imminent passing out parade. The rank was in fact an honour bestowed for the best all round performance by a boy entrant. The recipient was granted the awesome privilege of leading his entry's passing out parade in his role of Parade Commander. Needless to say, competition for this exalted rank was extremely fierce between the four Sergeant Boys and included tryouts on the parade ground to assess which of them would best fill the Parade Commander role. We lesser mortals didn't have to concern ourselves too much with this competition, since it was played out in the rarefied atmosphere to which we didn't aspire, but there was a small measure of reflected glory in belonging to the squadron that begat the Flight Sergeant Boy for any given entry. The honour fell to one of the other squadrons for the 26th entry's passing-out parade, so there was no glory to be had for 3 Squadron this time around. But our turn would come next time around, although it was still three and a half months in the future, when our own Dave Williams of the 27th entry would win the honour of wearing the small gold Flight Sergeant Boy's crown above his three stripes.

The Flight Sergeant Boy now called the parade to attention. Meanwhile, the Duty Orderly Sergeant waited at the base of the flagpole, holding the Royal Air Force ensign that was attached to the lanyard by which he would hoist it to the top of the flagstaff at the given signal. For a few seconds, there was an unearthly silence following the loud crunching noise of multiple boots stamping in unison on gravel, as the parade came to attention. In this quiet aftermath, the Parade Commander's chest swelled as he drew in a deep breath. Then the silence was broken.

"Slope arms!" He bawled, his chest returning to normal size as he forcefully expended the air from his lungs across his vocal chords.

To a man, we all responded by shouldering our rifles. The Parade Commander took another few seconds to survey the scene, seeming to savour the heady feeling of his power. Then, taking another deep breath, he bellowed, "General salute—present arms!"

The Parade responded by bringing rifles into the Present Arms position. This drill movement was characteristically noisy, caused by the sound of many hands slapping twice in succession against the rifles, as we transferred them from our shoulders into a vertical position, front and centre of our bodies. The simultaneous crunch of many left boots stamping into an angled position behind the right heel punctuated the final part of the Present Arms movement. The Parade Commander now performed an about-turn and snapped up a stiff salute in the direction of the flagpole. At the same time, the Station Band struck up with a rendition of the Royal Air Force anthem. We held the Present Arms and the band continued to play as the Royal Air Force ensign was raised to the tip of the angled jib that jutted out from the main pole, from where it waved gracefully in the light breeze that wafted across the Square. At that point, the Orderly Sergeant, still holding the lanyard on which he had raised the flag, snapped both arms to his sides in the position of attention. The band ceased playing, whereupon the Flight Sergeant Boy called out, "Paraaade…slo-ope arms," whilst simultaneously snapping his saluting arm back down to his side.

When an air of silence replaced the staccato sounds of the slope arms drill movement, the Flight Sergeant Boy Parade Commander gave the command to order arms. This initiated another brief round of rifle-slapping, gravel-crunching noises, followed by a brief silence that was broken only by the small sound of gravel being ground as the Parade Commander swivelled around in an about-turn to face us. Squaring himself up, he then ordered us to stand at ease whilst remaining at attention himself; he then performed another about-turn that brought him around to face the flag once more, before standing himself at ease. We now awaited the arrival of the Reviewing Officer.

We hadn't been waiting long before a large, immaculately gleaming black car, flying the distinctive flag of an Air Vice Marshal, glided slowly along the road towards us from the direction of Station Headquarters. When it reached the first entrance to the Square, the car turned and motored onto the hallowed ground, a white wispy plume of exhaust now visibly swirling around behind it. The car drew level with the saluting dais and eased to a stop. A sergeant stepped forward and used his left hand to open the rear passenger door, whilst saluting with his right, as an Air Vice Marshal emerged from his seat within the car and straightened up. He was resplendent in his full dress uniform, complete with ceremonial sword, medals and the small cruciform insignia of a knighthood that dangled from a ribbon around his neck to rest on the knot of his tie. The Air Vice Marshal was immediately approached by the Parade Commander, who marched up to him with a stiff jerky gait, coming to complete halt before throwing up an equally stiff salute. The AVM returned the salute in a casually relaxed manner and then briefly exchanged some words with the parade commander. Meanwhile, the car that had delivered him now glided smoothly away and off the Square, its wispy little exhaust plume fluttering behind like a puppy's wagging tail. With the initial pleasantries observed, the AVM turned and with an easy grace climbed the three steps to the dais, brought himself around to face the parade and then stopped in a position of attention. Once again, the Parade Commander ordered a General Salute and the band struck up with a fanfare to welcome the distinguished visitor, who returned the salute in the same casual manner as before by gently touching the fingertips of his right hand to his temple.

At the conclusion of the general salute, after which we had been stood easy and then brought to attention a few more times, the Parade Commander informed the AVM in loud, clipped military enunciation, "The 26th entry is ready for inspection, sir!"

With that, the AVM descended from the dais to perform his role of Reviewing Officer and after having observed a few preliminaries, went about the business of inspecting the 26th entry. This was the most tedious part of the whole process, during which everyone on parade was obliged to stand perfectly still for a very long time—although the Station Band lightened the monotony a little, by playing a variety of martial music as the inspection progressed.

We had been taught not to move out of place whilst on parade, but to raise our heels slightly off the ground from time to time to relieve pressure. It was usually during this part of a parade that a number of people would pass out in a rather different manner from that which was intended. This "passing out" was with eyes closed and mouth gaping open, as their knees sagged and they sank to the ground like a loosely-bagged sack of potatoes. Someone, usually the person standing next to them, would break ranks to assist the unfortunate individual back to his feet and then escort him to the rear of the parade ground where medics stood by to render first aid in the form of a glass of water. It was considered a stroke of good luck to have the person beside you faint on parade. If you possessed enough alertness to move quickly, it was possible to be first person to reach him and render assistance. The reward for this selflessly noble gesture was the opportunity of stretching your own legs as you gently helped the poor fellow off the parade ground.

Finally, the inspection was over. Salutes and inaudible words were exchanged between the Parade Commander and the Reviewing Officer and then it was time for the 26th entry's triumphant march past. In a normal colour raising parade, every squadron would march past the reviewing stand, but on this occasion only the graduating entry would have that honour. We of the lesser entries, on the other hand, had one final task to perform before the parade could end. Both squadrons of the boys who would soon be men were brought smartly to attention and given the command to right-turn. The gravel crunched as something like a hundred pairs of boots swivelled to face in the new direction, immediately followed by the loud report of their other boots stamping down in forceful contact with the parade-ground surface. The order to march was called out and the Boy Entrant Trumpet Band struck up with a special march composed especially for the 26th entry's pass-out. The marching squadrons headed off in a direction away from, but parallel with, the reviewing stand. Meanwhile, we of the supporting squadrons were marched into two formations that faced each other across several yards and were perpendicular to the dais.

When the first squadron of 26th neared the edge of the parade ground, they were ordered to "left wheel". But they had hardly started marching in the new direction before another command ordered them to "advance in review order, left turn". The squadron, as one man, made a marching turn that transformed them from a long column into three ranks marching line abreast. This took them in a new direction; directly past the reviewing stand where the Reviewing Officer waited, left hand resting on the hilt of the sword that hung in its scabbard at his side. As the first squadron neared the dais, an order was given to "slow march". The members of the squadron checked their right arms to their sides and immediately made the transition to "slow time". Nearer to the dais, the Parade Commander, marching at the front and centre of the first squadron, called out the order, "Eyeee-sss right!"

Every head but two turned smartly to the right and at the same time the parade commander's right arm snapped up into a salute, which he held as the squadron continued marching past the reviewing stand. The only people who continued looking straight ahead were the marker and guide at the end of the front and rear ranks nearest the reviewing stand. It was their job to keep the squadron heading forward in a straight line and at the same time provide a reference that the other marchers needed to enable them to maintain the alignment along the ranks. As they passed the Reviewing Officer, he returned the salute and held it until the squadron had completely passed the front of the dais. Then it was "Eyeee-sss front!" and all heads snapped back to the forward-looking position. The first squadron marched a little way farther in the line abreast formation, as the second squadron repeated the 'slow march' and 'eyes-right' behind them, then the first squadron was given the order to 'quick march' before changing from line-abreast to 'column-of-route', which meant another marching turn to bring them into column formation once more. Another left wheel was ordered to bring them back towards the starting point, but by now we had formed the Guard of Honour on either side of their route off the Square. As they approached, we were ordered to 'present arms' and so they passed between our ranks with such wide smiles on their damned smug faces that it was sickening to those of us who would still have to suffer through several more months of boy entrant life before we would be in the same enviable position.

Following their passing-out parade, the 26th didn't waste too much time in shaking the dust of St. Athan off their feet. That afternoon, groups of people attired in brand new battle dress, adorned with brand new LAC insignia, could be seen making their way around the station. They clutched blue clearance cards in their hands and wore broad smiles across their faces that would probably take several weeks to fade away. Gone were the colourful wheel badges and the coloured discs from behind their RAF beret hat badges. The chequered hatbands had also been removed from their SD hats and replaced by standard black RAF hatbands, which by their very mediocrity helped signify the wearer's elevated status to the regular RAF service.

By late afternoon the now ex-26th had all cleared the station to enjoy a few weeks of well deserved leave before reporting to their new stations for real-life duty. Their passing left a power vacuum at St. Athan, but already the 27th were feeling the heady scent of long awaited Senior Entry status. That evening, they publicly claimed their inherited kingdom by noisily parading through the camp singing and shouting slogans in praise of their entry. Worse was to follow later, after lights out.

We were back to the dark times of nightly raids and bed tipping, but this time it was a little worse. When we had arrived into the Wings, the 26th had already enjoyed the first fruits of senior entry status, so although we had suffered through some billet raids after lights-out, the novelty had already started to wear off for them. Now, with the 27th, we were going to experience it from its infancy and that was much worse than our tribulations under the 26th. For one thing, we were no longer a bunch of anonymous sprogs whose faces were nothing more than a blur. Many of us, yours truly included, had managed to piss off more than a few of the 27th during our short time in the Wings, for reasons real or imagined. They knew who we were, they knew where we lived and they had bided their time until now.

On that first night of the 27th's ascendancy to senior entry, a huge raid took place and this time prisoners were taken! I could hear their feet pounding on the floorboards of the corridor towards our billet, but not just feet and muffled voices. The raiders were calling out the names of specific individuals to be targeted. I clearly heard my own name called out, at first by one person but then taken up as a chorus by the others. They sounded like hounds baying when one of them has picked up the scent of an unfortunate fox. "Carlin, Carlin, let's get Carlin!" I cringed and waited helplessly for whatever fate lay ahead of me. It was going to be a long, long night!

They came into the billet with torches flashing around and made straight for where I lay. My bed was thrown over and I found myself in the now familiar situation of picking myself out of an entanglement of blankets, sheets and mattress.

"Okay, Carlin," said a voice that I vaguely recognized, "time we had you up on court martial."

Two of them dragged me to my feet, pinioned my arms to my sides and then force-marched me out of the billet, into the corridor. A catcalling rabble followed behind as I was taken to the common room where a table, with three 27th entry members seated behind it, occupied centre-stage. Elsewhere in the room several of my fellow-29th entry members were being held under guard by the new senior entry, who were also jeering the ongoing proceedings. Evidently, I wasn't the first to appear before the court that night.

When my turn came, the escort manoeuvred me into a position in front of the table to face the seated "judges". The proceedings pantomimed a real appearance on a charge, but involved much more intimidation. Various people shouted at me to stand up straight at attention, while others accused me of looking disrespectfully at the judges. My name was read out from a "charge sheet" and then "evidence" for the prosecution was recited by one of the judges. It amounted to the fact that I had been disrespectful to several of the 27th entry members at various times during these past few weeks. This was probably true because I was a normal flippant teenager.

We got through the evidence and, not surprisingly, I was found guilty as charged. Now for the punishment.

The pronouncement came. "Boy Entrant Carlin, you are sentenced to jump off this table," said the first judge.

"Wait a minute," said another, "that's too easy. I think he should do it blindfolded!"

The third judge vigorously agreed, prompting the first judge to make pretence of thinking about it before agreeing to go along with the majority decision.

Addressing my escort, he commanded, "Take him outside and blindfold him well."

I was force-marched back out to the corridor where a scarf was placed over my eyes and tied around my head. It came down my face almost to the end of my nose so that I couldn't see out underneath the way children do when they're playing blind man's buff. When they were satisfied that I couldn't possibly see anything and I can only imagine that they tested me well, I was taken back into the "court martial".

Then several pairs of hands hoisted me in the air and lowered me down onto the Formica tabletop.

"Okay, you're in the middle of the table," a voice informed me, "move to the edge and jump."

I hesitated. The fear of injury was terrifying.

"If you don't jump, you're going to get a cold bath," said the voice.

Which would be worse, I wondered? At least with a cold bath there would be little risk of getting hurt. I continued to ponder my options, but a few seconds later some hands started nudging me away from my spot in the centre of the table. I resisted, but the hands were insistent. It began to look as though the cold bath option had been withdrawn and I was going to have to jump—or be pushed. My feet felt for the edge and at the same time the hands stopped nudging and held on to me instead.

"You're at the edge now," I was told. "There's nothing in front of you. When we let go, all you have to do is jump."

Easier said than done. Now I was shaking, trying to summon the courage to take this literal leap in the dark.

"It's all right, we won't let anything happen to you," the voice encouraged, "show us you're a man!"

Then another voice that I recognized as one of my own entry-mates piped up from somewhere in the room, "C'mon Carlin, you can do it. We had to do it too, so don't let the 29th down!"

A chorus of "Yeah's" followed this challenge, coming from the others that I'd noticed in the room earlier. That kind of did it for me. I bent my legs and crouched, trying to imagine how high I was off the ground so that I could consciously make the normally instinctive compensation needed to absorb the shock of landing. I tried to launch but my feet seemed glued to the table when the rest of my body tried to spring forward. I crouched again and failed again.

"Come on, or we'll push you off," the voice said, "We haven't got all night!"

I got down in the crouch position again and this time leapt blindly into space. Shock! I was expecting a short time interval of maybe a second between launching and landing, but there was none at all: my feet met solid ground almost as soon as they lifted off the table and I fell forward heavily onto the linoleum floor. That was the first shock, but it was immediately followed by a second surprise when a huge burst of laughter suddenly filled the room. I tore the blindfold off and then saw why I'd landed sooner than expected and the reason for the laughter. The tabletop was sitting on the floor with its legs removed. I had never been more than three inches off the ground the whole time that I'd been agonizing about making the jump!

My tormentors laughingly ushered me to the side of the room to join the other erstwhile victims and by this time I was laughing myself, but more from relief than from amusement. Then the next prisoner was brought in and I was able to see how it had all been pulled off. As soon as he was out of the room, the "judges" got up from the table and brought the tabletop with them. The legs had simply been propped into place with the whole rickety structure craftily supported on the knees of the three people seated at it. Next they laid the tabletop on the floor and then called for the blindfolded prisoner to be brought into the room. Four of the 27th grabbed him, one on each leg and one on each arm and then they lifted him high, purposely moving him around so that he would be disoriented. Then, when they lowered him onto the table it seemed to the unsuspecting prisoner that he was standing on a table a few feet above the floor.

There were motioned signs for no one to laugh and the poor guy was then subjected to the same goading that I had undergone just a short time previously. Then, when everyone had been through the "punishment", we were allowed to return to our billets and go to bed, but only after having to remake them as a result of the initial raid.

The next morning we awoke to find a white bed-sheet hanging from the very top of the 100 feet high water tower, with "27th Entry" crudely painted on it in large black characters. It flapped up there in the breeze for a whole week and no one ever found out who put it there, or even how the person or persons unknown managed to get to the top of the tower, because the door that gave entry to the internal stairway was always securely locked. We could only guess that one or more brave if foolhardy souls must have risked their necks for the glory of "The Entry" by scaling the outside of the brickwork structure under cover of darkness. Or maybe they had assistance from the St. Athan-based RAF Mountain Rescue team, which sometimes used the water tower to practise rope climbing. The banner was finally taken down, but in getting it up there in the first place, the 27th certainly scored a major propaganda point.

Mac, the 26th entry boy for whom I bulled, passed out with his entry, but that wasn't the end of my servitude as a bull boy. On the evening following the night of the court-martial, Mick, one of the 27th approached my bed-space carrying his tunic, beret and boots.

"Hey Paddy, you're going to bull for me, aren't you?" He asked smilingly, using a name by which many people addressed me because of my Irish origins.

I happened to like Mick. He was a sort of role model for me, in a similar way that an older brother frequently is for a younger male sibling. I agreed, feeling that I didn't have much choice in the matter anyway. Besides, it would only be for about four weeks, until the 30th entry moved up to the Wings. When that happened, the "duty" would be gladly handed over to one of their number.

* * *

In Workshops we moved from cockpit internal lighting to aircraft external lighting. There were the navigation lights, red for Port, green for Starboard and white for the tail. As with so many things, there's a little more to simple aircraft navigation lights than a person might suspect. They aren't just coloured lights stuck indiscriminately on the extremities of the aircraft. In fact, the lights serve a more important purpose during night-time navigation, especially in the years that preceded sophisticated aircraft anti-collision radar systems. Each light was masked in a way that made it visible only when viewed from a certain angle from a horizontal viewing position; 110 degrees for both Port and Starboard lights and 140 degrees for the tail light. The angles of all three lights add up to 360 degrees. This arrangement makes it possible for an observer in one aircraft to deduce the approximate heading of another aircraft at the same altitude in the night sky. If he can see a red and a green light at the same time, it means that the other craft is approaching on a collision course. One green and one white light, or one red and one white light, indicate that the aircraft is on a parallel course and directly on the observer's left or right side. A single red or green signifies that the other aircraft is travelling on a parallel heading in the same direction as the observer's aircraft, but behind his own position. A single white light indicates that the observer is viewing the other aircraft from the rear.

Then there was the retractable landing light, the type "J" I believe. This light was mounted in the underside of the wing and designed to be flush with the wing surface when retracted during normal flight. A small integral DC motor drove a mechanism that extended the light into two selectable positions: "Land" or "Taxi". Because the light was only supposed to be extended at low airspeed, it incorporated a clutch device that caused it to disengage from the mechanism if the light was lowered into the slipstream whilst the airspeed was too high. When this occurred, as it frequently did, the disengaged light would be pushed back into the wing by the force of the air against it and could only be reset by operating the light to its "Retract" position before it could be extended again.

We also learned about Downward Identification Lights. This was a set of three separately coloured lights, each of which could be operated in Morse code fashion or simply left on "steady". The purpose of the lights was to visually communicate with someone on the ground whilst maintaining radio silence, either by Morse code or by displaying a pre-arranged colour code as a means of identification.

After learning about these external lights, our task was to wire the components of the circuit together, using wiring diagrams and then find "snags" that had been deliberately set by the instructor. A favourite "fault" was to cause the high airspeed clutch to disengage on the landing light and then challenge us to determine why the light wasn't lit in the down position. It was tempting to assume it was for the most obvious reason—that the bulb had burned out—but a more careful analysis of the situation would reveal that the mechanism was disengaged. Since the micro-switch that completed the circuit to the bulb was attached to this mechanism, it hadn't moved to the position where it would close to light the bulb. Exercises such as this taught us to think before jumping to conclusions, which could waste a lot of time and resources in later operational situations.

Wiring up navigation lights or identification lights and then getting them to work soon paled in comparison to the excitement of getting a landing light to extend, after having wired it up, and then seeing the intense light beam turn on as it swung down into the "Land" position. We were still a few months away from getting an even greater kick out of the 24-way bomb gear system, which could be programmed to drop bombs from an aircraft in several different patterns. Although they wouldn't let us play with real bombs, the electrical release mechanisms made a very satisfying din as they operated in rapid succession. But for the moment, we had much more mundane stuff to learn—like batteries for instance.

Batteries just sat there and did nothing. There were no flashing lights, no clicking relays, just nothing. Yet there was a mountain of information to absorb regarding these passive black, oblong shapes. Although they didn't appear to do much, they were just as important to an aircraft's electrical system as a car battery is to a car. But unlike a car battery, which is largely ignored until it becomes a problem, aircraft batteries were removed every two weeks and replaced with a freshly charged set. And the task of replacing them was a large part of an aircraft electrician's duties. We needed to know that they contained a corrosive solution of distilled water and sulphuric acid and that any spills needed to be neutralized and then promptly cleaned up. But there was more to know about them. In the thorough technical training traditions of the RAF, we learned about the materials that went into the manufacture of a battery, the chemical processes that took place during their charging cycle and the reverse processes that occurred as this chemical energy reconverted to electrical energy.

'Instruments' was slightly more interesting. This topic referred to meters, such as voltmeters and ammeters, which exhibited activity when power was applied to them, unlike the static immobile batteries. There was quite a lot to learn because of the different types of internal mechanisms that are used in the various meters to make their pointers move and the ways in which different types of meters are connected in circuits. But regardless of the subject, my trade knowledge gradually increased as we progressed further along the path towards our eventual pass-out. In my case, this was a minor miracle considering how little I knew when I first applied to become a Boy Entrant.

An instructor supervises a trainee Electrical Mechanic (Air) who is engaged in servicing a 12/24-way bomb control system.

CHAPTER 8

The Seductive Call of the Trumpet

The Easter break intervened just a little more than one week after the 26th Entry's passing-out parade—Easter Sunday fell on 21st April that year—giving everyone a welcome respite from the 27th Entry's mad senior-entry rampage.

Easter marked the end of the winter term and time to take a short break before starting the spring term. For this reason, a 96-hour pass and a free travel warrant were granted to all those wishing to spending the long-weekend of Easter at home. Most of the English and Welsh lads took advantage of this opportunity, but it was impractical for those of us who hailed from the further reaches of the Kingdom to make the trip, because additional travel time could not be added to the pass. There were compensations, however. From "after duty hours" on Thursday the 18th of April until 2359 hours (midnight) on the following Monday, the camp was almost deserted. Discipline was at a minimum: we could stay in bed for as long as we wanted and didn't have to make our bedding up into bed-packs whenever we finally decided to drag ourselves out of our "pits". Breakfast was at a later hour and, because there were so few of us, the cooks were very willing to provide a little more individual attention to our culinary desires. Instead of being faced with the mass-produced, pre-cooked plastic eggs that we were used to seeing, eggs were cooked to order and the atmosphere in the mess, like everywhere else on the camp, was altogether more relaxed and easygoing.

Mick, the 27th lad for whom I bulled, decided to stay on camp for the Easter break, even though he lived somewhere in southern England and could easily have made the journey home in a relatively short time. Perhaps it was an 18-year-old's gesture of independence, especially since he had a girlfriend in Barry. On Easter Saturday, he invited me to travel into Barry with him on the bus, because even though I was his "Man Friday", we had become quite friendly. He introduced me to Phyllis, his girlfriend and all three of us sat chatting over a prolonged cup of coffee at a café near Barry railway station that many of us frequented.

By this time, my "Man Friday" role for Mick was nearly at an end, because two weeks later, on the 4th of May 1957, the 30th entry moved into the Wings from ITS. In the process, they assumed the dubious honour of replacing the 29th as junior entry, which certainly didn't cause me any unhappiness at being freed from my demeaning role as personal valet to Mick—even if I did like him. But more importantly, this was another small step on our way to becoming the senior entry. My billet received at least four of the new juniors; Boy Entrants Brown, Allen, Acton and Taff Jones. They fitted in well and soon became accepted as valuable members of our small Hut E7 community.

*　*　*

It was John Birch who got me interested in the trumpet band. He had joined the band almost as soon as we came up to the Wings. I envied how he was able to casually stroll into class all by himself, after everyone else had been marched there by the class leader several minutes earlier. He would remove the mouthpiece from his trumpet and put it in his pocket, before dangling the trumpet from a peg on the coat rack at the rear of the room. I had also noticed that whilst most of us formed up in the morning for the work parade and then suffered through the button inspection, the band just ambled loosely together into a semblance of ranks, where they chatted and tested their musical instruments until it was time to march to workshops. If they endured any inspection at all, it was a very casual affair and nothing like the microscopic scrutiny to which non-band members were routinely subjected.

Birchy would often say to me, "You should join the band Brian. It's a ruddy good skive."

Birchy always called me by my first name, unlike most other people who just called me Carlin, or "Paddy" if they were feeling friendly towards me, and he always said "ruddy" instead of "bloody". He was like that with other swear words too; always saying "frig" instead of the more commonly used "f-word", in contrast to nearly everyone else who, by this stage, "effed and blinded" like proverbial troopers. Usually, I just smiled and made some excuse when he encouraged me to join the band, because I couldn't play the trumpet. But then one day, just a few weeks before Easter, I became a little more interested. Maybe it was because I'd been put on jankers for having dirty buttons—a fairly regular occurrence by now—and saw the band as a means of avoiding the morning button inspections.

"How can I be in the band," I asked Birchy, "when I can't even play a trumpet?"

"It doesn't matter about not being able to play," he replied, "you just learn as you go along." He then thought for a moment before continuing, "There's a lot of frigging people in the band who can't play, but they just make it look as though they can. We all just practise together until we can play the tunes." Then he added, as an afterthought, "We're going to Earls Court in June."

"What's Earls Court?" I asked naively.

"You've never heard of Earls Court?" He asked the question a little scornfully, as though everyone but the remotest of cave-dwellers had heard of it—and perhaps kids like me, fresh from the bogs of Ireland.

"No, I haven't." I admitted.

John Birch liked nothing better than to snootily lecture someone on a subject that he believed the other person knew nothing remotely about.

"It's at a big indoor arena in London where they hold horse jumping shows and things like that," he loftily informed me. "And every year they hold the Royal Tournament there, which is a kind of big show put on for the Queen. All the Services take part in it and bands from all the Services come to play and do figure marching," he continued. "And this year the St. Athan trumpet band has been invited to play," he ended on a triumphant note.

Little did John realize that he had unwittingly pressed just the right button to launch my recruitment into the band. One of my greatest ambitions at that time was to visit London. The possibility of being able to go there with the band was all the encouragement I needed.

"How do I join?" I asked.

"Well, you can just come with me to band practice on

Tuesday night and talk to the Trumpet Major," he offered.

"Okay," I said, "I'll come with you."

By the time Tuesday night came around I still hadn't changed my mind. In fact I was more afraid that I wouldn't be accepted, despite Birchy's assurances that they took all comers. So, with some anxiety, I accompanied him over to No. 4 Squadron, where the band practice room was located. It wasn't really a very difficult place to find on band practice night—you only needed to follow your ears. The night air was filled with the sound of trumpets squawking out competing tunes, frequently interspersed with flat notes and other terrible sounds reminiscent of elephants suffering from extreme flatulence. All the while, drummers beat out various staccatos on their tenor drums and cymbals clashed as though the other noises weren't quite loud enough.

Birchy introduced me to Trumpet Major Davison, who wore four inverted chevrons on his right sleeve, surmounted by a small brass badge that was in the form of two crossed trumpets.

"Can you play a trumpet?" Davison asked, emphasising the word "play" as though he already knew the answer only too well.

"No," I replied, half expecting to be told that I couldn't join, because I still did not truly believe what Birchy had been telling me.

"Well, you'll have to learn quickly—we're going to Earls Court in June," responded Davison.

"I'll try," I said, smiling and nodding enthusiastically, both at the same time, but hardly believing what I was hearing.

"C'mon then. Let's get you fixed up with a trumpet, so that you can start practising right away."

As he said this, the Trumpet Major turned and walked towards a storeroom, motioning that I should follow him. I eagerly shadowed him to the storeroom and was soon holding my very own brass trumpet. This, I thought, will be my passport to London and will give me freedom from future button inspections. Although thrilled to get the trumpet, I had to admit to myself that as a musical instrument it had seen much better days. The large flared end looked as though it had been pushed very hard up against something solid, which gave it a crumpled appearance instead of the smoothly curved belled-out shape that one usually associates with a trumpet. In fact, dents covered most of the entire trumpet body. It was also in dire need of an energetic application of Brasso to replace its dull, thick patina with a brassy gleam more in keeping with its military duties.

The type of trumpet used in Boy Entrant bands was an E-flat cavalry trumpet, which is a very simple "straight through" type of instrument, lacking the valves that are apparent on trumpets used by professional musicians. The instrument consists simply of two elongated loops of brass tube with one end holding the mouthpiece and the other end flared out into the familiar "trumpet" shape. When being played, the trumpet was grasped in the right hand, around and halfway along the upper elongated part of the loop. The other arm remained at the player's side when he was standing still, or was activated in a normal swinging motion when marching. A rope-like binding, consisting of interwoven strands of red and gold coloured fibres, was wound tightly around and along the whole length of the lower elongated part of the loop. Two large tassels, one at the beginning and one at the ending of the binding, hung below the trumpet when it was being held in the playing position.

"Here, you'll need this too," said Trumpet Major Davison, as he handed me a silver mouthpiece. "Always take the mouthpiece out and keep it with you when you're not playing or marching in the band, because it'll get stolen if you don't," he warned. "Okay, you can go and start practising now," he said, giving a small wave of his hand in a gesture of dismissal.

I tried a practice blow, but nothing came out of the trumpet end except the sound of my breath. That came as something of a surprise. I'd been expecting to make some kind of trumpet noise, remembering how toy bugles made noise just by blowing into them when I was a child. Feeling a little defeated, I found John Birch again and asked him to show me how to play. Birchy removed the mouthpiece from his trumpet and blew into it, making a kind of squawking noise.

"You have to do it like that," he said. "You kind of spit into it at first to get it started, then keep it going, although you don't actually spit *spit*, if you know what I mean."

I wasn't quite sure what he meant about not *actually* spitting, but went along with it as though I did.

He continued, "Then, every time you need to take a breath, you have to spit again to get it started."

I put the trumpet to my lips and spat into it. Nothing much happened.

"No, you have to tighten your lips. Like this," and he grimaced with his lips pulled tightly against his teeth.

I tried again and managed a few pathetic squawks. Feeling a little more confident now, I asked, "How do you make the different notes?"

"You change the shape of your lips," he explained. "Tighten them for the higher notes and looser for the low notes. Go on, give it a try," he urged.

I tried, but not too successfully. This wasn't as easy as I thought it would be. There was going to be a lot of practise ahead before I would be able to make any kind of useful contribution, but I enjoyed being in the band and especially the more relaxed discipline that surrounded it. Now I was able to come into class with Birchy, instead of having to march in separately with the others under the control of dour-faced Willie Burns. Likewise, we were able to leave by ourselves when classes were finished and make our way to where the band formed up. Although these might seem like small freedoms, they were well worth having in our rigidly disciplined world.

In addition to achieving the knack of playing a trumpet, there were lots of other things I needed to learn as a band member. Leading Boy Entrant Featherstone was the Drum Major. He led the band by striding out in front, cradling the four-foot long, silver-capped mace in his right arm. Whilst marching, we would periodically strike up with a tune from our repertoire, requiring the participation of all trumpeters and drummers. Between tunes, the trumpets and drums were silent, except for the bass drummer who continued to beat out the step on his drum with a single drumstick.

When Featherstone wanted us to commence playing a new tune, he took hold of the mace by its bottom end and held it vertically above his head, with his arm stretched upwards as far as he could reach. This was the signal for the side tenor drummers to play a series of drum-rolls they called "two threes and a seven", drrr-drrr-dit, drrr-drrr-dit, drrr-drrr-drrr-drrr-drrr-drrr-dit. Up to this point, each trumpet player carried his trumpet tucked under his right upper arm, with his right hand grasped around the forward-facing mouthpiece. The first short set of drum-rolls was the signal to swivel the right hand around to grasp the instrument in the playing position. At the second set of drum-rolls, the trumpet arm was extended horizontally forward with the mouthpiece pointed upwards. At this point, the Trumpet Major in the rear rank, where he marched with the better trumpet players, would yell out the name of the tune we were supposed to play. At the final and longest set of drum-rolls, the trumpet was brought to the lips and we then waited for the end of the final drum roll as the signal to start playing. In the early stages of my band service, however, "playing" was little more than making discordant squawking noises as I grappled with the task of trying to coax the right notes from my trumpet.

There was no sheet music to play from, even if we had known how to read it—the music was all learned by ear. One of our tunes was known as "The Marseillaise", which had a passing resemblance to the French national anthem. Then there was "The St. Louis Blues". Around that time, the United States Air Force Band had recorded a swinging version of this famous tune, which was very popular on the camp "radio" system. We tried to emulate it, but could never quite match the quality of the USAF band's performance. One other tune that comes to mind is "Roll me Over in the Clover", which was abbreviated just to "Roll me Over" when its name was yelled out by the Trumpet Major.

Drum Major Featherstone invariably contributed his own virtuoso performance with the mace. Much of the time, he would use it to indicate the change in direction when we needed to make a turn, or to signal other visual commands to those of us following behind him. But when he wasn't doing this, he twirled the mace around in front and behind his back, sometimes tossing it in the air and then catching it, in much the same tradition as Scottish regimental pipe-band drum majors.

There was usually time for only one tune in the short distance between the billets and the workshops. After having played it, we each tucked our trumpets back under our arms and continued to march along in silence, save for the sound of the bass drum beating out the step. When Featherstone needed to bring us to a halt, he lifted the mace horizontally above his head and held it there between his two outstretched arms. At the same time, he commenced marking time by marching on the spot and then we proceeded to do likewise. All the while, the bass drum continued to beat out the step until Featherstone raised the mace by one hand, into a vertical position above his head, grasping it by the silver ferrule that encased its lower few inches. He then jerked it rapidly in a few short, horizontal movements. The bass drummer audibly mimicked these movements by beating out a rhythm of two double beats, two single beats and one final double beat, boom-boom, boom-boom, boom, boom, boom-boom! On the final double beat, the band stopped marking time and came to a halt. Featherstone then abruptly let go of the mace and allowed it to drop vertically, only to catch it neatly in the cradle of his right arm before performing an about-turn to face us and dismiss us to our classes.

Rehearsals for the Royal Tournament started almost as soon as I joined the band. The bands of both 1 and 2 Wings were combined into a single massed unit and arrayed in eight columns instead of the usual four. This was the formation in which we would represent St. Athan at the tournament. Twice weekly, on Mondays and Wednesdays after tea, band members were assembled on the parade ground to practise the figure marching routine that we would eventually perform at the show, under the direction of the band officer, Pilot Officer Read and instructor Corporal Naylor.

Corporal Naylor had felt inspired to develop the routine whilst watching a chorus girl routine on the "Sunday Night at the London Palladium" television programme. He didn't exactly want us to perform high kicks, but was impressed by the fluid formation changes that were part of the chorus girls' performance. This inspired him to develop a figure-marching routine that would continuously change as we marched, without any verbal or visual commands being given. Unfortunately for him, we weren't the London Palladium chorus line and so our early attempts at figure marching predictably degenerated into chaos. The good corporal and Pilot Officer Read must each have been tearing their hair out as they watched us stumble around, crash into one another, or fail to make turns when we were supposed to. But after a few practice sessions we started to get the hang of the routine and before long were fine-tuning and polishing it to perfection.

When we had achieved a reasonable level of competence, an area of the parade ground was marked out to mimic the boundaries of the Earls Court arena in which we would be performing. We began the figure-marching routine as soon as we entered this mock arena, led by three drum majors, with Featherstone out in front as the main leader and the other two drum majors just a few steps behind him. I'm not sure how it came about that we had three drum majors when there were only two bands, but when we initially marched into the arena area, they formed the three points of a broad triangular pattern, with Featherstone at its apex. The two secondary drum majors synchronized their mace twirling movements with those of Featherstone as they marched along the length of the mock arena. Then, when Featherstone neared the opposite end, he doubled back and started threading his way through the ranks of the other marchers, who were still heading in the original direction. Each of us continued marching until we also reached the same turning point, whereupon we too doubled back, until eventually the whole band was marching in the opposite direction. We performed this manoeuvre once more at the other end of the "arena" and then headed back in the original direction. But this time, when we got to the centre of the arena, the four inner ranks performed a marching about-turn and emerged from the rear of the formation, going in the opposite direction. No sooner had the original formation developed into two separate formations, than the two outer ranks of each formation started splitting off at a tangent so that were all heading in separate directions, towards the four corners of the arena. While this was going on, the marchers in the remaining four inner ranks marked time until the tail ends of the outer columns drew level with them, then each of these ranks joined on to the end of an outer column so that now four single columns of marchers were heading towards the four corners of the arena.

The break-up of the original tight formation into four separate columns was the first part of Corporal Naylor's choreographed routine that included many variations of counter marching, figure of eights and crossovers that flowed into and out of one another so that the patterns continuously changed throughout the routine. The *piece de resistance* came when we formed a giant Boy Entrant wheel badge with the bass drummer at its centre, which stretched from one edge of the arena to the other and slowly rotated. Finally and seamlessly, we would then resume the original eight-rank formation before marching out of the arena area. Corporal Naylor did a truly magnificent job of coaching us in the performance of the whole routine. As originally envisaged, it was executed with only one command being given at the beginning and nothing more until the final halt was given on our exit from the arena.

At first, we concentrated on learning the figure marching routine, but as our grasp of the intricate movements improved we were required to start playing our band instruments as well. This added a new challenge to grapple with, because it was now necessary to concentrate on what we were playing in addition to maintaining our position in the formation.

Meanwhile, the band continued to lead the daily parade to and from workshops, which helped me to get some desperately needed practise towards elevating my trumpet-playing to at least a basic level of competency, before going to the Royal Tournament. It was a slow process, but I was progressing nicely and all would have been well if I hadn't suddenly been promoted to Corporal Trumpeter.

Earning a "band rank" was a difficult undertaking, even though it had standing only within the band. There were four ranks above that of basic trumpeter: Leading Trumpeter; Corporal Trumpeter; Sergeant Trumpeter; and Trumpet Major, which was the highest attainable. Rank was indicated by inverted chevrons on the right cuff of the person's tunic, surmounted by the small brass badge in the shape of crossed-trumpets. It was the same badge that ordinary trumpeters wore on their upper left arm. Actual rank was denoted by the number of chevrons: one for Leading Trumpeter, two for Corporal, three for Sergeant and four for Trumpet Major. A candidate for promotion to any of these ranks was required to demonstrate his ability to play the trumpet—during a "play-off" before a committee of higher-ranking trumpeters—at a level of competency that was deemed the minimum for that particular rank. As with promotion to normal ranks, it was usually a prerequisite that a candidate would be promoted one rank at a time and only after he had spent a reasonable amount of time in his current rank. Considering all of this, it might be difficult to imagine how someone like me, who had only recently joined the band and could only hit the right notes more by accident than intention, could possibly receive a sudden promotion to the rank of Corporal Trumpeter, whilst conveniently leapfrogging the intervening rank of Leading Trumpeter in the process. Well, it had nothing whatsoever to do with my ability to play the trumpet and more to do with the overall appearance of the band—a case of fluff without substance, conceived to create a certain visual imagery.

It seemed that Pilot Officer Read, while doing his homework on military bands, had noticed an abundance of decoration on most other "professional" bandsmen's uniforms. This translated to lots of braid, stripes, badges and all manner of uniform decoration that gave the appearance of overdone icing on a fancy cake. He had also noticed that there was always a cadre of senior bandsmen populating the rear two or three ranks of every "proper" band. The uniform sleeves of these rear-rankers were heavily adorned with stripes, badges and insignia, whereas the other bandsmen were progressively less and less heavily festooned the further the eye travelled forward through their ranks.

Pilot Officer Read desired to impress our potential audience with a similar make-up of obviously senior band members in the rear ranks, to make us appear more like "pros". Unfortunately, there were hardly enough band members endowed with the necessary sleeve decoration to make up even one paltry rank. Our officer therefore conceived the idea of awarding temporary seniority to some of his boys, sufficient to make up a number of complete ranks of "senior" members. I had already been automatically assigned to march in the third row from rear, by the "sizing" process, and now Pilot Officer Read decided to populate this row exclusively with Corporal Trumpeters. The row behind mine was to be made up of Sergeant Trumpeters and the last row would be a mixture of Sergeant Trumpeters and the two Trumpet Majors, whilst those in the row to my immediate front would all be Leading Trumpeters. All other trumpeters forward of this would hold no rank and therefore minimal arm decoration. The same rank "adjustments" were applied to the drummers, who marched in the three front ranks of the band. In this way, Pilot Officer Read aimed to richly enhance the band's visual impact, so that it would be able to hold its own with the big boys. What he hadn't bargained for was the human element, manifesting itself as a torrent of outrage from the band members who had actually earned their stripes the hard way—by playing off for them.

I first learned of the new promotions during practice one evening, when Corporal Naylor handed me a chit and two sets of double chevrons. The chit informed me that I had been temporarily awarded the rank of "acting" Corporal Trumpeter and that the chevrons should be worn immediately. I was thrilled at receiving the unexpected promotion and, on my return to the billet, set about the task of sewing the new stripes onto the right cuff of both tunics. When in place, they contrasted with the single proficiency stripe on my left cuff, giving me a slightly unbalanced appearance, but that was how it had to be.

At the next band practice, those of us who had received the windfall promotions turned up proudly wearing our new stripes, but the effect on the more senior members of the band was not quite what we expected. Although their fury was directed at Pilot Officer Read, their first action was to take it out on those of us who, in their eyes, had been undeservedly promoted. Soon after arriving, I found myself surrounded by a group of angry senior trumpeters. They cordoned me off, together with one or two other "instant" corporals and sergeant trumpeters, and half dragged, half pushed us into a quiet corner where, one by one, we were challenged to demonstrate that our playing ability matched the level required to legitimately earn our stripes.

One of the Sergeant Trumpeters, a Scot, confronted me. "Let's hear ye playin' 'Marseillaise'," he demanded angrily.

I put the trumpet to my lips and tried to play the tune, but the notes issuing from the instrument were falteringly wide of the mark, even allowing for the stressfulness of the situation.

"All right, that's enough o' that! Play 'Roll me Over'," my tormentor now challenged.

Once again, I could only produce a miserably poor rendition of the tune.

"Ye canny play well enough to be a Corporal Trumpeter," he scorned, "ye need tae take them stripes off yer arm!" He glared angrily into my eyes as he hurled out the words.

The other "rapid promotion" candidates fared no better than I did and by the end of the impromptu play-off, all of our accusers were demanding that we remove our stripes. But here, at least, we were able to stand our ground, reinforcing each other as we insisted that we'd been specifically ordered to wear them. We won that challenge, but it was only Round 1. The still-angry senior band members then went as a group to buttonhole Corporal Naylor, giving full vent to their injured feelings when they had managed to corner him. Naylor heard them out, then he and Pilot Officer Read went into a huddle. Finally, they came up with a compromise that was proposed to all of us at the end of band practice. Their solution to the dilemma was that the undeserved promotions would be effective only during our appearance at the Royal Tournament and that we would have to remove the stripes until just before we actually set out for the event at Earls Court.

I was a little disappointed at losing my not-so-hard-won stripes, but a welcome calmness and serenity returned to our band community, allowing us to concentrate on perfecting the figure marching routines and improve our playing of the repertoire, in readiness for the Royal Tournament. And so it would have continued, except that our practice sessions were interrupted for a two-week period by the annual Boy Entrant Summer Camp at RAF Woodvale.

* * *

Ah, Summer Camp! Of all my experiences as a Boy Entrant, this was by far the most enjoyable.

On 22nd May 1957, the entire Boy Entrant population of St. Athan departed from Gileston railway station on two specially chartered trains. Our destination was Woodvale, an idyllic RAF station located just four or five miles southwest of Southport—a relatively genteel seaside resort in the county of Lancashire. Woodvale was positioned in close proximity to the posh Royal Formby Golf Club and was separated from it only by the railway tracks that carried a frequent electric train service between Southport and the distant city of Liverpool. The picturesque little Freshfield railway station was located a short distance from the Woodvale camp, providing us with a convenient and economic means of travel to and from Southport. It can't be said that we descended on this peaceful setting like an unexpected tidal wave, because Woodvale had also been host to our Cosford brethren for their summer camp, during the two-week period immediately prior to ours. Maybe it would be more correct to say that the invasion of the Woodvale area by boy entrants continued unabated for another two weeks after Cosford's departure.

It is entirely likely that British Railways knew exactly what they were letting themselves in for, by agreeing to put on specially chartered trains. But, reflecting on the events that took place during the journey, it was probably just as well that we were segregated from normal civilized society, because the journey from St. Athan was not without its own excitement. After all, this wasn't exactly jankers—we were going on an RAF sponsored holiday, the prospect of which created an atmosphere of youthful exuberance. First, however, we were paraded in the Gilestone railway station yard to receive a briefing from Wing Commander Ranson, who was to be our Commanding Officer for the duration of summer camp. We were stood at ease.

"Okay, pay attention," one of the NCOs bawled, as the Wingco climbed gingerly up on a stack of railway sleepers, all the better to be seen and heard.

"Boys, I want you to remember that you represent the Royal Air Force and Royal Air Force St. Athan in particular," he intoned. "So that means that you must be on your best behaviour and respect British Railways property during the journey to Woodvale. I don't want to hear of any acts of vandalism. Is that understood?" He didn't wait for an answer, but continued, "And we don't want any toilet rolls streaming out of the train windows like we had last year. If that happens, there'll be trouble. Now let's go to Woodvale and enjoy ourselves! That's all!" Then he turned to the lead NCO and said, "All right sergeant, dismiss them and get them on the train."

The sergeant took over, "When I give the order to dismiss, you will proceed onto the station platform in an orderly fashion. Izzat understood?"

"Yes sergeant," we chorused.

"When on the platform, you will spread yourselves out along its whole length and not congregate in one area! And keep back from the edge of the platform until the train has arrived and come to a complete stop. Izzat understood?"

Again, we chorused, "Yes sergeant!"

"There are some box lunches over there," and he pointed to somewhere behind us, "Pick one up as you go onto the platform and you better look after it because that's all you'll get to eat until you get to Woodvale."

Then the sergeant drew a deep breath and in his best parade ground voice bellowed, "Paraaaaade, dis-miss!"

We broke ranks and headed towards the three-tonner that the sergeant had indicated. Its cargo area was piled high with white cardboard boxes. I took one of the boxes from an airman who was handing them out from the tailboard of the lorry and then filed through the narrow station entrance, to wait with the others for the train's arrival.

Earlier that morning, we had packed the last of our kit—all of it—into our kitbags. There had been orders to paint a large coloured blob on the bottom of our kitbags as a means of identifying the squadron to which they belonged. The kitbags that belonged to our squadron were identified by a red blob, presumably to match the colour of our wheel badge disc. We also learned that while we were away having fun at Woodvale, members of Durham University Air Squadron and some units of the Air Training Corps would temporarily occupy our accommodation at St. Athan, which explained why we had been ordered to take all of our kit with us, even though most of it wouldn't be needed at Woodvale.

Now, as we stood on the station platform in the cool morning air, impatiently waiting for the train to make its appearance, there was a mild buzz of conversation, but it was mostly forced. We were really all feeling preoccupied, frequently peering along the railway line, hoping to catch our first glimpse of the train when it came into view. After what seemed like an age, but was probably only about fifteen minutes, the dark shape of the locomotive came into view. I could only see the locomotive, but not the maroon coloured carriages that followed behind, as it came directly towards us. At first the train looked like a small speck, framed by the semi-circular opening of the short tunnel that guarded the approach to the station, but it grew steadily larger until only its dark shape filled the tunnel opening. Then it was through and into the light, dragging its carriages out of the tunnel behind it like some magician pulling maroon streamers from the dark interior of his top hat. The engine puffed and hissed loudly past us, its driver's oil-smeared face grinning in our direction as we stood on the little railway station's platform. I could feel the wave of heat and caught the whiff of steam intermingled with smoke and oil—a hot kind of smell unique to steam engines of all kinds—as it passed in front of me. Then, when the carriages were alongside the platform, the train came to a halt with a prolonged screech of its brakes and an extra loud hiss of released steam that shut off as suddenly as it had begun. All seemed silent for a moment and then everyone sprang to life. Carriage doors were quickly thrown open and a loud hubbub ensued as we embarked on our summer adventure.

Some of us were detailed to load kitbags and other assorted baggage into the guard's van and then we were all aboard. A whistle blew, a green flag waved from the rear end of the train and we lurched off on our 250-mile journey. For a second or two, the large driving wheels of the locomotive spun rapidly on the shiny tracks, as the driver deliberately used the heat of friction to burn off moisture that had condensed from the steam onto the wheels and railway track. Then they slowed down and gripped the rails to move the train, slowly at first, but gradually gathering speed to accelerate it at a steady rate along the track.

We sat in compartments that were typical of British Railways of that era. There was ample space for six passengers on high-backed sofa-like seats, with armrests that could be folded up or down depending on the whim of the traveller. Three seats faced forward, opposite three that faced rearwards. There was just sufficient floor space to allow someone to walk carefully between the passengers seated on both sides of the compartment. Four framed photographs adorned the wall-space above the seats, as was typical for railway compartments. Usually, these were landscape scenes of places that could presumably be travelled to by train. A mirror filled in the centre space of each wall, between the landscapes. Luggage racks made from what appeared to be deep-sea fishing net were firmly installed above the pictures and it was into these that we tossed our small packs and box lunches before settling down on the seats. A small Formica table protruded from just below the large picture window that filled most of the carriage's outside wall. Two small sliding windows were situated above the main window, with a small sign advising passengers not to open them any wider than the two arrow marks engraved on the sign. This, the passenger was assured, would provide ventilation without any draught. A sliding door, glazed only in its upper half, sealed the compartment off from a corridor that ran the length of the carriage. The corridor connected with similar corridors in the other carriages, so that a person could walk the full length of the train if he or she was so inclined. Both ends of the carriage housed a toilet with a sign that read: "Do not use toilet while the train is standing at a station", as did all the other carriages, except that in many such toilets some wag had usually obliterated the word "not".

Wing Commander Ranson's admonishment not to stream toilet paper out of the train windows very quickly proved to be a waste of his breath. In fact, no one had probably even thought of it until he put the idea into our heads. By the time the train had reached a reasonable speed, the first solitary streamer of white paper flapped past our compartment window. It wasn't solitary for very long. Soon, increasing numbers of other toilet paper streamers joined it, as every toilet roll on the train was sacrificed to make the train look like some kind of football special hurtling northwards out of Wales.

Apart from the toilet paper streamers, which were eventually lost as the wind snatched them away and replacement supplies became harder to find, the only other incident of note was the broken window.

The five-hour train journey was boring, but most of us managed to pass the time by occupying ourselves with activities like reading, talking, playing cards, or exploring the contents of our white cardboard lunch boxes, in the hope that they might contain an appetizing treat instead of something just basically edible. (Disappointingly, when it came to the latter, all hope was dashed when I found that it contained only an apple, a bottle of orangeade and two sandwiches, one of corned beef and the other containing a thin wafer of processed cheese, but both displaying the curled up corners indicative of advanced sandwich age.) At least that was typically how we occupied our time in my compartment, but in a nearby compartment we could hear the activity level steadily becoming more raucous. The loud noise coming from the compartment continued for quite some time, but then suddenly there was a sound of breaking glass that seemed to come from both inside and outside the train simultaneously. We all looked up from what we were doing and someone said, "What was that?" Another answered that maybe someone had thrown a glass bottle out of the window, but no sooner had this been said than we heard the sound of several pairs of feet running along the corridor in our direction. The next thing we knew, several people rushed past the window of our compartment clutching what appeared to be their personal belongings. From the state of their dress—shirtsleeves and collarless in most cases—they were obviously in a hurry and it didn't take Sherlock Holmes to deduce they were rushing away from where the sound of the breaking glass had originated. One of them slid the door of our compartment open and hurriedly sat down on a vacant seat.

"Hey, I've been here all the time if anybody asks," he panted breathlessly. He paused for a moment to catch his breath and then added by way of explanation, "Somebody just bust a window. We were messing around and then somebody accidentally knocked it out."

Curious to see for ourselves, a few of us got up and went along to the abandoned compartment for a look. The scene that greeted us was pure mayhem: wind was howling into the small confined area through a large jagged hole in the centre of the windowpane. Shards of broken glass were littered everywhere and loose pieces of paper whirled around like frantic seagulls circling a trawler. Having quickly taken it all in, we returned to our own compartment, since there was little point in hanging around to risk taking the blame.

The British Railways train guard soon found out about the broken window and came to investigate. He was alone at first, but then went off and returned a little later with one of our officers and an NCO. Shortly thereafter, all three of them came along the corridor, stopping off at each compartment to ask if any of us had been in the compartment when the window had been broken, or if we knew who did it. Naturally, everyone denied having been there, or of knowing how it had happened. Shortly afterwards, the train made an unscheduled stop at a small station, where a more thorough investigation was held by the British Railway police. It seemed as though the culprit or culprits must have eventually owned up, because a few police constables were seen conversing earnestly with two ashen-faced downcast-looking youths, whilst taking down lengthy notes in their small notepads.

Meanwhile, a couple of British Railways workers boarded the train, carrying a large sheet of plywood, which they somehow fixed over the broken window. After more than an hour's delay, we resumed our journey with the plywood patch in place and a much more subdued atmosphere aboard the train.

Late afternoon saw us finally arriving at Freshfield railway station, the nearest stop to our camp at Woodvale. It felt wonderful to finally be able to stretch my legs on the platform, after having travelled for somewhere around six hours. When the kitbags had been unloaded onto the platform, the train chuffed off to lick its boy entrant-inflicted wounds, leaving us standing there on the platform in a glorious blaze of summer sunshine.

For a while, the NCOs and officers milled around in a small group, talking amongst themselves, before ordering us to form up in ranks of three on the road immediately outside the station. We were then marched along a narrow road that ran parallel to the railway line, towards Woodvale. At first, the area around us appeared to be upper middle class residential, but as we marched along the road towards camp, the landscape opened out to take in the airfield to our front and wooded sand dunes on our left, on the far side of the railway line. After having marched for about a mile, we arrived at the tent encampment on a grassy area of the airfield between the main runway and the railway line. The tarmac road suddenly came to an end, but continued on as a dirt track across the grass and through a gateway in the fence bordering the airfield. We stumbled along this track for a few yards, after entering through the gateway, until we came to tarmac again when we reached the western taxiway or peri-track—short for perimeter track—that ran through the centre of the small tent city. All around us were neat rows of small olive-coloured ridge tents, interspersed here and there by larger mid-brown marquees. This was to be our home for the next two weeks and it certainly looked as though it was going to be a lot more fun than going to workshops every day.

Our column was brought to a halt somewhere in the middle of the encampment and we were immediately given our tent assignments, six people to a tent.

"Pick up a safari bed from the pile here, then take it and drop it in your tent along with your kit. When you've done that, come to the mess tent and we'll get you something to eat," announced our corporal, before dismissing us.

I grabbed one of the olive-coloured canvas bundles that the corporal had indicated. It was about three feet long, six inches in diameter and felt as though there were rods of some kind wrapped inside the canvas. Actually, the ends of four steel rods poked out at an angle for about eight inches from the top and bottom of the bundle and I could feel some shorter rods hidden inside. Clutching our beds and small-packs, we stumbled around looking for the tents to which we'd been assigned. I eventually found mine and threw my stuff on a spot at one end of the tent, essentially staking my claim to that particular bed-space. The tent measured 14 feet by 14 feet and each safari bed, when assembled, was approximately 30 inches wide and 6 feet long, so there wasn't a lot of room to spare in the confined area. Headroom in the tent was 7 feet, which meant that we could at least stand upright.

I made my way back to the mess tent marquee, where the messing arrangements were considerably different from those that we were accustomed to back at Saints. A field kitchen had been set up next to the marquee, where the cooks sweated over wood-fired stoves as they busily cooked an evening meal for our hungry mob of teenage boys. The mess tent itself contained several rows of collapsible wooden tables and chairs set out on the grass "floor". Before long, we were sitting at those very same tables, tucking into a meal that was a lot tastier than anything we'd experienced in the St. Athan mess.

After having finished eating, I extricated my kitbag from the huge pile of similar bags that had been dumped near the mess tent and somehow get settled into my new accommodation. I knew that I needed to familiarize myself with some small but important details, such as the location of the latrines and ablutions—the area where we washed—but first I needed to assemble my safari bed. Untying the tapes that held the canvas bundle together revealed a collection of metal rods, some of which were sewn into the canvas of the bed and others which were free. The rods held captive by the canvas incorporated a number of sockets into which other rods, both captive and free, needed to be inserted for full assembly of the bed. It was as taxing as a very simple jigsaw puzzle and before long I was testing my fully assembled safari bed, which proved to be comfortable and very lightweight.

Comfortable as they were, the beds had a notorious reputation for being very unstable and were prone to tipping an unwary occupant unceremoniously onto the ground at the slightest provocation. I'd heard about this from some of the senior entry boys who had been to summer camp the previous year, so I decided to see for myself. They were right! The mere act of just lying down on the bed was comparable to getting into a small boat. The secret of maintaining stability was to initially place one's bum on or as close to the exact middle of bed as possible. Too much to one side and you were tipped out sideways. Likewise, plunking yourself down too near to either end caused the bed to behave like a seesaw, with the seated end swiftly depositing the sitter on the ground and the other end rising high in the air. Getting into bed at night was an acquired skill and even then, as we all soon discovered, managing to do that successfully didn't guarantee immunity from being tipped out later if an occupant suddenly shifted his weight without being careful to do it gently. Learning to sleep in one of these beds was much like a sailor having to gain his sea legs, but after a few nights we all got the hang of it—most of the time, anyway.

The long journey from St. Athan to Woodvale and then the business of getting settled into the new accommodation had taken a heavy toll on our energy. It had been a long day and most of us were glad to turn in for the night by the time "Lights Out" was sounded. It was still daylight because we were getting near to mid-summer, which was just as well, since there was no lighting in the tents. That first night was a new but not unpleasant experience, if I ignore the number of times that I found myself dumped on the floor because of the safari bed's instability. (We didn't need senior entry raiding parties at Woodvale, because the beds came with their own built-in self-tipping feature.) I dozed off with the sweet aroma of grass and fresh air in my nostrils, but also feeling slightly claustrophobic due to the close confinement of the tent. Occasionally, there was a brief rattle and whoosh of air as an electric train sped past on the railway line not more than a hundred yards away from where I lay. But these things didn't prey on my mind for too long—I was asleep within a few minutes.

At 0630 hours next morning, I awakened from my slumbers to the sound of "Reveille" being played on a trumpet. That came as a surprise in the grogginess of my sleep-filled mind, but I soon remembered that there was no Tannoy system in our primitive environment and that it fell to us trumpeters to play "Reveille" in the morning and "Lights Out" last thing at night. Fortunately for me, I wasn't "duty trumpeter" on that first morning, but my turn would come around more than once during our summer camp.

I had been doing quite a bit of trumpet-playing practice and, even if I say so myself, had become reasonably proficient—if not quite up to Corporal Trumpeter standards—by the time we set out for summer camp. But this morning all I had to do was get up, get washed and be ready for parade at 8:30 to find out what the day had in store for us at this RAF version of Butlin's Holiday Camp.

I fell out of bed (getting out gracefully would take a few more days' practice) and grabbed my towel and toiletries before heading for the latrines and ablutions. The latrines took some getting used to. The urinal was just a trench dug in the ground hidden behind a canvas screen. I wondered what it would be like if I had to go during the night. The thought of missing my footing in the dark and stumbling into the trench didn't seem very appealing—yugh! By contrast, going for a "number two" meant using one of the chemical toilets—the "thunder buckets"—that sat in a row in a nearby marquee. There wasn't much privacy in there and the smell was enough to make anyone gag. Definitely not the place I wanted to sit around in to catch up on my reading!

The ablutions turned out to be a row of open-air washbasins, with cold water supplied by the operation of a hand pump. I washed my face, neck, ears and hands and brushed my teeth, but didn't need to shave—at sixteen, I only needed to shave off the little bit of bum-fluff that sprouted along my upper lip about once every three or four weeks. Back in the tent, I donned the dress of the day: P.E. shirt and shorts under denims and my webbing belt clipped around my waist. My plimsolls and beret completed the outfit, as I headed off to the mess tent for breakfast.

In the breakfast queue, I shuffled along over a trail of bruised, trampled grass, finally getting to the place where the plates were stacked. I picked up the top plate and held it out towards the boy entrants in kitchen whites who were serving out the food. One of the kitchen staff was frying eggs on a hotplate that formed part of the servery. I asked him if he could splash some hot fat over the top of my egg—I didn't like the clear jelly stuff on top and always scraped it off my egg at the St. Athan mess—and he cheerfully obliged. There was no choice at St. Athan: the eggs were fried somewhere in the cavernous recesses of the kitchen and brought out to the servery on a tray. There was little other option there than to point to an egg that appeared to have less clear albumen on top than the others, in the hope that the server would feel charitable enough to scoop up the indicated egg and deposit it on your plate. Here at summer camp, it was a different matter: we were being positively pampered. I passed along the line of servers, getting my plate loaded with streaky bacon, canned plum tomatoes and fried bread, then moved on to the cereal. After putting a ladleful of cornflakes into a cereal bowl, I headed for the milk urn that stood by itself on a table near the entrance to the mess tent. That was a mistake. Halfway there, a gust of wind blew up and took most of the cornflakes out of my bowl. There was nothing I could do about saving them because my other hand held a plateful of cooked breakfast, so I turned around and went back to the large carton of cornflakes and filled my bowl again. This time I put the cereal bowl under my other plate to shield it from the wind. That seemed to work, but by the time I was finally able to sit down and eat, I discovered that the cooked breakfast had become stone cold. Such were the joys of open air breakfasting on that first morning, but experience is a great teacher and I had at least learned how to prevent my cornflakes from becoming airborne.

At 0830 hours we were directed by a corporal boy to form up in threes, by entry number, on an open grassy area in front of our tents. After the usual right dress, we were stood at ease and then "stand easy" to await further information on whatever morning activities we would be undertaking. During the short time that we had been on parade, I had noticed a small group of RAF Regiment sergeants—the famous Rock Apes—standing nearby. Therefore, it came as no great surprise to discover that we would be under their supervision for most of our daily "adventures". The Rock Ape NCO huddle broke up when all of the "entry" flights had been given the "stand easy" and each NCO headed towards his assigned flight of boys. One of them inevitably approached our flight and stopped in front of us with a friendly grin on his face.

"Good morning!" He bellowed.

Hardly anyone responded and those who did only managed a very tame "Good morning, sergeant".

The grin vanished. "When I say 'good morning,' I mean 'good morning!' he roared. "Now let's hear it again and this time put some bloody life into it! Good morning!"

"Good morning, sergeant!" We yelled.

"Again!" He shouted, "and louder this time!"

"Good morning, sergeant!" This time we yelled it about as loud as we could.

"That's better," he said, the grin returning to his face. "Now, let's tell you…"

That was about as far as he got before his voice was suddenly drowned out by the gravelly growl of an aircraft engine being given full throttle, somewhere off to our left. All heads swivelled to look in the direction of the sound, just in time to see a Spitfire start its take-off roll from the end of the runway that passed across our front. The fierce growl got louder and increased in pitch as the aircraft came closer to our position. It lifted off the runway, just before reaching the point that would bring it directly in front of us, the undercarriage retracting even as the wheels seemed to have just barely left the ground. When it drew level with us, we caught the full impact of the naked sound waves that were being thrown off by the propeller-blade tips: a sound so powerful that it vibrated our teeth, our bodies and even the very ground beneath our feet. A swirl of condensed vapour whipped backwards from the spinning propeller as it clawed greedily at the moist morning air, pulling the fighter forwards and upwards in a shallow climb. Then, after passing in front of us, the spine-tingling sound of the powerful Merlin engine became steadily lower in pitch and more throbbing. As its growl grew fainter with distance, I thought I could even make out the crackle of exhaust from each of the individual twelve cylinders. We watched it, heads now turned to our right, as the Spitfire grew smaller and smaller until it became nothing more than a small speck against the sky, but the low throaty beat of its engine was still audible long after the plane itself had disappeared from view. The whole episode had started a buzz of excitement amongst us. Spontaneous comments like, "Wow, did you see that?" and "A SPITfire!" flew from many mouths, to no one in particular; we just needed to say something that paid homage to that mystical moment. But the sergeant didn't let it go on for too long.

"Silence in the ranks," he shouted, "remember you're on parade!"

That brought us back down to earth and our attention back to what he had been about to say a few minutes earlier.

Later, I learned that there were actually three Spitfires based there and that they belonged to the Meteorological Flight. The weather kites, as they were called, flew daily and each of these occasions was a very special event to be savoured. Indeed, I never got tired of seeing that graceful shape in its natural element and hearing the somehow deeply satisfying growl of a Merlin engine at full throttle. At the time, I recognized it as just a Spitfire, but I've learned since then that all three were PR Mk XIX Spitfires and they were the last three of this famous aircraft to see operational service in the RAF. In fact, that year, 1957, was their final year, which probably means that we unknowingly witnessed a small piece of RAF history when we saw them in operation during our short stay at Woodvale.[1]

"Pay attention lads," the sergeant's grin was replaced with a more serious look, "we're going for a route march on the beach. So I want you to go back to your tents and get your denims and hats off and leave them there, then report back here on the double, just in your P.E. gear."

On our return, we discovered that a second Regiment sergeant had joined the party to assist the first sergeant.

---

[1] For the fate of the Woodvale Spitfires, see Appendix 2

Together, they set us off marching along the tarmac peri-track on our way to the beach. As we were marching, the sergeants began encouraging us to sing a marching song. I think that one of them may even have started us off on our first song, but soon we were all singing "Green Grow the Rushes-O". It consists of something like ten or twelve verses, but I can only remember the first five, which go like this:

> I'll sing you one-O
> Green grow the rushes-O
> What is your one-O?
>
> One is one and all alone,
> And ever more shall be.
>
> I'll sing you two-O
> Green grow the rushes-O
> What is your two-O?
> Two, two, the ruddy SPs
> Covered all in blanc-ho-ho
> One is one and all alone,
> And ever more shall be.
>
> I'll sing you three-O
> Green grow the rushes-O
> What is your three-O?
> Three, three, arrivals!
> Two, two, the ruddy SPs
> Covered all in blanc-ho-ho
> One is one and all alone,
> And ever more shall be.
>
> I'll sing you four-O
> Green grow the rushes-O
> What is your four-O?
> Four for the squadron markers
> Three, three, arrivals!
> Two, two, the ruddy SPs
> Covered all in blanc-ho-ho
> One is one and all alone,
> And ever more shall be.
>
> I'll sing you five-O
> Green grow the rushes-O
> What is your five-O?
> Five for the blankets on your bed and *
> Four for the squadron markers

Three, three, arrivals!
Two, two, the ruddy SPs
Covered all in blanc-ho-ho
One is one and all alone,
And ever more shall be.

*This line was frequently replaced with "Five for the wank stains on your bed and...."

We marched south and when the perimeter-track curved away to our left we continued in a straight line across the airfield grass, until we picked up the sandy dirt-track by which we had first arrived at the tent encampment. But instead of continuing on to where the track became a tarmac road, we were brought to a halt before a wide gateway in the fence separating the camp from the railway line. The singing stopped as one of the sergeants opened the gate and then looked up and down the line to make sure that there were no approaching trains. When satisfied that all was clear, he signalled to the other sergeant to march us across the level crossing. Both sergeants then stationed themselves so that one watched out for trains coming from the north, while the other guarded the southern approach.

On reaching the far side of the railway line, we passed through a second gate, which the first sergeant had opened in advance of our crossing. After passing through this gate, we began to encounter loose sand. The sand made it progressively more and more difficult to keep in step, as we began to make our way between sand dunes and pine trees towards the sound of distant waves breaking on a shore. Then, just when marching any further seemed to be next to impossible, one of the sergeants called out for us to break step. Shortly after that, we emerged onto a long wide beach.

As we moved away from the sand dunes, but continued to head in the general direction of the Irish Sea, the sand gradually became damper and firmer. Both sergeants began calling out the step again, "Left, right, left, right," making us resume marching order. When we reached the seashore and were only a few yards from getting our feet wet, the first sergeant lead the column into a slight turn that brought it parallel with the shallow breakers. No sooner had this happened than the second sergeant called out, "Double," and we were off at a trot along the long beach, the wind in our hair and the firm damp sand underfoot. It was an exhilarating experience and somehow set the tone for what summer camp was all about: fresh air, fitness, team building and good clean fun.

We ran for what must have been five miles all told, before returning to the level crossing and back across the tracks for our midday meal. The singing picked up again as soon as we got back on the grass, but this time we needed no encouragement—it just issued forth spontaneously.

That afternoon, we were assigned to be the camp fatigue party, washing dishes and tins at the mess tent, picking up litter around the camp and helping to empty the rubbish bins. Thankfully, we weren't expected to empty the thunder buckets—that dubious privilege belonged to a contractor who came around each day with a tractor drawn tank-on-wheels. It was always advisable to stay upwind of him whilst he made his rounds.

There were two good things about being on the fatigue party; one was that we finished early and the other was that the cooks prepared a special meal for us before the rest of the herd turned up for tea. Being finished early and having a square meal under our belts gave Butterworth and me the idea of going to explore Southport. The electric trains ran every half hour, so all we needed to do was get out of our denims, get washed, put on our best blues and then catch the next available train. It wasn't very long before we were standing on the Freshfield station platform with only a few minutes to spare before the next train was due.

"You know," said Butterworth, "If I went across to the other platform I could be home in Liverpool in a very short time." I looked at him, wondering if he'd changed his mind about Southport. "But I'm not going to," he continued, "why would I want to go there?" He asked rhetorically. I understood. His home life had been as unhappy as mine.

"No, we can have a much better time in Southport," I replied.

We both grinned and at that moment the Southport-bound train swept almost silently into the station, its arrival announced only by the squeal of its brakes.

Southport seemed to be a more genteel place than Barry Island, but the one thing that both resorts had in common was a funfair, which we made a beeline for as soon as we got off the train. And there we revelled in the attention of girls of around our own age, who were attracted to our uniforms. They were mostly holidaymakers and out for the afternoon without their parents. The girls' fascination with our uniforms gave us the perfect opportunity to break the ice, enabling us to 'chat them up' very easily. From there, it was only a short step to take two of them on some of the more exciting rides, where they pretended to be scared and cuddled up to us. We, like the gentlemen that we were, put our protective arms around them to make them feel safe. For the whole afternoon, it was one thrill ride after another with the sweet young ladies clinging to us for dear life. Then we went with the girls to a secluded spot for a little snogging—and whatever else we could reasonably get away with.

CHAPTER 9

The Royal Tournament

The very next morning it was my turn to be the duty trumpeter and the first order of business was to play Reveille. But if it takes a trumpeter to wake up the camp, then who wakes up the trumpeter? Actually, the arrangement was fairly simple. Six of us had been nominated to be 2 Wing's trumpeters during summer camp and we were therefore all housed together in the same tent. The duty trumpeter for a particular day placed a white towel across the end of his bed before turning in for the night and then, in the morning, the camp Orderly Corporal was supposed to come to the tent and wake him up. It was a good arrangement in theory and had actually worked for the previous morning's trumpeter. But something went sadly wrong on this particular morning, because the Orderly Corporal for that day failed to make an appearance at our tent. I slumbered on, oblivious to all. Fortunately, one of the other boys woke up and after glancing at his watch he realized that Reveille was late by a good ten minutes. Seeing the white towel still in place across the foot of my bed, he vigorously shook me awake. Since there was no time to get dressed, I hurried out of the tent, dressed only in pyjamas, with my trumpet clutched tightly in my hand and headed for my place of duty at the camp flagpole. The Orderly Officer and Orderly Sergeant were already hoisting the colours—the RAF Ensign— when I arrived there and worse yet, the Wing Commander had put in an appearance, wanting to know why Reveille hadn't been sounded. He gave me a disgusted look as I rushed forward, dressed only in my PJ's.

"The Orderly Corporal didn't wake me, sir," I tried to explain, but my mouth was dry from just having woken up, so all that came out was an incoherent mumble.

"Get on with it," he growled, "and never let me see you show up on parade looking like that again!"

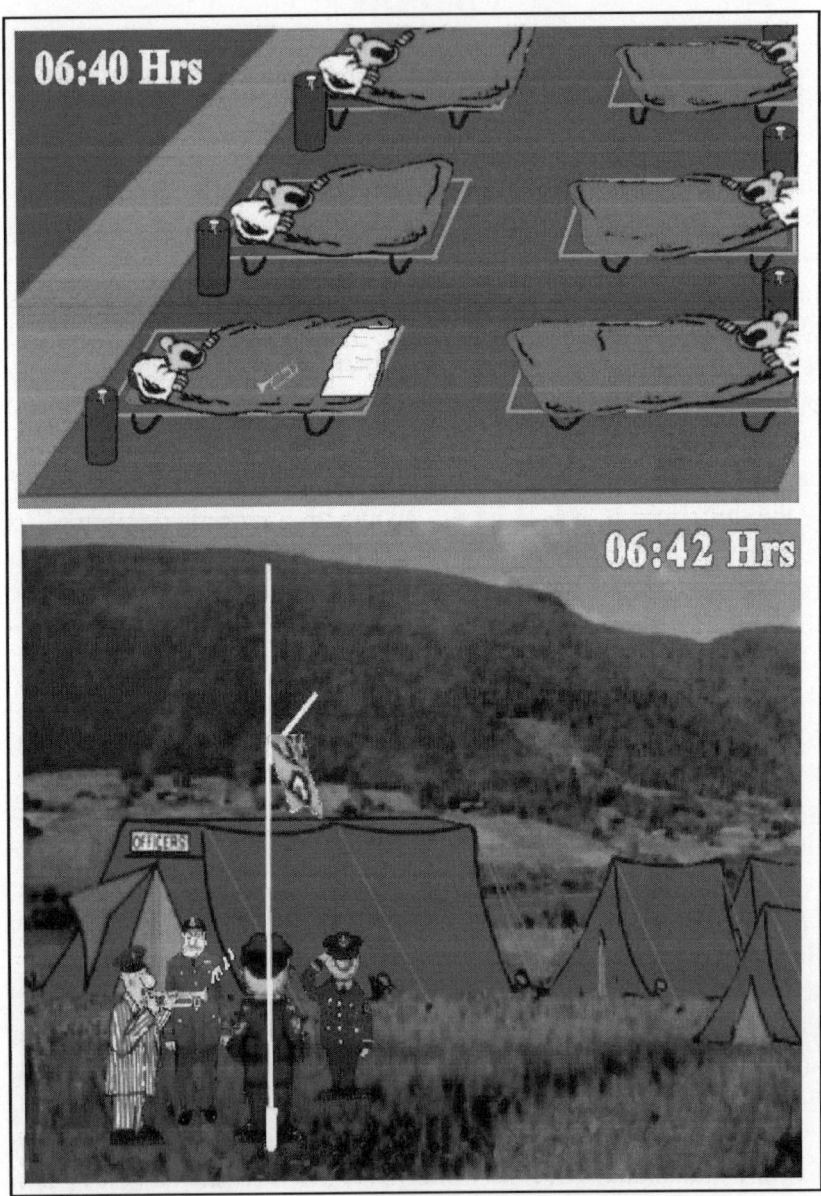

Late Summer Camp Reveille
As envisioned by "The Chequered Band" cartoonist, Mickie Collins.

Being greeted by the Wing Commander was bad enough, but my troubles were far from over. I pushed the mouthpiece into the trumpet and put it to my lips. The metal was stone cold in the chilly morning air and, to my horror, I found that my lips felt paralysed and I couldn't make them change shape to play the notes. All I seemed to be capable of squeezing from the trumpet were some unearthly discordant noises. But at least I achieved the desired effect of awaking my slumbering fellow-campers, although it certainly wasn't Reveille by any stretch of the imagination.

Not surprisingly, all of the good advice came after the event. One of the more experienced trumpeters in the tent said, "When you have to play Reveille, you should keep the mouthpiece in bed with you all night, so that it's warm when you come to play it in the morning."

It was advice I would certainly remember when my next stint as duty-trumpeter came around, but right at that moment I was just feeling glad that I hadn't been put on a charge for any of the breaches of good order and discipline that I'd dragged through the dust that morning. Let's see: late on parade; improperly dressed on parade; incompetent playing; and I'm sure the Wingco could have come up with quite a few more things if he had decided to throw the book at me. I was dead lucky that he let me get away with just a curt remark.

* * *

One of the main objectives of summer camp, from the RAF's point of view, was to teach us about teamwork and to show us how to pool our combined initiatives for efficient problem solving—like the compass-reading exercise that our RAF Regiment sergeants put us through one day, for example.

We were divided into small teams, given a hand-drawn map and a compass, taught how to take compass bearings on prominent features and then navigate a complicated course by following the compass bearings noted on the map through a series of area landmarks, such as a high sand dune or distinctive pine tree. It was a lot of fun, as most of the activities were and at the same time taught me, for one, how to find my way by using a map and compass.

Another exercise was the task of setting up a means of transferring personnel and equipment across a "ravine", using nothing more than ropes, poles and pulleys. The sergeants coached us on how to set up a trestle-like structure on each side of the ravine, braced with ropes and pegs, which we then used to support a strong line strung across the ravine. The acid test came when someone was supposed to make a trip across this makeshift bridge to prove that it was fit for its purpose, by riding on a crude sling contraption that we'd rigged up to travel along the line on a pulley. We were so confident in our own handiwork that there were absolutely no volunteers, but then we managed to persuade a young National Service Pilot Officer from the Education Section to make the first trip across. We were all chuffed that the bridge held up under his weight and that he made it safely across. But then, we knew all along that he would.

All of our daily adventures were carried out under the supervision of the RAF Regiment and as they marched us to and from our tent encampment we became so accustomed to singing our marching songs that, after the first day, we did it without any need of their encouragement. And, along the way, many of us had acquired staves and stout walking sticks. These we ornamented by cutting designs into the wood or bark with our penknives. In keeping with the atmosphere of a more relaxed discipline, each Entry made its own distinctive flag, which was carried high by one of the lads at the front of each column on our marches. When one Entry column met another, there was much light-hearted banter between the two groups, with lots of flag waving and gesturing. The Regiment sergeants seemed to enjoy this as much as we did and actively encouraged us to have pride in our respective Entries.

On one particular day, we were taken to the Altcar army shooting range for rifle practice. This was a 100-yard range that made our 25-yard range at St. Athan seem like a shooting booth at a funfair. The targets were much larger to compensate for the greater distance and the aiming point area was manned. Each time anyone fired at his target, a coloured disc on the end of a long pole would materialize upwards from behind the sand bunker at the target base, to indicate the general area in which someone fired at a target and then, when the inevitable disc-on-a-pole appeared, would blast away at it to see if we could hit the moving target. It was a lot more fun than shooting at a boring bulls-eye target, but also a total waste of time. Later, when I saw some of my Entry-mates sporting their marksman badges, I felt a tinge of regret that I hadn't also used my time at the Altcar range a little better to earn a marksmanship badge.

It was at Woodvale that I experienced the wonderful sensation of flight for the first time in my life. The aircraft was an Avro Anson—a monoplane powered by two radial piston engines.

On the day of the flight, a group of us were taken to the Station Flight dispersal area where we were each fitted with a Mae West and a parachute and then instructed on how to use

SUMMER CAMP, 1957, AT WOODVALE
Testing a rope bridge, a reliability and initiative project

A brave Pilot Officer tests our rope bridge. The author is the tallest of the group on the right, between Richard Butterworth on the right and Howard "Ginge" Brown on the left.

them. The parachute harness would be worn throughout the flight, but the parachute pack was kept separately at a convenient point aboard the Anson, where it could be readily clipped on to the front of the harness in the "unlikely event of an emergency". We then waited for the aircraft to return from its previous flight.

It wasn't too long before the Anson landed on the runway and then taxied around the perimeter track into the dispersal, where we waited. The butterflies in my stomach became more agitated by the moment. A ground-crew member held up two yellow marshalling bats and as the Anson taxied straight towards him, he repeatedly waved them up and down in semaphore fashion to guide the pilot. When the aircraft was almost on top of him, he lowered one bat but continued waving the other. At this signal, the aircraft turned around in its own length to face in the direction from which it had just come. Another ground-crew member, waiting a short distance away, then began waving his bats when he came into the pilot's view. But he only brought the aircraft a short distance forward before holding both bats straight above his head as a signal for the pilot to brake and come to a stop. Both men then ran and placed chocks in front of the main wheels, to prevent it from rolling forward if the brakes were accidentally released. They then wheeled a short set of steps up to the passenger cabin door, after which one of them climbed up the steps and opened the door. Very soon a group of Boy Entrants emerged, one or two of them clutching small brown paper bags that they had obviously used in a moment of gastric distress. Now it was our turn, as we were ushered towards the steps and up into the Anson.

On entering the passenger cabin, my sense of smell instantly registered an aroma that was peculiar to military aircraft of that era. The bouquet was complex but not unpleasant. Some of it was given off by the rubber insulation that sheathed the aircraft's electrical wiring, but it also combined other fragrances that were too difficult to separate and identify. Yet these smells, when combined together, became a signature aroma that was instantly associated with aircraft. Once smelled, it imprinted itself on my sub-conscious, never ever to be mistaken for anything else as long as I live. The encounter with this aroma, on entering the Anson, added further to my sense of excitement at the prospect of "slipping the surly bonds of earth and dancing the skies on laughter-silvered wings". [2]

As with all passenger aircraft of that time, there was only a single central aisle that sloped upwards from the tail end of the Anson. I made my way up the slope grabbing at the backs of seats on either side to help me make the climb, before taking my place in a seat where a crew member indicated that I should sit. It was a comfortable passenger-aircraft type of seat, which wasn't very surprising since Ansons were commonly used during that period as "station communications aircraft", which was something of a euphemism for the station commander's personal executive transportation. The passenger cabin contained ten seats in two single rows down each side of the cabin, each adjacent to a square-shaped window that permitted good viewing for all passengers.

When all were aboard, the sergeant aircrew member, who had earlier directed me to my seat, stood at the front of the cabin and instructed us to fasten our seatbelts. He then proceeded to lecture us on the safety procedures we would need to follow in any of the "unlikely events" (that phrase again) that we would have to bail out, or otherwise be forced to evacuate the plane in an emergency on land or in water. Meanwhile, the ground-crew slammed the door closed and then it was chocks away! The sound of the engine picked up in intensity as the pilot opened the throttles for a brief period, then he released the brakes and the plane lurched forward and started rolling at a steady clip in the direction of the perimeter track. As we trundled along, the propellers appeared to be just fluttering around because the engines needed to run only at idling speed to keep the craft moving. Then, after about five minutes of taxiing, we reached the end of the runway but came to a stop before actually moving onto it. The pilot checked each engine in turn by running it up to full power, then throttling back. When it seemed that he was satisfied, the brakes came off again and we taxied on to the end of the runway, with the tail simultaneously swinging around

---

[2] Paraphrased from the poem "High Flight" by John Gillespie Magee, Jr. See Appendix 3

through ninety degrees so that we were now pointed in the right direction, ready for takeoff. Both engines came up to full power and we lurched off, as everything around us in the cabin began vibrating and rattling. Within a few seconds, the tail lifted off the ground, bringing the cabin to a level position. Then, as we gathered speed, the bumps on the runway became fewer and fewer, giving an increasing impression of weightlessness, until finally the main wheels cleared the ground and the ride became a lot smoother, although the occasional dip seemed to leave my stomach several feet above where it was supposed to be. The aircraft still vibrated from the exertions of its two radial engines, as the "Anny" struggled into the air in a shallow climb. It wasn't a Spitfire, but I couldn't have been more excited if it was.

The noise of the engines seemed to become muffled until I swallowed, unwittingly equalizing the pressure between my inner and outer ears, which immediately brought the noise back again at full volume. My forehead was pressed to the window as I watched the ground dropping away and the fields, houses and cars became a miniature landscape. It was a bright clear summer day, so nothing was hidden from our view as the aircraft banked around to the right and headed towards the coast. I could see that we were turning and that the attitude of the plane had changed as one wing dipped and seemed fixed on a point on the ground far below. Since I was sitting in one of the right-hand seats, my brain told me that I should feel myself being pressed against the fuselage, but I was very conscious of the fact that my body felt absolutely no sensation of gravity and it was just as though I was sitting in a level position instead of at a steep angle. The Anson levelled off as we crossed the shoreline, putting us out over the Irish Sea. Then we made another right turn before levelling off again so that we were now flying north, parallel with the coastline.

The aircrew sergeant had stayed in the passenger cabin with us and he now started pointing out some landmarks, shouting most of the time to make himself heard above the noise. He indicated Southport as it came up on the right-hand side, prompting someone seated on the left side of the aircraft to come over and crowd up to the window at which I was seated, so that he could see. Shortly after that, the land faded away to our right as we crossed an expanse of open sea. Over in the distance I could make out a silvery ribbon of water that contrasted brightly with the dull grey of the land that surrounded it. As my eyes stayed with this shining arrow of light I realized that it was a river. And, as we drew abreast of it, the sliver of silver pointed directly to the east, reflecting the morning light and then just for a split second, glinted with even greater intensity as it suddenly caught the sun's direct reflection. Then, while my gaze was still locked on the river, we regained the coastline again on the other side of the estuary.

"There's Blackpool Tower," the sergeant called out.

My eyes became glued to the tall brown skeletal structure of the famous tower, as it seemed to slowly pass by on our right. This was the first time I'd ever seen Blackpool Tower in real life and I mentally marked it off as "done" on a longstanding mental list of famous places or things that I just had to see.

After flying past the tower, the aircraft banked to the right and flew a half circle around it, then levelled off as we headed in the opposite direction. Now we were over land, with the seaward side to our right.

"Look, there's Warton and that's the P-1 down there," said the sergeant, suddenly and excitedly, as he peered out of the window nearest to him.

He was referring to the new top of the line supersonic fighter aircraft that would later be named the "Lightning," but which at this moment in its history was still undergoing flight-testing and had not yet entered into RAF service. I knew a little about it and looked down with great anticipation, expecting to see the sleek secrecy-enshrouded aircraft. But I could see nothing except mediocre looking buildings that were probably hangars. It was a big disappointment and yet, judging by some of the comments around me, a few of the others had actually seen it. After that we saw fields and villages, roads with cars and lorries crawling along like ants, but nothing else of great note.

Soon the Anson started descending and my ears started to pop as the pressure on them changed. We'd been told to swallow when this happened, so now I swallowed hard each time successive waves of pressure caused my ears to feel uncomfortable. The pilot levelled off after a while and then I heard the engines being throttled back and saw the flaps go down as the aircraft slowed. Before long, there was a loud thud with an accompanying increase in the wind noise. These sudden noises were alarming, but the sergeant must have noticed the frightened look on several of our faces, because he quickly shouted out that it was only due to the wheels being lowered. The ground started to get closer and closer, then a quick flash of the white threshold markings passed underneath, to be immediately replaced by the dark grey of the runway tarmac. We floated above the surface for a few long-seeming seconds and then the wheels touched the surface with a gentle bump. Now the tail started to settle down onto the runway and soon the tail-wheel hit with a smaller bump. The Anson coasted along on the ground with both propellers fluttering around in idle, until we reached a convenient exit point on the runway. There was a faint squeal of brakes as the pilot used differential braking to yaw the tail around and point us towards the exit, then we continued taxiing back to the dispersal and waited for the door to be opened before disembarking. In all, the flight lasted for only half an hour, but I had found it very exciting and would have gone back up again without a moment's hesitation, if that had been a real possibility.

* * *

The weather was glorious during the entire two weeks of our summer camp, which encouraged me to make the trip into Southport every evening that I could afford the train fare and have a little left over to spend when I got there. But, coming up to payday, the cash situation was usually stretched a little thin, so Southport wasn't always an option. Fortunately, there were other things we could do on warm sunny evenings that required no cash outlay. We frequently charged around in the sand dunes near the beach, sometimes defending the higher ones against all-comers like a teenage version of "King of the Castle". It was a great way of having fun while burning off some youthful energy.

We would really have preferred to meet some girls, but there didn't seem to be too many around in the immediate neighbourhood of the camp.

Evenings in the camp could also get boisterous. Once, as dusk was falling, there was a brilliant flash of light from the direction of the electric railway line. I heard next day that someone had thrown a safari bed onto the track and the bed's metal frame had fallen across the live centre rail and one of the main rails, short-circuiting them. As a result, the electric train service was out of action for several hours and Boy Entrants once again came under the very unwelcome scrutiny of the British Railways police, although I don't think they ever found the culprit on this occasion.

The weekend saw us flocking into Southport *en masse*. There were lots more girls around during these two days, and the sight of our uniforms seemed to attract them like bees to honey. But the uniforms also attracted some attention that we could well have done without. Teddy boys from Liverpool came to Southport at the weekends as well and they didn't like us for many reasons. The image we presented to the world was the complete opposite to theirs. We were smartly dressed in our uniforms and had short, well-kept hair. Teddy boys, on the other hand, dressed in slouchy loose "drape" jackets, drainpipe trousers, thick crepe soles and long greasy hair. The older generation saw them as a threat to traditional values (along with rock 'n' roll), whereas Boy Entrants exhibited the image and values of the older folks (but little did they know that we also liked rock 'n' roll). Scuffles broke out in several places, but were usually broken up by the civilian police. I didn't have the misfortune to get into a scuffle, but came as close as I wanted to on the only Saturday that I was there.

Three or four of us were walking along on one of the main Southport thoroughfares, talking amongst ourselves and generally minding our own business, when we suddenly became conscious of being surrounded by several tough-looking individuals dressed in Teddy boy clothes, all of whom looked a few years older than we were. One of the toughs produced a flick knife and started playing with it, repeatedly making the blade spring out by pressing the release catch and then folding the blade back in again, obviously trying to intimidate us—and succeeding.

"Oh look at the little Brylcreem boys," mocked one youth, who appeared to be the leader. He made a grab for one of our SD hats, but the wearer saw the move coming and grabbed it off his own head and clutched it to his chest. We all followed suit, knowing that they would try to snatch someone's hat.

"How much money have you got?" The gang leader demanded and with this he made a menacing step towards me, his face not more than six inches from mine.

"None," I stammered weakly, betraying the fact that I was scared.

"Liar," he snarled and then grabbed me by the lapels of my tunic. It seemed that I was going to have to fight whether I wanted to or not; I was worried about the flick knife and whatever other weapons they might be carrying. One of the others started patting my pockets, trying to find if I had a wallet. At this point, I began to think that my chances of getting out of this situation unhurt and without being robbed weren't very promising. But help arrived when it was needed most, like the cavalry arriving in the nick of time. Only it wasn't the cavalry that arrived, it was two Southport Bobbies, one of them a sergeant and the other a constable. Both were dressed in their summer attire of blue shirts with rolled-up sleeves.

"What's going on here?" The sergeant demanded, but no one answered. The question was redundant anyway, because the situation was very obvious. The gang leader still had a good grip on my lapels and didn't seem in any hurry to let go.

"Let him go," the sergeant ordered. Reluctantly, the Teddy boy released me, shoving me away as he did so. "Now, move along," the sergeant commanded and then turning to us, "you lads get on your way too! That way!" He pointed in the opposite direction to the one taken by our attackers.

Scowling, the Teddy boys started ambling off in a deliberately unhurried fashion that was intended to show their contempt for authority, but as they walked away one turned and spat in my direction. A large ugly green lump of sputum landed on my trouser leg at about calf level. Angry as I was at this insulting act, I realized it could have been a lot worse, so I turned and walked away with the other lads in the direction indicated by the police sergeant, which happened to be towards the railway station. I don't know about the others, but it took me quite a while to stop shaking after what seemed to be a narrow escape. At the railway station, I made a beeline for the public toilets and gingerly removed the disgusting gob of spit from my uniform, using plenty of toilet paper in the process. There was some talk around camp about a large group of us going into town armed with our webbing belts and doing serious battle with the Teds, but it was all talk and nothing ever came of it.

On the whole, this unpleasant episode was an isolated one and didn't mar the good feeling I had about Southport. Ironically, that very same weekend I met someone who was more than just the usual run-of-the-mill type of girl. Her name was Jennifer and, not surprisingly, I met her at the funfair. When I first came to Southport I had decided just to have a good time and pursue a policy of love-'em-and-leave-'em in the belief that two weeks wasn't long enough to get serious with anyone, but Jennifer had a quality that attracted me and made me want to get to know her better. And she was different in another way; she actually lived in Southport and wasn't just a fleeting holidaymaker. That had an immediate advantage, because she was there all the time that I was (if anything, it was I who was the fleeting holidaymaker). For the remainder of summer camp I took every opportunity to spend time with her. Most of the time I went into Southport at the end of our daily activities, cash situation permitting. But to make it easier on my meagre finances, she sometimes made the trip to Freshfield by electric train and we walked on the beach together, talking and laughing as we dodged the small wavelets that tried to catch us by surprise and overwhelm our unwary feet. Then, when we got tired of that, we kissed and cuddled in a secluded hollow amongst the sand dunes until it was time for Jennifer's train back to Southport.

All good things come to an end, and so it was with summer camp. The wonderful time that I spent there was easily the highlight of my entire time as a Boy Entrant. We were blessed with near perfect weather during the whole of our stay, which is very surprising, given that our predecessor campers from Cosford suffered cool rainy weather that mysteriously came to an end at the same time as their summer camp finished. Just as mysteriously, the rainy season resumed as soon as we struck camp and headed back to Wales. Maybe it helped, on some higher plane, that our home station was named for a saint.

Jennifer and I said goodbye, temporarily, and we promised faithfully to write to each other; a promise that we both kept for a long time. I would see her again, although it wouldn't be for quite some time after I completed my Boy Entrant training.

For most of the boys, summer camp lasted an enjoyable two weeks, but not for the trumpet band members. We departed for St. Athan on the 1st of June, a few days ahead of the main contingent, because we needed to make some final preparations for our appearance at the Royal Tournament. As a farewell gesture, we all joined together as a group to play our final Last Post. By this time I'd taken the good advice offered to me earlier and kept my trumpet mouthpiece warm in bed with me throughout the night, so that my subsequent renderings of Reveille sounded a lot sweeter than the first attempt—if Reveille can really be described as "sweet".

The Last Post was a much nicer piece to play and on that final evening we put everything we had into it because we knew that it truly was the Last Post for us. Six of us formed up around the flagpole and at a nod from the senior trumpeter we played it out, the notes bringing moistness to our eyes though we tried hard not to show it. When the final notes had faded away, we sadly lowered our trumpets and then shook hands with each other in mutual congratulations for a job well done. Summer camp was over for us.

Our return to St. Athan that Saturday was quite a different experience compared to the jubilant journey to Woodvale of two weeks earlier. This time there was no special train to take us there. Instead, our small group was issued with travel warrants to be exchanged for normal British Railways train tickets and a travel allowance for food. An NCO was also detailed to accompany us to make sure we got there safe and sound, or to keep us from getting up to mischief, or probably both.

We started off by taking the electric train service to Liverpool, which was in the opposite direction to Southport. That by itself was reason enough for a heavy-hearted feeling as the train pulled away, putting more distance between Jennifer and me with every clickety-clack of its wheels on the rails.

Much bull awaited us at our destination, because of the need to get our kit all cleaned and made ready for the big event. We had already been informed that a full dress rehearsal was planned for the coming Tuesday, which would be our last performance before appearing at the Royal Tournament itself, on Thursday the 6th of June, 1957.

At Liverpool we changed trains, taking the mainline train to Barry, then a change at Pontypool Road and another change at Barry to get us to Gileston, where we waited around for ages until an RAF bus came down from the camp to pick us up and deposit our weary bodies at the Guardroom. Finally, there was a long walk to our billets, carrying our heavy kitbags. On entering my billet, it seemed as though I'd never been away and that it had all been a dream, although it was eerily quiet without the others, who were still enjoying themselves at Woodvale.

On Sunday, we attended band practice, during which we went through all the marching routines to clear away any mental cobwebs that might have accumulated during summer camp. Corporal Naylor seemed satisfied, after going through the routine a few times and called a halt. Now it was time to receive the special kit that would embellish our uniforms for the big event. Each of us was issued with a white webbing belt, a white bandsman's music pouch complete with a white leather shoulder strap and what looked like a large tangled clump of red and gold rope-like material, complete with tassels, that was similar to the binding on our trumpets. Like the others, I was supposed to wear the small music pouch across my back by draping the shoulder strap from my right shoulder across my chest. It was purely for decoration because, as I've already mentioned, we didn't use sheet music to play our trumpets.

The red and gold rope material, when untangled, turned out to be braid that was to be worn on our uniforms. One end of the rope was knitted into a kind of epaulette that I had to hand-stitch onto the crest of my tunic's left shoulder. When that was accomplished, it resulted in the two tassels hanging down on the outside of my upper arm from the epaulette. The other end of the braid was also knitted into a shape that was thinner and longer than the epaulette. It had a loop at the very end by which means it was attached to the top button of my tunic underneath the buttonhole. Then, between these two extremities, a pair of single ropes was passed over my head and worn loosely around the neck like a lanyard. A pair of white gloves completed the whole ensemble. Altogether, the heavily-overdone braid with the white belts and gloves, when added to our chequered hatbands, wheel badges and stripes, certainly brightened up the uniforms, giving us the appearance of a delegation of Generals from some far-off banana republic.

Oh and I nearly forgot to mention that I got a new trumpet to replace my sadly battered horn. I don't suppose it was quite the thing to appear in the prestigious Royal Tournament playing something that resembled a ragman's battered old bugle. The new instrument was flawless in its curved lines and I took unusual pleasure in applying some Brasso to polish the yellow metal to an eye-catching gleam.

There was other work to do as well. My uniform needed pressing to give the creases a razor-edge appearance and I needed to clean my boots, buttons and badges until they gleamed and then sew the braid epaulette onto the shoulder of my tunic. After that, the white belts and music pouch needed a fresh coating of white blanco. All of this had to be completed by Tuesday, when we were to be put through our paces in the full dress rehearsal.

Tuesday arrived and just to add a little stage fright to the whole proceedings, the Station Commandant, Air Commodore Perkins and his wife, as well as a very large group of officers and their families, attended the event. I'm pleased to say that all went well and we completed the rehearsal without anything going seriously awry. Our audience treated us to a hearty round of applause as we marched off the parade ground, making us feel proud and ready for the greater challenge ahead.

The next day was another day of continued preparation involving more Brasso and black Kiwi boot polish. On top of all this, the main contingent of boys returned from summer camp. I sat on my bed cleaning and polishing as chaos swirled around me; people unpacking kitbags, making up beds and talking as they tried to get settled back into life under a solid roof. I watched and cleaned, going about the normal routine that I'd already adjusted to a few days earlier and mildly resenting the mayhem that had arrived with these Johnny-come-latelys. The irritation was partly justified because I had an early start next morning, since the band would be leaving at 0700 hours on a specially chartered motor coach for the journey to Earls Court, so I needed to get a good night's sleep. Alas, it wasn't to be.

Bed check settled everyone down and it seemed as though all would be well. The lights were turned off and before long the billet fell quiet as everyone went off to sleep. I don't know what time it happened, but I was awakened by a peculiar sound that seemed to be coming from the end of the room. It sounded like a scratching, fumbling sound and then I realized that someone was down there in the darkness mumbling to himself.

"Where's the flap?" The voice said, over and over. This puzzled me in my half-asleep state, but I suddenly understood when I heard the unmistakable sound of someone peeing in the same general area where the voice had been muttering.

"What's going on?" I called out. This woke up most of the other sleepers and then someone switched on the billet lights. The mystery piddler was revealed for all to see. He was one of our new 30th entry boys, standing sheepishly in a puddle of urine that was spreading widely around him in all directions.

"I thought I was in the tent," he explained, "and I couldn't find the flap to go out for a piss."

"Well, you better get it cleaned up," said Leading Boy German, who had appeared in the doorway to find out the reason for all the sudden noise.

The Phantom Piddler, as he came to be known after that, set to work and cleaned up his mess, but it was a good hour before we were able to turn the lights out again and the whole episode cost me the loss of some badly needed sleep.

Next morning, the 6th of June 1957, I was awakened at 0530 hours, having booked an early call at the Guardroom on the previous evening. The early call procedure was identical to what I had experienced at summer camp—the Orderly Corporal made the rounds of billets where early calls had been requested and woke up those who had stretched a white towel across the foot of their bed before going to sleep. After being roused from sleep by the Orderly Corporal's gentle but forceful hand shaking my feet, I got up, washed and dressed and then headed to the mess for an early breakfast. Many of the other band lads were already there, but no one was talking very much at this ungodly hour of the morning. The only sounds that disturbed the pre-dawn quietness were the occasional loud clanging of pots and pans that echoed off the tiled walls of the mess kitchen and the rattling and rumbling of the steam being forced into the hot water tank that we used to wash our mugs and irons.

With breakfast over and a few puffs on a Woodbine to complement the food, I made my way to the Guardroom with the others. All of us were dressed in the full regalia that we would be performing in that evening and were thankful to be spared the nudges, stares and sniggers of the other camp inhabitants, who were still comfortably tucked up in their beds. Two luxury motor coaches that had been hired from a Barry company were waiting for us, so I climbed aboard, trumpet in one hand and small pack containing my overnight stuff in the other and settled into the comfortable softness of the luxury coach seat. At 0700 hours, the driver started the engine and we pulled out through the main gate on the first leg of our journey to London. The plan was to stop for a meal at the RAF Halton apprentice school just outside Aylesbury in Buckinghamshire, before continuing on to Earls Court. Nestling down in the snug comfort of my seat and being rocked by the smooth suspension of the coach, I soon fell asleep, although it was broad daylight by this time. Falling asleep was due in no small part to the effects of being disturbed the previous night and then from having to get up earlier than usual. But although I enjoyed the nap, it caused me to miss seeing many of the towns and villages that we sped through on our way east towards Aylesbury. I think most of the others were sleeping too, because the unusual quietness allowed me sleep for at least an hour. Then I awoke and was able to enjoy the unfolding scenery as we sped along. It was late morning when we arrived at Halton, where arrangements had been made for us to have our midday meal. We were also going to return there to spend the night in a "transit billet" after our Earls Court performance, since it would be too late to return to St. Athan that same evening.

As we climbed down from the coach, a vaguely familiar figure detached himself from a nearby group of apprentices and approached us. He was grinning from ear to ear and I suddenly realized that it was Jock Murray, one of the boys who had originally been with us in ITS. He had been awarded a well-deserved place at the Halton apprentice school for doing exceptionally well in the education test that had been administered to us in those early days. Jock had apparently recognized the chequered hatbands that identified us as St. Athan Boy Entrants (apprentices wore solid colour hatbands) and on coming closer had recognized a few of us with whom he had briefly shared the ITS experience. We shook hands and talked and joked around for a while, comparing notes on St. Athan and Halton. He inquired as to what we were doing at Halton and why we were wearing all the "scrambled egg". We explained about the Royal Tournament and, in turn, learned from him that the Halton bagpipe and trumpet band would also be appearing there another evening. He had many questions about Saints and about some of the friends he had left behind on being transferred. He also half-heartedly complained that his apprentice training would take three years, but it was easy to tell that he didn't really mind the extra time because of the higher prestige he would gain by graduating as an apprentice. After several minutes of animated conversation, Jock said that he would have to go. In saying goodbye, he told us how nice it was to see all of us again and then, with a wave of his mug and irons, hurried off to join his apprentice friends.

The food in the Halton Apprentice Mess turned out to be remarkably similar to the fare we were accustomed to back in our own St. Athan mess, but we were hungry and wolfed it down. Then, when everyone had finished, we climbed back aboard the coach and set off once again, this time south-eastwards towards London. At first, the going was swift as we travelled through open countryside, small towns and villages, but gradually the landscape became increasingly built-up, with much more traffic in evidence, as we neared the big city. Eventually, our rate of forward movement slowed to a snail's pace as the coach stopped and started through a series of multiple traffic lights.

By mid-afternoon we were feeling restless and hungry, so Pilot Officer Read asked the coach driver to stop at the next café that he saw, to give us a break and get something to eat. Shortly afterwards we pulled up outside a modest eating establishment, into which we gratefully flocked after scrambling eagerly out of the coach. It must have seemed quite a sight as we all trooped inside, dressed in our heavily-decorated uniforms. Pilot Officer Read insisted that we needed to be properly dressed, with tunics buttoned up and SD hats worn properly, so that our appearance would not be unbecoming to the good name and order of the RAF. The two sweet middle-aged ladies who ran the café were clearly puzzled by this sudden invasion and even more puzzled as to our origin. One of them eavesdropped on a conversation that I was having with one of the other band members, thinking that I didn't notice. She then approached the second lady, saying in a quiet but clearly audible voice, "I don't know *who* they are Doris, but they speak with a beautiful brogue. They must be from Scotland."

We both laughed at this and later told the others that we'd been mistaken for the Scottish Air Force.

The ladies may not have known who we were, but they knew how to take care of our grumbling stomachs. Large platters of sausage, egg and chips washed down with mugs of decent tea soon took the edge off our hunger and thirst. Then we were on our way again, reaching Earls Court around 1700 hours—ten hours after we'd set off that morning from St. Athan. I had been looking forward to seeing the famous sights of London, but was disappointed at seeing nothing more than the type of ordinary buildings and streets that are common to any city. There was no Big Ben to marvel at, no Buckingham Palace or Tower of London and although we were so close to the centre of London that it seemed almost impossible to miss these famous landmarks, we didn't see a single one of them.

Earls Court was a much larger place than I had imagined it to be. There were people in military uniforms of every description all around us and military equipment from tanks to aeroplanes to horses. The coach dropped us off near the exhibition area and we were then given leave to explore the various service exhibitions for about an hour, before reporting to the arena assembly area—the equivalent of backstage. Then, at around 1830 hours, we all converged on the specified meeting point to prepare for our entrance and grand performance at 1900 hours.

The atmosphere in the assembly area was hectic and the air filled with distinctly equine aromas. I found myself dodging cavalry horses and field artillery pieces as soldiers dressed in ornate uniforms hurried around attending to their mounts, brushing and combing the flanks of the gleaming, sinewy animals. Others brought buckets of water to the stalls where the dark feisty horses were prancing around at their tethers like highly strung prima donnas, as they waited for their turn in the limelight. A thick carpet of dark brown sawdust covered the entire floor; probably to make the footing better for the pampered horses, or perhaps to make it easier to clean up after them.

Pilot Officer Read and Corporal Naylor were waiting for us and had apparently used the time to survey the arena where we would be performing. They had some news for us.

"Gather round lads and pay attention," said the diminutive Pilot Officer.

A few people continued talking, seemingly unaware that everyone else had fallen silent in anticipation of what the officer had to say. Those around them quickly shushed them to be quiet.

After pausing long enough to make sure he had our undivided attention, he began, "We will be going on first as the "opening act", so as soon as we've finished here I want you to get formed up at the arena entrance and be ready to start." He paused for a moment, read something from a small piece of paper that he held in his right hand, seemed to gather his thoughts and then continued, "Corporal Naylor and I have made a survey of the arena area. We were distressed to find that some equipment has been set up in the arena for one of the later events and so the area available for our figure-marching is only about half of that in which we practised."

This was something of a bombshell. We had practised marching in a certain size area that we expected to be near enough identical to the real thing. Would we be able to carry it off in an area size that we weren't used to? And even if we could do it without some disaster befalling us, the half-size area seemed to indicate that we would finish in only half the time allotted for our routine.

Pilot Officer Read continued, "Corporal Naylor has suggested that when you reach the end of the routine, continue on and start all over again without stopping. Do you think you can do that?"

"Yes sir," several people answered.

"Okay then, that's what we'll do!" He announced triumphantly, apparently with the utmost confidence in our ability to get faultlessly through the amended routine, even though it was a major departure from what we had diligently practised week after week. "Now lads, I want you to put on your best show ever and make St. Athan proud of you," he continued. "Good luck! Now go and form up for your entrance."

With that he walked towards the entrance to the arena, where the massive doors that temporarily hid us from the arena area dwarfed his slightly built figure. We followed behind him and then formed up in our eight ranks, facing the closed doors, with our trumpets on our hips in the "at-ease" position. At some unseen signal, the massive doors began to slowly glide open and while they were still moving, Drum Major Featherstone gave the order for us to quick march. As always, we stepped off with the left foot as our drummers beat out their two threes and a seven and by the time we actually entered the arena we already had our trumpets to our lips and had started to play.

The repertoire had been well established during our many practice sessions and we had memorized the names and order of tunes to be played. These included, but weren't limited to, *Swinging the Prop; Come and Join Us; The Marseillaise; On Ilkley Moor B'at 'At; Swinging the Cat; Roll me Over in the Clover;* and *The St. Louis Blues March.*

The sawdust that covered the backstage floor area also covered the entire floor of the arena and while it may have been good for the horses, it made the act of marching very difficult for Boy Entrants. Instead of the hard even surface that we were accustomed to, there were humps and hollows, hard spots and soft spots. At first I thought I would stumble and fall in an embarrassing heap on the arena floor, as I'm sure my fellow bandsmen also thought, but I got used to it and made adjustments to my stride that compensated for the difficult surface. What I found more irritating than marching on the sawdust was the sparsely-occupied spectator seating. Perhaps disappointed is a more appropriate word to describe my feelings, because most of the seats were empty, although people were slowly trickling in to fill them. It seemed that after all the build up we had been subjected to, not to mention the hours of practice that we'd put in, we weren't playing to anything remotely resembling a packed house. But then I thought of it in another way—we were there! We had made it to London and were appearing at the Royal Tournament, even if we were just the warm-up act, playing and figure marching while the audience members were finding their seats, as they probably anticipated the more interesting main events that would come later in the programme.

We went into the figure marching routine, resplendent in our braid and regalia, as our leaders and markers made adjustments for the smaller area in which we were forced to operate. It all worked out well. Our Boy Entrant wheel badge figure was smaller in diameter than the one we'd practised, so we had to slow up the pace and almost mark time as our wheel rotated. Then, when we came to the end of the routine, at the point where we would normally have marched out of the performing area after reforming back into our eight ranks, we just went straight back into it again. It wasn't necessary to repeat the musical repertoire because the trumpet majors and Corporal Naylor had allotted enough tunes to last for the entire duration of the display. In the end, we proudly completed our mission of bringing Boy Entrant trumpet band music to the masses and if by chance any of them might have been watching, they probably wouldn't even have noticed that they had just witnessed two performances for the price of one.

It was customary, at the end of each performance, for the display members to form up facing the royal box and then their officer would take his place out in front of them and give a salute to the royal personage in attendance. At the end of our performance, Pilot Officer Read, who had been waiting somewhere in the background, marched out in front of the band and, standing stiffly to attention, threw a text book style salute in the direction of the royal box. Alas, Her Majesty the Queen wasn't there to take it. In fact, no royal personage was present, not even a minor one. A senior officer filled in for her instead. That was a little disappointing too, because we'd been told that we would be performing before the Queen.

After leaving the arena, our little officer gallantly congratulated us on a fine performance and commended us for the skilful manner in which we'd changed the routine to accommodate the reduced performance area.

"And now, lads, you can stay and watch the rest of the tournament."

With that, we were ushered to a block of seating that had been especially reserved for us and watched an enjoyable show, the likes of which I'd never seen before.

It was fantastic! Each of the United Kingdom services was amply represented in all of the performances, but added to that were service groups from the Commonwealth, some of them keenly military and others colourfully exotic.

The show began with the Royal Navy Field Gun Competition. A large group of naval ratings, dressed in their traditional short-sleeved, collarless white gun-shirts and bell bottoms gathered into white gaiters above their boots, ran into the arena and started setting up the very same equipment that had hampered our performance only minutes before. This was accompanied by a fast paced rendition of *"You Can't Get a Man With a Gun"* over the arena sound system.

The Field Gun Competition involved teams from various ships and naval bases, each team consisting of eighteen naval ratings. The object was to manhandle a field gun and its gun carriage a number of times from one end of the arena to the other. The problem was that they had to get it over two 5-foot high walls and across a wide intervening 28-feet long "chasm". The complete gun assembly was too heavy to get over the walls in one piece, so part of the race involved disassembling it and then moving it over the walls in its component pieces. Both teams had obviously practised the drill many times and when a loud explosion signalled the start of the race they soon set to at removing the gun barrel and wheels from the gun mount, at the same time detaching the mount from the limber—the forward wheeled part of the carriage that supports the ammunition box. Then various groups of ratings skilfully manhandled their limber over the first wall by running the shaft, by which it was pulled along, over the top of the wall until the wheels of the limber came hard up against the obstruction. In doing this, the towing end of shaft arced upwards until it could go no further. Almost immediately, two of the men climbed atop the wall and launched their body weight against the tee-bar that formed the end of the shaft, pivoting the heavy parts of the limber upwards until the wheels could be pushed over the wall. Some of the other team members rigged up a tightly suspended rope line between the two walls and then one man hung onto a small trolley contraption riding atop the line on two grooved wheels that whizzed him from one wall to the other. But he wasn't just joy riding; he carried both of the heavy gun mount wheels with him, one suspended from each shoulder. A tag line on the trolley enabled it to be pulled back to the starting position, where four other team members suspended the gun mount from it, using a rope sling. Then all four men balanced precariously on the gun mount, whilst hanging onto the trolley handles, as they rode it to the second wall.

Meanwhile the limber group had pulled their carriage across the intervening ground, before removing its wheels and manhandling the parts through a narrow gap in the second wall. This was closely followed by the gun mount, which was then reunited with the wheels that had already been taken through the gap. As the pieces arrived at the other side of the second wall, the teams worked furiously at reassembling their gun in a firing position, with the limber at some prescribed distance away. And then, when the assembly was complete, one member raced to the limber, opened the ammunition box and retrieved a round that he cradled in both arms as he bolted back to the gun position. The gun team muzzle loaded the blank round and when all was ready, one of the gunners yanked on a lanyard, firing off the round with a deafeningly loud explosion that temporarily filled the arena with a large expanding cloud of blue smoke. But no sooner had the round been fired, than the runner raced back to the limber for another round so that the procedure could be repeated. In all, each team fired off three rounds. Then, a brief rest only to be interrupted by a bugle call and they were off again, repeating the same drill, but this time in the opposite direction. Three more rounds were fired off at the end of that run and then another rest period. Soon, the bugle sounded again and one more run was made, but instead of firing off some more rounds, the teams raced the gun and limber combination down the sides of the arena instead and across the finish line to complete the competition.

The audience was going wild, cheering the teams on. Apparently, different naval stations competed at each performance and on this particular night it was Chatham against the Fleet Air Arm. I couldn't make my mind up which team to cheer for—my father's home port had been Chatham when he'd served in the Royal Navy during the war, so I felt I should support them. But I was torn by loyalty to my aviation brothers of the Fleet Air Arm. In the end, the familial association won and I supported Chatham, who went on to win by a very close margin.

Both teams were visibly exhausted by their heroic efforts and breathed heavily whilst a senior naval officer faced the royal box and saluted the royal person. It wasn't Her Majesty the Queen, but another member of the Royal Family; the Princess Royal, I think. After this brief rest the teams departed the arena pulling their gun carriages with them, as the arena sound system played *"All the Nice Girls Love a Sailor"*, much to the amusement of the wildly applauding audience.

The next event was also staged by the Royal Navy. It involved a number of manned scenes, acted out under the bright cones of spotlights that illuminated them one at a time and in isolation from the otherwise darkened arena. The scenes started with one that depicted the manned gun deck of Nelson's ship and ended with the portrayal of a guided missile being fired from a ship.

It took the arena crew several minutes to remove all the scenery and props after the lights came up, which gave the audience time to stretch their legs before the Royal Marines' massed bands entered in a breathtaking spectacle of precision marching and stirring music.

Five combined Marine bands paraded through the arena as one, seeming to fill it entirely. There must have been around 250 individual players, each of whom was dressed in the customary dark blue dress uniform surmounted by a white tropical helmet. We were treated to an amazingly varied repertoire of music, most of which was military, although some pieces like *"Ave Maria"* clearly were not.

After the Royal Marines had made their exit through the great doors, the arena turned quiet for a short time, but before long the doors slid silently open again to permit a large troop of mounted Royal Household Cavalry to enter the arena. Each trooper carried a lance in the vertical position, with a pennant fluttering at the top near the sharp end. As if the pageantry of the cavalry in their plumed helmets and shiny breastplates wasn't enough, they were led into the arena by the colourfully dressed Royal Horse Guards Kettledrummer astride a huge horse that, we were informed by the announcer, was named "Hannibal". Two large, heavy-looking, ornately decorated, silver bowl-shaped drums slung across the horse's shoulders were being beaten with the type of padded drumsticks used for bass drums. Four trumpeters, garbed in the same colourful uniform as the kettledrummer, rode in a row immediately behind him. The drummer beat out the rhythm for the troop as he led them all the way to the centre of the arena, where they eventually came to a halt. Such a spectacle was rarely seen, except during the Queen's

Birthday Trooping of the Colour ceremony, or other rare State occasions. By this time, a solemn hush had fallen over the audience and so all was quiet when the four trumpeters raised long, straight, silver herald-trumpets, that each dangled a banner bearing the Royal coat of arms, to their lips. They paused in this position for a moment and then played a fanfare that resounded throughout the great cavernous hall. That done, they departed the arena, led by the kettledrummer and we were left alone with two troops of the Household Cavalry—the "Blues," wearing royal blue tunics and red plumes on their helmets and "Royals," who wore red jackets that were offset by the white plumes atop their helmets.

What followed was a musical ride by the 32 mounted riders that lasted for several minutes. Harnesses jingled and hooves pounded on the sawdust-covered arena floor as they trotted and cantered through a series of intricate manoeuvres, during which the horses narrowly missed colliding with each other by miraculous split second timing, as their columns interwove and criss-crossed in the centre of the arena. Gleaming helmets and breastplates glinted under the bright overhead lights, as the cavalry troopers turned and wheeled in time with the music. The long horsehair plumes that streamed from the pinnacles of their helmets danced and bobbed in rhythm with the horses' body movements.

As a finale, the kettledrummer and trumpeters solemnly re-entered the arena to perform a closing fanfare, during which the officer in charge saluted the Royal Box. Then the entire troop of cavalrymen slow-marched their horses out of the arena, to the steady boom of the kettledrums and thunderous applause of the spectators.

But even the noble horses of the Royal Household Cavalry are subject to the call of nature, which wouldn't have been so obvious if the pomp and circumstance that we had just witnessed hadn't been immediately followed by the unheralded entry of an overall-clad gang of shovel-wielding, wheelbarrow-pushing young soldiers, who expeditiously scooped up the still-steaming horse detritus, much to the amusement of the audience, who gave them a heartfelt round of applause as they quickly departed the now-clean arena just as swiftly and silently as they had arrived into it.

When the next display group entered the arena, it appeared that the pooper-scooper crew had been wasting their time, because this event also featured horses. The thick layer of sawdust on the arena floor couldn't entirely deaden the sound of thudding hooves as three separate teams of The King's Troop, Royal Horse Artillery thundered through the open doors. Each team, consisting of six horses harnessed in pairs, was pulling a field gun behind it. What seemed very unusual was that all three horses on the left side of each team carried a rider, who was dressed in an ornate Hussar uniform. Unlike the cantering Household Cavalry, these teams galloped around the arena at a very fast pace, turning and twisting the field gun through many intricate manoeuvres. Given the tight area in which they were required to perform, such sharp turns at speed would probably have been impossible without the three riders each controlling his pair of horses. In fact, there was no other way to guide the horses since the gun that they pulled had no place for a driver to sit.

Up and down and around and around they galloped, gleaming harnesses jingling and hooves thudding in the sawdust of the arena floor. The Hussars' uniforms made ours look plain and nondescript, in spite of our braid and white belts. The cap they wore was the most distinctive part of their uniform, being like a flat-topped Busby with what appeared to be a flap hanging over the right side from the crown and surmounted by a stiff plume that stood several inches vertically above the headgear. The uniform itself could hardly be described as nondescript. If anything, it resembled a uniform that could have been worn by Cinderella's Prince Charming, with its high-necked collar and several narrowly-spaced horizontal rows of ornate gold braid that covered the chest area of the tightly fitted jacket. Epaulettes of gold-braid adorned the shoulders and an intricate design in gold piping decorated the lower arms of the sleeves.

No doubt there was much history behind the uniform and wearing it certainly didn't detract from their skill as horsemen, as they wheeled their teams to interact with each other and in time with the music that played over the sound system. They performed intricate figures-of-eight and crossovers at a speed that seemed to suggest that a writhing heap of horses, Hussars and field guns could occur in the centre of the arena at any moment. But nothing like that happened and they completed the display without mishap. The pooper-scoopers made another appearance, greeted by some light laughter and applause from the audience.

We were then treated to a massed pipe band made up of a number of Irish regimental bands. Even though I was Irish, this was a little unusual for me. Growing up, the only pipe bands I'd seen had been tartan kilt-clad in the Scottish tradition. But these pipers wore plain light brown kilts and long green cloaks. I love pipe music and enjoyed the Irish pipes just as much as the Scottish. And they played Irish tunes that had a deeply nostalgic familiarity, all the more so because it had been a long time since I had heard many of them.

Although there were a large number of other events, let me just describe one more that honoured the island of Malta, GC and made a big impression on me.

It began with the arena plunged into darkness as props were rushed in under cover of darkness. Then, in the darkness, the deep resonant voice of actor Jack Hawkins came over the arena loudspeakers. He spoke of how the small island nation had been such a thorn in the side of the enemy during the Second World War, because it sat astride Field Marshal Rommel's supply routes between Italy and North Africa. About half of Rommel's supplies were sent to the bottom of the Mediterranean by the Maltese forces and this became such a problem for the German High Command that they ordered Malta to be either bombed into oblivion or invaded and captured.

The island was pounded day and night by endless air raids and seemed ready to fall, but incredibly refused to give in. King George was so awed by the courage of the Maltese people that he awarded the George Cross to the island for its valour. But the decoration, impressive as it was, didn't help too much—they needed reinforcements, especially fighter planes to beat off the German and Italian bombers. British and American aircraft carriers then arrived off Tunisia, bringing several squadrons of Spitfires which were to be flown off the carriers, land, refuel and then take off as soon as possible to avoid being knocked out while they were still on the ground. But first the bomb craters in the Maltese airfields had to be filled in, so that the fighters could land.

The display depicted how the entire population of Malta went out onto the airfields and runways to fill the holes, repairing them to provide a landing place for the Spitfires. At one point, spotlights illuminated an anti-aircraft gun emplacement and we heard and saw a realistic simulation of the gun crew firing at enemy bombers. Then another set of spotlights focused on the arena entrance, as a real Spitfire taxied into the display area. Thinking back on it, there must have been some stagecraft involved because the aircraft's whirling propeller should have kicked up a cloud of sawdust, but this didn't happen, so I really don't know how the fighter was made to behave so realistically. Anyway, it taxied up to the gun emplacement where a crew of Royal Air Force, Army and Navy personnel swarmed over it, performing the refuelling and arming operations. Then, when they were complete, the Spitfire taxied back out of the arena and we heard a simulation of the sound of its engine at full take-off power, as it climbed into the sky to do battle.

Jack Hawkins spoke again to pay tribute to Malta and, as we heard his voice for the second time that evening, spotlights lit up a huge replica of the George Cross that hung over the arena. We were told that from that time on, Malta has been formally known as Malta, GC.

All too soon, the Royal Tournament was over. At that moment I felt that having been able to watch such a great spectacle more than made up for the disappointment that I had felt earlier about our band only being the warm-up act. And after watching the quality and professionalism of the other participants, I felt that it had been a privilege to have even been included in the same show.

We wearily made our way out of the arena and climbed aboard our coach for the journey back to RAF Halton, where we would spend the night. There wasn't much to see as the coach sped through increasingly empty streets, heading out from the centre of the city. Street lamps flashed past and I think I fell asleep in the soft comfort of the snug seat. At Halton, we hastily made our beds and tumbled into them exhausted. It had been a long but eventful day.

CHAPTER 10

Coffee and Biscuits with Mr. D

Our return to St. Athan coincided with the Whitsun holiday weekend, during which the majority of boys were able to go home on a 96-hour leave pass. For those of us who hailed from the far-flung corners of the British Isles, the travel time needed to get home and back within the 96-hour period made it an impractical proposition. But life is full of compensations and we could at least look forward to a few fleeting days of easier life on camp and a lot less competition when it came to wooing the local girls.

I remember being at Barry Island that weekend in warm sunny weather, where Paddy McGowan and I practised a little of our Irish charm on a couple of attractive Welsh lasses. Paddy came from Portstewart—a small seaside resort about five miles from my home town and had recently come up to the Wings as a member of the 30th Entry.

Our uniforms, coupled with good grooming, were our greatest assets when it came to attracting girls, so a smartly turned out appearance with well-shined buttons and boots, together with well pressed trousers and tunics was a "must". Anything else that could be used to enhance this basic appearance, without making us targets for the constantly-patrolling snoops, was an advantage. By rights, I should have removed my temporary corporal trumpeter stripes, now that the Royal Tournament was over. But with no one around to challenge my right to wear the stripes, I conveniently "forgot" to remove them for the duration of the long weekend, hoping they would make a big impression on the fair sex.

It seemed to work, because Paddy and I spent a great Whitsun weekend as a foursome in the company of some girls we met. In retrospect, it's probably a safe bet that the stripes had absolutely no influence on the young lady that I had somehow managed to impress, but they certainly helped to boost my self-confidence and, in the end, that's what seems to count most in all of life's challenges.

Paddy McGowan (left) and the author at Barry Island during the Whitsun break, 1957. The Corporal Trumpeter stripes on my right sleeve cuff were soon to be removed.

It was just as well that the long weekend had been pleasant, because the week that followed didn't start off very well. On the first day back in Workshops after the break, Corporal Tech. Turnbull, my class instructor, passed on a message that I was to immediately go and see Mr. Dimbleby, the Warrant Officer in charge of our training. My stomach suddenly felt knotted up on hearing this and I immediately headed towards Dimbleby's office, anxiously pulling on my beret as I left the classroom. On my way there, I recalled Ginge Brown's description of "having coffee and biscuits" with the big man. It sounded funny at the time, especially when it was happening to someone else, but now it looked as though the joke was on me and it didn't seem funny in the slightest.

On arriving at Mr. Dimbleby's office, I knocked timidly on the open door, causing him to look up and see a very nervous Boy Entrant standing in the doorway, clad in denim overalls.

"Carlin?" He asked.

"Yessir." I answered.

"Come in lad," he said, not unkindly, "and shut the door."

I stepped across the threshold into the small office, gently closing the door as I did so and came to attention in front of his desk.

"Okay, you can stand at ease lad," he said, peering up at me over his half-rim glasses.

He was a slightly rotund middle-aged man and although, from a distance, I had at first mistaken him to be a Warrant Officer, it was now obvious that the insignia on the cuff of his tunic was not a Warrant Officer's "Tate & Lyle"—the RAF slang for the Royal coat of arms worn as a badge of rank by WOs. It was actually a slightly different insignia that incorporated the Royal Coat Of Arms surmounted by a small gold RAF eagle, with the combination enclosed within a larger laurel wreath. This, in fact, was the badge of Master Aircrew. In other words, he had served as an aircrew member, achieving a rank equivalent to that of a Warrant Officer. On the left side of his chest, just above a double row of campaign medal ribbons, he wore the "brevet" of a Flight Engineer. This was a small disc-shaped piece of black cloth inscribed with a white letter "E" inside a gold coloured laurel wreath. From the left side of the disc, a single feathered wing jutted upwards at an angle, its tip pointing towards the wearer's left shoulder. In my personal gallery of heroes and villains, this put him on the side of the good guys—non-commissioned aircrew members were heroes to me.

Following his instruction, I stood at ease, but felt far from really being at ease. Mr. Dimbleby—the Mister title was commonly accorded to Warrant Officers and Master Aircrew—picked up a manila file folder from his desktop and methodically paged through the paperwork inside, frowned and then looked up at me.

"These trade test marks are very disappointing Carlin," he said, in a stern voice.

"Yessir," I mumbled, by way of acknowledgement.

"What happened?" He asked.

"Didn't study hard enough, sir," I replied.

"And why not?" He retorted.

"I'm in the band sir, and we were practising for the Royal Tournament," I offered by way of explanation.

"Oh, the Royal Tournament," he said, nodding his head slowly and pronouncing the words in a mock upper-crust voice. This little piece of sarcasm effectively deflated any hope I had that band practice would be accepted as a legitimate excuse for my poor academic performance. Dimbleby pushed himself up from his chair and came around the desk to where I stood, studying the open file folder that he held in both hands as he walked.

"Do you want to pass out with your Entry?" He asked, the tone of his voice suggesting that the answer had better be yes.

"Yessir," I replied truthfully.

"Well, lad," he said, his face now only inches from mine, "if I were in your shoes, I would give up the band and start reading my notes a lot more. You might still be able to pass out with your Entry, but only if you work very hard from now on."
He walked back around his desk and settled down into his chair before continuing, "The best advice I can offer you is to give up the band. Some people can combine the band *and* their trade training, but you're not one of them. You need to concentrate on the thing that's most important and leave band

playing to those who can do both." He paused, then, "Do I make myself clear?"

"Yessir," I quickly replied, immensely relieved that I wasn't going to be relegated to the 30th Entry.

"Okay, Carlin, you can go back to your classroom now, but think very seriously about what I've told you."

"Yessir," I replied, and with that I came to attention then turned and walked out of his office.

The air in the workshop area seemed much cooler and the atmosphere less claustrophobic than it had been just a moment ago, in the confines of that small room. I had already known, before being invited for "coffee and biscuits" with Mr. Dimbleby, that I'd fared badly in the end of term trade test. The Squadron Leader who had interviewed me during my Induction had warned that the subject matter in my chosen trade as an aircraft electrician would be difficult and that I would have to work very hard to pass the course. Well, he was right. We had long since passed through the simple topics like navigation lights and other 24 volts DC equipment.

Some weeks previously, we had entered into the realm of alternating current, or AC as it was more commonly known. Direct current had been difficult enough, but in the end it was easy to understand. You flipped a switch and the current flowed through the circuit and did the work. There were formulas like Ohm's Law and mnemonics such as Maxwell's right-hand corkscrew rule to memorize, but they were relatively simple to grasp. Alternating current, on the other hand, behaved in mysterious ways. It wasn't just satisfied with the resistance in a circuit. Oh no, it had to behave weirdly with coils and suchlike, creating something else called reactance that was treated like resistance, but couldn't be measured directly with an ohmmeter and was only present when AC was applied to the circuit. Not only that, alternating current *alternates*—it changes from positive to negative several times a second. On aircraft this change from positive to negative then back to positive and so on, occurs 400 times every second. For certain circuits this so-called frequency can be as much as 1600 cycles per second. On top of that, there are all kinds of mathematical relationships to contend with that involve things like the square roots of 2 and 3, or pi, or the sines and cosines of angles, all of which make quick mental arithmetic calculations all but impossible.

Memorising all the important formulas and being able to use them in calculating things like voltage, power and reactance required lots of study and concentration. The sad truth now confronting me was that band practice for the Royal Tournament had taken up far too much time—time that would have been much better used in studying and learning the skills of my trade, to help me get successfully through the phase tests. Obviously, my band skive was a luxury I could no longer afford, so I promptly handed in my trumpet and removed the little crossed-trumpets badge from my sleeve. The corporal trumpeter stripes had already been removed by this time.

There was some consolation in that I had at least managed to elude relegation to the 30th Entry, but such a close call didn't leave me totally unscathed. Because my trade test results were so low, the proficiency badge that most others were awarded was withheld in my case. When Corporal Longfellow handed out sets of two miniature chevrons that were to replace the single inverted chevron worn by most of us on the cuff of our right sleeves, there wasn't a set for me. My name was called out, filling me with hope that I would get the second stripe anyway, but Longfellow only handed me my permanent pass without the stripes. When I looked inside the pass, I saw that an entry had been made in the authorization space for the second badge, but it was unsigned and a line had been neatly drawn through it. The message couldn't have been plainer: I needed to earn that badge and the only way to do that was to study hard, starting off by making sure that I passed the weekly classroom tests.

* * *

Workshop practice was a regularly occurring feature of our training. Its purpose was to develop our skills in mastering the practical side of our chosen trades, so that we would be useful members of a servicing team when we went out into the regular air force, instead of just being useless human encyclopaedias of technical information. By this time, we were learning and practising the intricacies of making soldered connections to multi-connector plugs and sockets. It took considerable skill to neatly solder individual wires into the reverse ends of between 12 and 15 of the tightly-spaced pins that were packed within a diameter of approximately one and a half inches. Using too much solder would always result in large blobs of the material jutting out from the connections, just begging to cause short circuits between the pins. Applying insufficient heat to a joint during the soldering process, however, would eventually result in oxidisation between the solder and the pin, causing a gradual increase in electrical resistance at the connection that would create problems later on.

During this particular period of workshop practice, some of my classmates discovered an easy way to make some extra money. The activity that they pursued in this regard might seem worthy of much praise and admiration, except for one very minor problem—they weren't earning the extra cash. Instead, they were quite literally making it!

The pins on the multi-pin plugs that were provided to us for soldering practice were arrayed in a circular pattern, over which small waxed-cardboard protective caps in the shape of old-fashioned pillboxes were fitted, to save the pins from damage during storage and handling. Apparently, someone in the class noticed that the diameter of these little cardboard pillboxes compared very closely with that of a two-shilling coin of the realm. A murky light must have lit up in this person's head, prompting him to share his ill-found observation with a few others. And so the counterfeit scheme was hatched.

About four people formed a small consortium to experiment with the pillboxes, when the instructor wasn't looking. Most of us knew what was going on, even though we didn't actually participate in manufacturing the dud coins, but because of the code of silence that binds most teenagers, we didn't say anything about it to those in authority.

The consortium used the little cardboard caps as moulds, melting solder on a soldering iron and letting it drip into them. At first they tried making just one, using a real coin for comparison. Then, when they believed that they had reproduced the correct diameter and thickness, they tried out their prototype "two-bob bit" on the YMCA cigarette machine. It didn't work right away, so they were obliged to do some fine-tuning, but after some trial and error, finally achieved success. Then, there was no stopping them. They set about mass-producing more coins, deluging cigarette machines all over the station with dud coins and then very proudly, but very stupidly, showing off their ill-gotten gains to all and sundry.

Perhaps if the YMCA folks had found only an occasional dud coin in their cigarette machine, they might have treated it as a minor irritant, but the colossal raids on the machine's takings couldn't be easily ignored. It wasn't very long before the matter was reported to the Snoops, who then called in the SIB—the Special Investigation Branch—who were much snoopier than the Snoops.

It couldn't have taken too much head-scratching for the SIB to figure out where the fake florins where coming from, so the next thing we knew was that all of us were being called into an office one at a time, to be interviewed. The miscreants confessed after one or two days of this treatment, probably thinking that they would be punished by a week or so on jankers. But if this is what they were thinking, they were in for a nasty shock. Word came down from on high that this was a serious offence and all of those involved were sentenced to several days of detention in the Guardroom. Not only that, but their crime would appear on their records for a specific number of years after the event. This was a departure from the normal procedure by which the records of minor transgressions—the type that earned an "award" of jankers—were destroyed when the Boy Entrant graduated from training.

By all accounts, having to do time as a prisoner in the Guardroom was a very unpleasant experience. I'm thankful that this particular misfortune never befell me, but I did hear first-hand from others unlucky enough to spend some time "inside". I also had a few opportunities to get a small taste of the Guardroom experience during some of my sessions on jankers, when a number of us would be sent there to perform fatigues.

Mind you, this only happened when there were no "guests" in residence and the Snoops needed some outside labour to maintain their highly-bulled floors and brass-work in the pristine conditions that seemed to make them feel comfortably at home.

Prisoners in detention were incarcerated in small single-occupancy cells with a thick, heavy steel door that shut off their contact with the outside world. The door was featureless on its cell-side, save for a small peephole. The peephole was closed off by a small hinged cover on the exterior side of the door that permitted someone to view the interior of the cell, but prevented the inmate from seeing out. A tiny window of frosted glass, high up on the outside wall, permitted only a little daylight to penetrate the cell's dim interior.

The sleeping arrangements were certainly not designed for comfort—consisting only of a raised wooden platform without a mattress. A rectangular-shaped piece of wood with a shallow hollow scooped out of its upper surface was permanently affixed to one end of the platform to serve as a pillow. The edges of the hollow were rounded off as a small concession to comfort on this otherwise Spartan bed. The only other permitted comfort was the use of sheets and blankets, which of course were required to be made up into a bed-pack every day, including weekends.

A prisoner's day started at 0530 hours, when he was awakened by one of the night shift Snoops. It was usually a rude awakening, initiated by the illumination of the single stark light mounted high up on the ceiling. After getting washed and dressed, all under constant supervision, a prisoner would be ordered to perform a session of fatigues, typically bumpering the Guardroom floor and then making tea for the Snoops. At least he would get a cup of tea for himself, if the Snoops weren't feeling too mean-spirited.

At around 0730 hours, a couple of boys from his squadron, who had been specifically detailed for this duty, would arrive to escort him to the mess for breakfast. When marching there, one of the boys took up position in front and the other at the rear. In a way, it was a mildly comical sight as all three marched through the camp in a line, like a mother duck and her two ducklings. Whilst in the mess, the prisoner was kept isolated from everyone else except his escort as he ate his meal.

Prisoners were still required to participate in the normal daily class activities, but were marched to and from these by the escort. After workshops, they were kept busy with more fatigues, until being confined to their cells early in the evening, where they were expected to study and transcribe notes from that day's class-work. "Lights out" for cell inhabitants came early, at around 2100 hours, but I suspect they welcomed the darkness that enabled them to get some sleep and put another day of their sentence firmly behind them.

* * *

Mid-summer of 1957 brought the 27th Entry near the end of their training and the time for selection of the Flight Sergeant Boy. As always, one senior Entry member in each of the four squadrons had risen to the exalted rank of Sergeant Boy. In No. 3 Squadron, to which I belonged, Dave Williams became the anointed one.

Dave didn't seem to be cast in the same mould as the other sergeant boys of my experience—past, present or future. To begin with, most sergeant boys were tall strapping fellows, but Dave was of average height to the point of appearing diminutive in the company of the other three sergeant boys. The difference didn't stop there—Dave was also popular with most of the lads, which wasn't always the case with other sergeant boys. Although strict in the disciplinary sense, when he caught someone in a minor breach of the rules, he was much less inclined to pull out his little pad of Forms 252 to put them on a charge than his predecessor. More often than not, he would let the miscreant off with a caution.

Each sergeant boy was top dog in his own squadron, but with the Entry's passing-out parade approaching, it was time for one of them to be elevated to the unique rank of Flight Sergeant Boy. This rank, denoted by a small brass crown worn above the three sergeant stripes, carried with it the awesome privilege of being the Parade Commander at his Entry's passing out ceremony. This meant being in full command of the entire passing out parade, from start to finish—a task normally carried out by the Station Warrant Officer on all other parades of similar significance.

All four of these young men who were contending for the prized rank of Flight Sergeant Boy had gained their sergeant stripes by the achievement of excellence in their trade test results throughout all of their training; by acting responsibly and never committing any disciplinary infractions; by maintaining above-average personal grooming and appearance and by exhibiting mature leadership qualities. In Boy Entrant language, the word "keen" was commonly used to sum up all of these attributes.

Permanent staff in each squadron usually identified people with such characteristics shortly after their arrival in the Wings and then began the process of cultivating them like potential prize-winning plants. The first step for these keen chaps was a promotion to Leading Boy, which usually put them in charge of a billet and rewarded them with the privilege of their own private bedroom, or "bunk" and a modest pay increase. Several boys would receive such promotion, but only two of these would gain further promotion to Corporal Boy, to be put in charge of either 'A' Flight or 'B' Flight, their vacated Leading Boy positions being filled by further promotions from the ranks. Eventually, one of the Corporal Boys would be selected as the squadron Sergeant Boy, with another cascading series of promotions to fill the gaps left by his elevation.

At every step of the way, the previously-mentioned attributes were the yardstick by which these individuals were measured and subsequently promoted, so it may be surprising to learn that these were not the qualities used to select one of the four sergeant boys for elevation above his peers to the unique rank of Flight Sergeant Boy. In fact, the greatest factor in deciding who would win this most coveted of ranks hinged around which of them had the loudest voice when it came to calling out commands on the parade ground.

In order to demonstrate their parade-ground voices, all four sergeant boys were obliged to participate in a "shout-off" on the Square, before a judging panel of drill instructors. Each candidate was required to bellow out a number of the commands that would actually be used during the passing out parade. The person who was able to shout the loudest, the clearest and whose voice lasted the longest was selected as the anointed one. Much to everyone's surprise, our own Dave Williams was the clear winner and so it came to pass that, for the only time during my entire stay at St. Athan, No. 3 Squadron had the proud honour of producing a Flight Sergeant Boy.

The 27th Entry's passing out parade followed soon after, on the 25th of July, 1957. The Reviewing Officer was Air Marshal Sir George Beamish, Knight Commander of the Most Honourable Order of the Bath (KCB) and Air Officer Commanding-in-Chief, Technical Training Command—the Command to which we all belonged whilst in training. Sir George was a fellow Irishman from my home county of Londonderry, although I wasn't aware of that at the time, and had enjoyed an illustrious career during both war and peace.

The passing-out parade went very much along the same lines as the 26th Entry's ceremony, the most boring part of it being the Reviewing Officer's inspection of the graduates. Of course, several non-graduates also passed out, but in a completely different sense. Were they really fainting, or just skiving so that they could stretch their legs? We'll never know.

Later, after the parade, it gave me an uplifting feeling to see the 27th Entry residents of our billet change out of their Boy Entrant uniforms for the last time and into their Leading Aircraftsman service uniforms. The black crepe hatbands and cloth LAC badges didn't appear as colourful as the chequered hatband and wheel-badge discs, but from my point of view, they had greater intrinsic value. I was sorry to see our 27th Entry graduates leave. On the whole, that particular Entry had been a relatively gentle bunch of people, especially those with whom I had shared a billet and although they had frequently asserted their senior-entryhood, it was rarely done in a mean-spirited manner. Those of us who were forced to remain behind shook hands and congratulated our friends as we said our goodbyes to Mick, Titch Eyles, Dave Ward, "Taff" Williams and our Leading Boy—Gerry German. We were sad to see them go, but pleased

THE REVIEW—No. 27 ENTRY
Reviewing Officer : Air Marshal Sir George R. Beamish, K.C.B., C.B.E.,
Air Officer Commanding-in-Chief, Technical Training Command

Air Marshal Sir George Beamish inspects members of the 27ᵗʰ Entry during their Passing-Out Parade. Leading Boy Entrant "Gerry" German is nearest the camera. Next to him is Boy Entrant Mick Sumpter.

and relieved that the over-played LPs of Bill Haley (together with his Comets) and the Platters, also went with them. I was fated to have a brief surprise encounter with Mick a few months later, but I never set eyes on any of the others from that day forward.

That evening, after the last stragglers of the former 27th Entry had left the 28th camp for good and the permanent staff had left it for the day, the 28th Entry held a parade to celebrate their brand new Senior Entry status. This was a raucous procession that wound its way around the entire camp, appearing to grow larger every few feet, like a human snowball rolling downhill.

When the 27th Entry became Senior Entry, I accepted it in a fatalistic kind of way, and I'm sure my fellow Entry members did likewise. We were just new to the Wings then, so being a kicked-around junior Entry seemed to be something that we just had to accept. But when the 28th became Senior Entry, I felt a sense of intense irritation with them. After all, we'd been through all of this already with the 26th and 27th Entries and didn't really feel like dealing with all the after lights-out raids, or the cocky king-of-the-castle attitudes that the 28th assumed from the moment the graduating Entry had marched off the parade ground. In a soul-searching moment, I would also have to admit to feelings of envy. We were now so close to being Senior Entry ourselves, that the sight of these other "upstarts" celebrating while we still had to wait for another three months grated harshly on the nerves.

Meanwhile, the 28th wasted no time in flexing the muscles of their new seniority. They soon set about subjugating the junior Entry by holding mock trials, before which many of the 30th Entry were hauled to defend themselves against mostly dreamed-up charges. The 30th were probably terrified, as we had been before them, but nobody was physically harmed, although many were "sentenced" to involuntary cold baths and similar humiliations.

The 29th were immune from these activities, probably because many in the 28th couldn't really afford to get on our bad side. Already, several of them had been relegated to our Entry because of their poor phase-test results and although these individuals were still considered to be members of the 28th by their former entry-mates and enjoyed the same privileges, they were conscious that such protection would evaporate with the passing out of the 28th. Others, as yet not relegated, knew they could still suffer that fate if they didn't pass their final trade testing, so not one of them wanted to burn any bridges. It was a different story after lights-out, however, when absolutely no one was immune under the cover of darkness. The 28th carried out a massive raid on that first night, drunk on the elation of their new status as Senior Entry. Everyone was subjected to the indignity of being unceremoniously tipped out of bed, including yours truly. This time, instead of being scared, I was irritated at having to put up with this night after night as the 28th indulged their collective ego, for what seemed to be a much longer time than it had been with the previous two entries. The only thing keeping my spirits up was the thought that this would be the last time my Entry would have to suffer it.

* * *

Bill, one of the 29th Entry boys in my billet had formed a friendship with Ben, another boy in the billet who had been relegated to our Entry from the 28th Entry. When the 28th became the Senior Entry, Ben assumed their "privileges" according to the unwritten boy entrant code, even though he was now a member of the 29th Entry in the eyes of the authorities. As an extension of their friendship, Ben apparently felt that he could share his new-found 28th Entry privileges with Bill in such things as endowing him with the right to sit with Ben in the Senior Entry seats at the Astra. Although gratingly irritating to his fellow-entry members, Bill's acceptance of these privileges was fairly innocuous. But Ben's sharing of Senior Entry privileges with Bill went just a little too far when it came to playing Senior Entry pranks on people of other Entries, especially when the targets were members of Bill's own 29th Entry. It was in this context that they both plotted an ill-considered prank against my friend Richard Butterworth, who probably appeared to be an easy target because of his small stature.

It happened during the time when Air Ministry workmen were replacing the aging asbestos-based thermal insulation with new glass fibre insulation on the pipes that distributed hot water throughout the camp. Many of us, who were curious enough to examine this new type of insulation, picked some of it up from the ground where it had fallen, only to quickly discover that it was very nasty stuff. When handled, the hair-thin glass fibres unfailingly pierced the unprotected skin of our hands and then broke off at the surface, leaving behind small lengths of fibre embedded under the skin that caused maddening itching and irritation for several days afterwards. No amount of hand-washing would remove the fibres and so they remained until nature somehow dealt with the problem in its own way.

On learning that the glass fibre was imbued with these rather unpleasant characteristics, Bill and Ben came up with the idea of using it to play a prank on Richard. But with the short-sightedness typical of youth, they didn't think it through very well, with the result that the prank turned out to be anything but funny.

With a supply of glass fibre stashed and ready to be used, the pranksters waited for an opportunity to implement their plan, which came one evening when Rich and I went to see a film at the Astra. With the coast clear and probably with no witnesses around, they put a generous sprinkling of glass fibre in between the sheets of Richard's bed.

When Rich and I came back to the billet after the film had finished, we still had an hour or so to go before bed-check, so we got our uniforms ready for the next morning's working parade inspection and then lay around on top of our beds reading or chatting. We noticed knowing glances between Bill and Ben, but failed to connect them to anything in particular. It's possible that we checked for an "apple pie" bed, which was a harmless and popular prank that was sometimes played on people who were out of the billet for a lengthy period in the evening. It involved remaking the victim's bed in such a way that it appeared deceptively normal, when in fact the bottom sheet had been folded back up over itself and the top sheet folded downwards towards the foot of the bed. The blankets were then pulled back over the sheets in normal fashion and the tail end of the bottom sheet (which was now at the top of the bed) turned down to make it appear to be the top sheet. When the unsuspecting victim tried to get into bed, he found that he could only get his feet halfway down under the sheets before encountering the fold. Usually, this was just about the time for lights-out, so he had the annoying task of having to strip off his blankets and sheets to remake the bed.

But, if indeed we checked, it seemed that we found no evidence of an apple-pie and so the glass fibre lay undiscovered, waiting to do its nasty work later. The Orderly Corporal came into the billet and made his routine bed-check a few minutes before lights-out. Then, at 10 o'clock, the Tannoy announced "Lights out!" and with that, Leading Boy Tunstall, Gerry German's replacement, came into the billet and ordered everyone into bed before turning off the lights. As usual, we listened to the *"Last Post and Evening Hymn"* as it played over the broadcast system. There was always a little chatter that tapered off as we dropped off to sleep.

But sleep didn't come easily for poor Richard. In fact it didn't come at all. Multiple sharp brittle glass fibres began to pierce his skin and then break off to leave small irritating pieces of glass embedded in his flesh. He tossed and turned, but the more he moved around the worse the problem became, until most of his body seemed to be on fire. There were stifled snickers from the surrounding darkness as the anonymous perpetrators relished the sounds of his discomfort. Hearing them didn't make his suffering any easier. After about an hour of this torture, he got out of bed and went to take a bath. By now, he realized the cause of the unbearable itchiness and his immediate preoccupation was to find some relief. Half an hour later he came back to the billet sobbing audibly and uttering a few choice obscenities aimed at his unknown tormentors. Obviously, bathing hadn't helped, which wasn't very surprising since the fibres were too deeply embedded in his skin to be washed off.

At first, Richard tried to get dressed, but the clothing only seemed to make the irritation worse, so he gave up on that idea. Instead, he donned a pair of P.E. shorts and then wrapped his groundsheet around the upper part of his body, before setting off on the long trek to Station Sick Quarters at the other side of the camp, where he hoped the medics would be able to do something to ease his suffering.

Richard didn't return to the billet and his bed of horrors again that night, nor did he show up for workshops next morning. In fact, we found out later that he'd been admitted to the nearby RAF Hospital.

The doctors and nurses treated the inflamed areas of Richard's body with soothing creams and ointments and at the same time questioned him as to how he had come to be in that condition in the first place. Without giving anyone away—not that he knew who the culprits were anyway—he told the medics that someone had put the glass fibre into his bed as a joke. The medical staff didn't seem to think it was very much of a joke and took a much more serious view of the incident. First thing next morning, the telephone in our Flight Commander's office rang shrilly. When Flight Lieutenant Grafton picked it up, the Hospital Medical Staff briefed him on Butterworth's situation and the very uncomfortable night that he had spent.

On returning to the billet at lunchtime, after my midday meal, I expected to find Richard waiting there, but he was still missing. This left me continuing to wonder what had happened to him, but my thoughts on the subject were soon disturbed by the sound of several heavy, purposeful footsteps entering the billet. This intrusion seemed to portend something unpleasant, but before my consciousness could register anything else, the first of the intruders, Corporal Longfellow, barked the order, "Stand by your beds!"

Everyone in the billet leapt to his feet, most of us hastily donning our tunics and fumbling with the buttons and belt so as not to be "improperly dressed". Sergeant Savoury followed behind Corporal Longfellow into an atmosphere that had suddenly been transformed from relaxed to electrified, as both NCOs clumped up the centre of the billet floor. But there was more to come. The light streaming through the open front doorway was eclipsed by another figure, but there was no need to guess the identity of the new arrival because we all recognized the slightly rotund silhouette of our Flight Commander, Flight Lieutenant Grafton.

As the officer entered at a relaxed pace, Corporal Longfellow yelled out, "Billet, att-en-SHUN!"

Immediately, we all came to attention as Grafton walked casually to the centre of the room and paused for a moment, seemingly gathering his thoughts. Then he began, "Last night, Boy Entrant Butterworth was admitted to the hospital." He paused for effect and then continued, "Butterworth was suffering from a painful skin condition brought on by a stupid prank played on him by one or more of his fellow boy entrants." Another pause and then, "To his credit, Butterworth was either unable or unwilling to name the instigator of this deed, but I know as certain as I'm standing here that it was someone in this billet." He paused again and then spoke in a slightly lower but somehow more menacing tone, "This may have seemed to be a huge joke to whomever was responsible, but let me assure you that it was a very serious prank to play on an unsuspecting individual." Grafton allowed his words to sink in for a few moments before continuing, "Now, I want the person or persons responsible to prove that they are men, by owning up here and now." He glared around at all of us, and even though we were standing at attention with our eyes looking straight ahead, I could still feel the intensity of his laser-like gaze as it raked around the room.

Almost immediately, Ben took a step forward. Bill hung back for a few seconds, but then he also took one pace forward. Both now stood prominently in the centre of the floor waiting, as we all did, for the wrath that would surely descend on them. Inwardly, I felt both relief and surprise. Relief, because we were no longer all suspect and surprise because I had never suspected either of these two individuals, especially Bill who was, after all, a member of our own Entry.

Grafton walked across to where they stood, going first to one and then the other, each time standing directly in front of the person at a very close distance to silently glare directly at them. Both were bright red.

Finally, he stepped back. "Do you realize that you put a poor fellow in hospital and caused him a great deal of suffering?" The question was directed at both.

"Yes Sir," they both mumbled. Then Ben added, "We only did it as a joke Sir, and didn't think it would hurt him like that."

"Is that so?" The Flight Commander retorted, "Well, there's no place in my Flight for stupid jokes like that and you're both going to spend a little time on Defaulters' Parade to make sure you understand that! You're also going to apologize to Butterworth when he recovers and can return to his duties. Is that clear?"

"Yessir," they both replied in penitent voices.

Flight Lieutenant Grafton then turned and fixed his eye on Sergeant Savoury, "Sergeant Savoury, put these men on a charge."

"Sah!" responded Savoury, reaching into his left breast pocket for the little pad of Form 252s that all Discipline NCOs carried with them. With that, the Flight Commander turned brusquely and left the billet. Meanwhile, the sergeant's radar locked on to the two hapless culprits, streaking towards them as accurately and deadly as a guided missile.

"Roight you two, let's 'ave your twelve-fifties," he demanded, referring to their Form 1250 service identification cards. Then, looking around at the rest of us, he announced in his broad cockney accent, "The rest of you lot—get your stuff togev-vah and get aht on pa-ride. On the double!"

Grabbing our overalls and books, we all tumbled out of the billet and onto the road. In one final glance backwards before leaving the billet, I saw Bill and Ben standing with hang-dog looks as Savoury copied the information from their 1250s on to the 252 charge forms.

Later that afternoon Butterworth returned to class. I was dying to talk to him and find out what had happened, from the time that he had left the billet to go to Station Sick Quarters. Finally, at break-time, he told me the whole story.

Walking into Station Sick Quarters had been quite a surprise to the medics, who weren't accustomed to very much activity after lights-out. They quickly sized-up the situation and began swabbing him down with a cool-feeling lotion, probably calamine, which eased the itching. But he was still in agony and most of the skin on his trunk and legs looked an angry red inflamed colour. Going back to his bed in the billet was obviously out of the question and besides, he needed ongoing treatment, so they took him over to the hospital. He spent the next two days and nights there, receiving further ministrations from pretty nurses, in stark contrast to the male medics that most of us were used to seeing at Station Sick Quarters. The best part, from Butterworth's point view, was that his stay in hospital was all a legal skive, even though he had suffered in agony for the first few hours. He was completely unaware of who had put the glass fibre in his bed and was surprised when I told him that it was Bill and Ben, but he wasn't displeased when he learned of their lunchtime encounter with Flight Lieutenant Grafton.

When we returned to the billet that evening after Workshops, Bill and Ben were already busy cleaning brasses and webbing before getting attired to go on the first jankers parade. Apparently, there had been little time lost from the time that they were put on the charge until they were marched before the Flight Commander to formally answer to it. Flight Lieutenant Grafton proceeded to throw the book at them, subjecting them to a stern lecture before "awarding" the maximum sentence of seven days jankers that his status of Flight Commander permitted. They were lucky to get off with that, because inflicting personal injury to someone else could very easily have put both of them in the Guardroom for an uncomfortable spell, if they had been remanded up the chain of command to the Wing Commander.

A silence descended on the billet the moment that Butterworth entered, but the two janker-wallahs immediately approached him and offered their very sincere apologies, which Richard graciously accepted. Then they all shook hands and that was the end of it, except for the jankers.

* * *

Not long after the fibreglass incident, Butterworth had to make a return visit to the hospital, but he wasn't alone this time. During mid-summer of 1957, the Asian flu pandemic, which was sweeping around the world that year, invaded Britain. By the time September rolled around, it had found its way into South Wales and to Royal Air Force Station St. Athan.

Initially, those who succumbed were few in number, but the virus was highly contagious and within one or two weeks the entire camp population was severely affected. Station Sick Quarters worked overtime to process the hordes of Boy Entrants who were turning up on the daily sick parades. In fact, the sick parades, which usually consisted of no more than five or six blokes, competed in size with the workshops parade. Eventually, anyone suspected of harbouring flu symptoms was despatched immediately to Station Sick Quarters, instead of having to wait until the next day for the routine daily sick parade at 0830 hours.

The Station Sick Quarters medics soon became highly efficient at handling the deluge of Asian flu patients, as I experienced first hand when, several days into the crisis, I came down with the dreaded symptoms: high temperature, headache, shivering, severe body aches and weakness. On arriving at

Station Sick Quarters, no one asked the nature of my complaint; instead I was brusquely told to sit down on one of the long hard wooden benches and before I knew what was happening a thermometer was thrust into my mouth. At the same time I was given a short form to fill out that required me to provide my name, rank, service number and a description of my perceived ailment, the latter being almost a formality. Within moments, the thermometer was whipped out of my mouth and inspected. The medic then took one brief look at me before ordering that I needed to take myself to the hospital. I never got as far as seeing the Medical Officer. The hospital was a considerable distance away but, like everyone else, I was expected to walk there, Asian flu or not.

During the time that the pandemic raged through St. Athan, those succumbing to it were so numerous that the hospital was forced to drastically increase its number of beds by expanding into a whole section of nearby empty billets. In normal times, these billets were used only to accommodate visiting parents during the passing-out parades. Now, they were full of sick boy entrants and frantic medics trying to cope with the sheer weight of numbers. I was directed to a bed in one particular billet and, before getting into it, was given some syrupy amber liquid in a small glass and a few pills. I had no idea what they were, but trustingly swallowed them anyway. Blankets, pillows and sheets were provided and the bed was already made up, so I got quickly undressed and into my pyjamas before sinking wearily into the bed and drifting off into a sweaty sleep that was full of strange dreams. I don't know how long I was out for, nor did I care. One medic or another periodically came by to wake me up to ask how I felt. I would groan when they shoved a thermometer in my mouth, whilst asking me if I felt warm enough. I always nodded yes, that I did, wondering why they didn't seem to notice the perspiration in which I was evidently drenched. But it was their reaction to my response that never failed to surprise me, because they would always throw another blanket on top of the mound that already covered me. This particular scene played out several times over the course of the next two days and not just with me. Everyone else confined to bed in the billet seemed to receive the same treatment. On reflection, I suppose the strategy was to either simply sweat the germs out of us, or kill the little buggers by making conditions too hot for them to exist!

On the first and second days, I just fell in and out of a coma-like sleep, not knowing what time of day or night it was, not feeling hungry, but always thirsty when I woke up. In addition to loading me up with more blankets, the medics came around with their little cups of liquid amber and pills, insisting that I sit up and take them. After struggling to sit up and take the medicine, I would crash back onto my sweat-soaked pillow as yet another blanket was piled on top of the huge and ever-growing mound that my aching body was already supporting.

On the third day, I was beginning to feel a little better and although my mouth tasted as though something had crawled in there and died, my state of consciousness seemed to be returning to something nearer normal. And I was hungry.

It now became obvious that other patients, who were in the later stages of recovery, but still not well enough to be discharged, were acting as orderlies to help the overworked medics. One of their jobs was to bring around the meals to those of us still confined to bed. The food, it turned out, was being brought over from both 1 and 2 Wing cookhouses by lorry, which must have been a logistics nightmare in itself. Individual plates had been prepared and stacked on top of each other, separated by those little metal rings that are commonly used in the catering industry. Because of the sheer numbers of patients and the few lorries assigned to ferry the food from the messes, breakfast was more likely to turn up stone cold at around lunchtime. Lunch was similarly time-shifted, as was the evening meal. It wasn't very appetising, but I was hungry and had little choice other than to eat it. Besides, I couldn't taste anything anyway.

Two days later, one of the medics pronounced that I was well enough to be up and about, so he told me to first go and take a bath and then get dressed. The recovering patient's "uniform" was pyjamas worn under a working-blue tunic, with plimsolls as footwear. For the next two days, I helped out with such duties as distributing meals, sweeping out the billet and making up beds for the new patients, who arrived to fill them as soon as they were vacated. Those of us in the process of recovering discussed amongst ourselves the excellent opportunity this pandemic presented for the Russians to attack Britain, because if the situation at St. Athan was anything to go by, the entire RAF was probably laid low by Asian flu. All of the ground defence training that we'd undergone would have been little use in putting up any resistance, since most of the camp was near comatose during those late summer weeks of 1957. Cold-war Russia seemed so far away from our little part of the world in those days, that it never occurred to us that they too were probably under attack by the very same microbes that had brought Britain to its knees.

After two days of dishing out food, rinsing dishes in the bath before stacking them in containers for their return trip to the mess and generally being at the beck and call of the medics, I was only too pleased when the duty M.O. (Medical Officer) pronounced me fit for discharge. Being able to wear my normal uniform again instead of pyjamas and plimsolls felt weird at first, probably because I had lost some weight into the bargain, but it felt good to be discharged from the temporary hospital and back in the normal world once more, even if I did still feel a little weak and shaky.

That evening in the billet, I was surprised to discover that more than half of the beds had become unoccupied in the days that followed my own forced absence. Classes at workshops were sparsely populated by the few of us who had recovered and those who had yet to succumb. The few instructors still with us were marking time until class levels returned to somewhere near full strength. Just to keep us occupied until that day came around, we were tutored on topics that had been previously covered, which was actually a heaven-sent bonus for someone like me, since I was able to receive almost personal tutoring on my weaker subjects.

The situation wasn't without other bonuses as well. We received more personal attention at the boy entrants' mess, not unlike the long weekends during which some of us had to remain at camp when the majority went home on 96-hour passes. It was easy to find a good seat in the Astra and there was scarcely a blue uniform to be seen on Barry Island, except for those few of us who took on the heroic task of ensuring that the teenage girls of Barry didn't pine away out of sheer loneliness. All good things come to an end, however, although it was nice while it lasted. Within a few weeks everything had returned to normal. Regular instruction resumed at the workshops, mess queues regained their customary length and life everywhere just got back to being crowded again.

* * *

In October of 1957, the 32nd Entry commenced their ITS training. The routine had become old hat by now. Suddenly there were hundreds of pounding feet running up the concrete pathway to the mess at lunchtime, when the brand new sprogs were dismissed by the drill instructors. What it meant for old sweats like the 29th was that we either had to train them to be respectful of our Entry status or wait until the rush had died down. Most of the time, it was easier just to remain in the billet for half an hour or so and then take a casual saunter across to the mess. Invariably, when I did this, the queue had melted away, enabling me to go directly up to the servery and get lunch in good time, without having to compete with the press of humanity.

* * *

When the October trees had taken on the golden colours of autumn, it signalled that the balmy summer weekends spent flirting with the Rhondda Valley girls on Barry Island were behind me. Soon it would be greatcoat weather again and that magical summer, when I was 16 and knew everything there was to know about everything there was, would fade into the background to become nothing more than a dusty memory that might occasionally be taken out and aired once in a while as the years rolled by.

The Rhondda Valley girls were a breed apart. They weren't shy by any stretch of the imagination, as many a boy entrant was destined to find out, much to his utter amazement.

The valley itself was a highly industrialised area just a few miles to the north of Barry, given over to coal mines and smokestack factories. Most of the teenage girls born and raised there went straight into factory jobs as soon as they had finished school at the age of 15. Apart from the few days off work at Christmas and Bank Holidays, their only escape from the everyday monotony of factory life was when all of the Valley coalmines and factories closed at the same time for the annual two-week summer holiday. One of the highlights of the girls' lives during this period of unfettered freedom seemed to be a day trip to Barry Island on chartered coaches. And day-trip they did, arriving in wolf-like packs with an apparent single-minded determination to enjoy every second of their day out. They loved boy entrants! The sight of our uniforms, coupled with the fact that we were around the same age, seemed to attract them like magnets. If a group of them caught sight of us—and they always went around in large groups—they were immediately in hot pursuit, until they caught up with us. Not that we exactly ran too fast, mind you. It seemed that every Rhondda Valley girl's ambition was to snatch one of our SD hats to be borne triumphantly back to the valley as some sort of hunting trophy. Thwarting this quest meant that we needed to be ever on our guard.

But the girls had a sexual agenda as well! In the process of trying to distract us as they attempted to steal our hats, they weren't always too ladylike and would often subject us to a group-grope. This, for us, was all part of the enjoyment— although we heard lurid tales that these same young 'ladies', egged on by older mentors, inflicted near-emasculation on any young, unsuspecting factory lad who might have made the tragic mistake of wandering into their all-female areas. The consequences were always sexual in nature, in ways that were very humiliating for the hapless young male victims.

In spite of these stories, I always enjoyed encounters with the Rhondda Valley girls and loved their high spirits and devil-may-care attitudes. But alas, it was only for that one short summer.

* * *

An air of grim dreariness settled over St. Athan with the onset of November's gloomy days; days that barely got light before dank darkness descended again. The Rhondda Valley girls had long since returned to their terraced houses, surrounded by factory smokestacks and their black-faced coal-mining men-folk. As they worked in the factories, perhaps they thought back to pleasanter balmy summer days spent at Barry Island, idly flirting with lads in blue RAF uniforms—helicopter pilots, as they might have been led to believe, maybe the occasional one with a little bit of an Irish lilt in his voice. Meanwhile, the very same "helicopter pilots" were huddled inside the protection of their working greatcoats as they battled against biting, horizontal, wind-driven rain that opposed their march to workshops, in their ongoing pursuit of technical knowledge.

November then gave way to December and thoughts of going home on Christmas leave loomed large in everyone's mind. Not only that, but the spirit of Christmas had begun to make itself felt. For one thing, there was to be a Christmas concert in the Astra for the inmates—starring none other than the inmates themselves.

When volunteers were called for, Richard Butterworth and I promptly decided to go into show business, notwithstanding the fact that we didn't possess a single ounce of stage talent between us. But performing in the concert sounded like such a good skive that we just couldn't resist it.

A notice came around inviting volunteers to present themselves at the Drill Shed on a certain evening for concert auditions—no previous experience necessary! Well, if they were looking for people with no previous experience, they had certainly come to the right place, as far as Richard and I were concerned. We eagerly made our way to the Drill Shed on the appointed evening, bubbling over with excitement at this opportunity to be discovered as big stars. The large group that had already gathered by the time we got there were busy adding their names to a list, under the supervision of the officer in charge of the concert. Eventually the list came into our hands and we entered our names, squadron and flight number in the appropriate columns. We left the "Talent" column blank, although in retrospect we could have legitimately entered "enthusiasm".

When everyone had signed up, the officer looked over the list and gave us a little pep talk. Then he split the "artistes" into smaller groups according to their talents, holding separate discussions with each group before dismissing them. Approximately twenty untalented lads remained, including Richard and me. The officer walked slowly back to where we were all huddled, half expecting that he would dismiss us. But instead, he smilingly divided us into two smaller groups and directed each group to start coming up with ideas for a skit that we could develop and then perform in the concert.

We scratched our heads for some ideas as the evening jankers parade started to form up, forcing us to move to a more remote area of the Drill Shed. Although the move was an inconvenience, it triggered a flash of inspiration in one of our number, who then came up with the brilliant idea for a dysfunctional janker-wallah parade skit. We all liked the idea and excitedly proposed it to the officer, who gave it his warm approval. What followed was a series of several evenings devoted to the development of ideas, scripts and repeated rehearsals for the ten-minute time-slot that we would be allotted on stage.

It wasn't difficult to pack the Astra when admission was free and so on the night of the concert, it was bursting at the seams. The "jankers-parade" team sat in reserved seats in the auditorium, able to enjoy most of the show until it was time to go backstage and prepare for our own presentation. It's always amazing how much talent there is amongst ordinary people and the boy entrant population was no exception. We were entertained by singers, acrobats, amateur magicians, piano players, guitar players, comedy teams and more than one skiffle band that used washboards and tea-chests as basic musical instruments (this particular form of music having been made popular around that time by the likes of Lonnie Donegan). Then it was our turn!

The curtain rose on our skit to reveal a straggly line of janker-wallahs in various states of disarray. One boy stood with a lit cigarette dangling from the corner of his mouth, another was heavily bandaged and on crutches, while yet another was dressed partially in uniform and partially in civilian attire. The Orderly Sergeant, as played by one of the group, was very timid and repeatedly requested the parade to come to attention, but none of the janker-wallahs paid him the slightest bit of notice as they busily interacted with each other. All of this was already getting laughs, but the appearance of the Orderly Officer brought the house down. In a stroke of casting genius, the concert officer had cast the smallest of our number, namely Richard, as the O.O. Rich really got into the role, as he marched confidently on stage and bawled at the parade to get fell in and stand to attention, achieving immediate compliance from the suddenly intimidated defaulters and gaining feigned admiration from the Orderly Sergeant.

The defaulters' inspection followed—this was the main thrust of the whole skit. Richard started at one end and picked on each member of the group for some problem or other, satirising the things that happen on real defaulters' parade inspections. One individual was ordered to turn out the contents of his small pack, which in real life was supposed to contain several specific items, such as pyjamas, small kit (toiletries), boot brushes and button stick. But this particular small pack was wide of the mark. Instead of containing the correct items, the audience was treated to the sight of multiple ladies' lacy undergarments tied together in a seemingly never-ending string that Richard laboriously dragged out from the interior of the bag. That got a big laugh. Our hero then asked another defaulter to hand over his canteen so that it could be checked to make sure that it was full of fresh drinking water. This was the favourite inspection item on a real defaulters' parade and heaven help the poor sod whose canteen contained water that didn't taste fresh, or if it wasn't completely full. Butterworth uncorked the canteen and raised it to his lips and pretended to take a swig, then staggered around the stage after taking a hefty gulp of something that was obviously much stronger than water. He steadied himself and recovered his composure, but just when everyone thought he was going to make a big scene with the unfortunate janker-wallah, he took another swig and then another until the canteen had apparently been emptied. Then, he gave it back to its owner and told him, with a distinct slur in his voice, that it was the freshest water he had tasted in a long time.

Sobering up remarkably quickly, he moved on to the next defaulter, a well-built lad who was at least six feet in height. Richard, all four feet of him, looked the tall lad up and down, supposedly inspecting his buttons. Then he leaned forward, bending over at right angles to his waist and appeared to inspect the tall lad's boots. Meanwhile, Lofty, as he was known for obvious reasons, leaned forward from his waist and bent down over the top of Butterworth so that the upper parts of both their bodies were parallel to each other. He remained there during the whole time that Richard was bent over, returning to the upright position with split second timing as Richard also started to straighten up.

The Orderly Officer inspects Lofty's boots in a scene from the Christmas concert skit.
As envisioned by "The Chequered Band" cartoonist, Mickie Collins.

Next Richard, apparently suspicious that something had just occurred which threatened his authority, came up very close to Lofty and assumed a confrontational stance. In response, Lofty pulled himself more erect and puffed out his chest in a silent yet assertive attempt to counter the pint-sized Orderly Officer's attempt at dominating him. Not to be outdone, the O.O. re-exerted his authority by peering upwards in the direction of Lofty's cap and announcing, "Boy Entrant, your hat badge is filthy," although he very obviously couldn't see the hat badge from his position. Then, with barely a pause, he turned to the Orderly Sergeant and barked, "Sergeant, take this man's name and make sure he has cleaned his badge by the next parade. And tonight, have him do his fatigues at the mess!"

As expected, this remark brought loud boos and catcalls from the audience because it was one of the worst fatigues that a janker-wallah could be given, usually involving the scraping of congealed food residue off cookhouse pots and pans.

The inspection continued until all of those on parade had been dealt with, sometimes to the defaulter's advantage and at other times to the Orderly Officer's. Meanwhile, I had been waiting in the wings for my cue. Alas, my great moment of fame was merely a brief walk-on part, but I tried to make the best of it. Unlike the defaulters, I was properly dressed in working uniform and, on making an entrance from stage right, I marched smartly across the stage to where Butterworth stood. He, meanwhile, had turned expectantly to face me. Of course my "keen" march across the stage brought loud boos from the audience, who all naturally identified with the underdog janker-wallahs. I came to a smart halt in front of Butterworth, giving a kind of little skip that drill instructors liked to perform when they came to a halt face-to-face with an officer. My arm came up in salute and quivered there for a few moments in exaggeration of another drill instructor favourite. Richard returned the salute. I then leaned forward and pretended to say something confidential into his ear, then straightened up and stood stiffly at attention.

"Bring him on," Richard loudly commanded.

I turned towards the wings, from where I'd just emerged and beckoned. At this signal, four brawny boys staggered out from the wings carrying a bed on which a "defaulter" apparently lay sleeping in his full janker-wallah regalia of webbing and large pack. They carried the bed to one end of the parade line-up and placed it gently on the ground. Richard approached the person on the bed, then came to a stop and took a deep breath and yelled, "Defaulter, wake up!" The person in the bed reacted in a startled fashion, as though he had been suddenly and rudely awakened.

"Why are you in bed, lad?" Richard inquired.

"I'm on light duties, Sir," was the boy's reply, as he simultaneously held out a crumpled piece of paper that was supposedly a much coveted light-duties chit.

"Oh, I see," retorted Richard, his voice heavy with sarcasm, "so you can't do any heavy work, eh?"

"No Sir," said the still-prone fellow, who also shook his head vigorously to give added emphasis.

"Well, in that case we'll send you to the mess along with Lofty and you can bake some fairy cakes while you're there. I think that should be light enough work for you!"

By this time the audience was laughing uproariously, including the Station Commander and several of the senior officers who had been seated in the front row. And, with that, the curtain came down on our skit, to thunderous applause. It couldn't have been a more fitting end to our career in show business.

* * *

Christmas edged ever closer, its imminent arrival having an increasing tendency to focus young minds on warm thoughts of very soon going home on leave. Meanwhile, the really cold winter weather had yet to set in. December was damper, greyer and more dreary than cold. We were getting up in darkness and then marching to work when it had barely got light, in a world filled with the perpetual drip of water from every inanimate object that possessed the slightest elevation above ground level. Premature nightfall enveloped our return from workshops in the early evenings. The surrounding darkness was lit occasionally by the headlights of passing cars that illuminated the non-stop drizzle, leaking continuously from the heavily laden clouds drifting eastwards from the Atlantic on their slow but relentless journey across the British Isles. But, at least there was one bright note to sweep away much of the dreariness in our otherwise depressed lives—the 28th would be passing out in mid-December and in doing so would hand over the baton of Senior Entryship to the 29th Entry—like an early Christmas present.

Most members of the 28th had mellowed considerably from the high spirits that we'd seen when they first became Senior Entry. They seemed to have come to the realization that it paid to be nice to the underdogs at this stage of the game. After all, they didn't want anything untoward happening that might detract from the joy of their upcoming graduation. And just to make sure, the soon-to-be graduates hoarded their white webbing, their carefully pressed best blues and their highly bulled boots under lock and key during this vulnerable period, when they weren't actually cleaning them or wearing them to dress rehearsals. Bull boys, who had been buried under mounds of drudge work in the past, were now relieved of their menial duties because of a sense of paranoia that seemed to grip those preparing to pass-out.

Several of the 28th would not be wearing white webbing belts during the passing-out parade. Instead of sharing in the euphoria with their fellow Entry members, they would be parading with the "supporting entries" in what must, for them, have been a very disheartening experience. That was because, for one reason or another, they had been unable to meet the academic standards necessary to graduate with their own Entry and had therefore been relegated to ours for one more attempt. A little tap-dancing was in order for them—up until now, they had been wrapped in the blanket of protection that their original 28th Entry membership bestowed. But that protection had very quickly evaporated with the 28th Entry's passing-out parade and these marooned individuals knew it. Now, their once-cocky attitudes had been replaced by a desperate outreach towards a more conciliatory accommodation with the Entry that would be adopting them for the next few months. It must be said that most made the accommodation with few problems.

By now, passing-out parades were becoming ho-hum. The only thing good about the 28th parade was that it meant the 29th Entry's passing-out parade would be next and more immediately that we would be the new Senior Entry just as soon as the 28th marched off the Square. And so, forming up in the farewell Guard of Honour for the very last time was just about tolerable. The 28th, of course, were all grins, just like the entries that had passed this way before them and those whose turn had yet to come.

We celebrated our new-found senior Entry status in much the same way as our predecessors. I would like to say that we were nobler than they and didn't stoop to such terrorizing activities as billet raids after lights-out, or mock courts martial of hapless junior Entry victims. But shamefully, we did—and revelled in it! I do feel, however, that the 29th Entry was much less vindictive than those who came before us. As far as I'm aware, no junior Entry member was harmed during any of our activities and most seemed to take the harassment in reasonably good spirits. Of course, that's a very subjective viewpoint and doesn't take into account the fear of the unknown that played such a major part in making the experience something of a nightmare for yours truly when I was a mere Junior Entry sprog.

CHAPTER 11

The Final Test

On our first full day as Senior Entry, Corporal Longfellow summoned all of us to the common room. He first lectured us on the responsibilities that came with our new status, most importantly that we were expected to play a supportive role to the permanent staff—a clear reference to himself and the other squadron NCOs and officers. We were to set a good example to the younger boys, weren't to bully them and so on and so forth. He then asked that we hand over our permanent passes (PPs) so that they could be annotated to reflect our latest and final proficiency badges—the small inverted chevrons worn on the cuff of the left sleeve.

I was still a one-striper, having been denied the second proficiency badge because of my unsatisfactory performance in trade tests during the summer term. That's when I had been skiving in the trumpet band instead of studying. My performance had definitely improved on account of giving up the band, otherwise I wouldn't have been sitting in that room on that particular day, but the new proficiency badge would only bring me up to a grand total of two stripes. That would still be one stripe short of the three chevrons needed to clearly proclaim my status as a member of the Senior Entry and attract the unquestioned respect and deference that came with it. With only two chevrons, I could imagine myself having to verbally convince subordinate entry members that I was indeed Senior Entry, since the normally accepted three-chevron indication wasn't in evidence. I needn't have worried, however.

During lunch break on the following day, Longfellow reconvened our common room get-together. When we had all settled down, he produced a large, bulky, brown envelope into which he stuck his hand and then began fishing out PPs that noticeably contained sets of chevrons folded between their two pages. When each individual's name was called out, that person came forward to receive the little blue document, together with his set of three stripes. Eventually, my name was called and I made my way up to the front of the room to where the corporal stood. He gave me a little smile as I reached forward to receive my pass and chevrons, but the significance of the smile was lost on me until I looked at the chevrons. They've made a mistake, was my most immediate thought, because there in my hand was a set of three stripes, instead of the two I had expected.

My heart pounded as I made my way back to my seat, expecting to be called back at any moment, when Longfellow realized he had made an error. But it didn't happen. Instead, he continued calling on others to come forward and receive their stripes. I got back to my seat and sat down, then gingerly opened the PP to check the annotation. With great relief, I saw that there was no mistake—a handwritten notation had been entered on the appropriate line, in blue fountain-pen ink, awarding me the third proficiency stripe. The Flight Commander's signature next to the entry, in darker coloured ink, made the award official.

I was very curious to know why they had decided to allow me to wear all three chevrons, but was afraid to ask in case it focused too much attention on the issue and that I might end up having the third chevron withdrawn. After a reasonable length of time had passed, during which the third stripe remained firmly attached to my sleeve, I was able to rationalize the whole situation. It seemed to me that the second and third stripes had been awarded concurrently, as recognition that I had worked hard to make up for lost ground in my trade knowledge. This rationale, coupled with Corporal Longfellow's knowing little smile when he handed me the stripes, convinced me that all three were mine to keep. Whatever the reason, receiving them was a tremendous boost for my morale, giving me the feeling that I had genuinely made it as Senior Entry.

* * *

The time for Christmas leave finally arrived and as always, the Irish and Scottish lads were granted two days' "travelling time", which enabled us to get away on the day before, when the local buses and trains were relatively easy to board. Just 24 hours later, queues for those very same buses and trains would be as long as tempers were short, when the majority of the Boy Entrant population would be released on leave.

Travelling across the Irish Sea was less of an ordeal than it had been the previous year. Many of us had discovered that the Heysham route, operated by British Railways, was superior to the Liverpool route in every way. The ships were newer and better appointed, the boat-train brought passengers right up to the dock and the harbour was directly connected to the open sea, which meant there was no lock system to add extra time to the journey. Heysham also lacked the pungent smell that characterized Liverpool, so I was spared from having to inhale the acrid fumes of Lime Street station. Another big difference from the previous year was that instead of staying in uniform, I changed into my civilian clothes as soon as possible after getting home.

The "civvies" were courtesy of a recent policy that granted Senior Entry the privilege of wearing civvies when off duty. The policy itself was a joke, because it also dictated that the civilian clothing would consist exclusively of a black or navy blue blazer, grey flannel trousers, white shirt and "suitable" necktie, which was every bit as much a uniform as our best blue. There was, however, an element of "status" attached to wearing civvies. Besides, normal civilian shirts with their attached collars meant not having to suffer the uncomfortable collar stud that pressed into my throat every minute of every day when in uniform. So now I had a modest wardrobe of "civvies" that I had been able to purchase, thanks to the princely sum of twenty-five shillings now received each week at pay parade.

It wasn't long before I looked up John Moore and Melvin Jackson. As always, Coleraine was about as lively as a graveyard after the shops closed at 6 o'clock in the evening, so we usually just hung around Main Street, talking and trading banter. It was while we were standing at the corner of Park Street and Main Street one weeknight that my eye registered a familiar figure coming towards us, easily recognizable under the bright fluorescent street lights that had replaced the dim gaslights of several years earlier. There was only one person that I knew of who walked with that unusual gait, but I still couldn't believe what my eyes were telling me until he came closer. Then I knew for sure that it was my old ex-St. Athan friend, Mick—the guy for whom I had bulled when the 27th first became Senior Entry. He was dressed in civilian clothes, but was instantly recognizable by his peculiar mode of locomotion that combined a strange loping gait with an awkward backward thrust of his right arm, (which had quite possibly resulted from a badly-set broken bone).

"Mick!" I called out.

He stopped and appeared puzzled, obviously taken aback that someone would know his name in this little Irish backwater of a town. Then he smiled in recognition, "Paddy Carlin," he declared, "what the hell are you doing here?"

"This is where I come from," I responded, a little defensively.

"I'm stationed at Ballykelly," he said, informatively.

"Yeah, I remember when you got your posting. That's when I told you that I came from Coleraine."

"Oh yeah, I remember now," he responded weakly, betraying the fact that he really didn't, "are you still at Saints?" He asked, quickly changing the subject.

My friends had fallen silent as the conversation proceeded and I suddenly became aware of how much out of place Mick's Home Counties accent must have sounded, to ears that were accustomed to hearing only the familiar brogue of my hometown.

"Yeah, we're Senior Entry now," I responded, slipping out of my thick native brogue and into a more easily understood hybrid accent that was neither Irish nor English, but somewhere in between. "We pass out in March."

"God, how time flies," he uttered. "Anyway, where's all the life here in Coleraine?" Suddenly changing the subject again.

"There's not much goin' on durin' the weeknights," John Moore suddenly chipped in, gregariously deciding to join in the conversation. "Coleraine's a long way tae come from Ballykelly. Ahsn't Lammavaddy a bit nearer fur ye?"

"Limavady's a one-horse town," countered Mick, "and the horse is dead! There's just nothing there!" It was a good remark and we all laughed, knowing that he was right on target about the little town of Limavady, about 20 miles east of Coleraine and much nearer to RAF Station Ballykelly. We all talked for a little while longer, Melvin not saying much, but John really wading in and enjoying the opportunity to talk to someone new, and "Anglish" at that. Then Mick said he'd have to be on his way and that he was going to see if there was any life in Portrush. He wished me good luck and we shook hands before parting, never to meet again. I couldn't wait to tell the lads back in the billet that I'd met him in my home town.

* * *

With Christmas leave behind me, I had three months until the passing-out parade in late March to get back into some serious work, if I intended to maintain momentum and pass out with my entry. After my "coffee and biscuits" session with Mr. Dimbleby, I had developed the habit of studying. This was especially important for the periodic tests that we were given at the end of each Phase. I usually teamed up with Richard Butterworth on these study sessions; we would take it in turns to compose questions to each other based on our classroom notes. This helped both the reader and the responder to cram knowledge into the nooks and crannies of our brains, in readiness for the real tests. At other times, the instructors would subject us to "mock" tests that helped us find out how much—or little—we knew about the subjects we were studying. The mock tests were always similar to the multiple choice "ballot" type of exam paper that we would have to pass as one part of the Final Trade Test—the other part of the test would be an oral "Board", but more about it later. On and exam paper, we were given four possible answers, A, B, C and D, for each question, only one of which was correct. The other three answers ranged anywhere from "almost correct" to "complete and utter nonsense".

The instructor marked the test by using a cardboard template that he placed over the answer paper. Holes in the template coincided with the correct answer boxes and the answer was counted as correct only if an "X" appeared in the hole. There was no waffling—the answer was either completely right or completely wrong. It was a popular legend that if someone, having absolutely no knowledge of the subject matter, took the test, they would statistically score around 30% correct. The passing mark was 60%, therefore the same statistical probability strongly implied that a candidate needed to possess a reasonable level of trade knowledge in order to successfully pass the test.

Our instructors were often able to obtain old Final exam papers that they would use to give us as mock tests. It was well-known that some questions appeared on more than one Final paper, so the instructors were diligent in hunting down these old papers to help us get "genned up" for the real thing. But in spite of this intensive tutoring, the Final paper was still considered difficult. It was a cakewalk, however, compared to the "Board"

As mentioned earlier, the Board was an oral test, during which a Trade Standards and Testing Section (TSTS) examiner grilled individuals on the full training-course syllabus, as they toured around the workshops together, stopping at various pieces of equipment and circuit boards. Some portions of the Board involved the diagnosis and rectification of faults on equipment that had been deliberately sabotaged by the examiner. Other segments consisted of verbal question and answer sessions concerning any and all of the equipment we had been trained on.

Since safety procedures and "trade practice" are also an important part of aircraft maintenance, not only were we grilled on these, but needed to observe them when carrying out any of the diagnostics or rectification called for by the examiner. Failing to do so could lead to a huge loss of marks. Because of the many possible pitfalls, we all understandably dreaded the Board more than the Final paper and spent a lot of time grilling each other on questions that an examiner might possibly ask.

But we still hadn't finished with the training syllabus. During this term, we covered Advanced AC Circuits that delved ever deeper into AC generators and their control circuits. This was important because aircraft were becoming more complex as the jet age took over from the piston engine era and the electrical systems were being called on to do more things. Continuing with low voltage DC systems would have required the use of heavier electrical cables to carry the increased loads; therefore modern aircraft of the day were being designed with high voltage AC systems that enabled smaller diameter cables to be used for distribution. Also, high-voltage AC could be easily stepped-down to low-voltage AC and then rectified to low voltage DC for the many circuits that still required it. Advanced AC circuits required lots of concentration because, like maths, it was a difficult subject that had little interest for the average person, at least until you grasped it and then it became almost elegant. But few would admit to thinking that way, except Charlie the class "swot".

"Airfields" was a much more interesting subject, because it was mostly non-technical and involved working with actual aircraft in an airfield situation. We were able to put into practice the procedures learned in the classroom, on how to interact with aircraft in hangars and on the equivalent of a flight line. This meant checking ejection seats before entering a cockpit and making them safe, if necessary. We were also placed in the challenging situation of directing real aircraft as they taxied towards us, using the big yellow marshalling bats for daytime operation and lighted "wands" to wave if it was dark—we didn't

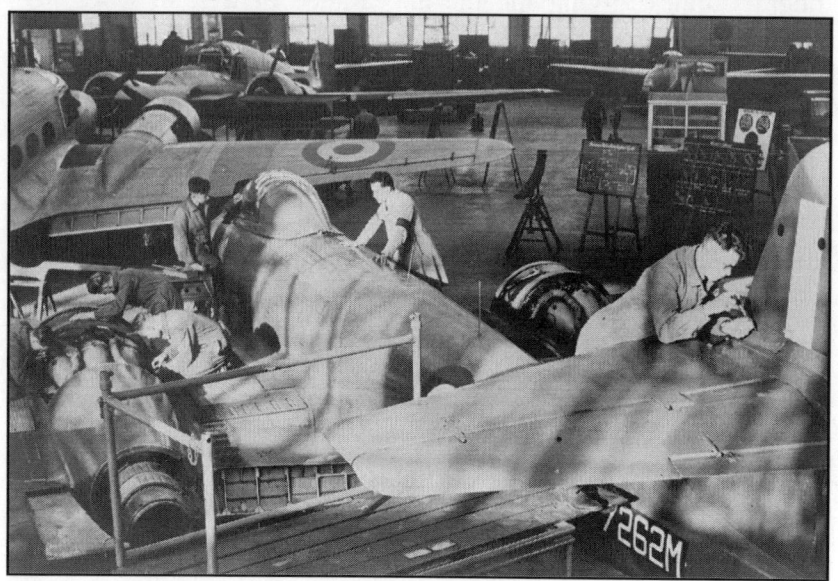

Boy Entrants perform servicing tasks on a Meteor in "Workshops". Other aircraft featured in the picture are two Ansons (upper left) and a Vampire (upper right).

actually practise in the dark but just used the wands during daytime to get a feel for them.

Practising marshalling in a classroom was easy, but was more difficult when I was faced with an aircraft taxiing straight towards me, its propeller whizzing around menacingly. On my first occasion, just being able to stay in place and do the job took a tremendous amount of self control. Inwardly, I felt terror-stricken and mentally struggled with the knot in my stomach to prevent it from travelling up to my brain, where it would almost certainly have flared up into a full-blown panic attack. That's what happened to some. I remember seeing one boy suddenly throw the bats down in the face of the advancing Piston Provost and run like hell across the airfield, putting as much distance as he could between himself and the threatening aircraft. It was even more intimidating when the person taxiing the aircraft needed to rev up the engine whilst making a turn. But while a strong primal instinct somewhere in the background was constantly telling me to make a run for it, I still had to focus my upper consciousness on the correct marshalling signals. Holding both bats upwards at 45 degree angles, giving me the appearance of a giant letter "Y", meant "come towards me, 'cos I'm your marshaller".

A turn was indicated by pointing in the direction that aircraft needed to turn with a bat held at horizontal arm's length, whilst repeatedly waving the other bat by moving only the forearm and keeping the upper arm in a horizontal position.

Extending the bats vertically upwards at arms-length in the air signalled "Stop" and an "emergency stop" was indicated by rapidly waving the bats above the head in a criss-crossing motion—the more frantic the motion, the more urgent the need to stop.

Marshalling was a heart-in-the-mouth experience, but after going through it a few times, it started to get exciting and by the time I had completed the Airfields Phase, there was a distinct feeling of having really earned my spurs. I just wonder what my thoughts might have been in those moments if only I could have seen several years into the future, when I would be routinely putting this particular training into practice while marshalling huge four-engined jet bombers, often at night and along dark taxiways, whilst being blinded by the intense beams of light directed straight at me from the Vulcan's twin taxiing lights.

There were many other activities involved in the Airfields Phase, most of which involved the excitement of working as ground-crew during aircraft movements, but there was a boring side to it as well. It came in the form of aircraft documentation that we needed to know about and learning how the various levels of servicing were organized. There would be no more certain cure for insomnia than to discuss these activities now, but learning how to make entries in the Form 700 did allow us some room for a little humour.

Each aircraft in service had its own Form 700 servicing record book that minutely recorded its daily state of readiness. Every maintenance activity performed on the aircraft was logged in this book. It also served as a means for aircrew, or anyone for that matter, to report a fault or "snag" affecting the aircraft's serviceability. Anyone who serviced the aircraft in any way was obliged to sign for the deed in the Form 700.

One section of the "700" was reserved exclusively for snags. In real life, someone, usually an aircrew member, would make an entry to log a specific fault encountered during a flight. The corresponding line on the opposing page was reserved for the servicing personnel to "clear the snag" by entering a brief description of the action taken to rectify the fault. We, of course, were given dummy Forms 700 on which to practise making and clearing invented entries. Intense competition existed between us and the other classes as to who could come up with the most creative entries. One supposed fault that I remember stated: "Engine missing"—referring to a misfiring of one or more cylinders on a piston engine. On the Rectification page, someone had cleared the snag with: "Engine cowling opened and engine found to be still there." Maybe it doesn't seem very amusing now, but at the time it seemed hilarious to a bored classroom of teenage boys.

* * *

During the final term of training, we were subjected to a steep increase in the amount of physical training we received. This may have been to toughen us up before unleashing us into the regular RAF, so that we would have enough stamina to run around an airfield, marshalling aircraft from dawn to dusk. But there could have been another reason—perhaps it was because during the short time we'd been at St. Athan we had physically transformed from boys into young men (my 17th birthday occurred during this final term) and were in need of more intense conditioning, to keep pace with our changing physiques. Whatever the reason, however, we were subjected to a five-mile route march, in boots and at the double, every day for several of the final weeks. And when we weren't out on route marches, the PTIs filled an hour of every day with a rigorous circuit-training regime. This consisted of step-ups on benches, weight-lifting, push-ups and chin-ups, for timed periods—all at different stations in the gym. When the PTI blew his whistle, we were expected to move to the next station in the circuit and begin the new activity. There was no escape. Apparently, we were going to have muscles whether we wanted them or not.

It wasn't just the RAF that acknowledged this change. There was a world of difference between now and just a year ago, in how members of the opposite sex seemed to behave towards me. There were less giggles now—replaced by more meaningful looks. Gaynor was a good example of this. She was one of the girls who served behind the counter in the NAAFI canteen and was perhaps older than me by a year or two. Gaynor was nice-looking and what might be described as pleasantly plump in the areas that tended to catch a young man's eye—and she knew it. Somewhere around the time that the 29th became Senior Entry, she began to get friendly towards me. At first it started with a special little smile that was always there to greet me when I came to buy something. Then, before long, she wanted to know my name—that sort of thing. After telling her, she always called me Bri-yan, in a sing-songy way, with the heaviest emphasis on the second syllable, in typical Welsh fashion.

There was a jukebox in the NAAFI and Gaynor really liked it when someone played the record that was currently number one on her personal hit parade. On one particular evening, I came up to the counter to buy a snack.

"Hello Bri-yan," she said from the other side of the counter, flashing me a big smile.

I placed my order and we chatted for a few moments. Then she asked if I would put some money in the jukebox and play the record she was longing to hear. I don't think I liked the particular artiste and must have hesitated because she suddenly took hold of my hand and squeezed it gently, pleading, with a sweet smile on her lips. It wasn't working, although I appreciated the hand-holding. Next thing I knew, she put my hand on her breast and squashed it deeply into the yielding softness, pleading once again as she did so. Let me tell you, Gaynor's action was shrewdly calculated to have an immediate and electrifying effect on the 17-year-old male libido and it certainly worked—yes, she got to hear her favourite record.

That same jukebox very nearly killed me—quite literally. It was one of those squat, curvaceous chest-high Fifties affairs, all aglow with multicoloured lights, that no self-respecting "caff" would be caught open without. The mechanism that manipulated the black 45-rpm vinyl records was clearly visible through the transparent plastic half-dome that enclosed most of the upper part of the jukebox. Watching the mechanism move along the library of records and then select the disc that you had just paid to hear was all part of the experience. Once the mechanism arrived at the selected record, it paused. Then an arm plucked the disc out of the stack and swung it out into a clear area, swivelling it into a horizontal position in the process. The turntable rose up on a long shaft, lifting the disc up with it as it passed through the circular holder in which it reposed. The turntable continued onwards and upwards in its travel, beginning to rotate just before the disc made contact with the stylus. Then the music began to play, but only after a short introductory hissing noise as the needle followed the lead-in groove that took it to where the music was recorded.

The reverse occurred when the music had finished. On reaching the end of the recording, some mechanism triggered by the stylus arm caused the turntable to cease revolving and begin sinking. The disc was neatly deposited back into its holder as the turntable passed through on its downward journey, as it continued on to its resting place. The mechanical arm that had first swung the disc holder out into the path of the turntable now cranked in the opposite direction, returning the disc back into stack from whence it had originally emerged, to become just another anonymous black vinyl platter in the line-up. And that was it, until another coin in the slot launched the sequence all over again.

It was my fascination with the mechanism that nearly had me checking in at the pearly gates several decades too soon. It was one of those weekends—perhaps a 96-hour pass weekend—when few people were on camp. I was sitting on a chair near the jukebox, whilst nestled up against the central heating pipes that ran around the wall of the NAAFI, clutching one of them in an effort to keep warm because it was a cold wintry day. Except for me, the entire NAAFI was deserted.

Normally, the rear of the jukebox was protected from tampering fingers by a solid-looking cover that was locked in place. But on this particular day, the cover was unlocked and open. In fact it had been like that for several days. And boys being boys, someone had discovered that a small pushbutton inside the jukebox would launch the mechanism, neatly sidestepping the usual tiresome protocol of having to deposit a coin in the slot. The discoverer of this interesting, but little-known quirk had unselfishly passed instructions around on how a person could easily avail himself of the free service, with the net result that not a soul had paid to have a record played in many days.

Having the free-play jukebox all to myself and while enjoying all my favourites—not to mention Gaynor's—I allowed my attention to wander to the mechanism, marvelling at the clever yet simple operations it performed whilst plucking the selected record out of the stack and presenting it to the stylus for playing. After watching the arm swinging the record holders out into the path of the turntable for the umpteenth time, I wondered what might happen if I tried to impede its motion. With that idle intent in mind, I reached into the jukebox with the extended forefinger of my left hand, moving it forward to push against the arm as it swung yet another record out of the stack. My other hand still grasped the central heating pipe for the welcome warmth it provided.

I never really discovered whether or not the force of my finger impeded the arm's motion, because the next thing I remember was groggily coming awake and wondering where I was, as though from a long dreamless night's sleep. But instead of being snugly tucked-up in bed, I found that I was lying on the polished linoleum floor of the NAAFI, quite some distance from the jukebox (which was happily belting out some popular song or other) wondering what the hell I was doing there. There was a sense of some kind of discontinuity and I had no idea how long I'd lain there, but it must just have been seconds because the record was still playing. The NAAFI counter was closed and the shutters pulled down, so there was no one else around. I sat up, taking a few moments to try to remember the last thing I'd done before "going to sleep". Then I saw the jukebox and recalled that my last thought was to wonder what would happen as I reached out to touch the mechanism. It then dawned on me that I had just been dealt a powerful electric shock from what was apparently the unearthed metal frame of the machine. The current from the jukebox must have travelled right across my chest on its path to earth, by way of the central heating pipes and the shock was powerful enough to hurl me several feet across the NAAFI floor. God must have felt merciful towards me that day, because the shock could so easily have been fatal. But I survived and other than feeling a little shaken at the time, there seem to have been no ill effects, except for the nuisance of having knives, forks and spoons sticking to my hands when I try to lay the table for dinner—just joking, of course.

* * *

During the month of January, the 32nd Entry graduated from ITS and came over to the Wings. It was from this crop of sprogs that we, the high and mighty Senior Entry, selected our bull boys. I must confess to taking advantage of the unwritten tradition that enabled Senior Entry boys to have someone else clean their kit, without reward. After all, I'd served my time when I too was a sprog and therefore felt every bit entitled to this very unofficial perk. But not everyone did. Richard Butterworth, to his everlasting credit, refused to have anyone else clean his stuff. His point of view, being somewhat different from mine, was that he didn't like it when he had to do it, so he wasn't going to inflict the same indignity on someone else. At the time, I thought he was making a very foolish choice, but with the passage of years I've come to believe that he was the better man for taking such a principled stand. That's not to say that I was harsh to Adam, my bull boy. In fact, we became friends in the same way that Mick and I had been friends when I was his bull boy.

* * *

Although I had so far managed to remain in the 29th Entry, having narrowly missed relegation to the 30th (thanks to Mr. Dimbleby's invitation for "coffee and biscuits"), I certainly didn't feel secure in the belief that graduation with the Entry was a foregone conclusion. Occasionally, however, these feelings of insecurity were forced to take a back-seat by morale-boosting incidents that strongly encouraged me to make the grade at the first attempt. One such experience occurred early in the term, when Corporal Longfellow called all of us to the common room and then handed out forms on which we were invited to indicate our first, second and third choices of the RAF stations to which we would like to be posted on completion of our training. We were advised that there was no guarantee of ending up at any of our three choices and that this exercise was simply like buying a ticket in a raffle for three prizes, in which the ticket-buyer was not assured of a win. My first choice was RAF Ballykelly, near my home town and the second was RAF Aldergrove, near Belfast. I don't recall my third choice, but, as events turned out, it was of little consequence anyway. Nevertheless, participating in this particular ritual boosted my morale and made me determined to pass the Final Trade Test as I visualized myself arriving at my new station, ready to reap the rewards earned after the rigours of Boy Entrant training.

* * *

A few weeks later, when we were about halfway through the term, it became time for the Final Trade Test—the focal point of our entire training. I had looked forward to this event ever since coming to the Wings, but also dreaded it. For weeks, most of us had been burying our noses in notebooks day and night, yet even on the morning of the Final Paper itself, not one of us could resist a frantic eleventh-hour flick through pages of notes, seeking to reconfirm some difficult-to-remember information that "just might come up".

There was a solemn sense of occasion associated with sitting for the Final Paper that did nothing to settle the swarm of butterflies in the pit of my stomach. After being marched to the Education Centre at the appointed hour, we were assigned by name to specific classrooms. Seating in the classrooms was arranged in such a way that no two people of the same trade sat anywhere near each other. Education officers, who had taken on the role of the invigilators, ceremoniously handed out new, freshly-sharpened pencils.

The Final Paper, as I've already mentioned, was a multiple-choice type of question paper. The answer sheet consisted of 100 numbered rows, each containing four blank boxes. Each row represented a question on the paper. The columns formed by the quarter-inch square boxes were labelled A, B, C and D. This sheet of paper was placed in front of us after we'd taken our seats. The classroom invigilator then came around and placed a question paper face down on each desk. We were ordered not to turn the question paper over until told to do so, but were permitted to read the instructions at the top of the answer sheet. We already knew them by heart at this late stage in our training—"Select one of the options, A, B, C or D as the correct answer from the four alternative answers given for each question, then place two diagonal lines from corner to corner to form an "X" in the box represented by the column-letter and question-number coordinates unique to that answer".

We were allowed one opportunity to correct a wrong answer for each question by drawing a circle in the box in which we had mistakenly placed the "x" and then putting another "x" in what we now thought was the correct box. The invigilator also advised that we should periodically check that the row number on the answer sheet agreed with the question number we were working on, since it wasn't uncommon for someone to skip a line as they worked through the test, making the likelihood of correct answers from that point onward little better than if they were pure guesses, with failure a very strong likelihood.

The invigilating officer kept a watchful eye on the clock as it approached the fateful hour and then, as soon as the minute and second hands lined up exactly on 1000 hours, he pronounced that we should turn our papers over and begin the test. There was a quiet rustle of paper, immediately followed by an unearthly silence that would last for up to two hours. It was only interrupted by an occasional small sound, like a dropped pencil, that sounded like a thunderclap in the otherwise deathly quiet room. Heads were bowed as those of us taking the exam urged every available neuron to leap heroically across impossibly wide synapses and create the necessary flow of information needed to achieve, at the very least, the magic 60% mark that would spell the difference between pass or fail. At stake was the difference between a triumphant transition to the regular service, or a humiliating relegation to the 30th entry.

At about an hour and a half into the test, the heavy blanket of silence was broken by the sound of a chair being scraped on the floor as someone stood up. The invigilator looked up expectantly as one of the examinees approached him and handed over his completed paper. After a short interval, another chair scraped and another paper was turned in. I was still struggling through the test, racking my brains on many of the questions, as I tried to match them to correct alternative answers. Even if you knew the subject like the back of your hand, the question could still be answered incorrectly due to carelessness in reading it or the answers. And if all the answers to a question appeared equally correct, it was a clear sign that you were in deep trouble, leaving just one tried and tested option—eeny, meeny, miney, mo...

The frequency of papers being handed over increased, until finally I was able to put an "x" on my selection to question number 100. A quick look over the question paper, which was so fleeting as to be worthless and I was done, one way or another. This time it was my chair that made a noise as I stood up and handed my hopes and dreams over to the invigilating officer. I noticed that a good few still remained bent over their papers, so I tiptoed out of the room as quietly as possible. Then it was back to the billet and the inevitable post-mortem with the other lads. We recalled questions from memory and then discussed what answers we'd given. Sometimes my heart sank as I realized that a particular answer I had selected was wrong and at other times my spirits soared when I was able to confirm that I'd got one right. All in all, I felt I had a fair chance. Not a "dead-cert" pass, but a feeling that I'd done all right. But, of course, we had yet to face The Board.

If sitting for the Paper was nerve-racking, it was at least civilized and predictable by being set for a certain time of day, for a particular duration and consisting of no more or less than 100 questions. But not so with taking the Board, which involved spending an unpredictable amount of time alone with one of the formidable senior NCOs from TSTS, the Trade Standards and Testing Section, who could ask as many or as few questions that he considered necessary to ascertain the extent of our knowledge. Since there were only a few of these examiners and many of us, we were obliged to wait until called individually. Awaiting my turn to be marched in front of a firing squad could have been worse, but only marginally so.

There were two waiting areas, which were used in serial fashion. The main holding area was our classroom in Workshops. Here we sat, frantically going over our notes and quizzing each other on how certain types of equipment and complex circuits operated. A TSTS senior NCO would come into the classroom every hour or so and read off perhaps half a dozen names from a clipboard. The chosen few would then rise and

follow him to a smaller holding area close to where the Board
was actually being held.

My name was eventually called as one of a group of six,
so I dutifully stood up and followed the Senior Technician who
had come to summon us. All six of us were as joyless as
condemned men being herded to the scaffold. Only Charlie, the
class swot who wore his beret pulled down over his forehead,
seemed to be excited by his anticipation at what was to come.
We were led to a small cubicle in the main practical application
area of the workshop where, over the past few months, we had
undergone practical training on the equipment. Consoles of
aircraft electrical apparatus surrounded us on all sides and in the
centre of the workshop stood the grounded Hawker Hunter jet
fighter that I'd crawled over many times during various phases
of instruction. The sight of all this was very familiar, since we
had spent many hours in that same location. That investment of
time would now be put to the test, when the TSTS examiner
began prying and probing to determine the depth of knowledge
that we had managed to absorb.

On entering the cubicle, we were told to wait there until
an examiner came and called for us by name. And so, having
brought our notebooks with us, we settled down once more into
the relentless task of trying to cram every last little scrap of
knowledge into our heads.

Very soon, a Chief Technician appeared at the door of the
cubicle and announced a name. A boy entrant stood up and then
followed the grim-faced NCO, who had turned and walked off in
the direction of the equipment consoles. Shortly afterwards,
another NCO came to the door and our number was reduced by
one more. We waited for perhaps a quarter of an hour before a
third examiner came into the cubicle, looked at his clipboard and
then called out the name of the third victim. Another agonizing
period of waiting and then the first boy came back. He looked
ashen and as he came into the cubicle we all anxiously asked
him: "How did you do?"

He rolled his eyes upwards as he picked up his
belongings, "Tough," was the only response we got before he
hurriedly exited the area.

"Carlin!" Oh my god, it was my turn. I looked up to see the grim-faced NCO who had made an appearance after our initial arrival in the cubicle, now framed in its doorway. Just my luck, I thought.

"Chief," I responded, whilst rising from the uncomfortable wooden chair. As before, he turned and started walking away from the cubicle, apparently confident that I was bringing up the rear. He came to a halt on reaching the equipment consoles and turned to face me, clipboard poised in one hand and a pen in the other.

"Carlin?" He asked.

"Yes, Chief."

"What's your service number?" I told him and he wrote it down on the clipboard. He continued writing for a few moments as I stood there, feeling awkward, exposed and vulnerable. When he had finished he lowered the clipboard and started walking towards one of the consoles.

"Okay, let's start here," he announced. "Can you name this piece of equipment?" As he said this, he placed his hand on a black-painted metal object that consisted mostly of nine-inch square cooling fins. Its rectangular base was bolted to a paxoline board and the various electrical wires connected to its terminal strip were banded neatly together, before disappearing into a hole drilled through the paxoline. They re-emerged through similar holes drilled at other locations on the console, from where they were connected to the terminal strips of adjacent black boxes. The colour of the equipment wasn't particularly significant, since all aircraft electrical equipment of that time was painted black.

"It's a type 23 voltage regulator, Chief," I responded, knowing that this was only the preliminary question to a whole series that would test the depth of my knowledge, probing for chinks and flaws.

"What does it do in this circuit?" He asked.

I then went on to identify the circuit as the P3 generator power circuit used on four-engine aircraft and that the output voltage of each engine driven generator was controlled by one of these type 23 "slave" regulators, in a "master-slave" control system. A question and answer session ensued, during which I was able to confidently explain that the "master" regulator controlling all four slaves was a type 32 voltage regulator. We then got into the intricacies of voltage equalizing and load sharing and as I answered his questions, it felt as though there were two people inhabiting my body. One, a kind of stranger, was confidently expounding on all of this knowledge in answer to the Chief Tech's questions and the other, whom I perceived as the real me, was watching with mouth agape in awe at this amazing performance by my alter ego. Luckily for me, the examiner was only aware of the first persona as we finished with the P3 generator circuit.

A feeling of calm confidence had descended on me by this time and in a way, I was enjoying the experience. We moved along the row of consoles to where another type of voltage regulator squatted on the flat workbench. Here, the vertical paxoline board behind the bench wasn't equipped as a console furnished with aircraft electrical components. Instead, it was configured as a tool-board of a type known as a shadow-board. Silhouettes of various common hand tools had been painted on the board to visually indicate which tool belonged in that space. The tools were held on the shadow-board by spring clips on or around the "shadow." All of the tools were in place as we approached the bench, so the shadows weren't plainly evident. We stopped in front of the voltage regulator and the Chief Technician looked down at it. I followed his example.

"I want you to do a mechanical setting on this," he said, placing a hand on top of the regulator for emphasis, as he had done before.

The task was an easy one. The basic aircraft voltage regulator of that era was an electro-magnetic device that compressed or relaxed a "pile" of carbon washers in order to increase or decrease the current flowing to the generator's magnetic field. The mechanical setting was a coarse initial adjustment, from which finer adjustments could be made to achieve the correct output voltage from the regulator when power was applied to the unit. We had been taught the procedure, which involved screwing the magnetic core all the way into the regulator until it bottomed and then screwing it out until two threads showed. Then, at the other end of the regulator, screwing the pile compression screw in until it gently made contact with the pile and then unscrewing it three-quarters of a turn and locking it. That was the extent of the mechanical setting. But simple though it seemed, there was a need to be wary because this type of question concealed a hidden trap that our instructors had frequently warned us about—although we had been taught the procedure, we weren't supposed to perform it from memory. Instead, we were required to refer to the appropriate servicing schedule and follow a step-by-step set of instructions whilst performing the task. If I didn't ask for the servicing schedule, I would lose marks.

"Can I please have the servicing schedule, Chief?" I asked.

Without a word, the Chief Tech immediately opened a drawer in the bench and produced a sturdy cardboard binder containing the servicing schedule, which he handed to me. Then he made a notation on his clipboard. Turning to the first page of the servicing schedule, which I had laid on the bench beside me, I proceeded to make the mechanical setting, using the special non-magnetic screwdriver required by the servicing schedule. It's fair to say that I would probably have forgotten about the special screwdriver if I had failed to read the servicing schedule and that would have been two marks against me for the price of one.

We moved on to other things. Sometimes, I was asked to trace out complex circuits on wiring diagrams and explain how the circuits operated. At other times, I was instructed to perform other servicing tasks and as with the voltage regulator, there was always a need to be conscious of using the correct procedures and observing appropriate safety precautions.

For one such task, the examiner set me to perform a battery change on the Hunter aircraft that stood in the centre of the workshop. The job itself was easy, needing only a little exertion to lift the heavy batteries. But I was also being examined on whether or not I used the servicing schedule and observed the safety precautions that it included, with regard to working with batteries. Handling them was one thing, because of the corrosive acid they contained, but there was also a need to

Trainee Engine Mechanics take an oral "Board" during a trade test.

observe certain precautions when connecting and disconnecting them from the aircraft's electrical system. The negative battery terminal is always connected to the metal airframe, just as the same terminal of a car battery is always connected to the car body. The main reason for this is to save weight and expense by using the metal of the airframe as the return conductor to carry the current back to the battery for all circuits. When disconnecting battery cables, the negative side is disconnected first, to electrically isolate the battery from the airframe. This makes the creation of a hot spark due to an accidental short-circuit much less likely, which could otherwise easily happen if something metallic—perhaps a spanner—accidentally touched against some part of the aircraft frame while it was being used on the positive battery terminal. Sparks of any kind are something to be avoided around aircraft, where easily ignited aviation fuel is ever-present.

I disconnected the negative cable first, then the positive cable, before loosening off the bolts that clamped the two heavy lead-acid batteries in place. At this point, the examiner stepped forward and told me to assume that I had already removed the old batteries from the battery bay and had replaced them with new batteries. Now he wanted me to finish the installation. I then performed the procedure in reverse, first clamping the batteries in place and wire-locking the wing nuts that bolted them securely to the battery trays. Then I connected them up to the aircraft electrical system, reading the servicing schedule as I went along and making sure that reconnecting the negative cable was the very last item of the procedure.

I was now supposed to go into the cockpit and make sure that the instruments powered up when the battery isolation switch was operated to the "on" position. This action required that another very important safety precaution was observed. I climbed the ladder leading up to the cockpit. The Perspex canopy had already been slid all the way back on its rails, allowing free access into the cramped one-man space within. It only required a foot to be planted on the seat cushion down inside the well of the cockpit, followed by the other foot, before sliding down onto the seat while holding on to the top of the windscreen frame for support. Oh so easy! But there was one important thing to check first. Was the seat safe? Were the safety pins in the right places, making accidental operation of the ejection seat impossible? So, whilst still standing on the ladder and with one hand on the outside of the canopy, I peered through the clear plastic and saw that the large red metal disc attached to the pin was threaded through the triggering component of the ejection-gun firing mechanism, at the very top of the seat,0 to prevent accidental operation. So far, so good! Now, before stepping in, I needed to look down along the side of the seat to make sure the drogue gun pin was in place and then check for a safety pin in the alternative firing handle down on the front edge of the seat pan. Yes, they were both in place. I turned to Chief Tech Grim-Face, knowing full well that he was watching me like a hawk. "I've checked the seat Chief and it's safe." He nodded in understanding as I swung a leg over the lip of the cockpit and proceeded to enter. Then he came up the ladder after me, looking into the cockpit as I flicked the toggle of the battery isolation switch upwards and was rewarded by hearing a satisfying clunk coming from somewhere underneath the cockpit as the battery circuit breaker closed. Immediately, the aircraft's electrical circuits energized. Gauges suddenly sprang to life, gyros started to whir as they spun up to speed, the "generator failure warning light" glowed red and all three "undercarriage locked down" lights glowed green. The artificial horizon chattered erratically for a few moments before settling down and the G4B compass card whirled crazily until I reached out to press a small button that brought it to an immediate stop.

"Battery functionally checked Chief," I announced.

"Okay. What do you need to do now?" He asked.

"Sign the seven-hundred, Chief," I responded, referring to the aircraft's servicing record.

"Okay," he said, "turn the battery off and then go and do that."

We walked together to where the 700 lay on a bench near the Hunter. I searched for the correct page and then made the appropriate notation in the log.

The Chief Tech watched as I signed and dated the entry and then beckoned that I should follow him as he made his way to another console.

"I want you to perform a functional check on this circuit," he announced, indicating a console that was wired up as an engine starting system. Everything was there except the engine and the electric motor that turned it during the initial phases of a jet engine start-up.

The starting system was designed to rotate the engine slowly at first and then cause it to speed up in two separate stages, in much the same way that a car is taken from standstill to normal road speed through successive gear changes. But the speed changes in this case weren't achieved by changing gears. Instead, the electric current to the starter motor was initially kept low by inserting a very large resistance in the circuit. Then, when cued by a timing device, some of the resistance was automatically removed, causing the motor to turn a little faster. Finally, all of the resistance was removed and the motor was free to run up to its full speed. When the fuel in the engine ignited and made it turn faster than the electric motor, the starter system shut down.

Of course, all of this involved the participation of several electrical devices to make it happen and most of them were wired together, in faithful reproduction of the real thing, on the console that now confronted me. Other than the absence of a real engine and starter motor, the only other difference was a group of small, coloured indicator lights used to indicate the various stages of resistance as they were switched in and out of the starter motor circuit.

I asked for the servicing schedule and started reading it. All I needed to do was turn on the supply voltage to the console and then press the engine start button. The circuit should step through its three stages and then stop. But this was an exam and things weren't going to be that easy!

The first indicator light glowed, showing that the resistance had been inserted into the motor circuit and, in real life, the motor and engine would be starting their initial rotation. I could also hear the whir from the clockwork timing mechanism as it was being electrically wound up, but when several seconds had elapsed and the second indicator light remained dark. Uh, oh, I thought, looks like we've got a snag! The servicing schedule wasn't going to help here; this came down to tradecraft and the ability to think and work logically in order to track down the cause of the problem and then fix it.

First, I needed to check the obvious, although I knew in my heart of hearts that the cause of this fault was going to be anything but obvious. The second light hadn't come on, so the most obvious and the simplest course of action was to check for a failed bulb. I didn't know what Grim Face's expectation might be. Maybe I was supposed to deduce that it wasn't a simple bulb failure because of other less evident symptoms, so there may have been marks against me instead of marks in favour, but I had chosen a certain course of action and was determined to stick with it. I unscrewed the indicator light's lens cap and removed the small bulb. The tiny filament looked intact when I held it up to the light but I flicked a finger gently against the glass envelope anyway, just to check for the telltale vibration of a broken end. It still looked okay, but that didn't mean there wasn't a fault.

"Can I have an Avo please, Chief," I asked, referring to an Avometer, the brand name of a multi-meter used throughout the Service—the first three letters of its name was an acronym for Amps, Volts and Ohms. My examiner bent down and reached into a cupboard underneath the bench, withdrew an Avo and handed it to me. The way in which I handled this piece of test equipment would also be scored as marks for or against, so I proceeded carefully. The first thing I did was to lay it flat on the bench and check that it was zeroed, meaning that the pointer rested exactly on the zero mark when no measurements were being made. There was a ribbon of mirror that stretched across the face of the instrument parallel to the scale. To make an accurate reading, it was necessary to view the needle-thin pointer in such a way that it completely blocked its own reflection in the mirror. This ensured that the measurement was being viewed from directly above the pointer and not from an angle that would produce a false reading. I now looked down at the scale from directly over the pointer and immediately saw that it was several graduations off the zero mark. Peering down on the meter scale and with one eye closed to view the pointer accurately against the mirror, I carefully adjusted a small knob that mechanically moved the pointer until it hovered directly above zero. Having done that, I then rotated one of the two selector switches on the face of the Avo to read Ohms, a measurement of electrical resistance. This applied a small internal battery voltage to the two test leads connected to the meter, which could be used to test a circuit's continuity. Before testing the bulb, I briefly touched one of the metal probes at the end of a test lead against the probe on the other lead and checked that the pointer on the Avo swung all the way across the scale, proving that the meter was working in this mode. Out of the corner of my eye, I saw Grim Face making a note on his clipboard.

Satisfied that the meter was operational, I touched the probes to the contacts of the bulb and wasn't surprised when the pointer swung most of the way across the scale, confirming that the bulb was indeed "serviceable", in RAF jargon. That confirmed what I really knew all along—that there was a more serious problem with the circuit.

There was a circuit diagram pasted to the front of the console and it was to this that I now turned for help in finding the problem. Referring to the diagram while probing around on various terminals, I discovered that there was one particular terminal on a relay that was "dead" when a careful study of the diagram indicated that it should be "live". Aha, I thought, this looks promising. Picking up a screwdriver, I started unscrewing the small terminal stud to free the wire that was connected to it and immediately saw the Chief write something on his clipboard. Damn! I suddenly realized that the circuit was still live. Realizing that I should have turned the power off first, I mentally pictured marks being deducted for poor tradecraft and failure to observe proper safety precautions. Feeling a little rattled, I immediately reached over and flicked the console power switch to "off" before continuing to unscrew the terminal. Then, when it was free, I pulled the wire out of the slot and noticed that a small piece of insulating tape had been wrapped around the end to simulate the fault. My spirits rose as I pointed this out to the Chief. He simply nodded and made another notation; a good one this time, I hoped. After having peeled the insulating tape off the wire and reconnecting it to the terminal, I powered the circuit up once again and then pressed the start button. This time everything worked perfectly. The time delay whirred, relays clicked and the three different coloured lights glowed in the correct sequence as the circuit performed its function.

After that, there were only a few more questions and tasks to be tested on, before I was told that I had completed the Board and could return to the classroom. With a feeling of great relief, mixed with some confidence that I'd done okay, I collected my notebooks from the waiting area and headed back to rejoin my mates in the classroom. Mates? As soon as I walked through the door, they pounced on me.

"What were you asked?" They all wanted to know.

I described everything about the Board that I was able to recall, the recollections coming in fits and starts, as the act of remembering some of the key events triggered a recall of many other questions I'd been asked, or tasks that had been set by my examiner. This worked for all of us, because those who were still waiting to take the Board wanted to get a feeling of what to expect and I was anxious to know how well I'd done. Being able to remember many of the questions helped me to get some badly wanted feedback from the others as to whether or not I had correctly answered them. In the end, I got the impression that I'd done reasonably well, but it wasn't a sure thing by any means.

* * *

There were two or three days to suffer through before we would learn how well or poorly we had performed in the Finals. In the meantime, most of us indulged in endless post-mortems, during which we sought to recall all of the questions that had been set on the Paper and asked during the Board and then try to determine whether or not we had provided the right answers. During these few days my spirits often soared with the realization that I'd answered a particular question correctly, but then crashed again when it seemed clear that I'd given wrong answers to others. And so, during those few days, my feelings swung erratically between the optimistic certainty that I'd passed and the gloomy pessimism of failure. Finally, word came that we were to report to the common room. As I entered with my fellow billet-members, the air of tense nervousness in the room was almost physical. There was none of the cheerful chatter and hubbub that usually characterized such get-togethers. Most faces looked strained and the few smiles that managed to appear briefly here and there were of the grim, tight-lipped variety. Attention was focused on Corporal Longfellow, who waited until he felt reasonably sure that everyone was present. Then his eyes ceased flicking around the room and he drew himself up to his full height.

"Okay, pay attention!" He said.

"Shushes" were uttered from various parts of the room, to silence those who, oblivious to the call to order, were engrossed in private, whispered conversations. But, for the most part, the statement was completely redundant since almost all eyes were already riveted on him.

"I've got the results of your Finals," he said solemnly.

He then proceeded to loudly read down through the list of names, announcing the percentage of marks that the individual had gained for both parts of the final exam. We needed to achieve a minimum of 60% for each part of the Final and relegation loomed large in the future of anyone who didn't make it past this milestone. In addition to the marks, Longfellow also announced the consequence of each result. For most it was LAC (Leading Aircraftsman) with automatic promotion to SAC (Senior Aircraftsman) within six months. A few, who had worked hard to gain exceptional marks, were rewarded with immediate promotion to SAC. Those who failed to meet the required percentage were either told that they were to be relegated to the 30th entry or, in the case of some who had already been relegated once, "cease training". The latter was another way of saying that the RAF didn't expect them to make it and they could either leave the service or transfer to another trade-group—one for which they might have a better aptitude.

As the results were being read out, the tense atmosphere in the room began to give way to one of whoops and loud gasps of relief mingled with a few groans, as pent-up feelings were released. At best, I was hoping to have squeaked through with a bare 60% on both parts of the exam and was overjoyed to hear that my marks for the Paper and the Board were both in the low seventies. Most of us had passed and those of us who did were now all busy pumping each other's hands in congratulation. At long last, we could wholeheartedly prepare for the upcoming passing-out parade with a renewed sense of fervour and mounting excitement. The ordeal was nearly over.

* * *

Within a few days of the results having been made public, we were marched to the Clothing Stores to be measured for the new uniforms that we would wear after leaving boys' service. The same little tailor who had originally measured us for our first uniforms when we were in ITS was still in attendance at the Clothing Store. To youngsters like us, the 15 or 16 life-changing months that we'd spent at St. Athan since we'd last seen him might have seemed like an eon, but to him it was probably nothing at all, since he had more than likely spent a major portion of his working life in the same occupation at that very same place. He was happy in his work, joking and chatting with us as we came to him one at a time, trying on our brand new "T63" Best Blue uniform and then the battledress-style Working Blue, both of which smelled of mothballs. All the while, we were admiring ourselves in the full-length mirror as he made small marks in the various places where the uniforms needed to be taken in or turned up. Like everyone else, I had received my new badges of rank from one of the Clothing Store clerks at the same time that they loaded me up with the new uniforms. They were still in my left hand when it was my turn to see the tailor, but he took four of them from me and stuffed two into a pocket in each of the new uniforms. These small two-by-three-inch rectangular pieces of blue felt cloth, on each of which was embroidered a two-bladed propeller in light blue silk, would be sewn onto the sleeves as part of the alteration process. I still had two more LAC badges remaining from the six that I'd been given, but I would have to sew these onto my greatcoat myself, after the passing-out parade.

* * *

As we of the rank and file were kept busy cramming as much knowledge as possible into our heads during the approach of the Finals, a gentlemanly tussle had been taking place at a slightly higher level. It was time for the permanent staff to select the 29th Entry's Flight Sergeant Boy—the person on whom they would bestow the honour of Parade Commander for the graduation ceremony. Eric Critchley, our own 3 Squadron Sergeant Boy, was one of the four contenders, as was Eugene Gilkes, the 4 Squadron Sergeant Boy. No. 1 Wing provided its two hopefuls in the persons of Sergeant Boy Stannard and Sergeant Boy Foster.

Critchley was of medium build, contrasted with Gilkes who was much bigger and of better build than any of the other entry members. This was noticeable right from the beginning, when the Clothing Store had initially been unable to provide him with a uniform that would fit his large frame. For a few days, during our time in ITS, he was obliged to go around dressed in denims until a uniform could be specially ordered for him. Eugene was smart and excelled in his training as a Navigational Instrument Mechanic.

Becoming a Sergeant Boy was no easy task because, in addition to academic excellence, it also required a perpetually faultless turnout, which meant always appearing in a well-pressed uniform, gleaming buttons and shining boots. Not only that, but his disciplinary record had to be spotless. No one who had spent any time on jankers could aspire to be a Sergeant Boy. In short, Eugene Gilkes well and truly earned his stripes, as did the three other challengers for promotion to Flight Sergeant Boy.

Now it came down to the four of them in the "shout-off" that would decide who would receive the coveted rank of Flight Sergeant Boy. Sergeant Boy Gilkes's large frame and deep chest worked to his advantage and he won the day by out-shouting the other three candidates into submission. So, now that we had our Flight Sergeant Boy, the parade rehearsals began in earnest. In fact, that's all that we had left to do, except for regular sessions of P.E. and of course the daily route marches—on the double.

As the first order of business, in preparation for the passing-out parade, we were issued with white webbing—a belt, bayonet frog and rifle sling, all of which had served in previous passing-out parades. We were also issued with a bayonet scabbard that fitted into the bayonet frog. The webbing items were all in need of white blanco and the scabbard badly needed one or two coats of black paint. Blancoing the webbing, polishing its brasses and painting the bayonet scabbard filled in some of the time between parade rehearsals. And, as if that wasn't enough bull to be getting on with, there were always our parade boots to be spit-and-polished, buttons and badges on our best blue to be cleaned to a dazzling sparkle, and long periods in the ironing room spent adding razor-like sharpness to the creases on our best blue uniforms and greatcoats. Ordinarily, all of this bulling would have been a huge chore, but because it was for our very own passing-out parade, the work was a labour of love. I now began to understand that the reluctance of the previous entries to set their bull-boys to work on these menial tasks wasn't so much the paranoia that I'd originally assumed, but was an extension of the passing-out parade ritual itself. I relished every moment spent endowing the webbing with a virginally white coating of blanco, took pride in the sharpness of the creases in my uniform and admired my distorted reflection in the mirror-like shine on the boots that I would wear for the parade.

CHAPTER 12

The Passing-Out Parade

We rehearsed for the passing-out parade every weekday during the course of the next few weeks, beginning from when we learned the results of our Finals. The gravel on the Square became intimately familiar, as we incessantly crunched around on it. For most of the rehearsals, we drew rifles and "pig-sticker" bayonets from the Armoury. The pig-stickers didn't look too impressive, since they were little more than 6-inch long sharpened steel spikes, but they fulfilled a purpose by enabling us to practise rifle drill with fixed bayonets. If nothing else, this helped to endow us with the ability to avoid stabbing fellow entry-members, or ourselves, during the actual parade. But before drawing rifles from the Armoury for the first rehearsal, we were put through the "Sizing" drill.

Sizing was necessary because, much to the distress of drill instructors and those of like mind, individual humans aren't all made the same height. And, if it were left to pure chance, the height profile of a formation of men would have a distinctly ragged appearance. Happily for the drill instructors, someone solved this irritating little problem by inventing a peculiar ritual known as Sizing. The sole object of Sizing is to transform the ragged appearance into a thing of beauty—at least in their eyes.

And so, on the first day of rehearsals, as we stood at attention in flights on the parade ground, our Squadron Commander, Sergeant Boy Eric Critchley, drew in a deep breath and commanded, "Squadron will size!"

Immediately our Flight Commander, Corporal Boy Spinks, executed a smart about turn and, now facing us, yelled an order that was echoed by the other flight commanders: "Flight, tallest on the right, shortest on the left, in single rank, size!"

The Sizing exercise took up several minutes, during which we initially broke ranks before taking our place in a single long line according our height. The single rank was then put through a series of intricate manoeuvres that ended up with a new three-rank formation, in which the very tallest of our members now occupied the end positions and the very shortest found themselves at the midway point. Those of us who were of varying degrees of intermediate height found ourselves graduated according to our stature. This was done in such a way that if an imaginary line touching the tops of our heads had been drawn from one end of the flight to the other, it would have traced a shallow concave curve. This was the sought-after result of the sizing drill and having achieved it, we were instructed to memorise our individual positions in the formation, relative to that of our immediate neighbours on both left and right. This was to be our permanent position in the flight, throughout all of the upcoming rehearsals and for the passing-out parade itself.

With Sizing out of the way, it was now possible to concentrate on the main purpose of the rehearsals, which was to endlessly practise the ceremonial drill involved in the passing-out parade, until we could do it in our sleep. Several months had passed since we had completed our basic training in ITS, when drill took up the major part of the training and we had understandably become a little rusty in the execution of many of the movements. So, we practised everything from marching onto the parade ground to our final march-past of the saluting dais in line abreast, which would symbolically mark our passing out of Boy Entrant service and into the regular RAF.

The line abreast march-past, alone, was quite a tricky manoeuvre. For this, we started off by marching in a column of threes towards the Station HQ end of the parade ground, before making a left turn—known as a right wheel—to snake along that edge of the Square. Then, at a pre-determined point, the Flight Commander gave the order, "Into line, left turn." Each individual then performed a marching left turn that resulted in an abrupt change of direction for the marching formation and also changed the flight's frontage from a column of three ranks to that of a line abreast formation, consisting of something like 15 files of three. It was as though a train, travelling along its track, suddenly changed direction and began to travel broadside at a right angle to the railway track. The flight, now moving in line abreast, marched past the dais whilst each marcher strived to do his part in maintaining the rank in a straight line. Difficult as it was to accomplish, the end result was nothing short of impressive as the marchers passed the saluting base at a slow march, with their eyes right and carrying rifles with fixed bayonets at the slope. As flight after flight passed the dais, from a distance they took on the appearance of a series of waves heading slowly towards a shoreline. The effect was much more visually stirring than a mundane march-past in column of route.

In the days leading up to the passing-out parade, we practised the line abreast march-past countless times. It had been a shambles to begin with. Every time the manoeuvre was attempted, it seemed that some individual or other misheard, or didn't act promptly on the word of command. The result was near total disaster as people cannoned into their neighbours, tripped over one another and sometimes fell in tangled heaps on the ground. But eventually, after the NCOs instructing us had torn most of their hair out, it had all come together and by the day of the actual parade we could almost do it in our sleep—flawlessly. The only remaining challenge was to try and stay in a straight line, which was difficult for a rank of fifteen or so people marching in line abreast when we could only check our dressing out of the corners of our eyes. At least it was difficult until we got the orders "slow march" and then "eyes right" on approaching the saluting base. The slower pace—and the fact that we could now see how we were dressed off—usually helped us to get in a straight line before we actually passed before the dais.

Finessing the line abreast march-past was quite an accomplishment, but it was all a waste of time, as things turned out in the end.

* * *

One afternoon, shortly after getting the results of our Finals, we were sitting on our beds cleaning buttons, spit-and-polishing our boots, or engaged in one of the other bull activities that had taken over our lives as we prepared for our finest moment. Suddenly, Leading Boy Powditch came rushing into the billet almost breathless with news.

"Everyone to E9," he exclaimed excitedly, "The postings are out!"

This was probably the most important news since learning our marks from the Finals. Button sticks and boot polish were hurriedly discarded as we doubled to the Common Room, "properly" dressing ourselves as we ran—collar studs were fastened, slackened-off neckties pulled back into place and tunics buttoned up—all at the gallop. Several members of the squadron Disciplinary staff were there, Corporal Longfellow presiding. We weren't the first, but weren't the last either, so it was with a sense of growing impatience that we waited for the stragglers to make their way into the room. When it was apparent that every last one of the available 3 Squadron 29th Entry members had gathered in the hut, Longfellow cleared his throat. Immediately, a great silence fell over the assembly as we waited in anxious anticipation of what he had to say.

"You will no doubt be pleased to hear that I've got your postings," he smiled, holding up a piece of unfolded foolscap in his right hand. "Okay, pay attention." This was a redundant phrase, if ever there was one.

The corporal then proceeded to read out surnames from his list, each followed by the name of the station to which that person had been posted. Some received so-so postings, even as others were more fortunate and got really plum postings. Nobby Clarke, who hailed from London, had requested Northolt, home of the Queen's Flight, which was almost in his backyard. He got it! Others less fortunate heard that they'd been posted to 32 MU, the Maintenance Unit on St. Athan West Camp (we were on East Camp), which meant they weren't going to move too far away. Many received exciting postings to Fighter Command stations or Bomber Command stations.

Eventually, Longfellow came to my name. "Carlin!"

"Corp," I shouted out in response.

He glanced up momentarily, as he had with everyone, "Shawbury, Flying Training Command."

That was it. He quickly moved on to the next name on his list. Shawbury? I'd never even heard of it! Someone nearby must have seen my puzzled look because he whispered that it was near Shrewsbury in Shropshire. I wasn't too sure where that was either and suddenly wanted to see a map of England, so that I could find it. And Flying Training Command? That didn't sound very exciting or glamorous. No Hunters or Valiants to work on there. Probably stuff like Chipmunks or Piston Provosts. But at least it wasn't 32 MU, which was something to be thankful for. Conflicting thoughts ran through my head—I was going somewhere that I'd never heard of that didn't sound too exciting, but I was getting away from St. Athan, which was good. Suddenly conscious that Richard Butterworth's name was being called out, I listened just in time to hear that he was also being posted to Shawbury. Well, that was good news. At least we were friends and would have a lot of fun finding out all we could about our future new home, in the weeks before the passing-out parade. I looked across to where he was sitting, only to see him grinning and giving me a thumbs-up sign, so I grinned back as I returned the gesture.

* * *

On Tuesday evening, the 25th of March 1958, two days before our passing-out parade, we had another ritual to observe. This was the 2 Wing Graduation Dinner, traditionally given by the Wing Permanent Staff for the graduating entry. Our fellow graduates over at 1 Wing were also attending their separate Graduation Dinner at the same time.

We all looked a sharp bunch in our best blues, as we entered the 2 Wing Boy Entrants' Mess to take our places at tables that had been laid up in a way that we'd never seen before. The usual bare Formica surfaces of the long refectory tables were covered by white tablecloths, on which place settings of cutlery, serviettes and souvenir menus were set out. Bowls of fruit and sweets adorned the centres of each table, alongside circular tins stuffed full of cigarettes, in subtle acknowledgment of our new adult status.

There was no need to queue up at the servery for this meal. We were instructed to be seated instead, whilst our former officers and NCOs good-humouredly assumed the role of our waiters. They welcomed us, made sure we were seated then disappeared in the direction of the kitchen. Moments later they reappeared, carrying bowls of cream of tomato soup, which they then served as our starter course. For our part, we just tried to ignore the occasional thumb slightly immersed in the creamy red liquid, as the soup bowls were set down before us and just hoped that our "waiters" had washed their hands before handling the food. And then for a time, the air was filled with the loud clinking of 120 stainless steel spoons making contact with 120 white porcelain bowls, as the soup course was consumed and enjoyed to the last drop.

Next, steaming plates of turkey and roast pork, both with the proper accompaniments, were carried from the kitchen to our tables. The menu from the event records, for posterity, that these dishes consisted of Roast Turkey with Forcemeat Stuffing and Bread Sauce or Roast Pork with Sage & Onion stuffing and Apple Sauce. Both dishes also included Chateau Potatoes, Potato Duchesse, Cauliflower & White Sauce and Garden Peas. Never ever had we eaten so well at the Boy Entrants' mess. The buzz of conversation quietened down again for quite a while as we tucked into the dish of our choice—which, in my case, was turkey. There was a brief respite after everyone had finished this course before the desserts made their appearance—fruit cocktail with ice cream, followed by cups of coffee in *real* cups instead of "Mugs, China, Airmen, for the use of". At the same time, platters of cubed cheese and crackers were brought to the tables for those of us who still desired something to nibble on.

As we sat back with full stomachs, drinking from our cups of coffee, the Wing Commander took the floor. He proceeded to praise us for being such a fine bunch of future NCOs and stated how proud he was of us. He reeled off a number of statistics—how many of us had been initially inducted versus how many had successfully completed the training. Surprisingly few had fallen by the wayside, although those who did were replaced by relegations from the 28th entry, so the actual number that we lost to attrition was concealed to some extent. The Squadron Leaders of both 3 and 4 Squadrons then said a few words and after that it was time to mingle, chat and enjoy the free cigarettes. Boys, NCOs and officers wandered around from table to table, shaking hands, autographing menus and engaging in an enjoyable session of socializing.

As the event drew to a close, Sergeant Savoury called for our attention and then announced in his cockney accent that we would be starting our clearance process in the morning and that we needed to report to hut E9 at "oh-ite-firty" (0830 hours) for further instructions. This meant that we would be making a start on the time-consuming process of walking around the station, visiting Section after Section, to have our blue clearance chits signed by each and every entity on the station that had any interest in the fact that we were about to take our leave of Royal Air Force St. Athan (and not a bloody moment too soon).

Gradually, the numbers thinned out as people began to dwindle away from the mess and make their way back towards their billets, bringing this significant rite of passage to an end. I couldn't help reflecting on how fortunate I was to be in that place, at that time. To hear it from the Wing Commander and the other officers, we were the *crème de la crème*—the future backbone of the Royal Air Force—the NCOs of tomorrow—and so the accolades went on. Later, but not too much later, most of us would make the painful discovery that in the wider world of the regular RAF this opinion of our own self-importance, with which we had been indoctrinated, didn't earn us too many fans amongst the non-Boy Entrant servicemen. This was especially true of the National Service "erks", who would very soon be showing us the ropes in the real world and who would typically entrust us with the very important responsibility of carrying their toolbags, in return for teaching us firsthand from their expertise. Some of us even made the grave error of confiding in these long-suffering National Servicemen of the high value in which the RAF held us and the destiny for which we had been groomed, only to find ourselves being instantly subjected to scorn and derision. But that was later. On the night of the Graduation Dinner, our egos were highly inflated and we were reeling on the heady wine of the praise and adulation to which we had just been subjected.

At 0830 hours next morning, we presented ourselves in hut E9, where the NCOs issued everyone with a 6-by-8 inch sky-

blue card that bore our name, rank and serial number. This was
the very same "Arrivals" card on which we had obtained
signatures on the day that we'd taken the Oath of Allegiance and
entered into Her Majesty's service. Now, however, we were
required to obtain approximately 30 "Clearance" signatures from
various Sections, on the reverse side of the card. A Section was
an entity in the lower rungs of the Station hierarchy that
performed a specific function. A few Sections had been crossed
out because they weren't applicable, but we were required to pay
all of the others a visit to obtain a clearance signature. Just to
complicate matters, some Sections could only be visited during
certain "opening hours," while some couldn't be visited until we
had obtained signatures from certain other Sections first. The
whole process required lots of time, lots of patience and lots of
walking and it was for all those reasons that Sergeant Savoury
wisely sent us out on the day prior to the passing-out parade. We
were required to be off the Station by "Sunset" on that very same
day, yet he knew very well that it would take us longer than one
afternoon to complete the clearance process.

Within minutes of receiving our blue cards, we set off in
little groups, walking around the station with the cards clutched
in our left hands, leaving our right hands free to salute any
officers whom we might encounter.

One of the first stops on our tour of the station was
Workshops, where we needed to clear from the Tool Store before
getting a signature from the Warrant Officer in charge of Trade
Training. Then it was on to the Boy Entrants' mess where a
signature was required to take us off the rations list. Next, it was
the Station Library and then the Padre's office, followed by the
Bedding Store—but we found that we couldn't clear from the
Bedding Store until next day, when we handed in our blankets
and sheets. Neither Pay Accounts nor the Station Orderly Room
would clear us either—the clerk at the little window in the
Orderly Room told us that he had to be the very last person to
sign our cards. By the end of the day, however, our little group
of walkers had been able to get most of the signatures, except for
those few that we couldn't get until the next day and a few for
which we had failed to present ourselves during "opening

hours". All the walking required lots of stamina and I began to wonder if the five-mile route marches to which we had been subjected for the past few weeks were really intended to toughen us up exclusively for this particular marathon ordeal. But however difficult and demanding the process, it was a task that brought all of us a great deal of excitement as we slowly but relentlessly broke open the chrysalis in which we were still trapped. On the morrow, we would finally be able to fly free as fully-fledged airmen in the regular service of the Royal Air Force.

That evening, I prepared my kit for the Big Day that would start in the morning. I did a final check of the shine on my boots, another session with buttons and Brasso, ran the iron over the creases in my trousers and checked the white blanco on my webbing. I wasn't alone. All of the other graduating boys were doing exactly the same thing. Finally, everything was ready. Then it was time for the very last bed check that I would have to suffer through, the very last lights-out and the final rendition of The Last Post over the station broadcasting system. There was a little nostalgia, but not much. The predominant feeling was one of long-suffering tolerance—that I had outgrown these petty and restrictive Boy Entrant rituals, but could tolerate them for just one more night, knowing that I wouldn't have to endure bed-check or lights-out ever again.

* * *

It would have been a fitting end to our training if the day of our passing-out had dawned bright and glorious. But sadly, it didn't. As we made our way to breakfast, the pale early morning light was filtered through a heavy blanket of fog that had descended over the countryside during the night, replacing the rain and drizzle of the previous day. Sometimes a light fog would lift shortly after sunrise, but not today. This was a persistent pea-souper and during our initial assembly at 0800 hours we were informed that the parade would be held in the Drill Shed instead of on the Square. It was an ironic turn of events, because our ITS passing-out parade had also been held in the same indoor venue for the same reason—"inclement weather". Fortunately, we had rehearsed an indoor version of the passing-out parade once or twice, just in case of the bad weather that was an all too real possibility at this time of year. Given our preferences, we would much rather it had taken place on the Square. But no matter. Ever since the arrival of the 29th Entry at St. Athan, the smooth, well-oiled machinery of No. 4 School of Technical Training had focused on moving us successfully towards this point in history. And now, at 0800 hours on 27th March 1958, the time had finally arrived when we could fasten the pristinely white webbing belts around our waists and then fall in on the road outside E7 for the very last time. But instead of going to Workshops with notebooks and denims tucked under our left arms, we marched to the Armoury carefully carrying our spotlessly white rifle slings in our left hands. Once there, we would pick up the rifles and bayonets needed for the ceremonial rifle drill associated with our passing-out parade.

On arriving at the Armoury, we were dismissed and directed to form a queue at one of the doors in the Armoury building. The door was open and those ahead of me were already shuffling through it in single file. When I crossed the threshold, it was necessary to pass an Armourer, who stood at a table handing out unsheathed bayonets to each of us in the line as we went by.

I immediately slid mine into the shiny black scabbard that dangled from the bayonet frog on my webbing belt—on the left side and slightly to the rear. We continued to shuffle forward, still in single file, until we reached two more Armourers who were busily handing out Lee Enfield .303 rifles. I accepted the one offered to me and then, with a little more shuffling, exited the Armoury through another door out into the foggy air once again. Resuming my memorised position in the flight once more, I opened and closed the rifle bolt six times to make sure that the weapon was unloaded, just as I had been trained to do, and then pointed the muzzle of the rifle harmlessly skyward before pulling the trigger to hear the action releasing with a loud click. Next, I attached the rifle sling, tightened it and then assumed the "stand-easy" position whilst waiting until everyone else was ready. At this point, both squadrons were arrayed along the road in front of the Armoury, six flights in all. Each squadron was under the command of a Sergeant Boy and each flight under the command of a Corporal Boy.

When it seemed that everyone was ready, the Parade Warrant Officer, Sergeant Boy Stannard, took up a position facing us at the midway point between both squadrons.

He briefly savoured the moment before taking a deep breath, "Twenty-ninth entry! Ah-tennn-shun!"

There was a loud crash of boots on tarmac as all 225 of us responded to his command.

"Stand at ease!" There was a second crash of boots, as we resumed the at-ease position.

"Prepare to fix bayonets!"

I groped for the hilt of the bayonet with my left hand, as did everyone else, and then withdrew it from its scabbard to hold it out at arm's length in front of me, with the gleaming stainless steel Bowie knife-like blade pointed upwards. This bayonet was no practice pig sticker—it was the real McCoy.

"Fix bayonets!" Shouted Sergeant Boy Stannard.

Steely blades flashed as I fitted the special receptacle in the bayonet hilt over the end of my rifle muzzle and then gave it a quarter turn twist to lock it into place with a loud click. My left hand remained there at the end of the muzzle, still grasping the hilt, until Stannard was certain that all bayonets had been properly affixed.

"Number twenty-ninth entry! Stand at ease!"

Our left hands came smartly around behind our backs as we resumed the normal at ease position.

Almost immediately, Stannard followed with the command, "Ah-tten-shun!"

As one, we pulled the rifles backwards into the upright position beside our right legs and came to attention. As we executed this movement, I couldn't help noticing out of the corner of my eye just how ominously close the tip of the bayonet came to my right armpit. Typically, one or two people would faint during a long parade such as this and I just hoped that it wouldn't be my turn today, because the idea of being accidentally impaled on my own bayonet was discomforting. I pushed the thought aside. Our bayonets were fixed and we were ready.

"Number twenty-ninth entry! SLO-ope ARMS!" Yelled Stannard.

In three movements that were executed in perfect synchronism, we brought our rifles from the position alongside our right legs to rest at a slope on our left shoulders, with the brass heel of the rifle-butt cradled in the gloved palms of our left hands.

Stannard then ordered, "Number twenty-ninth entry will move to the left in column of threes, LE-eft TURN!"

The words enunciating the order seemed to issue visibly from Sergeant Boy Stannard's mouth in little puffs of vapour, before quickly dissolving into the surrounding fog. In unison, we all pirouetted anti-clockwise in a quarter-turn. Stannard then executed a right turn and strode off to the head of the column, as Parade Warrant Officer. He disappeared from my view because of the fog, but I knew from previous experience that he halted and then turned to his right to face in the same direction as the members of the flight. Sergeant Boy Foster took up position behind him, as commander of No. 1 Squadron. At the same time, Sergeant Boy Eric Critchley marched into place at the head of No. 2 Squadron. In a likewise manner, the Corporal Boy flight commanders each moved to the head of their respective flights. When everyone was in position, Stannard yelled out an order, which sounded incomprehensible because of the muffling effect of the fog. But we all knew very well not to react to this command anyway, because it was really only addressed to the commanders of the individual flights, ordering them to each march their own formations forward in turn.

Since the combined 1 and 2 Wing Drum and Trumpet Band would have the honour of leading us to the Drill Shed, Drum Major "Nobby" Duff was the one who actually gave the first order to march. Almost immediately, the drummers beat out a tattoo of "two threes and a seven" during which the No. 1 Wing Trumpet Major, "Adgy" Barber, called out the name of the first trumpet tune to be played. The trumpeters began playing right on cue when the tattoo ended, whilst Drum Major Duff swung his mace with a practised flourish as he proudly led his Entry to the passing-out parade.

The No. 1 Squadron 'A' flight commander waited until the band had marched a few paces and then ordered his formation to march forward. Then, one by one, the other flights started marching as the flights ahead of them moved off.

When our turn came, Corporal Boy Spinks, who was in charge of my flight, turned his head slightly so that we could hear the order that he was about to give.

"'B' Flight, Number 2 Squadron...by the left, quick march!"

We stepped off on the left foot, pleased to be finally moving towards our moment of glory and happy to get some circulation moving through our bodies at long last. We badly needed to generate some warmth that would counteract the damp chilliness of the fog, which by this time had managed to seep through the fabric of our heavy greatcoats. We marched proudly, heads erect, right arms swinging vigorously, whilst our left forearms and hands remained immobilized and parallel to the ground, supporting the rifles resting on our shoulders. I could see very little ahead of me, except for a bristling forest of bayonet-tipped rifles that bobbed rhythmically together, reflecting the weight shift of the marchers from one foot to the other whilst they marched. Most of the flights ahead of us were enveloped by the surrounding dank greyness and it appeared that we were following them blindly into the grey oblivion. By now the faint boom of the bass drum was difficult to hear in our location far back down the column, so Spinks began calling out the step, *'eft, yoyt, 'eft, yoyt*. Similar but fainter calls from some of the boy NCOs leading the other flights reached my ears like echoes percolating through the denseness of the fog.

After a several minutes of marching, (*'eft, yoyt, 'eft, yoyt*), the huge monolithic shape of the station water tower began to take shape as it loomed out of the murk, taking on a progressively darker grey hue as we approached, in contrast to the unchanging light greyness of the surrounding fog. Nearly there! The Drill Shed was just across the road from the water tower. Ahead of us, I was just able to see the faint silhouette of

Drum Major Duff making a right wheel to lead the band down the slightly inclined concrete ramp that would take him to the large entrance-door and then into the Drill Shed. Shortly after that, we also made the same right wheel and followed the other flights down the ramp into the Drill Shed. Inside, the steady "boom-boom" beat of the bass drum, which was supposed to pace the march, actually defeated that purpose by echoing around the interior of the Drill Shed. It was impossible to separate the real drumbeats from the echoes, causing confusion and forcing the Flight Commanders to compete directly with the band by calling out the step even louder.

Ceiling-mounted floodlights brightly illuminated the interior of the Drill Shed, where it was also dry and relatively warm. Being inside and out of the fog was quite a relief. The dais, or saluting base, was set up along the wall nearest the road, which meant that after entering through the doorway, all flights left wheeled at specific points to form up in an array centred on the dais. On reaching our appointed position, we marked time until given the order to halt.

"'B' Fliiiiight, Number 2 Squadron…into line, LE-eft TURN!" Commanded Corporal Boy Spinks.

We turned and faced the saluting base, noticing that the Parade Commander, Flight Sergeant Boy Gilkes, stood near it, waiting for his cue to take command of the parade. Flanking the dais were two Standard Bearers, Corporal Boy Drinkwater of our squadron of Electrical Mechanics and Corporal Boy Crawford of 1 Wing, each Standard Bearer holding a No. 4 School of Technical Training Standard by his side.

When all six flights were present and facing the dais, Sergeant Boy Stannard marched to the front and centre of the parade, then turned and faced towards us.

There was a moment of silence, while he collected himself, then he barked out the order, "Parade! Order arms!"

In unison, we transferred the rifles from our shoulders into position alongside the right of our bodies—the noise of our hands slapping against the various parts of the weapon magnified by our number and amplified by the echo-chamber acoustics of the Drill Shed. The movement was finally punctuated by the dull *thunk* of the brass end caps of the rifle butts, as they made gentle contact with the concrete floor.

All seemed silent for a moment, but it was short-lived. For the next few minutes, we were brought to attention and then stood at ease several times, as dictated by ceremonial necessities of the parade. Eventually, the cue was given for the Parade Commander, Flight Sergeant Boy Gilkes, to take over command of the parade from Sergeant Boy Stannard.

More drill movements followed as Gilkes now put us through our paces, ending with the order that transformed our close ranks into open order, ready for the Reviewing Officer's inspection. When this had been accomplished, Gilkes momentarily surveyed the scene and then ordered the parade to stand at ease to await the arrival of the Reviewing Officer. The time was now 0930 hours.

We remained in this position for a few minutes, until Gilkes acted on a discreet signal from the sidelines by bringing the parade to attention once again and then giving the order to slope arms. As we performed the drill movement, both Standard Bearers hoisted the golden eagle-crested Standard staffs onto their right shoulders and then marched together towards the large door that we had entered several minutes ago. The sky-blue, golden-fringed Standards that they carried hung limply from the angled staffs and swayed from side to side with the bearers' motion, each displaying the school badge with the legend "Number 4 School of Technical Training RAF St. Athan" beneath it.

When the Standard bearers arrived at the doorway, they came to a well-rehearsed, simultaneous halt. Almost immediately, the Reviewing Officer, Air Vice-Marshal Hutton, appeared framed in the doorway. The Standard bearers then escorted the Air Vice-Marshal towards the parade centre, followed by two other figures. They were Air Vice-Marshal Spreckley, Commander of 24 Group—the Group to which we belonged—and Air Commodore Perkins, the commandant of No. 4 School of Technical Training—our headmaster in a sense, although he was an administrator rather than a teacher.

As the small party of Air Officers approached, Flight Sergeant Boy Gilkes took the deepest breath he could muster and

then called out, "Parade, general salute…pres-ent ARMS!" With
the last word of the command still on his lips, he turned to face
the approaching party, at the same time bringing his right hand
up smartly in salute as the crash of hands against rifles noisily
heralded our "present arms". At the same time, Trumpet Majors
Williams and Barber greeted the Reviewing Officer with a
resounding fanfare as he stepped up on the dais, turned to the
parade and saluted in response.

On completion of this portion of the ceremonial, Flight
Sergeant Boy Gilkes marched up to the dais and, whilst saluting
the Air Vice-Marshal, announced, "Numbers 1 and 2 Squadrons
ready for your inspection, SIR!"

AVM Hutton then descended from the dais as Gilkes
gestured towards No. 1 Squadron and accompanied the
Reviewing Officer as he headed in that direction, with the two
other Air Officers bringing up the rear. As the first squadron
endured inspection, the remainder of the parade was stood at
ease. Meanwhile, the station band, consisting of a number of
accomplished musicians, began playing the first of a number of
pieces from their repertoire of "music to inspect troops by." It
was pleasant to listen to and helped while away the time that it
took for the inspection party to wend its way along the ranks of 1
Squadron. Every now and then, the Reviewing Officer would
stop and talk to one of the boys. He would smile and chat in
relaxed friendly fashion, usually in stark contrast to the boy, who
would retain his stiff demeanour and stare fixedly ahead as he
responded to the officer. Occasionally, someone somewhere on
the parade ground would faint and crumple at the knees. No one
ever fell full length: that was a cartoon-like caricature. The
giveaway came when a person started swaying; before long his
knees buckled and then down he sagged, crumpling to the
ground in an untidy heap. Medics who were standing at strategic
points around the perimeter of the parade always rushed over to
get the poor unfortunate back on his feet and off to the side;
there he would be allowed to sit for a while and savour a
reviving drink of water. Fortunately, none of the fainters fell on
their bayonets, which seemed to ridicule the fear I had harboured
earlier. Meanwhile, the inspection continued relentlessly.

Trumpet-Majors Williams and Barber sound a fanfare.

After what seemed like a very long time, the party returned to the front of No. 1 Squadron at a quick pace. Salutes were exchanged and then Flight Sergeant Boy Gilkes led the group of officers towards our squadron. Sergeant Boy Critchley, who had been watching the approaching party out of the corner of his eye, brought us to attention. Overcoming the stiffness brought on by standing in one position for so long, we responded with a loud reverberating thud of boots on the smooth concrete of the Drill Shed floor.

"No. 2 Squadron ready for inspection, sir!" Critchley announced, as he turned to the Reviewing Officer and saluted.

"Carry on Sergeant Boy," the Air Vice-Marshal replied.

The same slow inspection procedure was repeated. As the great man passed closely in front of me, he glanced at me up and down, from my head to my toes. I studiously avoided his eyes and focused instead on the ornate white enamelled cross hanging from a crimson ribbon around his neck, to rest on the knot of his necktie—the cross signified his knighthood as a Companion of the Most Honourable Order of the Bath. My tactic seemed to work because he passed me by without stopping, leaving me with mixed feelings of both relief and disappointment: relief that he hadn't said anything to me and disappointment for exactly the same reason.

The inspecting party finished reviewing "B" Flight and then moved on to "C" Flight until, after another seemingly interminable age, the inspection ordeal finally came to an end. The Reviewing Officer and his party made their way back in the general direction of the dais, whilst Sergeant Boy Critchley detached himself from the group and returned to the front and centre of the squadron, from where he gave us the order to stand at ease. Meanwhile, the small group of Air Officers, accompanied by Flight Sergeant Boy Gilkes, continued walking until they reached the central position at the front of the parade, where they came to a stop. Gilkes turned to face the parade and brought us to attention. Having done that, he swivelled around on heel and toe to face the Reviewing Officer and then saluted him. The Reviewing Officer returned the salute in a more casual manner than the Flight Sergeant Boy's, while offering a few post-inspection comments that were inaudible to all but that small group of people out in front of the parade. Flight Sergeant Boy Gilkes thanked the Air Vice-Marshal and then requested his permission to carry on. Permission was granted before Air Vice-Marshal Hutton turned away to lead his companions back to the dais. The worst part of the parade was over and now the proudest and most uplifting moment of the ceremony was almost upon us.

Gilkes drew himself up to his full height, as he faced us. "Numbers 1 and 2 Squadrons, SLO-ope ARMS!"

The rifles were transferred to our left shoulders.

A few more orders followed that had us close up the ranks and then straighten them out. When this was all complete, Gilkes marched resolutely towards the dais and came to a classic parade ground halt just a few feet in front of the dais—facing Air Vice-Marshal Hutton—and saluted.

"Permission for the 29th Entry to march past, sir?" He enunciated in a precise military manner.

The Reviewing Officer returned the salute, "Permission granted. Carry on Flight Sergeant Boy."

Gilkes returned to his post. Now facing the parade, and pausing briefly to gather his wind, he gave the long-awaited order, "Numbers 1 and 2 Squadrons will march past in column of route, Number 1 Squadron leading. Move to the right in column of threes, RI-ight TURN!"

By rights, this order should have been "in column of flight," which would have been the precursor to marching past the dais in line abreast, as we had practised day after day on the parade ground. Disappointingly, there wasn't enough space in the Drill Shed to accommodate the line-abreast march-past and so we would have to march past in the less spectacular column of threes.

With a loud crashing noise that reverberated throughout the Drill Shed, the entire 29th entry executed a right turn. The Flight and Squadron Commander boy NCOs then marched smartly to the head of their flights and squadrons. Gilkes moved forward to take up position at the head of 'A' Flight of No. 1 Squadron, in front of Sergeant Boy Foster. On this cue, Corporal Boy Vickers gave the order that would start the march past.

"'A' Flight, by the left, quick march!"

Simultaneously, the Boy Entrant trumpet band started playing *The 29th Entry March* as the flight moved off. This piece had been composed especially for the march past by Drum Major Nobby Duff, Trumpet Major Mike Williams and Cliff Thomson.

When the 'A' Flight had made reasonable progress, the 'B' Flight Commander issued his order for 'B' Flight to march— and so it went on, until all flights of the graduating entry were on the march, *en route* to marching past the dais.

That was where the Reviewing Officer now stood, hand resting on the hilt of his sword, waiting to take the salute that we would present as we marched past him.

When the 'A' Flight Commander reached a certain marker, he turned his head slightly to his right and gave the order, "'A' Flight, SLO-ow MARCH!"

The marchers in the flight immediately ceased to swing their right arms, clamping them to the side of their bodies instead. At the same time, their pace of marching slowed to approximately half speed. This pace forced them to move forward in what appeared to be a series of jerks, instead of the freely flowing movement of the standard marching pace. With the transition into slow time complete and the marchers now within a few feet of the Reviewing Officer, the 'A' Flight Commander now gave the order, "'A' Flight, EYE-es RIGHT!"

All members of the flight immediately turned their heads sharply to the right, in order to meet the Reviewing Officer's gaze when they came abreast of him. The exception to this was the Guide in the front rank, whose job was to steer the flight on an unwavering course past the saluting dais. Meanwhile Gilkes, Foster and Vickers all raised their right hands to the peaks of their hats in salute to Air Vice-Marshal Hutton. The Reviewing Officer, having brought himself to attention, returned the salute, whilst his left hand remained resting on the hilt of his ceremonial sword.

Each flight marched past the dais in similar manner, receiving a salute from the Reviewing Officer in the process. It took several minutes for all six flights to complete the march and then return to their former positions, arrayed before the dais. The Boy Entrant trumpet band then ceased playing, creating an unexpected moment of eerie silence, which didn't last for very long. It was now time for the second major part of our ceremonial.

Gilkes turned and faced the dais once more, taking a deep breath before issuing the command, "Numbers 1 and 2 Squadrons will advance in review order, by the centre, quick MARCH!"

The trumpet band struck up as the 29th entry marched forward *en masse* for 15 paces, at which point Gilkes ordered, "Numbers 1 and 2 Squadrons, HALT!"

We came to the halt as the band abruptly ceased playing.

Gilkes called out his next order, "Numbers 1 and 2 Squadrons, general salute, pre-sent ARMS!

The Station band struck up, with a fanfare based on the first few bars of the Royal Air Force March. At the same time, Gilkes and the other 29th Entry commanders raised their hands in salute for the duration of the fanfare, while we in the ranks brought our weapons to the "Present Arms" position. Air Vice-Marshal Hutton and his fellow officers on the dais returned the salute, while the spectators rose from their seats and stood up as a mark of respect. When the fanfare finished, Gilkes ordered us to slope arms, which ended the salute.

And now it was time for the final act of the ceremony— arguably the best part of the entire ceremony. It began with Flight Sergeant Boy Gilkes advancing once more to the dais, saluting the Reviewing Officer and requesting permission for the paraded squadrons to leave the parade ground—the March-Off. Air Vice-Marshal Hutton returned the Flight Sergeant Boy's salute and granted permission. Gilkes then made an about turn, marched back towards us and halted when he arrived at his post.

"Numbers 1 and 2 Squadrons will march off in column of route! Into line LE-eft TURN!"

The order was smartly executed.

Gilkes then ordered, "NCOs, take post."

When everyone was in position, the Sergeant Boy in command of the supporting entries made an about turn and faced his charges.

"Supporting entries," he commanded, "PRE-sent ARMS!

Gilkes now gave us the order to march and simultaneously the Station Band struck up with "Auld Lang Syne". Gilkes, at the head of the column, wheeled to lead the flight out of the Drill Shed and into the drizzle that had replaced the earlier fog.

All three flights of No. 1 Squadron followed behind in turn, as the supporting entries maintained their "Present Arms" position. A happy grin spread broadly across my face and the faces of those around me that I could see. We were revelling in the same feeling of pure joy that had been visible on the faces of the 26th, 27th and 28th entries when they too had passed this way before us. I also had a good idea of the thoughts that were passing through the minds of the poor sods in the supporting entries, as they were forced to gaze on our brazenly smirking faces—thoughts that ranged anywhere from, "It's our turn next" to "I wish it were me!" And one day it would come to pass for them, just as it had come to pass for us after much patience and forbearance.

By rights, we should have had a proper Guard of Honour for our send-off, but it was impractical. The limited space in the Drill Shed forced the supporting entries to remain in place, instead of forming up into the traditional Guard of Honour that we would then have marched through, had the parade taken place on the Square. But it was a small loss compared to the major prize—the Passing-Out itself.

The first stop after marching off the parade ground was to return to the Armoury and hand in our rifles and bayonets. That's where we took the opportunity of breaking ranks to congratulate each other for the first time on successfully passing out of Boy Entrant service.

CHAPTER 13

Manhood Delayed

There was time to enjoy a quick "Woody" Woodbine, for those of us who had handed our rifles back in to the Armoury and now waited around for the others to do likewise. Quite a few of us were smokers, as was made evident by several small clouds of blue tobacco smoke that suddenly started appearing all around the exterior of the Armoury. The order to fall in soon came, however, so we got rid of the fags and formed up in our ranks once again, but minus rifles this time. After all the preliminaries of dressing off and turning into column of route were completed, we marched back to the Drill Shed. By this time the supporting entries had left the scene and were on their way towards the Armoury to return their weapons. For them, it was all over with nothing more to look forward to right now but a return to normal duties. Later in the evening it would be a different matter, but happily we wouldn't be there to witness the ascendancy of the 30th to senior entry status. For the moment, though, it was still the 29th Entry's day and there were yet more items pending on the Passing Out programme. The first order of business was to partake of some light refreshment, in the form of familiar urns of mess tea and trays of mess tray-baked sponge cake, kindly provided by the Station catering staff. Parents and other family who had attended the ceremony were also invited to join us. Half-an-hour or so passed by as we all stood around munching cake, drinking mess tea from disposable cardboard cups (also kindly provided by the Station catering staff) and answering the urgent call of nature, although not necessarily in that particular order of priority.

When it was time to get back to matters concerning the Passing Out proceedings, Permanent Staff NCOs gently shepherded everyone into the adjoining Astra cinema for the next phase of the programme. Once seated, the School Commandant, Air Commodore Perkins, took the stage to provide a plethora of statistical information relating to our Entry. Reading from a book, like Eamon Andrews in a performance of

"This is Your Life", he mentioned that 311 boys were initially inducted into the 29th Entry at St. Athan on Thursday the 18th of October, 1956. Of those, 28 transferred to RAF Halton for Apprentice training and the remaining 283 continued training at St. Athan. Although some members were lost along the way, replacements came via relegations from the 28th Entry and when it was time for our final trade test we were 244 strong. Sadly, some 19 boys didn't make it through the finals and of these, 17 were relegated to the 30th Entry and 2 were "CT'd"—an acronym for "Ceased Training". The Air Commodore then read out the names of individual Boy Entrants who had performed the best overall in their respective trades, whilst Air Vice-Marshal Hutton presented them with prizes in recognition of their achievements. In addition to the academic achievements, Flight Sergeant Boy Gilkes was also awarded a prize for coming first in general service efficiency.

When the prize-giving ended, the Air Vice-Marshal gave an address in which he congratulated us on our smartness on parade and successes in workshops, school and on the sports field. He then urged us to use the technical skills we'd learned for the good of the Service that had trained us and finally counselled us never to lose our curiosity, but continue to seek further knowledge and strive for excellence.

Appropriately motivated, we filed out of the Astra and formed up to march back to the billets, where Corporal Longfellow awaited us. He held in his hands a bunch of the coveted black crepe hatbands that we would now wear around our SD hats, to signify our transition to the regular RAF. In exchange, the corporal collected our chequered hatbands and the red and blue discs from behind our beret cap badges. As he was doing this, Corporal Longfellow told us to bring our white webbing with us when we cleared from the Flight office and with that we were dismissed in time for early lunch.

I was hungry, but there was something more urgent than food on my mind just at that moment. It was a matter of pride that I get changed into my brand new T63 uniform with my new Leading Aircraftsman badges neatly sewn on both sleeves and plop my equally new T63 SD hat, complete with its black crepe hatband, on my head. Everyone else was also changing into the new uniforms, before going to the mess for our last lunch at St. Athan-by-the-Sea. Excitement and elation took the edge off my appetite, so I didn't eat much in the end—just enough to stave off the sensation of hunger. Butterworth and I then headed back to the billet to pack our kit and finish the clearing process, so that we could say farewell to St. Athan and Boy Entrant Training as quickly as possible and begin our well-earned leave.

Most of our kit had already been packed and what little remained didn't take very long to stuff into our kitbags. We then gathered our blankets and bed linen together and piled our old "hairy" blue uniform on top, before carrying all of it out of the billet. First stop was the bedding store, to dump the bedding and obtain a signature on our blue clearance cards in return. The next stop was the clothing store; to hand in the old uniforms and likewise have an autograph added to our clearance cards. With both of those chores taken care of, we went back to the billet to get our white webbing and take it to the Flight office, so that we could clear from there. Corporal Longfellow took the webbing from us and smilingly wished us good luck as he signed the cards. We shook hands with him and said goodbye. When we got back to the billet, the 30th, 31st and 32nd Entry boys had returned from workshops for their lunch break. They commented admiringly and also a little enviously on our change of uniform and rank. Then one of them, a boy named Brown, came up to Richard.

"The lads wanted to give you something as a going-away present," said Brownie, "so we had a whip-round."

With that, he thrust a handful of cash towards Richard, who reached out and accepted it with a very surprised acknowledgement of thanks.

Brownie then went on to explain that Richard had always treated them fairly and had never used his senior entry status to lord it over them. It was a touching gesture and one that I'd never heard of before. It was the rule rather than the exception that junior entries were always glad to be rid of the outgoing senior entry and were hardly inclined to give them any parting gifts. I was glad for Richard to the extent that it brought a lump to my throat, but at the same time I inwardly noted that it was he and he alone who had been the recipient of the gift.

During the time that the 29th had been the junior entry, Richard had frequently been a lightning rod for bullying, scorn and derision. I'm not sure why this was, but maybe it was because his short physical stature housed a feisty nature that could very quickly put him at odds with anyone who raised his hackles. He didn't easily accept the role of being a bull-boy for the senior entry and made this well known to those who had expected him to uncomplainingly clean their boots and buttons and suffered the uncomfortable consequences as a result. It would have been very easy for him to exploit his senior entry status when that time finally arrived, as a way of compensating for the trials and tribulations he'd been forced to suffer. Not my friend Richard, however. Much to his credit, he turned down the opportunity of having junior entry members perform menial tasks on his behalf and made a point of cleaning his own kit and keeping his own bed-space clean.

By way of contrast, I had wholeheartedly embraced the privileges of senior entry-hood. In fact, my basic philosophy during that period was always to look out for number one, probably due to the tough childhood I'd experienced—on top of the "survival of the fittest" mentality permeating the Boy Entrant culture. Richard Butterworth had experienced a childhood every bit as difficult as mine and he had also suffered through the same bullying and humiliations that Boy Entrant service had dished out to me, perhaps even more so. Yet from somewhere deep within himself, he had adopted a philosophy that dictated compassion towards those in lesser circumstances than his own. The lesson wasn't lost on me. Although unaware of it at the time, I also received a gift from the junior entries that day. It was one that I believe stayed with me and in the years that followed helped me to develop a more respectful and compassionate attitude towards my subordinates, both in the service and later in civilian life.

We said goodbye to our former billet-mates, knowing we wouldn't see them again because we would finish clearing and be gone long before they returned from workshops. In fact, we had cleared from everywhere except the final two Sections: Pay

Accounts and the Station Orderly Room. So we now made our way to the Station Headquarters building, where both Sections were located. Before long, we emerged from the SHQ with our wallets stuffed full of back pay and the travel warrants needed to take us home on leave and then get us to RAF Shawbury when the two-week leave period was over. We felt as though we were walking on air heading back to the now empty billet, where our kitbags lay waiting on the stark stripped-off beds which up until that morning had been the one small piece of territory we considered our own. There was a brief sense of nostalgia, but it was soon over-taken by a greater sense of happiness at the prospect of finally leaving St. Athan.

The trudge to the main gate with kitbags on shoulders seemed effortless and it was the greatest thrill in the world to pass through those forbidding wrought iron gates as regular airmen for the very first time and also the very last time. The Snoops barely gave us a glance as we walked past the Guardroom, although I still felt the same sense of intimidation that experience had taught me to associate with running that particular gauntlet. Inwardly I tried to relax by reminding myself that we were no longer the lowest of the low in their eyes and were therefore less of a target, since we had managed to climb up one rung out of the primordial ooze. Nevertheless, I couldn't help feeling the awful anticipation of some SP bawling out, "You there, boy!" No such call came, however, so we crossed the road outside the main gate without incident and walked to the bus-stop to await the bus for Barry that would drop us off at Gileston railway station. We were free—free at last!

Butterworth travelled with me as far as Crewe and then we both caught separate trains, his was to Liverpool and mine was the boat train to Heysham for the trip across the Irish Sea to Belfast. We congratulated each other once again on our passing out of Boys' Service and said that we would see each other at Shawbury on the day we were due back from leave. We then parted company and went our separate ways. It was impossible to make any definite arrangements to meet up since we didn't know exactly what to expect when we got to Shawbury, but we knew it couldn't be too difficult and so just left it at that.

* * *

Going home to Coleraine on leave was a different experience this time. Not just because it would be my first return there as a fully-fledged airman in the regular RAF, but also because the actual homestead itself had moved since my previous visit. My family had moved out of the pre-fab that had been our home since 1947 and into a new council house nearby. The pre-fabs had been erected just after the war, as temporary council housing, and were designed to last for ten years. Now, just a little over ten years later, the council had built more permanent housing for its pre-fab tenants. A brand new street, named The Crescent, had arisen in an area of green fields adjacent to the pre-fabs, where I had played as a child. As each new house on The Crescent became available, a pre-fab family was moved into it and their former home immediately demolished. New and more durable council housing was subsequently built on the site of the old pre-fab development, but that occurred some time later.

I knew all about the move before going on leave, because Annie had given me the new address in one of her letters. Even so, arriving at the new house was a strange experience. It had two storeys, unlike the pre-fab, which had been a bungalow. The ground floor consisted of two rooms, one of which was the posh front "parlour" that was used only to receive visitors. The other room was the kitchen cum everyday living room at the rear of the house. It was rectangular in shape, about twenty feet by ten feet and was dominated at one end by a coal and coke fired range, which not only heated the room but also incorporated a boiler that heated water. The range was also the only means of cooking or boiling a kettle of water and consequently was kept alight day and night, summer and winter. The hot water was a nice touch. We never had that particular little luxury in the pre-fab except on bath nights, because the hot water tank there used an electric immersion heater, which cost too much to operate.

And even on bath nights, Annie wouldn't use it. Instead, she would boil a kettle of water on the gas cooker and then pour the contents into the bath, before adding enough cold water to bring it down to a tolerable temperature. The resulting volume of tepid water measured about three inches in depth—not exactly conducive to an indulgence in luxurious wallowing. Yes, the ability to enjoy a nice hot bath was indeed a luxury in the new house.

The upstairs accommodation consisted of three bedrooms, the bathroom and a separate toilet, but it was annoying to learn that my father's pet budgies were allotted a bedroom all to themselves, while the humans were squeezed into two rooms, just like it had been back in the pre-fab days. My brother shared the largest room with my father and Annie, while my sisters Veronica and Pauline shared the other bedroom. When home on leave, I had to share my brother's bed.

It was nice to get home and see the new house, but the novelty wore off after a few days and then I was ready and anxious to get back on the boat and discover what my other new home at Shawbury was like. The duration of my leave pass was for two weeks, however, which meant having to kick my heels around for all that time before being able to get on with that next big phase of my life. It also seemed that Coleraine was becoming just as irrelevant to me as I was becoming to it. It was as though a giant hand had scooped me out of a pond just 18 months earlier and the water had immediately closed in to completely fill the space I had formerly occupied. A few faint ripples were all that now remained and they were fading away with the passage of time. There was still a sense of duty to return home on leave, but it just didn't seem like "home" any more, especially since the house I'd known as home no longer existed. During earlier spells of leave I had dreaded the approach of the last day at home, knowing that when it finally came around I would be returning to St. Athan. This time, though, I wasn't going back to St. Athan because I wasn't a Boy Entrant any more—or so I thought—which made me feel that the last day of leave couldn't come soon enough. So when the time came to say my farewells, it was with a great sense of adventure and excitement, rather than the heavy heart I'd experienced on other occasions. Indeed, the feeling was one of impatient eagerness as I stood on the Coleraine railway station platform, waiting for the Belfast train that would take me on the first leg of the journey to my new posting at RAF Shawbury in the County of Shropshire. I didn't know exactly what to expect when I got there, but it certainly promised to be a lot more interesting than hanging around Coleraine just killing time. And as the train finally started pulling out of the station with me aboard, I silently cheered to be on my way at last.

* * *

The first part of the journey to Shawbury followed much the same route as I'd taken on previous trips back to St. Athan. First there was the sea leg from Belfast to Heysham and then the train to Crewe. From there, the new route diverged from the old. Instead of taking a mainline train to South Wales, I boarded a local train for the one-hour jaunt to Shrewsbury. The next and final leg was by Midland Red bus from Shrewsbury to RAF Shawbury, which was less than 10 miles from the city centre in a north-north westerly direction. It was still only early afternoon when I presented myself at the Guardroom to sign in. The Snoop on duty was less surly than those at St. Athan and after getting me to sign the Visitors' Book, he directed me to the transit billet and bedding store. My first stop was the transit billet, where I dumped my kitbag on one of the unoccupied beds—the one that seemed to have the least amount of sag in the middle. I noticed that another bed had been made up, but there was no sign of the occupant. Then I walked the short distance to the bedding store and drew out a set of blankets, pillows, bed linen and some eating utensils. After that, I returned to the billet to make my "pit". It was too late to report to the Station Orderly Room by the time all of this was accomplished, so I set out to find the NAAFI where perhaps I might be able to get a sandwich or something to eat, since I'd missed lunch at the airmen's mess.

When I returned to the transit billet, the occupant of the other bed had also returned. Not surprisingly, it was Butterworth, who had arrived earlier in the day. In fact, he had already been to the Station Orderly Room and begun his "arrival" process, but didn't get far because most of the Sections he needed to visit had closed for the day. We sat around and chatted about our experiences while on leave, until it was time to go for early tea at the mess. After that we spent some time exploring the station to find the important places, such as the camp cinema, and since the NAAFI seemed dead we decided to see the film that was currently showing.

The Shawbury Astra was much smaller than its namesake at St. Athan and the audience behaved quite differently as well. They joked around a lot more and there seemed to be much more camaraderie than the standoffish entry-ism that permeated everything in the Boy Entrant world, including going to the cinema. It was there that I first heard the standard RAF cinema audience's reaction to a particular screen credit that follows every "Tom and Jerry" cartoon—an Astra staple in those days. When the producer's name, Fred Quimby, appeared on-screen, the entire audience, as one, shouted out, "Good old Fred!" This, I found out later, was a universal ritual in the regular RAF, but it startled both of us on hearing it that first time. The feeling of being a part of this new adult community made me feel good inside. But I was tired after an almost sleepless night during the sea crossing from Belfast, so we had an early night and agreed to "arrive" together next morning.

After breakfast, I presented myself to the Station Orderly Room clerk. He munched his way through a bag of Smith's crisps as he otherwise silently noted my details, before handing me a blue card that looked exactly like the one I'd taken around to clear from St. Athan. My name appeared on the "Arrival" side, together with a list of the Sections I needed to visit. The Station Establishment would then be aware—and no doubt feel suitably reassured and relieved—that a fully trained LAC in the trade of Electrical Mechanic (Air) had now joined its strength. Richard waited around until I got my blue card and then accompanied me to the Sections he'd already visited, until I caught up to where he'd left off. After that, we tackled all of the other Sections together.

Probably the most important signature for us to obtain was identified on the Arrivals card as "Tech. Wing Adj." We would be working within Technical Wing, so the Tech. Wing Adjutant was responsible for assigning us to whatever duty we were considered best suited, in light of our hard-won qualifications. The Technical Wing Adjutant was a junior officer whose main job was to deal with the Wing's daily routine, on behalf of the senior officer in overall charge of the Wing.

After obtaining directions from one or two passers-by, we found our way to the Tech. Wing office in one of the large hangars on the perimeter of the aircraft ground-handling area, otherwise known as the Pan. The Wing "Discip." Sergeant took our blue cards and made some notes, then told us to wait a moment. With that, he disappeared through the doorway of an adjoining office. Very soon he returned and told us that we were to go in and meet the adjutant. We walked cautiously through the open doorway, then stopped and saluted. Simultaneously, our jaws must have hit the floor because the adjutant wasn't quite what we expected. She was a strikingly beautiful woman, a WRAF Flying Officer in her mid-twenties whose neat short dark-brown hair framed a face of such classical beauty that it could quite easily have belonged to a film actress. To say that I was absolutely stunned is only putting it mildly.

"Ah! Butterworth and Carlin," she said, looking up from her desk. She wasn't wearing a hat and Service protocol therefore dictated that she couldn't return our salute. Instead, she stood up and came around the desk, then reached out her hand to shake each of ours in turn.

"Which one are you?" She asked as she politely and gently shook my hand, her eyes twinkling with amusement at the impression she obviously knew she'd made on both of us.

"Carlin, Ma'am," I managed to stammer.

"And Butterworth I presume," she said, turning to Richard and holding her hand out for him to shake.

"Yes Ma'am," he replied in a voice that was every bit as shaky as mine had been.

"Welcome to Shawbury. We're very glad you've joined us," she said with a radiant smile that revealed her perfect white teeth. She returned to sit behind her desk before continuing, "Now, what trade are you?"

"Electrical Mechanics, Air, Ma'am," we answered together.

"Oh, gooood," she responded, "We can find plenty for you to do—we're a little short-handed in the Electrical Section at the moment."

We smiled politely at this observation. It was nice to know we were wanted.

The beautiful Flying Officer continued interviewing us. "Where did you do your technical training?" She asked.

"St. Athan, Ma'am," one of us replied.

"I see," she said thoughtfully and then continued in a more upbeat voice, "I'm a little familiar with St. Athan. So you were Boy Entrants then?"

"Yes Ma'am," we smilingly responded together.

"Have you come straight from there?"

"No Ma'am, we've been on two weeks' leave."

"Yes, but this is your first posting since finishing your training. Isn't that right?"

"Yes Ma'am."

"So, how old were you when you first started your training?" Her voice took on a more serious tone as she asked this question.

"Fifteen and a half, Ma'am," we both answered independently. This was more of a pat answer than an accurate one; I had been two months past the 15½-year mark when I joined the Boy Entrants' Service, whereas Richard had somehow managed to enlist one month before achieving the lower age limit.

"And how old are you now?" She asked.

"Seventeen," I answered.

Richard said nothing. In fact, he still had about another month to go before he would reach his seventeenth birthday in May.

"So you're not eighteen yet?" she asked.

"No Ma'am," we both answered.

She frowned at this and then looked down at some paperwork on her desk. "Then, technically speaking, you're both still Boys," she announced, still looking at the paperwork on the desk. Quietly, almost to herself, she said, "That could be a problem." When she looked up at us, the twinkling eyes had been replaced by a more serious look.

The Adjutant's pronouncement surprised, shocked and horrified both of us. We thought we'd left Boys' Service behind at St. Athan, so what was all this about? Could she possibly be thinking of sending us back there?

"Where are you billeted right now?" She asked.

"In the transit billet, Ma'am."

"Are you aware that QRs (Queen's Regulations) forbids anyone under the age of eighteen living in the same accommodation as adult servicemen?"

It was our turn to frown. After all, it wasn't our fault if we were breaking QRs. "We thought that was just when we were Boy Entrants at St. Athan Ma'am," I responded, speaking for both of us.

She gave a little laugh, "Oh no. It applies anywhere in the service." The laughter that had briefly flitted across her face was quickly replaced by a concerned look. "I'm not sure how we're going to deal with this, but for the moment you'd better remain in the transit billet. I'll have to get in touch with Personnel Records to see what we can do." With that, she looked towards the open door of the office and called out "Sergeant!" in a slightly raised voice.

The sergeant came through the door with an expectant look on his face. "Ma'am? He asked.

"Sergeant, Butterworth and Carlin are elec. mechs. They're going to be joining us, so can you please take them to the Electrical Section and introduce them to Chief Tech. Smith. We have a slight problem due to the fact that they're both under age, but hopefully we can sort it all out."

"Yes Ma'am," the sergeant responded. "Right lads, come with me."

We saluted before turning to leave the office. The beautiful Flying Officer smiled in response, but it was very brief and was replaced almost immediately by a look of determination as she reached for the phone on her desk.

The sergeant signed our blue cards after we followed him into the outer office and then handed them back to us.

"You need to go to the E and I Section next," he said, referring to the Electrical and Instruments Section. "It's in the next hangar," which he indicated by pointing in that general direction. "Go in through the fire doors on the airfield side and then turn right. It's a couple of doors down."

"Yes, Sergeant," we responded, then turned and made our way out onto the pathway that ran along the hangar frontage.

Chief Technician Smith, the NCO in charge of the E&I Section, possessed a seemingly pleasant disposition. He welcomed us to the Section and then introduced us to the other Section members, who were sitting around drinking what looked suspiciously like very strong tea from of an assortment of cups and mugs.

"Who 'ave you got there then, Chief?" One of them asked.

"Couple of lads straight out of St. Athan who are going to show you sorry lot how it's done," he replied with a grin.

"Wot? A couple of brats?" the first speaker retorted. "Cor blimey!"

This was the first time that we heard ourselves referred to as brats on account of our Boy Entrant pedigree, although it certainly wouldn't be the last. The two or three other men in the room behaved in a more friendly way towards us, as did the WRAF girl who was apparently also a member of the E&I Section. She was as thin as a rake and wore a battledress blouse and WRAF issue slacks. We found out a little later that she was known to all and sundry by the nickname of "Splitpin", because of her slim frame and very long legs. Her resemblance to a split-pin was accentuated by the slacks she was accustomed to wearing.

One of the other lads, a tall cockney named Bert who wore heavy horn-rimmed glasses, offered us a cup of tea, which we gladly accepted. He searched around until he found some grimy, tea-stained cups, which he rinsed out with hot water from the kettle by pouring a small quantity into each and then swirling it around before tossing it out into a white-enamelled tin basin that had seen much better days. He then filled the cups with some of the same strong-looking brew that the others were drinking, from an ancient brown-enamelled metal teapot.

"Milk and sugar?" He queried.

When we answered yes, he picked up a tin of condensed milk and poured a stream of its white syrupy-thick contents into each cup from one of the two holes that had been punctured in its top—although not too recently by the look of the yellowish, congealed gunk around the holes. He then added one spoonful of sugar per cup, shovelling it out of what appeared to be an old tin tea caddy and then briskly stirred both concoctions before handing them to us. I can't say it was the best tea that I've ever tasted, but it was wet and warm. I also appreciated the hospitality, since it was coming from people with whom we would no doubt be working in the very near future. We spent a little time with them, listening to their banter, most of which I suspect was put on for our benefit. Then, when we had finished our tea, or as much as we felt was necessary to avoid being impolite, Butterworth and I excused ourselves and went off to finish doing our rounds of the Station to complete the Arrival process.

We completed "Arriving" by lunchtime the next day and then reported for duty to the E&I Section early in the afternoon. The corporal in whose charge we were placed teamed me up with Bert, the tall cockney with the horn-rimmed glasses, and Richard was assigned to work with a spindly Senior Aircraftsman from Yorkshire who always seemed to have a liquid droplet dangling precariously from the tip of his thin beaky red nose.

Bert was a kindly sort of bloke who said to me in his strong cockney accent, "Stick wiv me, me old mite and I'll see yer oh-roight!"

Our job was to carry out pre- and after-flight servicing, change batteries and check and adjust the generator voltage during engine run-ups, all on Vallettas and Varsities, or "Pigs" as they were more affectionately known. He confided in me about Splitpin and how she would occasionally entertain her many male acquaintances in one of the Ansons. He warned me not to follow if I saw her going into an Anson and close the door. When I told Richard about this later, we were both afflicted with uncontrollable fits of laughter as we took turns in describing to each other how the Anson's tail-wheel might bounce around on the tarmac when Splitpin was busy "entertaining" her friends.

In recognition of my eighteen months of intense technical training and grooming as a future NCO of the Royal Air Force, Bert entrusted me with the awesome responsibilities of carrying his tool bag when we went out on a job and making the tea in the Section servicing bay. And although this chafed, I somehow understood that we all need to pay our dues. My father had told me long ago that serving time in a trade meant having to put up with menial stuff like this and that there was no option but to take it like a man.

In the evenings Richard and I went into Shrewsbury, since we were no longer fettered by the inconvenience of bed-checks. Shrewsbury was a picturesque town, more so than Barry, with many *olde worlde* buildings that were still in everyday use. On one of the major streets, we came upon an imposing statue of some important person. The statue stood on a massive cubic stone plinth on which was inscribed but the single name "Clive". We wondered who the heck this character Clive was, but it gave us an excuse to invent all kinds of tall tales about him to explain why the citizens of Shrewsbury had erected a statue in his honour. Later, we discovered that the statue commemorated Clive of India, who had been born in the Shrewsbury area. It was interesting to find that out, but it ruined the fun we'd been having inventing strange identities for him, or at least for his commemorative statue.

At the weekend, we ventured into the village that adjoined the RAF station and started getting to know the local young ladies, with some success I might add.

All in all, we liked Shawbury and the City of Shrewsbury and felt content with our technical duties. It seemed as though we had achieved perfect balance with the potential for interesting work and pleasant leisure activities. But as we blissfully enjoyed our new life at this wonderfully idyllic station, we were completely unaware of the urgent "signals", of which we were the subject, that were flying rapidly back and forth between the Station Personnel Records Section and Flying Training Command HQ. The exchange of correspondence continued for about two weeks, before the Brass arrived at a momentous decision. The first we knew of it was when, one day, the Beautiful One—the Tech. Wing Adjutant—summoned us into her presence once more. We were quite excited at the prospect of gazing on her flawless countenance again, never suspecting that the outcome of this meeting might not be quite as joyful as we expected. When we arrived in the outer office, the Wing Discip. Sergeant motioned us to wait and then popped his head through the doorway into the Adjutant's office, to let her know we had arrived. He then beckoned for us to go in. We entered her office, then stood at attention and saluted, somehow sensing the sombreness of the atmosphere at the same time.

"Stand easy," she said. Then, seeming to choose her words carefully as though she'd been rehearsing them, she began, "As I mentioned to you before, Queen's Regulations expressly forbid underage personnel from being accommodated with adult personnel."

"Yes Ma'am," we agreed.

"Well," she continued, "We've tried to make some arrangements to provide separate accommodation for you at Shawbury, but I'm afraid Command won't hear of it and has ruled that all of the underage personnel in Flying Training Command must be stationed at one place." Her voice dropped to a softer tone, "So, I'm sorry to have to tell you this, but you are both being posted to RAF Cranwell." She allowed us a moment for this to sink in before adding, "I'm sorry. We liked having you here and the reports I've had tell me that you seemed to be fitting in well, but I'm afraid there's nothing I can do about it." She seemed genuinely sorry as she said this, but then continued, "You need to report to the Station Orderly Room right away to begin clearing. We'll miss you and all I can do is wish you both good luck." With that, she sadly shook hands with both of us and smiled encouragingly. Crestfallen, we saluted her and then turned and left the office.

Two weeks! It must have been one of the shortest postings in RAF history and just when we were finding our feet and getting to know our way around. We hoped that Cranwell would be just as enjoyable as Shawbury, but we really didn't hold out too much hope in that direction. After all, it wasn't just "Cranwell"; it was the bloody *Royal Air Force College* Cranwell where officer cadets are trained before being let loose on the world. That could only mean one thing; tons and tons of bull.

* * *

Two days later, Butterworth and I stood dejectedly on a Shrewsbury railway station platform, dressed in our best blue uniforms and with all of the possessions we owned in this world packed into our cylindrical white canvas kitbags that now rested on the platform by our sides. We were waiting for the Birmingham train to take us on what would be the first leg of our journey to Royal Air Force College Cranwell in the County of Lincolnshire. It was a sad occasion, because we had fallen in love with Shawbury during our short sojourn there. There had been a welcoming feeling at all levels, both on the station and in the surrounding area and we had been settling into it very nicely, thank you, when the order to uproot us had come so rudely and abruptly from On High. The prospect of going to Cranwell, on the other hand, was none too encouraging. Several people had visibly shuddered when we told them of our new posting, which didn't do much in the way of helping us adopt an attitude of gleeful anticipation at the thought of going to our new home.

Several weary hours and a number of train changes later, we pulled into Lincoln Central station where we would make the last change for the final leg of the rail journey. Accidentally misreading the name of our next destination on the ticket as "Seaford," we scanned the timetable posted on a wall near the station exit, but couldn't find it listed. In desperation, we approached a uniformed official, who was quite possibly the Stationmaster.

"Excuse us please," I said. He looked at us sharply as though we were interrupting something important, but seeing that I had his attention, I continued, "We're supposed to be going to Seaford but can't see it on the timetable."

"Seaford?" He barked. His body language suggested that he was busy and didn't really want to be bothered by two little erks like us. "There ain't nowt 'round 'ere by that name, lad."

I held out my ticket so that he could see the name of the destination printed on it, but had to wait a few moments whilst his officious attention was directed elsewhere, before he condescended to look at the small green rectangle of cardboard in my hand.

"Oh, *Sleaford*!" He exclaimed, pronouncing it loudly in a slow theatrical manner as though he had solved a great mystery and was making everyone within earshot aware of how he had cleverly exposed our incredible stupidity. His patronising tone strongly suggested that if morons like us intended to travel in Lincolnshire it would help if we could at least get the names of its towns right. He must have enjoyed the moment, because it also gave him the heaven-sent opportunity to be rid of us.

"Need St. Mark's Station, lad," he continued gruffly, "train for Sleaford dunnit go from 'ere."

It was bad enough that we had to change trains, but we also had to change stations and in a city we weren't familiar with. "How do we get to St. Mark's station?" I asked.

"You'll 'ave to go oot the station exit," he indicated where the exit was as he spoke, "and then go to tha's left too-ards 'igh Street. Go to tha's left agin and cross o'er the crossing and it's aboot 'alf a mile on tha's ra-ight."

We thanked him for his grudging help, then threw our kitbags up on our shoulders and headed towards the station exit, proffering our tickets to be punched by the expressionless ticket inspector on our way out. Once outside the station, we turned left as instructed and soon came to the level crossing on High Street that the Stationmaster had mentioned. But the train we'd only just disembarked from was still at the platform and was apparently too long to fit all the way into the station, so the last few carriages blocked the crossing, preventing the gates from being opened to traffic and pedestrians. Instead of waiting until the train pulled out, however, we decided to use the pedestrian footbridge adjacent to the crossing. Climbing up the steps to the bridge level with the heavy kitbag slung over my shoulder was quite an effort, which was further complicated by trying to manoeuvre its awkward bulk in a way that avoided having it bumped into by the fast downward rush of hurrying pedestrians.

It was a relief for both of us to finally reach the level part of the bridge and start catching our breath, as we then started descending the easier downward flight of steps on the opposite side of the crossing. That's when I was rewarded by catching my very first view of Lincoln Cathedral. It stood majestically on the city's highest hill, overlooking the landscape descending into the valley below. It appeared tall, regal and serene above the common everyday goings-on of the hoi polloi below. The simple act of looking up and suddenly seeing this beautiful cathedral gave me a pleasantly strange feeling that seemed to resonate somewhere deep within my being. It was somehow like a sense of *déjà vu,* but not exactly, because I didn't get the sensation of having been there before. It was just a feeling of familiarity. The sensation is really difficult to describe, but the best way I can put it is that I suddenly knew I liked this city and wanted to return as often as I could. It's a good thing too, because Lincoln eventually became my second home. It was here that I met and married my wife Pam, it was where both of my daughters, Michelle and Sarah, were born and where I lived out a large portion of my life. But that's another story I intend to tell some other time.

St. Mark's Station was smaller than Lincoln Central and with fewer amenities. Eventually, our train for Sleaford arrived at one of the station's two main platforms. It was a local "milk" train that stopped at every small village station on the way, making the 17-mile journey spin out to more than an hour. Finally, we arrived at Sleaford in mid-afternoon and were pleased to discover that the bus terminal was directly across the street from the railway station. Well actually it wasn't so much a terminal as a series of buses parked by the kerb along the street. The buses were mid-green in colour and bore the seemingly quaint logo, "Lincolnshire Road Car Co. Ltd.", displayed prominently in yellow lettering along their flanks. It didn't take us very long to find a bus with "Cranwell Camp" displayed on its destination indicator and so we climbed aboard. A few minutes later, the bus conductor came aboard and approached us for the fare. We produced the bus warrants we'd been issued that morning by the Personnel Records clerk at Shawbury.

"East Camp or West Camp?" inquired the conductor.

We looked blankly at him. "Dunno. Can you drop us off at the Guardroom please?" one of us replied.

"That's East Camp," he said, taking our bus warrants and winding the little handle on his ticket machine to dispense a yellow paper ribbon consisting of two tickets. As this was happening, the driver climbed into his cab and then the bus juddered spasmodically for a few seconds as he coaxed its reluctant diesel engine into life.

"Hold tight," called out the conductor as he pushed the bell button twice in rapid succession. The ding-ding sound of the bell was drowned almost immediately by the harsh grinding noise of first gear being selected and with a jolt the bus set off, taking us on the last lap of our day-long journey.

As we travelled along its main street, I could see that Sleaford seemed to be a modestly-sized market town, but it was soon left behind as the vista evolved into that of a gently undulating countryside of green fields, woods and copses. The bus crawled along very slowly—probably at about 25 miles per hour, which was something we weren't used to. The Western Welsh buses travelled along at a fair clip and during my short stay at Shawbury, the efficient speed of the Midland Red buses hadn't gone unnoticed. Richard and I joked with each other about getting out and pushing or of being able to get there faster if we got out and walked, thinking that the driver was just a little too cautious and didn't want to put his foot down too hard. Later, I found that this slow speed was universal for the Lincolnshire Road Car Co. Ltd.—for reasons that have remained a mystery.

The road along which we travelled was the A15 to Lincoln and except for a short detour through the village of Leasingham, we stayed on this road for about two miles before making a left turn onto a "B" road. Just as we made the turn, I caught a brief glimpse of a signpost pointing in the direction that we were now taking. It read "Cranwell 2". I took this to mean that the distance to our destination was two more miles, but it was the wrong assumption. The sign really indicated the distance to Cranwell village—the camp itself was another two miles further on. After passing through the village, obvious signs of an airfield began to appear. First a control tower, then hangars and eventually clumps of buildings could be discerned as the bus slowly puttered towards them along the now arrow-straight road. The buildings became more identifiable as we got nearer and then we were passing between them—married quarters on the right and what appeared to be dilapidated red-brick barracks on the left. After a few hundred yards of driving in the built-up area, the bus pulled up at a bus stop with a long wavering squeal of its brakes that set my teeth on edge.

"Guardroom," sang out the conductor, as he looked in our direction.

I was expecting to see the typical main entrance of a Royal Air Force camp complete with gate, a headquarters building facing the entrance and a Guardroom strategically situated to monitor and control entry and egress to and from the station. But the bus had actually stopped at a place on the road where none of these traditional landmarks were obvious. There was, however, a long single storey building set back a few feet from the road and judging from the abundance of gleaming white paintwork and shining brasses, there was no mistaking that it was the Guardroom. We grabbed our kitbags and alighted from the bus and then heard the ding-ding sound of the bell and the conductor's "Hold tight" caution as the bus thundered off, leaving us standing there in a dense swirling cloud of black diesel exhaust fumes. Before picking up our kitbags again, we took a few moments to check each other's uniforms to make sure that everything was as it should be, before presenting ourselves to the Snoops inside the Guardroom.

The structure and location of the building was odd to say the least, but it wasn't until we walked into a passageway penetrating its midsection that I realized it was actually a railway station. I could see that we were really standing on a station platform. There was another platform facing the one on which we stood and between both platforms lay the track bed, minus rails and sleepers. This had apparently been the terminus of a spur line, probably from Sleaford, that at one time had served the station. But the tracks had evidently been torn up some time ago, although the path they had followed was still plainly visible, grown over as it was. From these clues, it wasn't difficult to deduce that the main form of transport to and from Cranwell must have originally been by train. And since the railway station was the camp's main access portal to and from the outside world, it only made sense for it to incorporate the Guardroom. Progress, no doubt encouraged by the Lincolnshire Road Car Co. Ltd., had consigned the train service to history's dustbin, but the Guardroom still remained as the lone survivor of an earlier era. Whether it had originally occupied the whole building, as it did now, or had completely taken it over later when the railway staff had abandoned ship, was entirely open to conjecture.

A dilapidated storehouse building provided a backdrop behind the opposing platform, although both were separated by an open area of weed-infested ground, blackened by coal dust that had been deposited there over the years. Far from the bull we had been expecting, this camp certainly didn't seem to measure up to the exalted reputation of the Royal Air Force College Cranwell. It was puzzling—to the extent that we began asking ourselves if perhaps there was some other Cranwell that we had been sent to by mistake. There was no mistake—we were definitely in the right place. But there were good grounds for our doubts because, as we were soon to discover, there really were two Cranwells. Both were in the same geographical location, yet one was worlds apart from the other.

We soon found ourselves at a counter, after having been directed through a doorway that opened off the passageway by a sign that bore the legend, "All Visitors Report Here", or words to that effect. The SP who came to the other side of the counter seemed to be expecting us when we identified ourselves, because he checked our names off against a list on a clip-board that he stretched over and retrieved from a row of similar-looking clip-boards hanging on a row of hooks along one wall of the room. When we had signed in, he gave us directions to the barrack block and room where we were to be accommodated. He also suggested that we go there first, drop off our kitbags and then go to the bedding store to pick up an issue of blankets and sheets. Thanking him, we retraced our steps back to the roadway as directed and then walked a few hundred yards further along the road in the same direction in which the bus had disappeared several minutes previously, until we came to another road leading into the camp. Strangely, there were no gates. Anyone could have walked right into the camp without being challenged. We soon found the bedding store, which was housed in a small building that came up on our right. Noting its location, we passed it by on the suggestion of the SP and, rounding a bend in the road, were confronted by a row of six or so barrack blocks each built in the configuration of the letter "H".

Not unexpectedly, the block we had been directed to was the very last one at the end of the row. As we walked along the road towards it, we noticed that all of the blocks were very old and were definitely of a pre-war vintage that had seen better days. They were also much larger than the neatly modern barrack blocks that we had seen, but failed to have been accommodated in, at Shawbury. We now also noticed the parade ground on our left. It had been hidden from our view by the storehouse building when we were at the Guardroom, because in fact the direction in which we were now walking had brought us around on the other side of the storehouse.

Eventually we reached the last barrack block in the row and entered it, to discover that the interior looked even worse than the exterior. It was a two-storey building incorporating eight barrack rooms in all, four upstairs and four downstairs. The barrack rooms formed the legs of the "H", whilst the horizontal crossbar contained the toilets, ablutions and various other utility rooms. The barrack room to which we'd been assigned was on the ground floor and was accessed by descending a flight of three steel-edged concrete steps to reach its floor level, indicating that the land on which the block was built must have sloped to some degree. The room was wide and cavernous, as were all the other barrack rooms in the block, seemingly designed to each house somewhere between 80 and 100 men. Right now, however, it contained 20 beds all crammed up near the entrance. A row of tall wooden lockers had been arrayed across the room, at the approximate halfway point, in such a way as to form a wall that cut off the unoccupied area. All but half a dozen of the beds were made up, signifying they were taken, so we picked the best two we could find from those remaining and dumped our kitbags on the bare mattresses before retracing our steps to the bedding store.

A little later we were making the long trek back in the opposite direction, this time peering over a pile of blankets, bed linen and pillows, as we headed back to get settled into our new home. It was while we were making up our beds that the corporal in charge of the billet put in an appearance.

"Hello-hello, who have we here then?" He remarked good-naturedly. "You must be Butterworth and Carlin. We've been expecting you."

He then introduced himself as Corporal Dillon and explained that this particular barrack room was reserved exclusively for under age ex-Boy Entrants. He went on to tell us that he was also an ex-Boy Entrant, although obviously not under age, and that he'd been selected as the corporal in charge of the billet for that very reason.

As the afternoon wore on, several other inhabitants of the barrack room, all of them under age ex-29th Entry members, showed up in dribs and drabs. Richard and I introduced ourselves and were repeatedly obliged to explain that we had been posted to Shawbury from St. Athan before being redirected to Cranwell because of our young age. Everyone commiserated with us on the stroke of misfortune that brought us to "Cranners", which didn't do much to make us feel any happier to be there. Most of them seemed to be radio or radar types from Yatesbury but at least five, Rowse, Simpson, Pyle, Melloy and May, were Airframe Mechanics from 1 Wing, St. Athan. All of us, it seemed, were doomed to live in this barrack room until we reached our 18th birthday, which for me was a long ten months away. So much for passing out into the men's air force.

We went to the airmen's mess for dinner with some of our new billet mates and listened as they explained the Cranwell camp layout. The first thing we learned was that there were two camps. We were billeted in dilapidated East Camp, which accommodated the Station's "other-ranks" support staff. By contrast, the officer cadets were accommodated at posh West Camp, which also contained Station Headquarters and Sick Quarters, as well as the Flight Operations area that included the aircraft servicing hangars. The road that we'd travelled by bus through Cranwell village to the Guardroom continued on past West Camp, which was on the left, before meeting up with the main Sleaford to Grantham road. The palatial-looking Cranwell College building was on the right side of this road, situated directly opposite West Camp. Airmen (the collective term for non-commissioned, non-NCO members of the RAF) were forbidden to fraternise with the officer cadets and were strongly discouraged from having any interaction with them, other than in the normal course of duty. For the cadets, this was the equivalent of the training that we had just completed as Boy Entrants, but at a much higher level. And they were treated with much greater respect than had been accorded us. Cadets wore officer-style uniforms but were easily identified by the white band worn around their hats, or the white disc worn behind the officer cap badge on their berets. They were addressed individually as "Sir" and collectively as "Gentlemen" by their drill instructors. Imagine that!

* * *

Next morning, we made the long trek to Station Headquarters on West Camp so that we could begin our Arrivals procedure. We were becoming quite the experts at this process by now, this being the fourth time we had either cleared from or arrived at a station within the short space of four weeks. Then, after returning our completed Arrival cards to the Station Orderly Room, we reported for duty to the E&I Section in Hangar 30.

The E&I Section was housed in two separate physical locations—the Instrument "bashers" inhabited the servicing bay that opened off the hangar on the west side of the north fire-door hangar entrance, whilst electricians occupied the servicing bay that opened off the east wall. We actually had to report to the Instrument Section because that's where the E&I Section office was located. There, we met Flight Sergeant Walker, the senior NCO in charge of the Electrical Flight. "Chiefy" Walker seemed a pleasant sort of man, burly of build and sporting a neatly clipped black moustache that completely covered his upper lip. He wore an aircrew brevet on his left breast, as did so many of the "command" senior NCOs of that era. It might have been a Flight Engineer's brevet, but time has dimmed my recollection of its exact designation.

Chiefy led us to the Electrical Flight, where he assigned Richard to the Aircraft Component Test Bay under the supervision of Les, a Junior Technician, whilst I was assigned to the Component Stripping and Servicing Bay in the room next door. My job was to dismantle aircraft electrical components— such as generators and voltage regulators—service and clean them and then pass them through a hatch in the wall, to be tested in the Test Bay. Technically, I was also under Les' supervision, but in fact I worked more closely with a Senior Aircraftsman (SAC) who had almost completed his two-year stint of National Service. And it was from this individual that I learned most of what I needed to do. The room in which I worked also served as the "crew room" for the electrical mechanics and fitters who worked on the aircraft in the hangar. They were supervised by a sergeant and three corporals. Listening to their banter and chumminess made me feel that I wanted to be a part of the team, working with them out in the hangar, but what became increasingly clear to me was that neither Butterworth nor I were going to be allowed anywhere near an aircraft until we at least reached our eighteenth birthday.

In September, six months after having passed out from St. Athan, we began visiting the Station Library every day to read the latest Personnel Occurrence Report (PORs). This was a daily list of the official promotions in rank and other significant occurrences for Cranwell-based personnel. The occurrence, whatever its nature, was effective only when it was published in PORs. We were anxiously anticipating our automatic promotion to Senior Aircraftsman so that we could start wearing our new badges of rank and, more importantly, receive the pay increase that went with it. Both promotions appeared a few days late by our estimate, but we soon forgot that on our way to the clothing store. There, citing the appropriate POR number as the authority, we requested the SAC badges so that we could replace the LAC badges that only six months previously had made us feel so proud.

In February of 1959 I once again started making daily pilgrimages to the Station Library to check PORs. This time I went alone, because of the three months' difference between my age and that of Richard. Having now reached my eighteenth birthday, I needed the official POR acknowledgement of my transition to the Regular Service before I could move out of the Boy Entrant barrack room and into the E&I Section barrack block.

When it finally appeared, Richard helped me to move my kit to the new accommodation. It was like moving from a Victorian dungeon to a modern luxury hotel because, although the E&I barrack block was identical to the Boy Entrant block on the outside, it had been completely modernized inside. The cavernous barrack rooms had been divided into several comfortable smaller rooms, each housing no more than five men. I felt sad that Richard had to stay behind in the Boy Entrant billet for another three months, but there was nothing to be done except commiserate with him, knowing that he too would make the transition in just three more months.

And so it was, that with very little ceremony, I finally made the official transition from Boy Entrant to Regular Airman—from boyhood to manhood.

EPILOGUE

For many years after passing out of Boy Entrant training, I made a conscious effort not to advertise the fact that I had been a "Brat". There were two reasons for this.

For one thing, my 18 month-long stay at St. Athan as a Boy Entrant had been anything but pleasant in the overall view and I would have preferred just to have forgotten all about it. Passing out and into the regular service was an enormous relief, even if fully-fledged official manhood took another few months to catch up with me.

The other reason can be summed up in the word "Brat." In general, the regular Royal Air Force did not welcome us with open arms. Instead, other servicemen most often referred to us scornfully as "brats" and sometimes, albeit less frequently, as "Trenchard's bastards". This reaction was probably due to the cocky attitude we had developed as a survival tool, during our eighteen-month long struggle to stay afloat in the world of Boy Entrants. The mistake was bringing it along with us into our new life, but we weren't to know any better.

After a "normalizing" period of several months, it seemed obvious that being an ex-Boy was not a helpful attribute when it came to integrating with other servicemen. So I consciously refrained from volunteering that information about my background and I suspect that most other ex-Boys did likewise.

It wasn't until many years later that I was mature enough to realize what a valuable contribution Boy Entrant training had made to the shaping of my life. Not that it was the be-all and end-all of everything, because it took me several more years to develop character and maturity, but it most certainly was the foundation. Nowadays, I fully believe that entering Boy Entrant service at the tender age of 15 was the most important step in my life. I also believe that many other former Boy Entrants would agree that this also holds true for them.

What qualities did we graduate with, that perhaps weren't there when we first joined?

Being thrust out into an unforgiving world at the age of 15 years certainly had an impact. Although the RAF took on the parents' role for our care, well-being and discipline, we quickly learned that there were no emotional strings attached. We had no one to turn to when the going got tough, therefore a sense of independence and self-reliance took root at an earlier age than may have happened had we remained at home with our families.

The fact that most of us stuck it out for the full eighteen months points to the spirit of endurance with which most Boy Entrants were imbued, although it has to be admitted that not everyone stayed. For the majority of those who continued on to the conclusion of Boy Entrants' training, self-respect was earned in passing out with the skills of a trade at our fingertips. This was something valuable that we had earned through our own hard work and endurance. Regardless of our origins, we knew that henceforth, we had the means to earn our own living.

There may be a perception in the minds of some people that members of military organizations react blindly and unquestioningly to orders from those in authority and are incapable of independent thought. Nothing could be further from the truth. We were encouraged to use initiative and logic to think our way through the kind of problems that would confront us when we entered the regular Service. Being trained in the ability to "think on our feet' was an important skill when it came to tracing the source of "snags", often under extremely stressful conditions, on increasingly complex aircraft systems. Such ability remains with a person as a valuable asset when it comes to making one's way in life after the RAF.

The military discipline to which we were subjected made our lives difficult at first, but when accepted it made them easier. Eventually, the discipline became ingrained into our personal makeup, transforming us from rebellious youths into citizens who abide by and respect the law of the land.

During training, we were constantly reminded that our work as aircraft technicians placed an awesome responsibility on our shoulders. The lives of airmen who flew in the aircraft we maintained and serviced were dependent on our dedication and conscientiousness. Careless work could very easily result in the failure of an aircraft to return from a sortie, with all the horrific implications involved. If we knew of anything that endangered an aircraft and its crew, we were aware of our moral duty to make that fact known, even if it meant exposing ourselves to the displeasure of others. One person in my experience did not abide by this code of conduct, as related earlier in the narrative, by failing to report that he had lost a tool in an aircraft cockpit. The result was almost disastrous for the pilot, who fortunately survived the incident. The person in question was justifiably banned from ever working on aircraft again. That was an isolated occurrence, however—every other aircraft technician that I ever worked with always upheld the strong tradition of responsibility for the lives of those who depended on his work. As Boy Entrants, however, it was implanted within us at a very early stage in our development, to remain there always.

The experience of successfully passing out of Boy Entrant training gave me a strong sense of direction. There was now a ladder which I could climb, with every rung attained by the achievement of clearly defined goals. To climb up the ladder one step at a time, it was necessary to gain increasingly higher levels of knowledge and experience. The experience came from spending a requisite amount of time on each rung, whilst evidence that the required level of knowledge had been acquired was proven by taking trade tests, sometimes after a further formal course of study. The same sense of direction led me to pursue further education during and after my transition to civilian life, and gave me the confidence to diversify my work experience into other fields, resulting in a long and successful civilian career.

All of this was more than I could have hoped for. As a naïve 15-year-old, the most I wanted was to learn a trade that I could follow after leaving the Service, but happily I got more than I bargained for. And so, if I had to do it all over again—I most certainly would.

Above, Boy Entrant trainee MT Mechanics work on a mobile airfield identification beacon and below, on a Hillman car engine.

Above, a Colour-hoisting parade at Summer Camp. Below, pre-war Boy Entrants undergoing practical training in Workshops.

Appendix 1

Life After Boy Entrants

In my RAF career, I progressed from Electrical Mechanic to Electrical Fitter and from Leading Aircraftman to Sergeant. I spent four years in Flying Training Command at Cranwell, then trained on Vulcan bombers prior to an expected posting to Florida as a member of the Skybolt Nuclear Stand-off Missile Trials Team. In December 1962, however, Skybolt was cancelled by the then Prime Minister, Harold MacMillan and President Kennedy. This was a great personal disappointment, but the upside was that I had finally escaped from Cranwell and subsequently worked on Vulcans, in Bomber Command, for the rest of my service—except for two interludes. In 1964, shortly after marrying my wife Pam, I was selected to take part in the trials of the P1127 Kestrel vertical take-off fighter—the prototype of the now famous Harrier STOL aircraft. At the end of the year-long trials I returned to Bomber Command but in 1966 I had an unaccompanied two-month stint in Borneo, followed by a 2-year posting to RAF Changi, Singapore, accompanied by Pam.

In 1968 I returned to Bomber Command and RAF Scampton. There were now just two years remaining in the twelve years of regular RAF service for which I had enlisted when the realization came that I needed more qualifications to further my career in civilian life. To accomplish that purpose, I successfully completed a course of instruction for an Ordinary National Certificate in Electrical Engineering, and continued with partial completion of the Higher National Certificate (HNC) course before leaving the RAF in February 1971 on my thirtieth birthday. I then gained a position as Electrical Draughtsman with a Lincoln company specialising in the manufacture of industrial gas turbine engines. My new company allowed me to complete my HNC and on achieving that qualification, I was promoted to Electrical Engineer. I stayed with the company for six years, during which time my two daughters came into the world. The economic demands of a small family ate up all our financial reserves and I tried taxi driving in the evenings to supplement my income, but the hours were long and the financial rewards not encouraging. I then took a 12-month contract as a Project Engineer with the Arabian American Oil Company in Saudi Arabia. The conditions were Spartan but the salary was easily four times what I had been earning in Lincoln. At the end of my contract I was offered a job as Applications Engineer in Houston, Texas, at a facility owned by my former company in Lincoln and on February 15, 1979 flew to Houston with my wife Pam and daughters Michelle (7) and Sarah (5). We had agreed we would only stay for one year in Houston to see how things worked out, but ironically, 27 years later, we're still in the USA.

I worked in Houston for the Lincoln-based company for two years and then accepted an attractive offer of employment with another company as Project Engineer. The new company was based in San Diego, California and in 1985 I was transferred there with promotion to Project Manager. Project Management suited me and I remained in that field of work with the same company for 19 years, before accepting early retirement in the year 2000. Since then we have continued to live in San Diego and our extended family of two daughters, two sons-in-law and four grandchildren also live in the San Diego area. Since retiring, I have developed another career as a self-employed training consultant to my former employer.

I look back on all of this with a feeling of satisfaction for having had a successful life and career and firmly believe that it was only made possible by the Boy Entrant training I received all those years ago.

Appendix 2

The fate of the Woodvale Spitfires

Whilst researching background material for this book, I discovered that the RAF Woodvale Spitfires eventually found their way to the Battle of Britain Memorial Flight, where two of them still thrill people to this day, as they thrilled me all those years ago. Here follows a brief history, excerpted from the Battle of Britain Memorial Flight web page on the Royal Air Force website: http://www.raf.mod.uk/bbmf/bbmfhome.html, and other sources.

The Battle of Britain Memorial Flight was born at RAF Biggin Hill as the Historic Aircraft Flight on 11 July 1957. On that date, three Spitfire PR Mk XIXs (PM631, PM853 and PS915) arrived in formation from RAF Woodvale via RAF Duxford, to join the sole surviving Hurricane (LF363). PS915 was immediately swapped for a Spitfire Mk XVI (TE330) on gate-guard duties at RAF West Malling, and then continued in that line of work later at RAF Leuchars and later again at RAF Brawdy. Some time later, the Flight moved to RAF North Weald for a short time and then to RAF Martlesham Heath, during which time PS853 also went to gate-guard duties, this time at RAF West Raynham.

After a short time at Horsham St. Faith (Norwich Airport), the Flight moved to RAF Coltishall in 1963, and shortly thereafter, Spitfire PS853 was returned to it. Coltishall then served as the Flight's home for the next 13 years.

In 1973, the Flight was renamed the Battle of Britain Memorial Flight, and in 1976 it relocated to its present home at RAF Coningsby.

Spitfire PS915 returned to the Flight in 1987, after being refurbished, but sadly, Spitfire PS853 was offered for auction to pay for the rebuilding of the original Flight member, Hurricane LF363. Then, during the winter of 1997, PS915 underwent major servicing at RAF St. Athan.

After leaving the Battle of Britain Memorial Flight in 1987, PS853 was grounded until 1989 and then, following extensive work, was fitted with a modified Rolls-Royce Griffon engine giving it a top speed of 439 mph and a ceiling of 45,000 feet. The re-engined Spitfire took to the air once again on 20 July 1989. In 1995, the aircraft was bought by a private individual, but it went up for sale a few months later, after his unfortunate death in a flying accident. The aircraft was bought by the Rolls-Royce Heritage Trust in September 1996 and is based at Filton Airfield, just across the road from the Rolls-Royce facilities in Bristol.

Appendix 3

High Flight, by John Gillespie Magee, Jr.

This inspiring poem is reproduced in full below, followed by a brief history of its author and how he came to write it.

> Oh! I have slipped the surly bonds of earth
> And danced the skies on laughter silvered wings,
> Sunward I've climbed, and joined the tumbling mirth
> Of sun-split clouds—and done a hundred things
> You have not dreamed of—wheeled and soared and swung
> High in the sunlit silence. Hov'ring there,
> I've chased the shouting wind along, and flung
> My eager craft through footless halls of air.
> Up, up the long, delirious, burning blue
> I've topped the wind-swept heights with easy grace
> Where never lark, or even eagle flew –
> And, while with silent lifting mind I've trod
> The high untrespassed sanctity of space,
> Put out my hand and touched the face of God.

The following history of the author and his poem was found on the "Time and the River" website:
http://www.geocities.com/everwild7/highflight.html.

"During the dark days of the Battle of Britain, hundreds of Americans crossed the border into Canada to enlist with the Royal Canadian Air Force. Knowingly breaking the law, but with the tacit approval of the then still officially neutral United States Government, they volunteered to fight Hitler's Germany.

John Gillespie Magee, Jr. was one such American. Born in Shanghai, China, in 1922, Magee was just an 18-year-old when he entered flight training. Within the year, he was sent to England and posted to the newly formed No. 412 Fighter Squadron, RCAF, which was activated at RAF Digby on 30 June 1941. He was qualified on and flew the Supermarine Spitfire.

"Pilot Officer Magee flew on fighter sweeps over France and air defence over England against the German Luftwaffe. Although the dark days of the Battle of Britain were over, the Luftwaffe was still on the job of keeping up the pressure on British industry and the country. At the time, German bombers were crossing the English Channel with great regularity to attack Britain's cities and factories.

On 3 September 1941, Magee flew a high altitude (30,000 feet) test flight in a newer model of the Spitfire V. As he orbited and climbed upward, he was struck with the inspiration of a poem—"To touch the face of God".

"Once back on the ground, he wrote a letter to his parents. In it he commented, "I am enclosing a verse I wrote the other day. It started at 30,000 feet, and was finished soon after I landed." On the back of the letter, he had written the poem "High Flight".

Just three months later, on December 11, 1941 (and only three days after the US entered the war), Pilot Officer John Gillespie Magee, Jr., was killed. The Spitfire V he was flying, VZ-H, collided with an Oxford Trainer from the RAF College Cranwell Airfield while over RAF Tangmere. The two planes were flying in the clouds and neither saw the other. He was just 19 years old".

Appendix 4

29th Entry, St. Athan, Graduation List
27th March, 1958

Airframe Mechanics

Allen, R. G.
Arnold, P. J.
Barber, A. O.
Betts, D. R.
Bloom, M. J.
Boyd, R.
Bradnum, P. J.
Burningham, L.
Carey, M. L.
Chaffe, A.F.
Chew, A. M.
Child, G. W.
Curtis, F. G.
Dingie, F. D.
Durack, G. B.
Eaton, T. E.

Forsythe, J.
Freaney, M. J.
Green, D. M.
Johnston, R. F.
Lawrence, L.
Lillington, P.
May, A. J.
McQuode, J.
Melloy, J.
Miller, P.
Mills, D. S.
Morris, P. G.
Nobie, P.
Pickering, G.
Potts, G. A.
Pyle, D. F.

Quint, R. A.
Rees, L. M.
Reynolds, D.
Rowse, V. G.
Simpson, N.
Slingsby, A.
Stannard, G.
Stone, P. R.
Tanner, D. E.
Taylor, M. S.
Urmston, P.
Walford, P. A.
Webber, P. N.
Whall, B. W.
White, R. W.
Wilson, C.

Engine Mechanics

Always, P.
Baldwin, F. H. M.
Bateman, M. A.
Bushell, A. J.
Collin, J. D.
Cox, V. H.
Crawford, D. A.
Gerard, M. B.
Hudson, D.

Humphreys, J. A.
Lidgett, T. W.
Marriott, N. B.
Maynard, P. J.
Middleton, R.
Moses, B.
Perrin, M. J.
Preece, P. J.
Rook, P. G.

Rossant, D. G.
Shade, J.
Trent, P. J.
Urry, C.
Vickers, M. J.
Vidler, P.
Walker, C. C.
Walmsley, D. L.

Armament Mechanics (Bombs)

Barnes, L	Fairbrother, K. R.	Porter, S.
Carpenter, S. R.	Hammond, B. A.	Riley, A. R.
Davis, P. S.	Hillman, B.	Sinclair, S. M.
Downing, G. L.	Jeffrey, J. W.	Tyler, B.

Armament Mechanics (Guns)

Adams, D.	Jenkins, A. J.	Pemberton, A. A.
Arnold, R. T. E.	MacGregor, A. G.	Pritchard, R. P.
Atkins, C.	Martin, A. D.	Spinks, D. A.
Bertram, W.	Mash, A. R. A.	Spurie, W. F.
Cowan, W.	Mills, A. R.	Watkins, A. J.
Gale, A. J.	Milner, D. H.	Wheatley, E. I.
Horton, T.	North, A. M.	Woodhams, J. H. C.

Instrument Mechanics (General)

Bolton, P. J.	Haslar, T. A.	Roberts, C. W.
Bragg, A. J.	Hesp, R. H.	Stovold
Dennis, A. F.	Hill, A. E.	Sutton, J. A.
Etherington, D. R.	Honiset, T. D.	Thompson, D. J.
Hand, R. T.	Kitchin, G.	Whiting, R. H.
Hann, R.	Lavin, T. P.	Williams, D. J.
Harrison, A. E.	McGrath, J.	Wrigglesworth, A. M.
Harrison, L. B. G	Reynolds, S.	

Instrument Mechanics (Nav.)

Anderson, A. J.	Gascoine, G.	Smith, P. A.
Cunningham, C.	Gilkes, E. A.	Sumner, J. P.
Dammery, T. W.	Graham, M. A.	Thorne, N. J.
Day, T. I.	Green, E. F.	Tovey, H. W.
Duff, W.	Newstead, P.	Williams, M. J.

General Mechanics

Allan, E. H.

Birch, R.

Cook, S.

Govier, P. D.

Gray, J.

Hilliman, R. C.

Hope, M. A.

Johns, K. F.

Laming, B. T.

Lepard, M. T.

Masters, J. W.

Meadows, D. R.

Platts, N. G.

Pryde, A. V.

M. T. Mechanics

Arthur, J. E.

Baker, D. L.

Barber, D. C.

Beardwell, J. G.

Clark, J. H.

Foster, C.

Garner, W. J.

Grindrod, B.

Milligan, D. J.

Nixon, J.

Roberts, S. A.

Rodgers, C. H.

Rogerson, J.

Tait, A. A. S.

Taylor, A. T.

Electrical Mechanic (Air)

Barker, M. J.

Barnes, T. B.

Bassett, R. J.

Brand, G. R.

Brown, H. N.

Burden, C. D.

Butterworth, R. R.

Callighan, F. J.

Carlin, B.

Chaplin, R. J.

Chinnery, C. R.

Chown, P. A. C.

Clarke, B. H.

Coaten, G. R.

Critchley, E.

Davey, K.

Disney, A. M. J.

Drinkwater, A. N.

Duff, R. A.

Edwards, N.

Fox, R. S.

Gillings, T.

Harvey, T. L.

Higgins, P. M. J.

Humphries, R. J.

Inglis, B.

Jackson, M. R.

Johns, M. W.

Johnson, N.

Jordan, R. S.

Levett, S. F.

Luckhurst, B. O.

Marlow, B.

Motteram, E. B.

Mowbray, M. J.

Nickels, R. V.

Oliver, M. H.

Persse, W. W.

Powditch, D. J.

Presland, W. E.

Priest, A.

Richardson, B.

Slatter, D.

Speer, R. E. J.

Staley, A.

Wiles, H. B.

Willis, T.

Woods, D. W.

Graduating members of the 29th Entry, 3 Squadron, 2 Wing, Electrical Mechanics (Air).

Back row (l to r)

Arthur Priest; D.J. Powditch; N Johnson; Derek Chinnery; D.W. Woods; F.J. Callighan; R.J. "Charlie" Chaplin; B. "Paddy" Richardson; M.H. Oliver; R.A. Duff

Third row (l to r)

Brian Marlow; P.A.C. Chown; M.R. (Bob) Jackson; B.O. Luckhurst; M.W. Johns; B.H. "Nobby" Clarke; T. Willis; A.M.J. Disney; R.S. Jordan; M.R. Jackson

Second row (all standing) (l to r)

R.R. Butterworth; S.F. Levett; R.S. Fox; K. Davey; N. Edwards; R.J. Humphries; G.R. Coaten; P.M.J. Higgins; W.W. Persse; M.J. Barker; C.D. Burden; E.B. "Ted" Motteram; D. "Spud" Slatter; R.J. Bassett

Front row (all seated) (l to r)

W.E. Presland; A. Staley; H.N. "Ginge" Brown; G.R. Brand; (Cpl. Boy) R.V. Nickels; (Sgt. Boy) E. Critchley; (Cpl. Boy) A.N. Drinkwater; B. Inglis; R.E.J. Speer; B. Carlin; T. Gilling

968714

Printed in Great Britain by
Amazon.co.uk, Ltd.,
Marston Gate.